ORIGIN MYTHS AND HOLY PLACES
IN THE OLD TESTAMENT

Copenhagen International Seminar

General Editor: Thomas L. Thompson, University of Copenhagen
Editors: Niels Peter Lemche and Mogens Müller, both at the University of Copenhagen
Language Revision Editor: James West

ORIGIN MYTHS AND HOLY PLACES
IN THE OLD TESTAMENT

A STUDY OF AETIOLOGICAL NARRATIVES

ŁUKASZ NIESIOŁOWSKI-SPANÒ

TRANSLATED BY JACEK LASKOWSKI

(TRANSLATION MADE WITH THE GENEROUS ASSISTANCE OF
'THE FOUNDATION FOR POLISH RESEARCH')

Equinox Publishing Ltd

London   Oakville

First published in Polish in 2003 as *Mityczne początki miejsc świętych w Starym Testamencie* by Wydawnictwo Akademickie DIALOG

English version published by

UK: Equinox Publishing Ltd., Unit 6, The Village, 101 Amies St., London SW11 2JW
USA: DBBC, 28 Main Street, Oakville, CT 06779

www.equinoxpub.com

First published 2011

Library of Congress Cataloguing-in-Publication Data
A catalogue record for this book is available from the Library of Congress

ISBN-10:   1845533348   (hardback)
ISBN-13:   9781845533342   (hardback)

Printed by Lightning Source

Contents

Preface

The nature of this work demands a few words of explanation. The text consists of nine chapters, of which the first and last are substantially different from the rest. The introductory chapter contains the subject of the work, its methodology, an explanation of meanings of the concepts explored, a brief (because of the extent of the material) review of the state of research related to the subject of this work, and an account of the sources. Chapters 2–8 are studies of the myths dealing with the origins (the aetiology) of holy places. Each one of them contains a general presentation of the archaeological material and of the information derived from extra-biblical sources related to the sanctuary under discussion. Following a recounting of the myth's contents comes a section containing elements of critical analysis of the text. The core of each chapter consists of two types of investigation. One aims to establish the probable date of the origins of the aetiological story or of the tradition from which it is derived, the other to analyze the myth in relation to its symbolic language and also to attempt to reconstruct the religious reality behind the myth.

Three of the seven studies of holy places have a slightly different shape. Chapter 6, dealing with Ophrah, contains a suggestion that the place be given a new identity. Chapter 7 deals with aetiological myths about Shechem and Gilgal. The justification for this is that there is a strong link between these centres; discussing them next to each other made for a coherent account. Chapter 8 contains not one but several holy places and their aetiologies. Despite the fact that it is impossible, on the basis of archaeological finds, to identify these places mentioned in the Bible, discussing them seems to be relevant in that not only did they play an important role in biblical tradition, but also they are crucial in the drawing of more general conclusions. The aetiologies of Galeed, Mahanaim, Penuel and the altar named Ed have been treated briefly but, in my view, in a way which allows them to be included in the general argument concerning both the date of their origins and the very structure of biblical myths dealing with the beginnings of holy places.

The final chapter is an attempted synthesis of the material under discussion. The emphasis has been placed—depending on the direction of the analysis of the texts—either on dating the myths in their first and final form as recorded in the Bible and, therefore, on the final redaction of the whole biblical text, or on speculations about the way these biblical myths were constructed and on their role.

In the appendix at the end of this work there is a table showing the most important elements of the myths discussed, and also a map marking the location of the places discussed in the book. For greater clarity I have also included the more important towns and other geographical points of reference, showing the territories occupied by the tribes living in Palestine (according to the biblical account). This should facilitate the reading of the text. The localization of the tribes is conventional and is not the result of separate research.

The individual chapters discussing the aetiological myths of holy places are linked to one another only to a small extent. Each one of them represents a separate study. Reading them may provoke some misgivings in the reader. This stems from the fact that the analyses included here consist only of a part of the research into the aetiological myths which are the subject of this work. Much more could have been added, but the necessity of retaining a cohesive presentation necessitated the selection of the material in such a way that it made the main theme clear. This work is not a definitive study of the subject. My aim was to raise a few questions and to try venture answers to them. To be sure, I have not dealt with all of the possible questions on the subject.

Acknowledgments

Thanks are due to many people and institutions for their help with the writing of this book. For their kindness and support I thank all the staff in the Department of Ancient History in the Institute of History at the University of Warsaw, headed by Professor Włodzimierz Lengauer. For advice and reading the text I would like particularly to thank Doctor Maciej Tomal and Doctor Marek Węcowski. Special thanks are due for her care and encouragement to Professor Ewa Wipszycka. Thanks are due for consultations and specialist discussions to Professor Piotr Bieliński, Professor Edward Lipiński and Professor Piotr Muchowski. I extend a special word of thanks to Professor Giovanni Garbini of 'La Sapienza' University in Rome; his advice and teaching have greatly influenced the shape of this publication.

This book was made possible by, among other things, foreign trips. I owe those to the Committee of Scientific Research, the Catholic University at Leuven, the government of the Republic of Italy and the Lanckoroński Family Foundation. My stay in Rome was particularly rewarding thanks to the good will of the directors of the Pontifico Istituto Biblico and the German Archaeological Institute.

English translation was possible only thanks to the generosity of the Foundation for Polish Research to which I owe gratitude. I would like to thank Thomas L. Thompson and Jim West for their advice, help and encouragement in preparing the text for publication.

Last but not least, I would like to thank my family very much for their support and help.

Abbreviations

AB	Anchor Bible
ABD	*Anchor Bible Dictionary*. Edited by D.N. Freedman. 6 vols. New York, 1992
ANET	*Ancient Near Eastern Texts Relating to the Old Testament*. Edited by James B. Pritchard. 3rd edn, Princeton, 1969
ANRW	*Aufstieg und Niedergang der römischen Welt: Geschichte und Kultur Roms im Spiegel der neueren Forschung*. Edited by H. Temporini and W. Haase. Berlin, 1972–
AOAT	Alter Orient und Altes Testament
ArOr	*Archiv Orientální*
ASOR	*Annual of the American Schools of Oriental Research*
BAR	*Biblical Archaeology Review*
BASOR	*Bulletin of the American Schools of Oriental Research*
BDB	Brown, F., S.R. Driver, and C.A. Briggs. *A Hebrew and English Lexicon of the Old Testament*. Oxford, 1907
BN	*Biblische Notizen*
BTB	*Biblical Theology Bulletin*
BZAW	Beihefte zur *ZAW*
CAH	*Cambridge Ancient History*
CBQ	*Catholic Biblical Quarterly*
CSCO	Corpus scriptorum christianorum orientalium. Edited by I.B. Chabot *et al.* Paris, 1903–
DCH	*Dictionary of Classical Hebrew*. Edited by D.J.A. Clines. Sheffield, 1993–
DDD	*Dictionary of Deities and Demons in the Bible*. Edited by K. van der Toorn, B. Becking, and P.W. van der Horst. Leiden, 1995
EA	El-Amarna tablets. According to the edition of J. A. Knudtzon, *Die el-Amarna-Tafeln*. Leipzig, 1908–15. Reprint, Aalen, 1964. Continued in A.F. Rainey, *El-Amarna Tablets, 359–379*. 2nd edn. Kevelaer, 1978
EAEHL	*Encyclopedia of Archaeological Excavations in the Holy Land*. Edited by M. Avi-Yonah. 4 vols. Jerusalem, 1975
EJ	*Encyclopaedia Judaica*. 16 vols. Jerusalem, 1972
HAR	*Hebrew Annual Review*
HTR	*Harvard Theological Review*
HUCA	*Hebrew Union College Annual*
IEJ	*Israel Exploration Journal*

JANESCU	*Journal of the Ancient Near Eastern Society of Columbia University*
JBL	*Journal of Biblical Literature*
JJS	*Journal of Jewish Studies*
JQR	*Jewish Quarterly Review*
JSOT	*Journal for the Study of the Old Testament*
JSOTSup	*Journal for the Study of the Old Testament*: Supplement Series
JSP	*Journal for the Study of the Pseudepigrapha*
JSPSup	*Journal for the Study of the Pseudepigrapha*: Supplement Series
JSS	*Journal of Semitic Studies*
JTS	*Journal of Theological Studies*
KAI	*Kanaanäische und aramäische Inschriften*. H. Donner and W. Röllig. 2nd edn. Wiesbaden, 1966–69
KJV	King James Version
KTU	*Die keilalphabetischen Texte aus Ugarit*. Edited by M. Dietrich, O. Loretz, and J. Sanmartín. AOAT 24/1. Neukirchen-Vluyn, 1976. 2nd enlarged edn of *KTU: The Cuneiform Alphabetic Texts from Ugarit, Ras Ibn Hani, and Other Places*. Edited by M. Dietrich, O. Loretz, and J. Sanmartín. Münster, 1995 (= *CTU*)
LSJ	Liddell, H. G., R. Scott, H. S. Jones, *A Greek–English Lexicon*. 9th ed. with revised supplement. Oxford, 1996
LXX	Septuagint
MT	Masoretic Text
NEAEHL	*The New Encyclopedia of Archaeological Excavations in the Holy Land*. Edited by E. Stern. 4 vols. Jerusalem, 1993
NIV	New International Version
NTS	*New Testament Studies*
OBO	Orbis biblicus et orientalis
OTP	*Old Testament Pseudepigrapha*. Edited by J.H. Charlesworth. 2 vols. New York, 1983
PEQ	*Palestine Exploration Quarterly*
RB	*Revue Biblique*
RSV	Revised Standard Version
SBLSP	SBL Seminar Papers
SHANE	Studies in the History of the Ancient Near East
SJOT	*Scandinavian Journal of the Old Testament*
StTh	*Studia theologica*
SVTP	Studia in Veteris Testamenti Pseudepigrapha
TADAE	*Textbook of Aramaic Documents from Ancient Egypt*. Edited by B. Porten and A. Yardeni. Jerusalem, 1999
TDOT	*Theological Dictionary of the Old Testament*. Edited by G.J. Botterweck, H. Ringgren and H.-J. Fabry. Grand Rapids, 1974–
VT	*Vetus Testamentum*
VTSup	*Vetus Testamentum*, Supplements
WBC	Word Biblical Commentary
ZAW	*Zeitschrift für die alttestamentliche Wissenschaft*
ZDPV	*Zeitschrift des deutschen Palästina-Vereins*

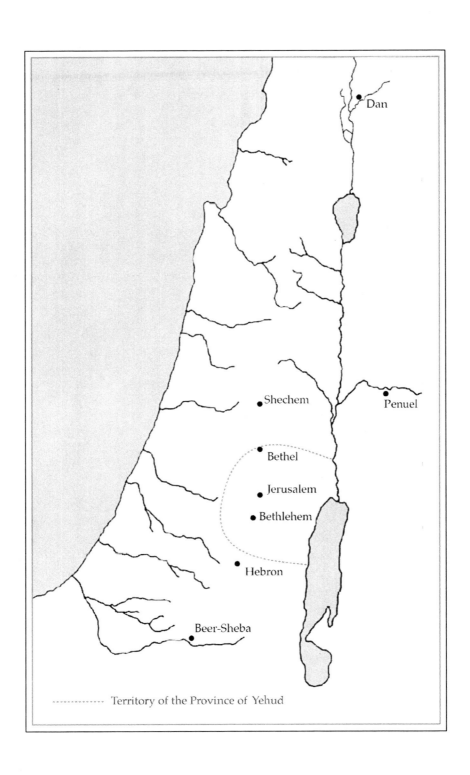

Dan

Shechem
Penuel

Bethel

Jerusalem
Bethlehem

Hebron

Beer-Sheba

----------- Territory of the Province of Yehud

1.
Introduction

The aim of this study is to analyse aetiological myths in the Bible that deal with the origins of holy places in Palestine as well as the circumstances of their inception. The conclusions will allow us, I think, to see the religion of the inhabitants of Palestine, as well as the changes introduced within the Bible, in a new light. I will start by defining the key concepts used in this study. I will then reflect on the limitations that the source text imposes on the work.

Myth

In view of the exceptionally extensive literature that has grown up around the definition of, and social role of, myth (with contributions from history, religious studies, anthropology, literary studies, ethnology and other disciplines), I make no attempt to undertake a synthesis of this subject. I simply present those views which have shaped my own approach to the study of myth. For the purposes of this study, however, I must set down a definition, albeit a tentative one, on which I based my choice of source materials. In this book, the word "myth" is understood to mean a *story which plays a particular role in the life of a society*. It is difficult to draw precise boundaries between a myth and, for example, a story or a legend. Nor is it possible to formulate a universal definition applicable to all eras and all societies. Furthermore, the sheer variety of contents and functions that myths have in different cultures forces us to resort to partial definitions which may apply to just one specific text. The distinguishing feature of a myth as opposed to an ancient story is that it has a special place in a society's consciousness. In religious thought, a myth is an account regarded as the truth. It is defined by its function, not its formal-literary qualities. For me, what is important is to examine the function that certain texts performed in an ancient society and not to look at the structural and formal elements that distinguish myths from other kinds of story.

The specific feature of a myth is its social reception. If a text is regarded by the society in which it functions as sacred, and therefore true, then we are dealing with a myth. This simplified definition is convenient but it does contain a danger in that it is left to researchers to determine whether or not a given text was indeed regarded as sacred. This kind of assessment creates difficulties in sociological and ethnographic studies, and it becomes particularly difficult (because of the paucity of source materials and their selectivity) in studies of the ancient world. The application of such a definition demands precision and the use of methods that allow it to be applied in a practical way, in this case to define a particular myth, which is to say one that was recorded in the Bible.

Myth in the Bible

The whole of the Bible has been (and is) treated as a sacred text. Following on from what I have said, the entire account should therefore be described as a myth. In this study, however, the Bible will not be understood to be "the word of truth" and so we cannot call the whole of the Bible a myth.

It is common knowledge that the biblical texts feature a wide variety of contents and forms. Our definition of myth is more applicable to some of these than it is to others. No-one will demur if we accept as a myth the account, for example, of the creation of the world (Gen 1:1–2:4a). The same applies to the material of the New Testament. Accounts of the birth, the teachings, the death and the resurrection of Jesus are articles of faith not called into question by believing Christians whose conviction it is that the Gospels contain the truth. This means that, using my proposed definition, they are myths. It does not, however, seem to be right to regard as myths the parables in the Gospels because they are presented in the form of metaphors. Faith is not needed here because the argument appeals directly to human reason; the text of the parable is presented not as a literal but as a rational address appealing to reason. The conclusion we can draw here is that it is a formal and necessary condition of a myth that it be received as a sacred text. A myth always appeals to faith and is not the subject of rational appraisal. Furthermore, if it becomes the subject of rational analysis and is not fully accepted by faith, then it stops being a myth. What it becomes then—whether it is literature, fairy-tale or make-believe—is not a question that concerns us here.

There is one other problem that needs to be resolved here, namely: how to establish whether or not a given people believe a text and regard it as sacred. An ethnographer can simply ask his informant. A historian, however, not having a contemporary account stating *expressis verbis* that such and such a faith exists, is in a more difficult situation and must be guided by his/her own investigative criteria. Despite the fundamental differences in the psychologies of ancient and contemporary peoples, we must not assume that people who are separated by eras, degrees of technical development and life experiences are significantly different. A historian must be equally wary of Eurocentrism and "modernocentrism." The people of ancient times were neither more nor less stupid, or wise, than their descendants of the nineteenth, twentieth and even the twenty-first centuries. Just like people of nowadays, they were capable of rational deduction and assessment. It is true that their religious thinking was more characteristically theirs, but that is not to say that they were incapable of reasoning logically. They were capable of perceiving contradictions and assessing the probability of phenomena which, even if understood, did not rule out the preservation of their faith.

Biblical myths have been defined here as accounts of events that took place in ancient times in a reality which, to a person thinking rationally, might appear to be fabulous or invented. These accounts relate events that never took place but which are completely real in terms of religious thinking, determined as it is by the faith factor.

Reservations have occasionally been expressed about applying the concept of myth (and other anthropological terminology) to biblical studies. They are not, however, justified in terms of scientific research. To a large extent they result from treating myth as a manifestation of a lower form of religious thought which in turn often reveals the researcher's own partisan approach. Anthropological terminology is, however, gradually entering Biblical Studies.[1] It was Edmund Leach who put forward the most persuasive argument in favour of granting equal status to myths that function among non-literate native Americans as well as those of the ancient Hebrews:

> Lévi-Strauss uses a narrow definition of myth which makes it appear that the myths of contemporary Amerindians are cultural products of an entirely different kind from the mythical-historical traditions of the Jewish people in the first century BC. My own view is that this distinction is quite artificial and that the structural analysis of the myth should be equally applicable to both the time of men and the time of Gods.[2]

1. J.W. Rogerson, *Myth in Old Testament Interpretation*, BZAW 134, Berlin, 1974.
2. E. Leach, *Genesis as the Myth and Other Essays*, London, 1969, 114 n. 8; see also J. Pitt-Rivers, *The Fate of Shechem or Politics of Sex: Essays in the Anthropology of the Mediterranean*, London, 1977, 126-30.

Aetiological Myth

We can regard as aetiology any explanation—on a religious basis—of the causes of, and circumstances leading to, the birth of a custom, law, place or any other thing or phenomenon. Every aetiology invokes some authority to give the truth it expresses its credibility. In the context of myths, this authority tends to be a religious one. Aetiology describes the causes and circumstances of the origins of any arrangement or institution whose inception demands (or is worthy of) explanation. It might appear from this, therefore, that the Bible in its entirety is of an aetiological character. It talks about the origins of various institutions; as a sacred text it is regarded as being the revealed truth; and in its account of the past it calls upon sacral authority.

The aetiological myths of the Old Testament are specified above all by the use of precise aetiological indications: "that is why X is called X," "to this day this place is named Y," "and he called this place Z" and so on. This, however, forms only part of the aetiological material. The aetiological function can also be seen in accounts which record the origins of various institutions, customs and laws but without such a form of words. Since the account is credible and talks of the first man to start viniculture, it means that it was indeed he who was the first to apply viniculture. The lack of an aetiological formulation does not alter the nature and function of the myth.[3]

To date, investigations of biblical aetiologies have concentrated on the internal ordering of their various manifestations, on analyses of them as a literary genre or on distinguishing the forms of words mentioned above when introducing accounts of their origin.[4] These literary-critical studies, although they have provided a formal ordering of biblical aetiologies, have failed to resolve several specific questions. They have not, for example, answered the question of whether the aetiologies are an archaic form of mythical explanations of reality, or whether they are later attempts at "rationalising" an explanation of reality of unknown provenance. Did these aetiologies aim only to explain the beginnings or did they play some other role?

---

3.   B.O. Long, *The Problem of Etiological Narrative in the Old Testament*, BZAW 108, Berlin, 1968.

4.   B.S. Childs, "A Study of the Formula 'Until this Day'," *JBL* 82 (1963): 279-92; *idem*, "The Etiological Tale Re-examined," *VT* 24 (1974): 387-97; A. Ibañez Arana, "La narración etiológica como género literario bíblico," *Scriptorium Victoriense* 10 (1963): 161-76; *idem*, "Las etiologías etimológicas del Pentateuco," *Scriptorium Victoriense* 10 (1963): 241-75; L. Sabourin, "L'étiologie biblique," *BTB* 2.2 (1972): 201-206 (English version "Biblical Etiologies," *BTB* 2 [1972]: 199-205).

The most important works on this subject are still the studies by Burke O. Long[5] and Friedmann W. Golka.[6] More recent works have not improved on the synthesis they reached more than thirty years ago in their research into the collection of books Genesis to 2 Kings.[7] Their aim was to research all the biblical material for instances of the aetiologies of various phenomena, places, institutions, names, nomenclatures and so on. Though there have been considerable changes in the field of biblical knowledge since the publication of their work, a whole series of conclusions and specific assertions remains valid.

Holy Places

In this work the term "holy place" is applied to all those places where—according to the Bible—ritual ceremonies were conducted. It is hard to establish their number since there was a wide variety of sanctuaries and temples in existence throughout Palestine. Just as the Bible changed shape through the centuries, so the religion of the inhabitants of Palestine underwent constant transformations. The biblical text itself provides information about numerous places where the Israelites worshipped various gods. The terms *bamah* and *bamot* indicate unnamed places of ritual. References to pilgrimages, holy days and sacrifices let us compile a catalogue of places where various religious practices were performed. My aim here is not to provide an exhaustive account of places of ritual in Palestine. The subject of this work is simply those myths which deal with the establishment of places that were regarded as holy at a certain period in Palestine's history. Evidence of the existence of a rite qualifies a place for this group, and the existence of a narrative explaining the beginnings of a rite qualifies it as an aetiological myth.

The Bible as a Historical Source

The Bible is a work compiled over the ages by a Jewish intellectual elite. Although the development of the biblical canon and the changes introduced into the texts over a period of centuries have not been exhaustively examined, we do know that it was a long, slow process and, from a certain point onwards, rigorously controlled. When we talk about the

5. Long, *The Problem of Etiological Narrative.*
6. F.W. Golka, "The Aetiologies in the Old Testament, Part 1," *VT* 26 (1976): 410-28, and Part 2, *VT* 27 (1977): 36-47.
7. P.J. van Dyk, "The Function of So-Called Etiological Elements in Narratives," *ZAW* 102 (1990): 19-33.

creation of a Hebrew canon we have to distinguish two periods. The first includes the formation of Judaism, from the return of the refugees from the Babylonian captivity to the destruction of the Temple in 70 CE. The second falls between the years 70 and 1008 CE, the period of mature Judaism as it moved through the phase of Pharisee domination towards the rabbinical phase. Like every division, the closing date of this period is purely conventional, marked by the creation of the oldest of the codices containing the complete Hebrew Bible preserved in its entirety in the Masoretic text (MT).[8] The so-called *Leningrad Codex* (which now probably ought to be called the *St Petersburg Codex*) is the crowning document of the Masoretes.

The MT, the oldest copy of which is in St Petersburg, was created in two stages. During the first stage, sources and texts were selected or abandoned quite freely, changes were made by adding or removing words or even themes. With the end of the Second Temple era, a collection arose which was ascribed to divine inspiration; what followed from this was the conviction that the Bible—being a text that came from God—could not be altered. The process of the canon's creation, that is to say, of the establishment of the list of holy books, probably ended in the first century CE, while the process of sanctification (in the sense of accepting the text's immutability) lasted for some time. This can be seen by comparing the Hebrew versions with the Greek or Latin translations. The considerable differences between the Septuagint (LXX) and MT show that editing was unrestrained in both languages. The finds in Qumran, which supplied biblical material from the end of the third century BCE and the first century CE, confirm that there were two trends in the editing of the texts, known by Qumranologists as proto-LXX and proto-MT.[9] Doubtless they do not provide a complete picture; nevertheless, just these two led to the creation of complete codices. In this context the state of the LXX codices is significant: the three oldest—the Sinai, the Vatican and the Alexandrian (fourth–fifth centuries)—feature differences which show the existence of various traditions in the textual accounts at the beginnings of Christianity. The effect, seen in the LXX codices, was the standardisation of the biblical texts by collating various versions, the best example of which is Origen's *Hexapla*. A different Greek text has been preserved in two Jewish translations: that of Aquila (from the first

8. Another turning point could have been the creation of the Aleppo Codex (c. 915 CE).

9. P. Muchowski, "Dwie kluczowe kwestie badawcze w studiach nad rękopisami biblijnymi z Qumran," *Studia Judaica* 4.1-2 (2001): 27-43; A. Tronina, *Biblia w Qumran*, Kraków, 2001.

quarter of the second century) and of Theodosius (the middle of the second century).

Decisions made after 70 CE by scholars and proto-rabbis not only shaped the canon of the biblical books, but also confirmed a particular version of the text. Talmudic tradition ascribes the shaping of the biblical canon to a group of rabbis gathered in Jamnia (Javneh). Although the date conventionally given for the end of this process is 90 CE, it is hard to imagine that it could have been finished so swiftly; it is safer, therefore, to stay with a less precise dating of its close as the end of the first and the beginning of the second centuries.

The history of the tradition's shaping did not end with the decision to select the canonical books or to accept the immutability of the Hebrew text; the freedom to choose different readings still remained because the text did not contain diacritic signs and in practice this meant that inter-pretation was dependent, insofar as the demands of grammar allowed it, on tradition. But tradition sometimes proved insufficient. As a result of the work of the Masoretes, Jewish scholars who standardised the Bible's text by introducing a system of diacritics, and by applying instructions and appropriate commentaries to the text, the MT assumed the form we know today. Consequently, what followed was that where hitherto there had been some freedom of interpretation, there was now a standardised rendition of the text.[10]

Research Paradigms: Religion and Biblical Historiography

Many of the fundamental axioms accepted in the study of biblical texts and the society of ancient Palestine have been challenged over the course of the last quarter century. This is equally true of Bible studies as it is of history and archaeology. Two factors have been the mainly responsible for this paradigm shift: archaeological discoveries and a revision of exe-getic theories that often dated back to the end of the nineteenth century.

Current historical research on the Bible tends to have a strongly criti-cal approach to the source text. In short, the Bible used to be regarded as a sure, that is to say robust, historical source (see the works by Alt, Bright, Albright). Contradictions were frequently glossed over and there are instances where texts from the Old Testament were used to support historical theories. The reconstruction of the past is currently based on information gleaned from a critical approach to the biblical text as well

---

10. I am talking here about interpretations of readings which changed the sense of the text and not about dialectical differences whose phonetic variation had no influence on the understanding of the text.

as from extra-biblical evidence.[11] It was a re-assessment of the Bible's value as a historical source that has been largely responsible for this change. The fact that it is a holy book does not mean that it contains historical truth. Nowadays it is treated as an expression of certain outlooks on life, sometimes even of propaganda, but not as an account of events or their faithful reconstruction.

One element undermining the traditional paradigms is the change in the dating of the biblical text. The first step in this process was the rejection of the so-called Documentary Hypothesis propagated by Wellhausen,[12] Gunkel[13] and Driver,[14] which proposed the existence of four sources (traditions) within the Pentateuch (sometimes expanded to the *Hexateuch*): J—the Jahwist, E—the Elohist, D—the Deuteronomist and P—the Priestly source. The J tradition was supposed to have arisen in the ninth century BCE, E in the eighth, D in the seventh, and P in the sixth century, during the Babylonian captivity. Criticism of this theory was directed primarily against its completely arbitrary and baseless dating. It has now been either totally rejected or partially amended because it has no evidence from external sources to support it. The theory of sources is currently confined to the assumption that there are two or three layers of the Pentateuchal text which can be separated by resorting to an internal critical analysis and analysis of the source. This source is generally described as being P and non-P, or P, J and pre-J. The shortcoming in this method of research stems from retaining the arbitrary nature of dating and the inter-relationships between the layers.[15]

The linguistic heterogeneity of the Hebrew Bible makes it impossible to show the evolution of the language. "The Biblical Hebrew language is the name of a literary norm which dominated the Hebrew tongue up to

11. M. Liverani, "Memorandum on the Approach to Historiographic Texts," *Orientalia* 42 (1973): 178-94; J. Van Seters, *In Search of History: Historiography in the Ancient World and the Origins of Biblical History*, New Haven, 1982.

12. J. Wellhausen, *Prolegomena zur Geschichte Israels*, Berlin, 1883 (English edition *Prolegomena to the History of Ancient Israel*, New York, 1957); *idem*, *Die Composition des Hexateuchs und der historischen Bücher des Alten Testaments*, Berlin, 1899.

13. H. Gunkel, *Genesis*, Göttingen, 1901.

14. S.R. Driver, *An Introduction to the Literature of the Old Testament*, Oxford 1897. See also G. von Rad, *Old Testament Theology*, trans. D.M.G. Stalker, New York, 1962; *idem*, *Das formgeschichtliche Problem des Hexateuches*, Berlin, 1938.

15. D.M. Carr, *Reading the Fractures of Genesis: Historical and Literary Approaches*, Louisville, 1996; J. Van Seters, *Prologue to History: The Yahwist as Historian in Genesis*, Louisville, 1992; *idem*, *The Life of Moses: The Yahwist as Historian in Exodus–Numbers*, Kampen, 1994.

the destruction of the second temple (70 CE)."[16] It is impossible to isolate, date or even so much as describe the various stages of the language's development on the basis of the Bible's Hebrew. It is equally impossible to perform even the smallest degree of textual dating, of the kind postulated by older works, by recourse to the criterion of whether the name of God appears as Elohim or Yahweh.

Another crucial element in Biblical Studies has been the use of anthropology and sociology in studies of the society of ancient Palestine. A transitional stage in this "anthropologisation" of contemporary Biblical Studies was the so-called Myth and Ritual School. This research tendency, represented by British and Scandinavian scholars, emphasised the text's meaning to the life of the society, and particularly to its ritualistic behaviour.[17] At the same time, research has been undertaken into reconstructing Western Semitic religions, to which archaeological finds (especially in Ugarit) have made an enormous contribution. The religion of the Semites proved to be far more complex than had previously been supposed, and the pantheon of their gods and their mythology much richer than the Bible's testimony had suggested. This has made many researchers address such questions: How was it that, in a world of extended polytheism, which occasionally took on the form of henotheism (as in the cities of Phoenicia), a monotheistic religion appeared? How far back do its origins stretch? To what extent did the pre-monotheistic religion differ from the beliefs of the Semitic world that surrounded Palestine? The answers given to these questions are various. Supporters of Albright's theory believe in the biblical account and the beginnings of monotheism in the time of the Hebrew settlement in Palestine,[18] assuming that the Bible conveys information about the origins of the cult of the Only One—Yahweh—when describing the history of the Israelites (the exodus from Egypt, the conquest and early monarchy). Other scholars

16. M. Tomal, *Język hebrajski biblijny*, Warsaw, 2000, 5; I am grateful to Dr Maciej Tomal also for the information that, philologically speaking, the Hebrew language can be described as "a set of linguistic norms," and efforts to separate it into concrete evolutionary steps prove misleading.

17. The most important representatives of this school, harking back to the tradition of Robertson Smith, are S.H. Hooke, *Myth and Ritual*, London, 1933; *idem*, *The Labyrinth*, London, 1935; *idem*, *Myth, Ritual, and Kingship: Essays on the Theory and Practice of Kingship in the Ancient Near East and in Israel*, Oxford, 1958, and also S. Mowinckel, *He that Cometh*, Oxford, 1956; *idem*, *The Psalms in Israel's Worship*, Oxford, 1962.

18. J.C. de Moor, *The Rise of Yahwism: The Roots of Israelite Monotheism*, 2nd edn, Leuven, 1997; R. Albertz, *A History of Israelite Religion in the Old Testament Period*, vols. 1–2, Louisville, 1994.

hold the view that religion was the factor that united the people who arrived in Palestine at the beginning of the Iron Age.[19] The theory which sees the beginnings of monotheism as coinciding with the formation of Israel's state and ethnicity, despite all differences, continues the scholarship tradition of Albrecht Alt[20] and Martin Noth.[21] The paradigm used in the study of the history of Israel has undergone considerable change and this, in turn, has changed the study of the beginnings of monotheism. Many historians have questioned the historicity of the patriarchs, and some have questioned or rejected the exodus from Egypt.[22] This process began as a result of fresh archaeological conclusions and new methods of Bible Studies.[23] The consequence of establishing a "new" history of Israel has been the introduction of a clear differentiation between literary narrative and historical account. It is now impossible to imagine a reconstruction of the history of Israel simply on the basis of biblical accounts. As far as historical studies are concerned, the biblical text has the same merit as extra-biblical written texts. Historical studies undertaken today must include the archaeological knowledge of a specific place as well as the reality of the world in which past events were played out. A biblical narrative can be accepted as a credible account only after it has been set alongside extra-biblical, and particularly archaeological, material. This is a result not just of moving the date of the text's creation (many scholars accept that though the text is of later origin, the oral tradition on which the work was based is credible), but of admitting that the Bible had certain aims which were not

19. N. Gottwald, *The Tribes of Yahweh*, New York, 1979.

20. A. Alt, *Die Ursprünge des israelitischen Rechts*, Leipzig, 1934.

21. M. Noth, *Das System der Zwölf Stämme Israels*, Stuttgart, 1930.

22. N.P. Lemche, *The Israelites in History and Tradition*, London, 1998; T.L. Thompson, *The Historicity of the Patriarchal Narrative: The Quest for the Historical Abraham*, BZAW 133, Berlin, 1974; *idem, Early History of the Israelite People: From the Written and Archaeological Sources*, SHANE 4, Leiden, 1992; G. Garbini, *History and Ideology in Ancient Israel*, New York, 1988; *idem, Il ritorno dall'esilio babilonese*, Brescia, 2001; *idem, Myth and History in the Bible*, London, 2003.

23. P.R. Davies, *In Search of "Ancient Israel"*, JSOTSup 148, Sheffield, 1992; V. Fritz and P.R. Davies (eds.), *The Origins of the Ancient Israelite States*, JSOTSup 228, Sheffield, 1996; D.V. Edelman (ed.), *The Fabric of History: Text, Artifact and Israel Past*, JSOTSup 127, Sheffield, 1991; archaeological findings are presented by N.P. Lemche, *The Canaanites and their Land: The Tradition of the Canaanites*, JSOTSup 110, Sheffield, 1990; *idem, Early Israel: Anthropological and Historical Studies on the Israelite Society Before the Monarchy*, VTSup 37, Leiden, 1985, and particularly I. Finkelstein, *The Archaeology of the Israelite Settlement*, Jerusalem, 1988; I. Finkelstein and N. Na'aman (eds.), *From Nomadism to Monarchy: Archaeological and Historical Aspects of Early Israel*, Jerusalem, 1994.

simply a "factual" examination of the past. The religious text which formed a theology was there to legitimise a system of values, a way of exercising power, and the establishment of a national consciousness. In the hands of the Bible's authors, the past was material to be freely shaped, and while they worked on it, they paid little attention to fidelity to reality. For the Israelites the stories of, for example, Egyptian slavery, the feast of Passover, the exodus from the land of the Nile and the conquest of Canaan were essential: they had to fulfil theological and political aims. It is hard, therefore, to accept them as an objective description of past events.[24]

This account of the state of the research into the history and religion of ancient Palestine, or more precisely of the changes in contemporary historiography, will explain the criteria used in the selection of the secondary literature discussed in the present study. Since this is not a detailed analysis of specific biblical places, I have refrained from giving references to the findings of the older schools of research. This does not mean, of course, that I am making a clean break between old studies and the new. I am simply explaining the selection of materials, based as it is on the research criteria I have outlined here. Discussion of which tradition concrete biblical texts belong to becomes pointless if the very validity of such traditions is rejected.

Limits

The starting point of this work was to pick out the biblical material that deals with the aetiological myths of holy places. The subject of analysis was, therefore, limited to those narratives which dealt with the beginnings of cults in various sanctuaries. Applying this restriction as a basis has meant that important centres, such as Shiloh or Mizpah, are not discussed because they do not have their own founding myths. Although the Bible often mentions their religious importance, it does not talk about their beginnings.

In selecting my material I limited myself to those centres whose location is known, in other words, to those places mentioned in the Bible which can be located on a map of Palestine. I followed this procedure largely to be able to confront the archaeological material with the biblical

---

24. See, e.g., the excellent article by J.A. Soggin, "Appunti per lo studio della religione d'Israele in epoca pre-esilica," in V. Angelo (ed.), *Biblische und Judaische Studien. Festschrift für Paolo Sacchi*, Frankfurt, 1990, 55-63, and also the brilliant seminal book by M. Smith, *Palestinian Parties and Politics that Shaped the Old Testament*, New York, 1971.

narrative about the beginnings and history of a given sanctuary. Because of this limitation, places associated with, for instance, the journey of the Israelites through the desert have been omitted. Since it is impossible to locate these places and, additionally, since we cannot recreate the history of the rites practised there on the basis of biblical material, any analysis of the aetiological story would have no purpose and no reference to reality.

I make an exception to this principle in Chapter 8, where I discuss the myths involving Galeed, Mahanaim and Penuel. I believe that by taking them into account, despite the lack of data about the history of these centres, I can delve more deeply into the whole question of the Bible's aetiology of holy places.

A separate issue is the exclusion of Jerusalem from this study, even though there is no suggestion that it cannot be located or that there is a lack of data about the sanctuary there.[25] It would certainly be correct to acknowledge that the fetching of the ark there by David and the building of the temple by Solomon are aetiological stories about the sanctuary in Jerusalem.[26] Jerusalem is a special case. It has been drawn into the nexus of Jewish religious thought as a cult centre and the capital of the state. An investigation of this subject would require a separate study and would far exceed the confines of just one chapter in this book, which is devoted to a study of centres which were in competition with, or hostile to, Jerusalem. In addition, this book is meant as a contribution to the continuing debate among biblical scholars and historians of Palestine about the extent, and form, of monolatry and about how widespread the idea of the exclusivity of Jerusalem's temple cult was.[27] It is widely accepted—by lay people and scholars alike—that Jerusalem was the most important religious centre in ancient Palestine. My aim is to analyse the stories about the beginnings of cult places which competed with it. Furthermore, by implication, my aim is to answer the question as to whether or not

25. Despite this optimistic assertion, it must not be forgotten that digs continue on a fragmentary basis in Jerusalem and it is not yet possible to draw any final conclusions about the sanctuary on the temple mount on their basis.

26. The Bible does not contain an aetiological myth to describe the beginning of a cult in Jerusalem. It could be that this centre was considered so holy that a myth about the beginnings of the cult of that place was quite simply superfluous.

27. Of the rich literature on the subject of Jerusalem and its religious significance, worth consulting, among others, are M. Haran, *Temples and Temple-Service in Ancient Israel: An Inquiry into the Character of Cult Phenomena and Historical Setting of the Priestly School*, Oxford, 1978; R. de Vaux, *Ancient Israel*, Vol. 2, *Religious Institutions*, New York, 1965.

Jerusalem really was such an exceptional or unique religious centre. Furthermore, it is to discover what purpose these stories served when, as seen from the standpoint of Jerusalem-centred authors (and editors), they could well be regarded as superfluous or even damaging.

The reader will discover that the biblical aetiologies of holy places are connected with the great figures of Hebrew tradition—the patriarchs, the judges, and heroes of the conquest of Canaan—though these figures are not linked to the beginnings of Jerusalem. The history of David's capital is, however, embedded in the history of the monarchy.

There is one more limit placed on this work, namely that the corpus of the source material has been narrowed down to the Pentateuch and the so-called Deuteronomistic History. The collection which includes the books of Genesis to 2 Kings comprises a compact set of texts which have been subjected to a unified redaction.

Aims of this Work

When I started studying the history and religion of the ancient Hebrews I asked myself several questions, ones which have led me to the writing of this treatise. First, how is it that the biblical text, decisively shaped by priests seeking to centralise the cult of Jerusalem, has preserved aetiological myths about other sanctuaries and how can this be reconciled with the criticism of unorthodox cult places found in the books of Kings and the Prophets? Secondly, how are the aetiological accounts constructed? Thirdly, are there any elements common to myths about different places? And finally, and most importantly, when did the mythical traditions about the establishment of specific sanctuaries begin and what were the circumstances that led to their preservation in the biblical text?

Archaeology has confirmed the existence of many cult places (for instance Arad, Lachish, Hazor) which were active at various times—from the Late Bronze through the Iron Age and to the Persian and Hellenistic eras. The Bible also mentions numerous religious centres (Shiloh, Nob, Carmel), but only in a few of these cases does it talk about their mythical beginnings. Is that because they were not important enough? Or maybe their aetiologies were not interesting enough? Why were the aetiologies of some sanctuaries preserved and those of others not? Could the decisive factor be the form of the myth, or the content? Or was it, perhaps, the historical situation in which the framework of the biblical canon was being constructed?

Summing up: I could say that the present study sets out to examine the forms of the aetiology of holy places, to sift from the aetiologies the mythical elements they contain, and to establish the time that they were begun and the reasons for their preservation of the biblical text.

Sources

The basic sources of this work are two versions of the Bible: the Hebrew edition of the MT is *Biblia Hebraica Stuttgartensia*, Stuttgart, 1997, while the Greek LXX is Rahlf edition. Individual narratives were also analysed by referring to a version of The Samaritan Pentateuch (SP) and the Aramaic targumim. A comparison with the versions in the Vulgate and the *Vetus Latina* was helpful in illuminating the texts and in establishing the original rendition of unclear passages. Similarly helpful were biblical texts uncovered in Qumran.

A lot of additional information was collected from non-biblical or apocryphal literature. The most valuable proved to be Flavius Josephus's *Jewish Antiquities*. Also useful were the book of *Jubilees*, *Genesis Apocryphon*, as well as *Seper ha-Yamin*, the Samaritan text corresponding to the biblical collection of Joshua and 2 Kings. Another source was the *Liber Antiquitatum Biblicarum (LAB)*, generally accepted as the work of Pseudo-Philo.

The biblical text has been given in Hebrew or Greek. The English version used here comes from the NIV. When my own interpretation of the text differs from that of NIV it is clearly pointed out.

I have also used the Samaritan Pentateuch in Abraham Tal's edition,[28] and the targumim[29] in editions by B. Grossfeld[30] and E.G. Clarke.[31]

Because the new publications of the volumes of the *Vetus Latina* are still in progress, I have used Petrus Sabathier's edition.[32]

The appropriate volumes of Discoveries in the Judean Desert series were consulted when dealing with the biblical fragments from Qumran.

---

28. A. Tal (ed.), *The Samaritan Targum of the Pentateuch: A Critical Edition*, vols. 1-3, Tel Aviv, 1980–83; *idem*, *The Samaritan Pentateuch: Edited According to Ms6 (C) of the Shekhem Synagogue*, Tel Aviv, 1994.

29. For more on the meaning of interpretation and the extent of the changes introduced by translators, see in M.L. Klein, "The Aramaic Targumim: Translation and Interpretation," in *Interpretation of the Bible: International Symposium on the Interpretation of the Bible*, Ljubljana/Sheffield, 1998, 317-31.

30. B. Grossfeld, *The Targum Onqelos to Genesis*, The Aramaic Bible 6, Edinburgh, 1988.

31. E.G. Clarke (ed.), *Targum Pseudo-Jonathan of the Pentateuch: Text and Concordance*, New Jersey, 1984.

32. *Bibliorum Sacrorum latinae versiones antiquae seu Vetus Italica*, Paris, 1751.

English translations of the non-biblical Qumran manuscripts follows those of F. García Martínez and E.J.C. Tigchelaar.[33] The text and English translation of Flavius Josephus are taken from the Loeb edition. The book of *Jubilees* is quoted from the translation by James VanderKam.[34] Citations from the *Genesis Apocryphon* follow Fitzmyer's standard edition.[35] The text of *Liber Antiquitatum Biblicarum* was consulted in two editions—those of Guido Kisch[36] and Charles Perrot and P.-M. Bogaert.[37] MacDonald's critical edition was used when citing the *Seper ha-Yamim*.[38]

A word of explanation is needed regarding the decision to write the noun "god" with a small initial letter. In the present work the reader will come across many gods worshipped in ancient Palestine and described in the Bible. Differentiating "god" in the case of El from "God" in the case of Yahweh does not seem to me to be justified, since they were both, according to the Bible, treated with equal reverence. By adopting this orthographic consistency I sought to standardise the account and to avoid the difficulty of differentiating between God and an unspecified divinity, which would have led to making a value judgment. The only exception is in the case of cited texts, where the orthography of the original has been retained.

33. F. García Martínez and E.J.C. Tigchelaar (eds.), *The Dead Sea Scrolls Study Edition*, Leiden, 2000.

34. James C. VanderKam (trans.), *The Book of Jubilees*, CSCO 511, Scriptores Aethiopici 88, Leuven, 1989.

35. J.A. Fitzmyer, *The Genesis Apocryphon of Qumran Cave I: A Commentary*, Rome, 1966.

36. G. Kisch, *Pseudo-Philo's Liber Antiquitatum Biblicarum*, Notre Dame, Ind., 1949.

37. C. Perrot and P.-M. Bogaert (eds.), Pseudo-Philo, *Les Antiquités Biblique*, SC 229-30, Paris, 1976.

38. J. MacDonald (ed.), *The Samaritan Chronicle No. II (or: Sepher Ha-Yamim) from Joshua to Nebuchadnezzer*, Berlin, 1969.

2.
Beer-sheba

Archaeological Data

In the history of Palestine, Beer-sheba—a town lying in southern Judah—has not always been part of the state(s). At the time of the migration of the Sea Peoples (thirteenth/twelfth centuries BCE), the lands on the boundaries of Judah and Negev were probably conquered by the Philistines or by one of the related tribes.[1] During the Judean monarchy a steady influx of the Edomite[2] people occurred and this intensified during the Babylonian period. By the fourth century BCE the population of Beersheba was already a mixture of Jewish, Edomite and Arabic peoples.[3] In this period Beer-sheba probably played some role in the network of the Persian administration; the discovery of fragments of Aramaic documents is evidence of this. Archaeological excavations have provided us with fairly exhaustive information about the history of the settlement in Beer-sheba. The layers of stratification indicate that although the first buildings in Beer-sheba went up in the thirteenth century, the settlement that existed there before the eleventh century was of marginal significance (strata I-8, I-9). During the Iron Age (strata I-2 to I-7) there was a fortified town there which was destroyed in the tenth and then the

---

1. J. Strange, "The Philistine City-States," in M.H. Hansen (ed.), *A Comparative Study of Thirty City-State Cultures*, Copenhagen, 2000, 129-39.

2. Bert Dicou, *Edom, Israel's Brother and Antagonist: The Role of Edom in Biblical Prophecy and Story*, JSOTSup 168, Sheffield, 1994, 180-81. See John R. Bartlett, *Edom and the Edomites*, JSOTSup 77, Sheffield, 1989; *idem*, "Edom in the Nonprophetical Corpus," in Diana Vikander Edelman (ed.), *You Shall Not Abhor an Edomite for He is Your Brother: Edom and Seir in History and Tradition*, Archaeology and Biblical Studies 3, Atlanta, 1995, 13-21; J.M. Myers, "Edom and Judah in Sixth-Fifth Centuries B.C.," in Hans Goedicke (ed.), *Near Eastern Studies in Honor of William Foxwell Albright*, Baltimore, 1971, 377-92.

3. Y. Aharoni, "Beersheba, Tel," in *EAEHL*, 1:167.

eighth[4] centuries (probably in 925 and 701 BCE). In the seventh century all that existed there was a small settlement (stratum I-1). Beer-sheba remained abandoned right until the Persian era, at which time it most probably became the site of a modest garrison (H-3). In the second century BCE settlement there becomes much more marked and it is from this period (H-2) that the discovered Hellenistic temple comes. The strategic position of Beer-sheba was exploited by both Herod the Great in the first century BCE and, in the second–third centuries CE, by the Romans who built reinforcements there.[5]

Excavations of the tell revealed the remains of an early Iron Age town. The structure, and traces of the older building discovered within the urban construction, are tentatively regarded as a sanctuary. Three facts support such an interpretation of the discovery:

1. the positioning of the building on an east–west axis;
2. the existence in front of it of a hardened courtyard (5 × 10 m) where the "horned" altar was supposed to have been;
3. the placing of the Hellenistic temple directly over the discovered remains.[6]

Biblical Information

The biblical text provides valuable material about Beer-sheba. The town is mentioned most often as a place lying the furthest south—as, for example, in the phrase "from Dan to Beer-sheba" (מדן ועד באר־שבע)— that is, from the far north all the way to the extreme south.[7] (The question

---

4. Cf. Ernst Axel Knauf, "Who Destroyed Beersheba II?," in U. Hübner and E.A. Knauf (eds.), *Kein Land für sich allein. Studies zum Kulturkontakt in Kanaan, Israel/Palästine und Ebirnâri für Manfred Weippert zum 65. Geburtstag*, OBO 186, Göttingen, 2002, 181-95, who opted for later times of destruction, not by Sennacherib, but in the early seventh century BCE.

5. Steve Derfler, *The Hellenistic Temple at Tel Beersheva*, Lewiston, 1993, 10-12. Cf. Yohanan Aharoni (ed.), *Beer-sheba I: Excavations at Tel Beer-sheba 1969–1971 Seasons*, Tel Aviv, 1973; Ze'ev Herzog (ed.), *Beer-Sheba II: The Early Iron Age Settlements*, Tel Aviv, 1984; *idem*, "Tel Beersheba," in *NEAEHL*, 1:167-73; Antoon Schoors, "The Bible on Beer-sheba," *Tel Aviv* 17 (1990): 100-109.

6. Ze'ev Herzog, "Israelite Sanctuaries at Arad and Beer-Sheba," in Avraham Biran (ed.), *Temples and High Places in Biblical Times: Proceedings of the Colloquium in Honor of the Centennial of Hebrew Union College–Jewish Institute of Religion. Jerusalem, 14–16 March 1977*, Jerusalem, 1981, 120-22.

7. Apart from the nine phrases of the "from Dan to Beer-sheba" kind, there is also another form, found, for example, in 2 Chr 19:4, where Beer-sheba is counterbalanced by Mt Ephraim, and in 2 Kgs 23:8, where mention is made of the defilement of altars "from Geba to Beer-sheba."

of which historical realities, if any, this turn of phrase refers to demands separate consideration.) Undoubtedly its popularity may be connected to the following phrase: "As surely as your god lives, O Dan! Or as surely as the god of Beer-sheba lives" (Amos 8:14).[8] Beer-sheba is mentioned as lying at the far south in 2 Sam 24:7 and in 1 Kgs 19:3 it is associated with the desert. Twice it is mentioned as the town inhabited by the descendants of Simeon (Josh 19:2; 1 Chr 4:28), and once as a town of Judah (Josh 15:28).[9]

In the LXX the Hebrew name באר־שׁבע is given as Βηρσαβεε. Only once does the LXX use the name Βηρσαβεε where it does not appear in the MT (1 Kgs 1:16). In this instance what we are dealing with is a curious misunderstanding, for the reference is to Bath-Sheba, the mother of Solomon, who is mentioned many times but only in this one case is her name altered to sound like the name of the town.[10]

There are several instances where name "Beer-sheba" appears in the MT (but exclusively in Genesis) when it does not do so in the LXX. The majority are references deriving from the aetiologies I will discuss later.[11] The only time the name appears outside Genesis and does not do so in the LXX, is Amos 5:5: "do not seek Bethel, do not go to Gilgal, do not journey to Beer-sheba. For Gilgal will surely go into exile, and Bethel will be reduced to nothing."[12] Instead of the anticipated transliteration of the proper name the translators of the LXX wrote φρέαρ τοῦ ὅρκου, that is, the "well of the covenant." Putting the name Beer-sheba into this verse is slightly anomalous because it breaks the internal analogy (the fall of the

---

8. Schoors, "The Bible on Beer-sheba," 105 considers that the juxtaposing of the names Dan and Beer-sheba in this verse is independent of the combination so characteristic of the Deuteronomistic History (DtrH); for more on the subject of "God of Dan," see the chapter on Dan.

9. The references in Neh 11:27 and 11:30 do not specify which of the tribes lived there. An attempt to explain this discrepancy is made, not entirely convincingly, by Schoors, "The Bible on Beer-sheba," 102-103.

10. καὶ ἔκυψεν Βηρσαβεε καὶ προσεκύνησεν τῷ βασιλεῖ καὶ εἶπεν ὁ βασιλεύς τί ἐστίν σοι.

11. Gen 21:14, 31, 32; 22:19–26:23; 26:33; 28:10–46:1; 46:5. *Nota bene*: in the LXX the name "Beer-sheba" does not appear even once in Genesis.

12. The presence in Syro-Palestine of the custom of pilgrimage as early as the Bronze Age is confirmed by excavations at Nahariyah. It is believed that the votive figurines of women found in the excavations of the temple remains were brought and offered there by pilgrims; see M. Dothan, "The Excavations at Nahariyah," *IEJ* 6 (1974): 14–25; Miriam Tadmor, "Female Cult Figurines in Late Canaan and Early Israel: Archaeological Evidence," in Tomoo Ishida (ed.), *Studies in the Period of David and Solomon and Other Essays: Papers Read at the International Symposium for Biblical Studies, Tokyo, 5–7 December 1979*, Tokyo, 1982, 139-73 (164).

city is not predicted here), as well as the external analogy to Amos 4:4 where only Bethel and Gilgal are mentioned.[13]

1 Samuel 8:1-5, a rather puzzling passage, provides further information about Beer-sheba:

> When Samuel grew old, he appointed his sons as judges for Israel. The name of his firstborn was Joel and the name of his second was Abijah, and they served at Beer-sheba. But his sons did not walk in his ways. They turned aside after dishonest gain and accepted bribes and perverted justice. So all the elders of Israel gathered together and came to Samuel at Ramah. They said to him, "You are old, and your sons do not walk in your ways; now appoint a king to lead us, such as all the other nations have."

We should bear in mind that Beer-sheba is not named among the Levitical towns (Josh 21), nor is it one of the cities of refuge (Josh 20). Why, then, should Samuel's sons be judges in this peripheral place since he himself was living in his mother town Ramah (1 Sam 1:1–15:34) and was active in Mizpah (1 Sam 7:11–10:17) or in Gilgal (1 Sam 11:15) which—as the narrative referring to the times of Saul suggests—functioned as administrative centres? Why, descending from the tribes of Levi but involved in the territory of Ephraim,[14] as they were, should the sons of Samuel of Ramah become judges over Israel in Beer-sheba? Is this a minor editorial emendation put there for some unknown purpose, or does the text perhaps suggest some links between the family of the prophet-judge Samuel and Beer-sheba?

There is a reference to Beer-sheba in one other place, namely, 2 Kgs 12:1-2 (see also the parallel 2 Chr 24:1-2): "In the seventh year of Jehu, Joash became king, and he reigned in Jerusalem forty years. His mother's name was Zibiah (צביה = Αβια); she was from Beersheba."

Aetiology

Genesis 21:22-33:

> (22) At that time Abimelech and Phicol the commander of his forces said to Abraham, "God is with you in everything you do. (23) Now swear to me (השבעה) before God that you will not deal falsely with me or my children or my descendants. Show to me and the country where you are

---

13. See H.W. Wolff, *Joel and Amos: A Commentary on the Books of the Prophets Joel and Amos*, Philadelphia, 1997, 109-10 n. k, 239; the author is convinced that the mention of Beer-sheba was of later origin and ascribes it to Amos's pupils; see also Schoors, "The Bible on Beer-sheba," 104.

14. The inconsistencies involved in the tribal affiliation of Samuel and his father Elkanah are discussed in R. Youngblood, *ABD, s.v.* "Elkanah."

living as an alien the same kindness I have shown to you." (24) Abraham said, "I swear it." (אשבע) (25) Then Abraham complained to Abimelech about a well (באר) of water that Abimelech's servants had seized. (26) But Abimelech said, "I don't know who has done this. You did not tell me, and I heard about it only today." (27) So Abraham brought sheep and cattle and gave them to Abimelech, and the two men made a treaty. (28) Abraham set apart seven (שבע) ewe lambs from the flock, (29) and Abimelech asked Abraham, "What is the meaning of these seven (שבע) ewe lambs you have set apart by themselves?" (30) He replied, "Accept these seven (שבע) lambs from my hand as a witness that I dug this well (הבאר)." (31) So that place was called Beer-sheba (באר־שבע), because the two men swore an oath (נשבעו) there. (32) After the treaty had been made at Beer-sheba, Abimelech and Phicol the commander of his forces returned to the land of the Philistines. (33) Abraham planted a tamarisk tree in Beer-sheba, and there he called upon the name of the Lord, the Eternal God.

Genesis 26:23-33:

(23) From there [Gerar] he [Isaac] went up to Beer-sheba (באר־שבע). (24) That night the Lord appeared to him and said, "I am the God of your father Abraham. Do not be afraid, for I am with you; I will bless you and will increase the number of your descendants for the sake of my servant Abraham." (25) Isaac built an altar there and called on the name of the Lord. There he pitched his tent, and there his servants dug a well (באר). (26) Meanwhile, Abimelech had come to him from Gerar, with Ahuzzath his personal adviser and Phicol the commander of his forces. (27) Isaac asked them, "Why have you come to me, since you were hostile to me and sent me away?" (28) They answered, "We saw clearly that the Lord was with you; so we said, 'There ought to be a sworn agreement between us'— between us and you. Let us make a treaty with you (29) that you will do us no harm, just as we did not molest you but always treated you well and sent you away in peace. And now you are blessed by the Lord." (30) Isaac then made a feast for them, and they ate and drank. (31) Early the next morning the men swore an oath to each other. Then Isaac sent them on their way, and they left him in peace. (32) That day Isaac's servants came and told him about the well (הבאר) they had dug. They said, "We've found water!" (33) He called it Shibah (שבעה) and to this day the name of the town has been Beer-sheba (באר־שבע).

What is characteristic of both narratives is that they are, to a large extent, very similar. This would indicate that we are dealing here with one story ascribed to two patriarchs concerning a covenant reached with Abimelech accompanied by Phicol—commander of the forces. In both accounts the etymology of the name "Beer-sheba" (באר־שבע) is derived from the numeral "seven" (שבע) and the verb "to swear an oath" (שבע). Both accounts use the same elements and this allows us to consider them jointly. What emerges is a picture where the following elements play a key role: a well, a covenant, the number seven and the toponym "Beer-sheba."

It seems that the story of Beer-sheba was originally associated with Abraham and only with time became ascribed also to Isaac.[15] This is supported by the fact that the composition of the account in Gen 21:22-33 is better constructed (the proper name of the place באר־שׁבע appears only after the introduction of the play on words באר, שׁבע). Also, Abraham's presence in the south of Judah is more likely than Isaac's because of his stay in Egypt.[16] This view would accord with that of scholars who regard the biblical Isaac as a character of secondary importance in comparison with Abraham and Jacob.[17]

The apocryphal book of *Jubilees* (the origins of which are put towards the end of second century BCE[18]) also contains a motif associated with the well in Beer-sheba:

> There he built an altar for the Lord who had rescued him and who was making him so happy in the country where he resided as an alien. He celebrated a joyful festival in this month—for seven days—near the altar which he had built at the well of the oath… During these seven days he was making—throughout all the days, each and every day—an offering to the Lord on the altar: two bulls, two rams, seven sheep, one goat for sins in order to atone through it for himself and his descendants. And as a peace offering: seven rams, seven kids, seven sheep, and seven he-goats as well as their (cereal-)offerings and their libations over all their fat—(all of these) he would burn on the altar as a choice offering for a pleasing fragrance. (*Jub.* 16:20-23)[19]

In later passages there is talk of Isaac's settling in the region of Gerar and his contacts with the Philistine king Abimelech (*Jub.* 24:8-13). The account in *Jub.* 24 relates closely to the contents of Gen 26 and follows the canonical text, while it also contains several fresh pieces of information. After the passage about the digging of three wells in the region of

15. Cf. John Van Seters, *Abraham in History and Tradition*, New Haven, 1975, 184-87.

16. *Nota bene*: the description of Abraham's meeting with Abimelech and the story of Sarah (Gen 20) are directly analogous with the story of events in Egypt (Gen 12:10-20).

17. See R. Martin-Archard, *ABD*, *s.v.* "Isaac." The marginalisation of Isaac can also be seen in *Liber Antiquitatum Biblicarum*, where Jacob is treated almost like the son of Abraham.

18. See James C. VanderKam, *ABD*, *s.v.* "Jubilees, Book of."

19. This and all subsequent translations are taken from VanderKam (trans.), *The Book of Jubilees*.

Gerar (*Jub.* 24:16-20) and about the well and the oath sworn in Beer-sheba (vv. 21-26), a diametrically different assessment of the Philistines is given:

> On that day Isaac realised that he had sworn an oath to them under pressure to make peace with them. On that day Isaac cursed the Philistines and said: "May the Philistines be cursed from among all peoples at the day of anger and wrath. May the Lord make them into (an object of) derision and curse, into (an object of) anger and wrath in the hands of the sinful nations and in the hands of Kittim." (*Jub.* 24:27-28)

Following this the curses continue and end with the sentence: "This is the way it has been written and inscribed regarding him on the heavenly tablets—to do (this) to him on the day of judgment so that he may be eradicated from the earth" (*Jub.* 24:33).

The fragments cited here appear to confirm the view that Abraham played the main role, and that Isaac's association with Beer-sheba was secondary.[20] In the first place there is a confusion of two figures: Isaac and Jacob (both of whom receive Abraham's blessing; cf. *Jub.* 22:1–23:5). Second, there is a direct reference to actions performed by Abraham: "There he built the altar which his father Abraham had first built. He called on the Lord's name and offered a sacrifice to the God of his father Abraham" (*Jub.* 24:23).

The duplication of the accounts about the beginnings of Beer-sheba does not prevent us treating the aetiological narratives analysed here as a whole.[21] Even if it were not possible to establish which of the patriarchs was more closely involved with this place, then the repetition of the mythical motif would fully justify the assessment of both narratives jointly.

It is hard to resist the impression that the whole story of the alliance between Abimelech and Abraham is derivative. It is also surprising that the numerous editor–translator modifications only too evident here have not eliminated it. There is a reference in Gen 21:33 to a name for god which is alien to Yahwism, namely, Yahweh El Olam (יהוה אל עולם).[22] This combination is surprising in that El Olam was a god who not only did not have to have any association with Yahwism, but who was, in

---

20. For another view, see de Vaux, *Ancient Israel*, 2:293; Schoors, "The Bible on Beer-sheba," 100-109.

21. E.A. Speiser, *Genesis*, AB 1, Garden City, NY, 1964, 203, is of the view that initially there was one story which was duplicated.

22. De Vaux, *Ancient Israel*, 2:293-94. On the subject of El Olam, see A. de Pury, *DDD*, *s.v.* "El-Olam"; von Rad, *Old Testament Theology*, 31.

fact, associated with solar and female cults.[23] It could be that some trait of this god was strongly allied to a cult practised in the sanctuary at Beer-sheba.

There can be no doubt about the importance of the part played in the aetiology of Beer-sheba by the word "well" (באר) or "wells." Here it should be noted that the translators of the LXX, in their attempt to maintain the relationship between the etymology of the place name and the events described in the narrative,[24] used the term Φρέαρ ὅρκου,[25] a translation of the Hebrew name Beer-sheba—"well of the covenant"[26]— instead of the place name itself.

The situation is complicated by the fact the Flavius Josephus gives a different account still. Writing the story that corresponds to Gen 21:27-33, he probably based his version on a proto-Masoretic text. In *Jewish Antiquities* we read:

> So Abimelech assigned to him land and riches and they covenanted to deal honestly with each other, swearing an oath over a well which they call Bêrsubai, that is to say "well of the oath": it is still so named by the inhabitants of the country (Καὶ Αβιμέλςχος τήν τε γῆν πρὸς αὐτὸν νέμεται καὶ τὰ χρήματα καὶ συντίθενται ἀδόλως πολιτεύσεσθαι ὑπέρ τινος φρέατος ποιούμενοι τὸν ὅρκον ὅ Βηρσουβαὶ καλοῦσιν ὅρκιον δὲ φρέαρ λέγοιτ ἄν οὕτω δ ἔτι καὶ νῦν ὑπὸ τῶν ἐπιχωρίων ὠνόμασται). (*Ant* 1.12.1)

Josephus's narrative, the equivalent of the stories in Gen 26:23-25, 32-33, looks as if it is drawn from a different source; for the author speaks of the meeting between Isaac and Abimelech (*Ant* 1.18.2) as taking place in the region of Gerar (Γεράρων) and omits the entire account of the building of the altar in Beer-sheba (Isaac does not go to Beer-sheba at all). According to Josephus, it was Isaac who journeyed into the region of Gerar where Abimelech greeted him and not the other way round, as given in the MT (Gen 26:26). Josephus (*Ant* 1.18) gives further details concerning Isaac's coming to Gerar and digging a well there. When Abimelech started to turn against him (*Ant* 1.18.2), Isaac moved from Gerar to Φάραγγα.[27] The name Φάραγγα seems to derive from the LXX version in Gen 26:17—καὶ ἀπῆλθεν ἐκεῖθεν Ισαακ καὶ κατέλυσεν ἐν τῇ φάραγγι Γεραρων καὶ κατῴκησεν ἐκεῖ—where the noun φάραγξ denotes a

23. De Pury, "El-Olam," 552-53.

24. N.F. Marcos, "Nombres proprios y etimologias populares en la Septuaginta," *Sefarad* 37 (1977): 239-59.

25. At Gen 26:33 the LXX reads Ὄρκος consistently instead of "Shibea."

26. See E. Tov, *The Greek and Hebrew Bible: Collected Essays on the Septuagint*, VTSup 72, Leiden, 1999, 175.

27. It could be that a trace of this motif can also be seen in Gen 26:16-17.

"valley." The Greek term φάραγγι Γεραρων corresponds to the MT form of בנחל־גרר, which is "in the valley of Gerar,"[28] and should not be rendered as a proper name.[29]

Further versions of Josephus's narrative inform us of the intensification of the hostility between Isaac and Abimelech (1.18), following which comes the motif of naming the wells:

> Then, when accident enabled him to dig unmolested, he called this well Roobot, a name which denotes "spacious." Of the former wells one was called Eskos, that is to say "Combat," the other Stena, signifying "Hatred." (εἶτα αὐτομάτου παραχόντος αὐτῷ τὴν φρεωρυχίαν ἀ νεπικώλυτον 'Ροωβὼθ τὸ φρέαρ ὠνόμασεν εὐρύχωρον ἀποσημαίνει τὸ ὄνομα τῶν δὲ προτέρων τὸ μὲν Ἔσκον καλεῖται μάχην ἄν τις αὐτὸ φήσειε τὸ δ᾽ ἕτερον Στένα ἐχθραν ἀποσημαίνει τὸ ὄνομα.) (*Ant* 1.18.2)

There are, then, three names appearing here: "Roobot," "Eskon(-s)," and "Stena."

Josephus's version combines into one whole the two accounts from Gen 26:1-21 and 26:22-35, mixing the events from Gerar and Beersheba. Here is the biblical text immediately preceding the aetiology that forms the basis of Josephus Flavius's account:

> (12) Isaac planted crops in that land [Gerar] and the same year reaped a hundredfold, because the Lord blessed him. (13) The man became rich, and his wealth continued to grow until he became very wealthy. (14) He had so many flocks and herds and servants that the Philistines envied him. (15) So all the wells that his father's servants had dug in the time of his father Abraham, the Philistines stopped up, filling them with earth. (16) Then Abimelech said to Isaac, "Move away from us; you have become too powerful for us." (17) So Isaac moved away from there and encamped in the Valley of Gerar and settled there. (18) Isaac reopened the wells that had been dug in the time of his father Abraham, which the Philistines had stopped up after Abraham died, and he gave them the same names his father had given them. (19) Isaac's servants dug in the valley and discovered a well of fresh water there. (20) But the herdsmen of Gerar quarrelled with Isaac's herdsmen and said, "The water is ours!" So he named the well Esek (Quarrel) (עשק), because they disputed with him. (21) Then they dug another well, but they quarrelled over that one also; so he named it Sitnah (Discord) (שטנה) (22) He moved on from there and dug another well, and no one quarrelled over it. He named it Rehoboth (רחבות), saying, "Now the Lord has given us room and we will flourish in the land." (Gen 26:12-22)

---

28. The Vulgate translates Gen 26:17 as "et ille discedens veniret ad torrentem Gerarae habitaretque ibi."

29. See Josephus Flavius, *Jewish Antiquities*, trans. H.St.J. Thackeray, London, 1958–65, *passim*.

The term given by Josephus as Ροωβῶθ (or, depending on the codex, as Ροωβώθ, Ροωβόθ, Ρυωβώς) also appears in the LXX as a transliteration of the Hebrew proper name (רחבות / רחבת, Gen 10:11, 36-37 and 1 Chr 1:48), from the root רחב ("to be extensive," "wide," "open").[30] In turn, as the equivalent of רחבות the LXX in Gen 26:22 uses the word Εὐρυχωρία,[31] that is, "an open space," "free space."

"Stena" (Στένα) in Josephus corresponds to the word Ἐχθρία in the LXX, whose Hebrew equivalent is שׂטנה (Gen 26:21).

"Eskon(-s)" (Ἐσκον) in Josephus is Ἀδικία in the LXX and עשׂק (Gen 26:20) in MT.

The names in the LXX, as in the Vulgate, are semantic equivalents of Hebrew terms whereas Josephus uses transliteration.[32] The following table shows the variations of the names of the three wells in the different versions of the story:

MT	LXX	Josephus	Vulgate	SP
עשׂק (to fight)	ἀδικία (misdeed)	Ἐσκον	Calumnium (insult, calumny)	עשׂק^{CJ} (to harass) עשׂק^A (to quarrel)
שׂטנה (accusation,[33] enmity)	ἐχθρός / ἐχθρία (hostility)	Στένα	Inimicitia (unfriendliness)	שׂנאתה^J / שׂטנה^C (enmity) שׂנתה^A (hindrance)
רחבות (open space)	Εὐρυχωρία (open space)	Ροωβῶθ	Latitudo (expanse, space)	רחבה^J / רחבות^C (spacious) / פתחיאתה^A (open)

The stories about the beginning of the cult around Beer-sheba include four wells bearing different names. The basis of the biblical etymology is the word באר־שבע, but just as significant are the other forms באר־עשׂק*, באר־רחבות*, באר־שׂטנה*.

We can place the constituent elements of the aetiological story regarding Beer-sheba into two groups: (1) those closely tied to the name's etymology, and (2) those not related to it but forming parts of the narrative. The first will include terms for: "seven" (שׂבע), "swear an oath" (שׂבע) and "well" (באר), the second all the other terms of which the most important are: "Abimelech," "covenant" (ברית), "lamb(s)" (כבשׂה),

---

30. As a proper name it appears in Gen 10:11.

31. This is one of numerous instances where Josephus's text is closer to the MT than to the LXX.

32. I write more about the meaning and role of well names later.

33. Thus, according to BDB, in Ezra 4:6.

"tamarisk" (אשל), "God Eternal" (יהוה אל עולם). The word "altar" (מזבח), even though it appears in the text (Gen 26:25), is not a key term because, first, its presence was associated only with Isaac, and, second, the covenant between Abraham and Abimelech, as well as Abraham's sacral act ("he called on the name of the Lord"), did not demand an altar. This object evidently became an essential element of the cult only during the editing of the Bible, and mentioning it in the text here is an example of its own kind of anachronism. Its derivative role in the story relating the origins of the holy place is also associated with the nature of cult practised there, which was most probably the basis of the aetiology of Beer-sheba.

It is also worth drawing attention to the appearance in Gen 21:30 of the term "witness" (עדה)[34] and to the sentence, "Isaac then made a feast for them, and they ate and drank" (Gen 26:30).

The numeral "seven" and the verb "to swear (an oath)" form the word-source of the name "Beer-sheba." The significance of their function in the narrative—whose theme is the forming of a covenant and the swearing of a mutual oath—means that even researchers who are usually sceptical about this kind of explanation treat it seriously. Although, of course, obviously the role of the words in the mythical story does not necessarily indicate any actual etymological links with the name of the place. Unfortunately, there is no evidence of the existence of the name "Beer-sheba" before the creation of the Bible.[35] However, such analogous names as "Beer-Lahai-Roi" (Gen 16:14) and "Beer-Elim" (Isa 15:8) indicate a strong probability that it did exist.

One also has to acknowledge the possibility that the numeral (with its evident symbolic meaning) and the verb appear in the aetiology of Beer-sheba only because of their homophony with the toponym. Although my own view is that the toponym was initially associated with the number "seven" and only later with the verb "to swear (an oath)," I shall try to indicate those elements that allow us to accept that their presence in the myth is not accidental.

34. See Chapter 8 for information about the construction of "an altar of testimony" on the Jordan.
35. N. Wyatt, "The Meaning of El Roi and the Mythological Dimension in Genesis 16," *SJOT* 8 (1994): 141-51. Wyatt (p. 142) presents an interesting hypothesis regarding the evidence locating Beer-sheba in an extra-biblical text. He claims that on the basis of Gen 12:33 Beer-sheba can be identified with *bt 'rm(in)*, a place mentioned in the record of Karnak as being one of the places captured by Sheshonk I in the years 925–924 BCE. This name might be read as *Bet 'Olam*, which tempts one to identify this place with the Beer-sheba mentioned in Gen 21:33.

To explain its meaning one must start by analysing the terminology used in the Hebrew Bible.

The feminine noun "well" (באר) is an essential element of both narratives and the motif of digging a well that appears in them both proves that the presence of the word is not accidental. In the Bible a well is most often written of as a life-giving reservoir of water:

> (16) From there they continued on to Beer (באר), the well (הבאר) where the Lord said to Moses, "Gather the people together and I will give them water." (17) Then Israel sang this song: "Spring up, O well! Sing about it, (18) about the well that the princes dug, that the nobles of the people sank-the nobles with sceptres and staffs." (Num 21:16-18)

A well is also a place of shelter:

> So the two of them [Jonathan and Ahimaaz] left quickly and went to the house of a man in Bahurim. He had a well (באר) in his courtyard, and they climbed down into it. (19) His wife took a covering and spread it out over the opening of the well and scattered grain over it. No one knew anything about it. (2 Sam 17:18-19)

It is obviously the case that a well with water in the desert indicates life:

> Then God opened her [Hagar's] eyes and she saw a well (באר) of water. So she went and filled the skin with water and gave the boy a drink. (Gen 21:19)[36]

Roland de Vaux claims that there were in Palestine Canaanite cults of water and that their holy places were associated with sources and wells.[37] At the same time one must be aware that the symbolism of the sea, which the Israelites crossed and which appears in the book of Exodus, decisively combines the element of the sea with the concept of Sheol.[38]

Related to the word באר is the Hebrew masculine noun בור,[39] which also denotes a well or a cistern. This noun may suggest links with the underworld; it is used several times, namely in sentences explicitly expressing the idea of an association between a well and the world of the dead: "But you are brought down to the grave (שאול), to the depths of the pit (בור)" (Isa 14:15); "O Lord, you brought me up from the grave

---

36. It is worth noting here that the desert where Ishmael is to die is described as "the desert of Beer-sheba" (Gen 21:14). It is also intriguing that in the MT the expression באר מים ("well of water") appears only in Gen 21:19; 26:19 and Song 4:15.

37. De Vaux, *Ancient Israel*, 2:277-78.

38. W. Wilfall, "The Sea of Reeds as Sheol," *ZAW* 92 (1980): 325-32.

39. *DCH*, 2:129-30.

(שאול); you spared me from going down into the pit (בור)" (Ps 30:4);[40] "Their graves are in the depths of the pit (בור) and her army lies around her grave. All who had spread terror in the land of the living are slain, fallen by the sword" (Ezek 32:23).[41] The well as a synonym for the underworld appears also in Lamentations: "They tried to end my life in a pit (בור) and threw stones at me; the waters closed over my head, and I thought I was about to be cut off" (Lam 3:53-54).[42]

The issue of the link between a well and the concept of the underworld has been the subject of many analyses.[43] A lot of attention has been devoted to it by Nicholas Tromp.[44] Tromp rejects Zorell's suggestion that Ps 40:3 contains an allusion to a well-Sheol, but he does see such an idea—associated with Isa 38:18[45]—in the text of Jer 38:6: "So they took Jeremiah and put him into the cistern (הבור) of Malkijah, the king's son, which was in the courtyard of the guard. They lowered Jeremiah by ropes into the cistern (ובבור); it had no water in it, only mud (טיט), and Jeremiah sank down into the mud." We read about the relationship between a well-Sheol and mud (טיט) in: "He lifted me out of the slimy pit (מבור שאון), out of the mud and mire (טיט היון)" (Ps 40:2) as well as "Rescue me from the mire, do not let me sink; deliver me from those who hate me, from the deep waters. Do not let the floodwaters engulf me or the depths swallow me up or the pit close (באר) its mouth over me" (Ps 69:14-15).[46] There are evident assumptions contained in such statements as: "then I will bring you down with those who go down to the pit, to the people of long ago. I will make you dwell in the earth below, as in ancient ruins,[47] with those who go down to the pit (בור), and you will not return or take your place in the land of the living" (Ezek 26:20); "…and

40. J.B. Curtis, "An Investigation of the Mount of Olives in the Judeo-Christian Tradition," *HUCA* 28 (1957): 137-80, sees in this an analogy to an address to the Babylonian god of the underworld—Nergal.

41. *TDOT*, 1:463-66 (456-66), where references are also made to Exod 12:29 and Jer 37:16.

42. N.J. Tromp, *Primitive Conceptions of Death and the Nether World in the Old Testament*, Rome, 1969, 67.

43. M. Held, "Pits and Pitfalls in Akkadian and Biblical Hebrew," *JANESCU* 5 (1973): 173-90; M.H. Lichtenstein, "The Poetry of Poetic Justice: A Comparative Study in Biblical Imagery," *JANESCU* 5 (1973): 255-65; see N. Wyatt, *Myths of Power: A Study of Royal Myth and Ideology in Ugarit and Biblical Tradition*, Münster, 1996, 109-10, where he discusses the symbolism of Ezek 26:20.

44. Tromp, *Primitive Conceptions of Death*, 66-68.

45. Isa 38:18 reads: "For the grave cannot praise you, death cannot sing your praise; those who go down to the pit (יורדי־בור) cannot hope for your faithfulness."

46. The image of the well closing its mouth is relevant to the further discussion.

47. It is worth noting the appearance of the term "eternal" (עולם) here.

consign to the earth below both her and the daughters of mighty nations, with those who go down to the pit (בור)" (Ezek 32:18).[48]

The use in Ps 69:16 of the noun באר is evidence that its meaning is identical with the noun בור.

What is intriguing are the numerous formulations showing the anthropomorphic concept of "well-Sheol." In Gen 29:2-3, there is a reference to the well's mouth (פי הבאר = στόματι τοῦ φρέατος), closed up by a large stone,[49] which might suggest the image of a well that devours, that is hungry and has to be fed.[50]

A well, or rather a pit, is mentioned also in 2 Sam 18:17: "They took Absalom, threw him into a big pit (הפחת הגדול) in the forest and piled up a large heap of rocks over him." The word used here is פחת, meaning "a hole in the ground, a pit," having a meaning close to באר / בור. פחת appears with an article only in 2 Sam 18:17 (χάσμα, βόθυνος), Isa 24:18 (βόθυνος), Jer 48:44 (βόθυνος) and also—in the plural (הפחתים)—in 2 Sam 17:9. The dictionaries translate פחת as "pit"[51] and that is how many editions of the Bible (e.g. KJV) translate it.

The Greek term βόθυνος, equivalent to the Hebrew word פחת, occurs in the following places in the LXX: 2 Sam 18:17; Isa 24:17-18; 47:11; Jer 31:28, 43, 44 (= ch. 48 in MT). In Isa 51:1 it stands for the Hebrew word בור, and in 2 Kgs 3:16 it applies to the word גב ("pit, ditch, trench").[52] From the time of Homer the words βόθυνος and βόθρος (*Odyssey* 10.517; *Iliad* 17.58) have been used not only in the meaning of a common noun ("well, pit") but have also been associated with chthonic cults. Porfirius (*De Antro Nympharum* 6) uses it within the context of offering sacrifices to chthonic gods.[53]

The word χάσμα in the LXX is a *hapax legomenon*. In Greek literature we find it as early as Hesiod (*Theogonia* 740), often combined with the descriptions of Tartarus.[54]

The reference in 2 Sam 18:17, where it talks of a well in a forest into which the body of Absalom is thrown, the symbolism of the prophecies of Isaiah[55] and of Jeremiah, as well as the Greek equivalents of the

48. See also Ezek 32:24.
49. See 2 Sam 17:19.
50. See Prov 22:14 and the previously cited Ps 69:15.
51. BDB, *s.v.*
52. In the singular it appears only in 1 Kgs 6:9; 2 Kgs 3:16; Isa 33:4; Jer 14:3.
53. *LSJ, s.v.*
54. *LSJ, s.v.*
55. Isa 24:17-18 reads: "Terror and pit and snare await you, O people of the earth. Whoever flees at the sound of terror will fall into a pit; whoever climbs out of the pit will be caught in a snare. The floodgates of the heavens are opened, the

Hebrew term פחת all testify to the cohesive symbolism of "well" (albeit denoted by different Hebrew words). The chthonic nature of this term, its use as a synonym for the grave, is beyond doubt. The well becomes an image of the grave and the underworld, a natural "entrance" to the underworld. To be in it is like being in Sheol. Water and mud, being symbols of Sheol, are a mirror image of the real bottom of the well. Many biblical texts confirm the linkage between the world of the dead and the symbolism of dampness and water.

There are two pieces of evidence to support the suggestion that offerings were made to chthonic gods in Palestine and that there was a sacrificial ritual associated with wells. Stewart Macalister, the archaeologist who led the excavations at the beginning of the twentieth century, discovered wells in strata III (1800–1400 BCE) and IV (1400–1000 BCE) which contained the remains of animals and humans at their bottom.[56] As the reconstructions he performed indicate, these were places of sacrifice. Sacrificial animals (or humans) were thrown in, and then they were stoned.[57] What is not known is whether the wells used for this had dried out or were still full of water.

If Macalister is right, then wells not only symbolised Sheol but also, as the gates to the underworld, they were places where people paid their devotions to the gods of the other world. These discoveries provide an explanation for the biblical passage about the stones thrown at the head of a man in a well (Lam 3:54). It could be a trace of ritual behaviour associated with a cult of the underworld gods: the person stoned in a well would have been offered as a sacrifice. If it were not so then we would have to deduce that the situation described in Lamentations is associated with punishment meted out to a criminal. But the presence in the excavated wells of animal as well as human bones would seem to suggest unequivocally that what we are dealing with here are the vestiges of a ritual sacrifice.

Traces of a chthonic cult whose key element was a well survived until the fourth century CE. Hermias Sozomen cites a letter from Constantine which contains the description of a pagan sanctuary in the region of Mamre:

foundations of the earth shake." The term "pit" used in this translation could be rendered just as literally as "well." This fragment demonstrates very vividly the whole chthonic nature of the symbolism associated with "well."

56. S. Macalister, *The Excavation of Gezer 1902–1905 and 1907–1909*, London, 1912, 2:397-401.

57. *Ibid.*, 397; this hypothesis was accepted by, *inter alia*, S. Cook, *The Religion of Ancient Palestine in the Light of Archaeology*, London, 1930, 82.

The place is open country, and arable, and without houses, with the exception of the buildings around Abraham's old oak and the well he prepared. No one during the time of the feast drew water from that well; for according to Pagan usage, some placed burning lamps near it; some poured out wine, or cast in cakes; and others, coins, myrrh, or incense. Hence, as I suppose, the water was rendered useless by commixture with the things cast into it. (*H.E.* 2.4)[58]

Though the sacrifices changed, the form of their offering remained the same. The throwing in of cakes, coins, or the pouring in of wine and aromatic oils can be explained as the relics of ritual sacrifices made to a god of the underworld. Incidentally, it may be mentioned that Sozomen's remark about the water in the well becoming unsuitable for drinking because of the substances thrown into it is surely the rationalisation of a historian, while the sentence "No one during the time of the feast drew water from that well" expresses a religious taboo and not a manifestation of concern about hygiene and health.

One other biblical motif associated with a well must be mentioned, namely, the story of how Joseph's brothers threw him into a well. The relevant biblical text says:

(20) "Come now, let's kill him and throw him into one of these cisterns (הברות = εἰς ἕνα τῶν λάκκων) and say that a ferocious animal (חיה רעה = θηρίον πονηπόν) devoured him. Then we'll see what comes of his dreams." (21) When Reuben heard this, he tried to rescue him from their hands. "Let's not take his life," he said. (22) "Don't shed any blood. Throw him into this cistern (הבור = εἰς τὸν λάκκον τοῦψον) here in the desert (אשר במדבר = τὸν ἐν τῇ ἐρήμῳ) but don't lay a hand on him." Reuben said this to rescue him from them and take him back to his father. (23) So when Joseph came to his brothers, they stripped him of his robe—the richly ornamented robe he was wearing—(24) and they took him and threw him into the cistern (הבור). Now the cistern (הבור) was empty; there was no water in it. (25) As they sat down to eat their meal, they looked up and saw a caravan of Ishmaelites coming from Gilead. Their camels were loaded with spices, balm and myrrh, and they were on their way to take them down to Egypt. (26) Judah said to his brothers, "What will we gain if we kill our brother and cover up his blood? (27) Come, let's sell him to the Ishmaelites and not lay our hands on him; after all, he is our brother, our own flesh and blood." His brothers agreed. (28) So when the Midianite merchants came by, his brothers pulled Joseph up out of the cistern (הבור) and sold him for twenty shekels of silver to the Ishmaelites, who took him to Egypt. (29) When Reuben returned to the cistern and saw that Joseph was not there, he tore his clothes. (30) He went back to his brothers and

---

58. Hermias Sozomen, *Ecclesiastical History*, repr., Kessinger Publishing Co., 2004.

said, "The boy (הילד[59] = παιδάριον) isn't there! Where can I turn now?"
(31) Then they got Joseph's robe, slaughtered a goat (שעיר עזים = ἔπιφον
αἰγῶν) and dipped the robe in the blood. (32) They took the ornamented
robe back to their father and said, "We found this. Examine it to see
whether it is your son's robe." (33) He recognised it and said, "It is my
son's robe! Some ferocious animal (חיה רעה = θηρίον πονηπόν) has
devoured him. Joseph has surely been torn to pieces (טרף טרף יוסף =
θηπίον ἥοπασεν τὸν Ιωσηφ)." (34) Then Jacob tore his clothes, put on
sackcloth and mourned for his son many days. (Gen 37:20-34)

This narrative employs a panoply of symbols.[60] The casting into the well
is synonymous with death. Joseph symbolically dies in a well without
water, and his father, weeping over his death, believes that he has been
torn to pieces by wild animals.[61]

The well (as a path to the underworld) is identified with the gates of
hell or even with Sheol itself. There is information in the Bible to indicate the existence of a sacrificial ritual involving the throwing of animals
into wells. For instance, in Ps 49:14 it is written: "Like sheep they are
destined for the grave (שאול), and death will feed on them. The upright
will rule over them in the morning; their forms will decay in the grave,
far from their princely mansions (שאול מזבל לו)."[62] A sheep (צאן) was a
typical sacrificial beast, hence the mention of sheep in Sheol has obvious
connotations of sacrifice, as does the sentence about throwing rocks/
stones at a person in a well (Lam 3:54). We have, therefore, a basis not
only for seeing in the presentation of a well an image of the world of the
dead, but also for reconstructing—by analogy, as did Macalister on the
strength of archaeological material—a ritual demanding the offering of
an animal as a sacrifice there.[63]

59.　From ולד ("boy").
60.　See Cristiano Grottanelli, "Giuseppe nel pozzo, I. Un antico tema mitico in
Gen. 37:12-24 e in RV I 105," *Oriens Antiquus* 17 (1978): 107-22; *idem*, "Giuseppe
nel pozzo, II. Il motivo e il suo contesto nel folklore," *Oriens Antiquus* 22 (1983):
267-90; G.R.H. Wright, "Joseph's Grave Under the Tree by the Omphalos at
Shechem," *VT* 22 (1972): 476-86.
61.　Further consideration of the mythological basis and possible ritualistic associations with this text have been included in the chapter on Shechem.
62.　It is worth pointing out that the noun זבל appearing here, "dwelling place"
(from the root זבל, "to honour," "to elevate"), is part of the name of the god of
Ekron, Baal-Zebul (2 Chr 1), as also of the name Zebulon (זבלון) and of Queen
Jezebel (איזבל), native of Sidon.
63.　*The Jerusalem Post* of 11 November 2002 published news of discoveries
made in the region of Philistia by a team of Israeli archaeologists led by Raz Kletter.
The discoveries, dated to the tenth or ninth centuries BCE, were at the bottom of a
well. If the presence of these cult objects was not the result of a secondary deposit,

The next element of the story associated with the origins of the holy place in Beer-sheba is the tamarisk. The Hebrew version of Gen 21:33[64] gives אשל, whereas the LXX uses the word ἄρουρα.[65] The term אשל also appears in 1 Sam 22:5 and 31:13 (with the difference that it has the definite article); in both cases in the LXX the Hebrew is substituted by the Greek term ἄρουρα. This is slightly surprising since the word ἄρουραψ denotes tilled earth or a certain expanse and has nothing to do with the name of a tree. The Greek term for tamarisk is μυρίκη.[66] It is therefore worth taking a closer look at these verses because an interesting change has occurred there.[67]

The Hebrew version of 1 Sam 22:6 can be translated as follows: "Now Saul (שאול) heard that David and his men had been discovered. And Saul, spear in hand, was seated under the tamarisk tree on the hill (תחת־האשל ברמה)[68] at Gibeah, with all his officials standing around him." The LXX reads καὶ ἤκουσεν Σαουλ ὅτι ἔγνωσται Δαυιδ καὶ οἱ ἄνδρες οἱ μετ᾽ αὐτοῦ καὶ Σαουλ ἐκάθητο ἐν τῷ βουνῷ ὑπὸ τὴν ἄρουραν τὴν ἐν Ραμα καὶ τὸ δόρυ ἐν τῇ χειρὶ αὐτοῦ καὶ πάντες οἱ παῖδες αὐτοῦ παρειστήκεισαν αὐτῷ. The Vulgate translates the phrase about the tamarisk as: "Saul [...] esset in nemore est in Rama."

The Hebrew version of 1 Sam 31:13 can be rendered as "Then they took their bones and buried them under a tamarisk tree at Jabesh (תחת־האשל ביבשה), and they fasted seven days."[69] The LXX has καὶ λαμβάνουσιν τὰ ὀστᾶ αὐτῶν καὶ θάπτουσιν ὑπὸ τὴν ἄρουραν τὴν Ιαβις καὶ νηστεύουσιν ἑπτὰ ἡμέρας. The Vulgate has: "sepelierunt in nemore Iabes."

then it is possible we are dealing here with another trace of the existence in ancient Palestine of a chthonic cult associated with a well.

64. For a review of the research on this fragment, see Schoors, "The Bible on Beer-sheba," 106-108.

65. R. Hayward, "Abraham as Proselytizer at Beer-sheba in the Targums of the Pentateuch," *JJS* 49 (1998): 24-37 (25-26).

66. See, for example, *Iliad* 10.466-67; 21.350 where the tamarisk is mentioned with reference to dead people.

67. For a comparison of other ancient translations of these parts, see J. Barr, "Seeing the Wood for the Trees? An Enigmatic Ancient Translation," *JSS* 13 (1968): 11-20; Hayward, "Abraham as Proselytizer," 27-29.

68. Following the LXX, Vulgate and modern translations (e.g. KJV), the term ברמה should be regarded as a proper name, "in Rama," and not as a common noun. Cf. the word-play between the words Saul (שאול) and tamarisk tree (אשל).

69. In 1 Chr 10:12 we see the phrase: "Then they buried their bones under the great tree (oak) in Jabesh (תחת האלה ביבש), and they fasted seven days."

The translation of the Vulgate, which uses the word *nemus*, or "wood," "forest," indicates that the term אשל is interpreted as "trees" (plural). This differs significantly from the MT, where the term תחת־האשל ביבשה—"under אשל in Jabesh"—excludes the plural form of the noun. This same noun *nemus* in the Vulgate serves to convey the Hebrew word אשרה, "pole" or "tree" (= ἄλσος, Judg 6:25; 26:30),[70] גנה, "garden" (= κῆπος, Esth 1:5; 7:8) and יער, "forest" (= δρυμός, 2 Chr 9:16). The Latin version does not explain the use of the Greek noun ἄρουρα.

Josephus in *Jewish Antiquities* (6.251 and 6.377) uses ἄρουρης, which might show, first, that he is relying on the LXX and, secondly, that he does not really know how to interpret the word. Unable to discover its meaning he has turned it into a proper noun. Difficulties with understanding the word אשל in Gen 21:33 are also signalled by Rashi, who writes: "Rab and Samuel differed in their opinion of what it was. The former considered it to be an orchard from which the fruit for food offered to guests came. The latter's view was that it was an inn where guests stayed and from which food for them came (*Sota* 10a). We can speak of 'pitching the inn' since we have a phrase speaking of pitching tents, as in Dan 11:45: 'He will pitch his royal tents [there]'."[71]

It will probably be impossible to establish why the noun "tamarisk" was replaced in the LXX with the noun ἄρουρα. It is likely that the translators found it difficult to understand, or that the associations provoked by it caused them to make profound changes to obscure the original meaning of the text.

1 Chronicles 10:12 contains a text parallel to 1 Sam 31:13, except that instead of the term "tamarisk," the word האלה, meaning "terebinth" or "oak," appears.[72] It is intriguing that the translators of the LXX should change the content of this verse so profoundly in the first book of Samuel, whereas for instance in 1 Chr 10:12 (= 1 Sam 31:13) they translated the Hebrew האלה[73] using the Greek δρῦς.

The matter is further complicated by one other problem associated with the symbolism of trees. Writing about Saul's burial place, the term האלה ("terebinth") is mentioned in 1 Chr 10:12, while in the parallel text in 1 Sam 31:13 the term האשל ("tamarisk") is used. The synonymy of these names, at least on the level of symbolism, is also confirmed by the

---

70. For more on this subject, see the chapter on Ophrah.

71. M. Rosenbaum and A.M. Silbermann (eds.), *Pentateuch with Targum Onkelos, Haphtaroth and Rashi's Commentary*, Jerusalem, 5733 (1973/1974), 92.

72. For more on the meaning of these trees, see the chapter about Hebron.

73. *DCH*, 1:273-74, gives the meaning of "terebinth." On the subject of in the meaning of האלה ("goddess"), see T. Binger, *Asherah: Goddesses in Ugarit, Israel and the Old Testament*, JSOTSup 232, Sheffield, 1997, 135-41.

targumim: the name of the tree in Gen 21:33 is translated as אילה by *Onkelos*, and in *Pseudo-Jonathan* as אשלא.[74]

James Barr's argument,[75] that the changes were introduced into the translations to avoid the association of אשל with אשרה, seems persuasive in the light of the fact that in the Vulgate the two words are rendered by just one—*nemus*—and also because not only was אשל ("tamarisk") asso-ciated with the goddess Asherah, but so was the symbolically twin term terebinth (אלה).[76] The association of terebinth with non-Yahwistic cults is confirmed in the Bible itself (see, for instance, Hos 4:13; Ezek 6:13).[77]

Paradoxically, אשל, via אלה, brings us back to the symbolism of the well. In Isa 15:8 we find the toponym באר־אילים ("well of terebinths").[78]

Unfortunately, we are unable to establish which of these trees—terebinth (*Pistacia lentiscus, atlantica*) or tamarisk (*Tamaris pentandra, Tamaris aphylla*)—could be more closely associated with Beer-sheba since archaeological traces of both have been found.[79]

The puzzling and seemingly deliberate use in the LXX of the term ἄρουρα to render the meaning of the word אשל, the symbolism associated with the world of the dead, and also the association with a well—all this could be evidence that the tamarisk was a tree associated with the underworld.

If we were to accept that there was an association in the minds of the ancient Hebrews between the two words שאל and אשל, constructed as they are using the same letters,[80] then we would be dealing with a further motif linking Beer-sheba with a cult of the underworld. Therefore it would point to the fact that, according to the biblical testimony (Gen 21:33), Abraham planted in Beer-sheba a tamarisk (אשל), a tree dedi-cated to a deity of the underworld, next to a well—the entrance to the

---

74. See Barr, "Seeing the Wood for the Trees?"

75. *Ibid.*, esp. 13-17.

76. K. Nielsen, *DDD*, *s.v.* "Terebinth."

77. There is a huge literature on the role of trees; see, for example, J.G. Frazer, *Folk-Lore in the Old Testament*, 3 vols., London, 1919, 3:30-60; K. Nielsen, *There is Hope for a Tree: The Tree Metaphor in Isaiah*, JSOTSup 65, Sheffield, 1989, 71-85; S. Ackerman, *Under Every Green Tree: Popular Religion in Sixth-Century Judah*, HSM 46, Atlanta, 1992.

78. The impossibility of identifying באר־אילים in Moab is broached by A.J. Ferch, *ABD*, *s.v.* "Beer-elim."

79. See I. and W. Jacob, *ABD*, *s.v.* "Terebinth"; see also, *ibid.*, *s.v.* "tamarisk." See too N. Liphscitz and Y. Waisel, "The Botanic Material of Iron Age I," in Z. Herzog (ed.), *Beer-sheba II: The Early Iron Age Settlements*, Tel Aviv, 1984, 116-17.

80. The word "Sheol" is most frequently written as שאול in the MT, but for instance in Num 16:30, 33 it appears as שאל.

world of the dead. In this context it is easy to understand the passage
dealing with the burial of Saul's remains beneath a tamarisk (1 Sam
31:13)[81]—a funereal tree *par excellence*.

Karel van der Toorn has suggested a different reading of Gen 21:33,
which is usually rendered "Abraham planted a tamarisk tree in Beer-
sheba, and there he called upon the name of the Lord, the Eternal God"
(Gen 21:33). According to van der Toorn, the text can also be read:
"Abraham planted a tamarisk tree in Beer-sheba and named it יהוה
אל עולם."[82] The sentence can indeed be interpreted this way. The phrase
קרא שם בשם is generally translated as "summoning the name,"[83] whereas
the verb קרא also expresses the activity of calling or naming. The weakness of the hypothesis lies in the fact that applying it to other passages,
using the same construction, undermines their sense. The text in *KAI* 10,
a dedicatory altar inscription, shows a close analogy to Gen 21:33, and
suggests that van der Toorn's hypothesis should be rejected.

The interpretation suggested by van der Toorn forces us to consider
the question of methodology. Specifically, we should resolve whether
trees were worshipped for their own sakes, or because they were inhabited by supernatural powers or divinities. James George Frazer, writing
almost a century ago about the tree cult in Palestine, was in no doubt that
their exceptional significance was a consequence of their being "inhabited" by divine powers.[84] Fifty years later, Mircea Eliade wrote: "It was
never the tree *itself* that was the object of worship but that which
'revealed' itself through the tree, what the tree contained within it and
what the tree signified."[85]

Studies devoted to the religions of the ancient inhabitants of Palestine
and related to trees and their place in the religiousness of the Israelites
have a disturbing tendency to see all trees as cult objects of various
kinds. It is of course possible, on the basis of biblical material, remnants
of material culture and of the literary culture of the Middle East, to show
that trees did have a cultic role and that they had a place in mythology.
We are, however, unable to establish what kind of cult it was. The statement that all trees were sacred is too general and it obscures the picture
of the nature of ancient religions. Even if every tree was perceived to

81. The burial of Saul's remains was accompanied by a seven-day fast.
82. K. van der Toorn, *Family Religion in Babylonia, Syria and Israel: Continuity
and Change in the Forms of Religious Life*, SHANE 7, Leiden, 1996, 257-58 n. 94,
259.
83. Gen 12:8; 13:4; 21:33; 26:25; Exod 34:5.
84. Frazer, *Folk-Lore*, 3:30-60.
85. M. Eliade, *Patterns in Comparative Religion*, New York, 1974, 262.

contain something sacred, then it surely was not the same something. The differences in nature were undoubtedly mirrored in the Israelite religious mentality—as certainly happened in other cultures as well. The problems around this question stem from the newness of the study of the mentality and religiousness of the Israelites and from the great selectivity combined with the modest amount of source data. The first difficulty is a methodological one. Historians who came from Bible Study Schools linked to Departments of Theology looked for divine premises and their research was subordinated to this presumption. This tradition led to the wholly predictable consequence of seeking manifestations of a proto-religion everywhere, be it in the shape of an ancestor cult or a cult of female divinities. It suggests that a sensible method of researching the religion of the ancient Israelites is accompanied by a conviction that, because we are dealing with very fragmentary and very non-objective material, we can never reconstruct a full picture of reality.[86] Our aim ought to be to reveal and describe an increasing number of pieces of the jigsaw so that the picture becomes more complete. When there is a fragment missing we should not deduce that the fragments that we do have will do to complete the picture. If we do not know what form a tree cult took, or in whose honour it was practised, then we simply do not know. And if we possess evidence testifying to some role of trees in the cult of a female divinity (Asherah), then it does not automatically mean that all trees should be regarded in our reconstruction as elements of the "feminine sacral."[87]

The material presented so far allows us to accept that the tamarisk and terebinth played some role in the chthonic and funeral symbolism of the Hebrews.

A further important element of the aetiological story of Beer-sheba is the figure of Abimelech (אבימלך) and the theme of the covenant (ברית) associated with it. The name "Abimelech" appears in the MT 51 times. It was the name of the Philistine king of Gerar (Gen 20–21 and 26), as well as of the king of Shechem—the illegitimate son of the judge Gideon (= Jerubbaal = Jerubbesheth,[88] Judg 8–10; 2 Sam 11:21). The LXX uses the form Αβιμελεχ for both Abimelechs and for Ahimelech (אחימלך).[89]

The heading of Ps 34 is interesting: "Of David. When he pretended to be insane before Abimelech, who drove him away, and he left" (v. 1).

---

86. Soggin, "Appunti per lo studio"; this is, it seems to me, a model way of reconstructing the religion of the Israelites.

87. Nielsen, *There is Hope for a Tree*; Ackerman, *Under Every Green Tree*.

88. More on the subject of this figure in the chapter on Ophrah.

89. See 1 Sam 21–23.

This sentence refers to the description in 1 Sam 21:11-15 of David's stay in Gath, from which we learn that David "pretended to be insane in their presence; and while he was in their hands he acted like a madman." The king of Gath, however, was not Abimelech but Achish (אכיש). Peter C. Craigie considers that this inconsistency disappears if one accepts that the name "Abimelech" is, in fact, the title of Philistine kings.[90]

In support of the claims by Craigie and Matthews[91] that what we are dealing with here are not names but titles is the fact that both Gezer and Gath were Philistine towns. A problem arises, however, in the case of Shechem and the potential links of the Philistine king with that town. There is no hint that Shechem was inhabited by the Philistines.[92]

Regardless of whether we see in Abimelech a specific figure (historical or mythical) or we concede that it is a monarchic title, the fact that Abimelech king of Gerar is mentioned in this narrative indicates a Philistine trace even though the name itself is Semitic and means "my father [is] king." It could be the Semitic equivalent of the term סרנים (from סרן*).[93] Information about the presence of the Philistines in the Pentapolis (the towns of Ekron, Gaza, Ashdod, Ashkelon, Gath) is consonant with the data indicating that along with other Sea Peoples they reached the south of Judah and spread into the territory of the Negev desert.[94]

There is no doubt that Abimelech of Gerar was a Philistine and it was with him, as a representative of his people, that Abraham and Isaac made the covenant. This fact might indicate the great antiquity of this narrative motif because in time the Philistines were absorbed by the Semitic organism surrounding them and already in the Persian era they were not identified as a separate *ethnos*. It appears that they absorbed much of the culture of the towns of Canaan during the Iron Age (including religion), but that they also made a considerable contribution of their own, including the knowledge of iron working, which they initially monopolised.[95] According to Trude Dothan, after the culmination of the Philistine

---

90. P.C. Craigie, *Psalms 1–50*, WBC 19, Waco, TX, 1983, *passim*. Cf. V.H. Matthews, *ABD*, *s.v.* "Abimelech."

91. Matthews, "Abimelech," claims that it could be the throne name of the kings of Gerar which would not explain the presence of the name in Ps 34:1.

92. See T. Dothan, *The Philistines and their Material Culture*, New Haven, 1982, 295-96.

93. H.J. Katzenstein, *ABD*, *s.v.*, "Philistines (History)"; see also. G. Garbini, *Note di lessicografia ebraica*, Brescia, 1998, 97-101.

94. H.J. Katzenstein considers that this can be deduced from 1 Sam 30:14; see also T. Dothan, *ABD*, *s.v.* "Philistines (Archaeology)"; *idem*, *The Philistines, passim*.

95. G. Garbini, *I Filistei. Gli Antagonisti di Israele*, Milan, 1997.

expansion in the middle of the eleventh century, there followed a gradual assimilation of Semitic models of material culture (especially Phoenician ones).[96] A relic of the Philistines is the name "Palestine" mentioned in Herodotus's *History* (1.105; 2.104) and later in Pliny's *Natural History* (5.12).[97] The survival of this term may (though it does not have to) indicate the vitality of the traditions associated with the Philistines despite their almost total assimilation into the dominant Semitic body. The rich biblical material is evidence of a vivid remembrance of them among the Hebrews. Unfortunately, the extent of "Philistinism" within the Pentapolis after the expansion of the Sea Peoples, dominated by the Phoenician element, remains unknown.

Bearing in mind how deeply rooted in the Bible the memory of the Philistines as the Israelites' foremost antagonists is, we should acknowledge that in time the term "Philistine" may well have been applied to peoples other than those to whom it referred originally. If the name of a people who no longer existed was indeed transferred to other groups as, in time, they became the Hebrews' arch opponents, then the dating of the narrative about Abimelech becomes impossible.

The subject of the covenant (ברית) which Abimelech agreed with Abraham and Isaac would require a separate study. What is pertinent to this work, however, is to look at the form this event took and at the role the animals mentioned in the text played in it. Does the story of the covenant between Abraham and Abimelech, and the circumstances surrounding it, have any link to the cult of a chthonic god? The description of how the place where they met was given its name precedes the information that "Abraham brought sheep and cattle and gave them to Abimelech, and the two men made a treaty" (Gen 21:27); in 21:28-30, seven lambs which Abraham set aside before giving them to Abimelech are mentioned. What did they need all these animals for—sheep (צאן) and oxen (בקר) and then those seven lambs (כבשׂת)—and what was done with them? There is no real analogy here to the story of the covenant that Abraham made with God (Gen 15:9-18), where mention is made of a heifer, a goat, a ram—all of them three years old—and also of a turtle-dove and a pigeon. From the context, it appears that the presence of the sheep and cattle (oxen) was linked to the ceremony of making the covenant whereas the lambs were excluded from it.

Undoubtedly what we are dealing with here are two separate rituals. The sheep and the cattle were there for the ritual of making a covenant (Gen 21:27), which was accompanied by a ritual feast (Gen 26:29-30);

96. Dothan, "Philistines (Archaeology)."
97. Katzenstein, "Philistines (History)."

but the purpose of the seven lambs is unknown (Gen 21:28). In response
to Abimelech's surprised question "What is the meaning of these seven
ewe lambs you have set apart by themselves?" (Gen 21:29), Abraham
explains that he had wanted to make of them a gift to him (v. 30). The
lambs have a purpose which is different from that of the other animals.
My own suspicion is its explanation is of a secondary nature and it was
introduced merely to create a new context; this served to excuse the
presence of the lambs after the covenant was made and after the feast.
But its presence in the aetiology of Beer-sheba's holy place is there for a
different reason.

כבשׂת ("lambs") is the plural of the noun כבשׂה, formed from the noun
כבשׂ ("ram").[98] The reference to lambs and to their part in this story could
be a consequence of the prosaic fact that the biblical editors knew of
such a mundane ritualistic practice or it could also be the trace of a
particular cult form deploying these animals. Lambs, often mentioned in
the Bible as sacrificial animals, always close a list of creatures destined
for sacrifice, as Christoph Dohmen noticed.[99] He also claims that originally lambs were used in the *'olah* kind of sacrifices, and only later in the
tamid sacrifices.[100] There is some controversy surrounding the nature or
form of blood sacrifices to be seen in the prophet's reprimands (Isa 1:11;
43:23; 66:3).[101] The biblical examples of the word "lamb" (כבשׂה) being
used testify to a certain ambivalence of approach towards this sacrificial
animal. It is my view that this ambivalence is linked to two facts. First,
the lamb was a sacrificial beast which took the place of a human.[102]
Secondly, the divinity to whom it was often sacrificed was a god of the
underworld.[103]

The word כבשׂה ("lamb") appears in the MT eight times (compare this
with כבשׂ, "sheep," which occurs 107 times), in Gen 21:28, 29, 30 in the
plural and in Lev 14:10; Num 16:14; 2 Sam 12:3, 4, 6 in the singular.

The verses in the books of Leviticus and Numbers contain apparently
standard prescriptions for ensuring the ritual purity of a sacrificial animal. Leviticus 14:10 mentions sacrifices associated with the treatment of
leprosy, and Num 6:14 states that "a year-old ewe lamb without defect"
is to be the offering for sins. Particularly interesting furthermore is a
fragment of 2 Samuel, coming immediately after the chapters describing
the seduction of Bathsheba by David and the death of Uriah:

98.   *DCH*, *s.v.* 4:360-61.
99.   *TDOT*, *s.v.* 7:43-52 (50-52).
100. *Ibid.*, 51.
101. *Ibid.*, 52.
102. *Ibid.*, 47.
103. *Ibid.*

The Lord sent Nathan to David. When he came to him, he said, "There were two men in a certain town, one rich and the other poor. The rich man had a very large number of sheep and cattle, but the poor man had nothing except one little ewe lamb (כבשה) he had bought. He raised it, and it grew up with him and his children. It shared his food, drank from his cup and even slept in his arms. It was like a daughter to him. Now a traveller came to the rich man, but the rich man refrained from taking one of his own sheep or cattle to prepare a meal for the traveller who had come to him. Instead, he took the ewe lamb (את־כבשת) that belonged to the poor man and prepared it for the one who had come to him." David burned with anger against the man and said to Nathan, "As surely as the Lord lives, the man who did this deserves to die! He must pay for that lamb (הכבשה) four times over, because he did such a thing and had no pity." (2 Sam 12:1-6)

The intriguing aspect is the number of times that death is mentioned in this fragment, something which many commentators have pointed out. First, David, having heard Nathan's metaphorical story about the taking of someone's property, states that the perpetrator "deserves to die" (v. 5). Then the prophet accuses the king of being guilty of Uriah's death (v. 9), following which he announces that his sin is forgiven ("you are not going to die," v. 13) but predicts the death of his son (v. 14).

Commentators on this fragment,[104] which is part of the history of succession, also draw attention to the legal resonance of the metaphorical story, on the literary motifs or textual interdependencies between the greater narrative elements and so on, while ignoring the motif of the poor lamb.[105] Only Uriel Simon makes a direct reference to the question of the lamb but from a slightly different perspective than mine.[106] He gives an account of a law that allows Bedouins living in the regions of Beer-sheba to take their neighbour's animal if it is needed to feed a guest. But one animal to which this injunction does not apply is a lamb, especially one

---

104. L.L. Lyke, *King David with the Wise Woman of Tekoa: The Resonance of Tradition in Parabolic Narrative*, JSOTSup 255, Sheffield, 1997, 145-58; G.H. Jones, *The Nathan Narratives*, JSOTSup 80, Sheffield, 1990, 96-101; P.K. McCarter, Jr, *II Samuel: A New Translation with Introduction, Notes and Commentary*, AB 9, Garden City, NY, 1984, *passim*; S. Lasine, "Melodrama as Parable: The Story of the Poor Man's Ewe-Lamb and the Unmasking of David's Topsy-Turvy Emotions," *HAR* 8 (1984): 101-24 (103-106); R.P. Gordon, *1 & 2 Samuel: A Commentary*, Exeter, 1986, 256-57; H.W. Hertzberg, *I & II Samuel: A Commentary*, Philadelphia, 1964, 312-13.

105. Lyke, *King David*, 147: "It is less clear why the text stipulates that he had bought the lamb... We are likely supposed to take all this description simply to indicate the tremendous value he put on the lamb..."

106. U. Simon, "The Poor Man's Ewe-Lamb: An Example of Juridical Parabole," *Biblica* 48 (1967): 207-42.

to which its owner is particularly attached. Evidence of this attachment would be to tie a collar round its neck or to keep it in the owner's tent.[107] Being unable to comment on the data given by Simon about the Bedouins of the twentieth century or to explain the inter-dependency between Bedouin law and the biblical narrative, I can only acknowledge the fact and reflect on the continuity of custom law in the Middle East which has survived despite the passage of time and the changes in religion.[108]

Lasine considers that the comparison in the story of the lamb with a daughter to be a literary *topos* expressing both a role reversal in dependency relationships and also the interdependence of man and animal. He also believes that Nathan's story is a literary fiction (*melodrama*) which cannot be regarded as a source of information about a historical reality.[109] Of course, I am not claiming that it was a common custom in Palestine to treat a sacrificial beast as a member of the family. Nevertheless it is intriguing to note that images of animals "dressed in human skin" and subsequently killed and eaten permeate literature (and mythology).[110]

We are no nearer to understanding the phenomenon—that the lamb "was like a daughter to him."[111]

It is possible that the story of the lamb (כבשׂה) in 2 Sam 12:1-6 is an echo of an ancient sacrificial ritual in which a lamb took the place of a human. The pairing of lamb and daughter underlines the relationship between the surrogate offering and a human being. The offering of human sacrifices, and especially children, was practised by the Western Semites, and there is evidence of it both in Palestine and among the Phoenicians.[112] It is in precisely this context—as an offering to a chthonic

---

107.   *Ibid.*, 226-32 (227-28).

108.   Cf. K.J. Cathcart, "The Trees, the Beast and the Birds: Fables, Parables and Allegories in the Old Testament," in J. Day, R.P. Gordon and H.G.M. Williamson (eds.), *Wisdom in Ancient Israel: Essays in Honour of J.A. Emerton*, Cambridge, 1995, 212-21 (216-17), where he accepts Simon's hypothesis adding (after von Rad) that the parable initially functioned as an independent story.

109.   Lasine, "Melodrama as Parable," 105-106. Similarly H. Hagan, "Deception as Motif and Theme in 2 Sm 9–20; 1 Kgs 1–2," *Biblica* 60 (1979): 301-26 (305-306).

110.   For more about phrases suggesting the "humanisation" of the lamb, see G.W. Coats, "Parable, Fable, and Anecdote. Storytelling in the Succession Narrative," *Interpretation* 35 (1981): 368-82 (371).

111.   W. Roth, "'You are the man!': Structural Interpretation in 2 Samuel 10–12," *Semeia* 8 (1977): 1-13. The structural analysis of 2 Sam 10–12 by Wolfgang Roth contains a few graphs which add little to our knowledge of lambs.

112.   See G. Bohak, "Classica et Rabbinica I: The Bull of Phalaris and the Tophet," *JSJ* 31 (2000): 203-16; L.E. Stager and S.R. Wolff, "Child Sacrifice at Carthage—Religious Rite or Population Control?," *BAR* 10 (1984): 31-51; G. Garbini, *La religione dei Fenici in Occidente*, Dipartimento di studi orientali.

god—that כבשׂה appears in the aetiology of Beer-sheba. The lambs mentioned in Gen 21 are not intended for the feast accompanying the ritual
covenant-making between Abimelech and Abraham, but are sacrificed to
the god of Beer-sheba. Hence Abimelech's surprise. Though the editors
have introduced mention of an altar, the text does not talk about a blood
sacrifice. I suspect that this is because the כבשׂה was not going to be
sacrificed on an altar but was to be offered to the god whose presence
was symbolised by the well—the gate of Sheol.

We have to ask ourselves whether it was the motif of the well and its
chthonic symbolism which initiated the whole story about the beginnings of the holy place in Beer-sheba, or whether it was rather the theme
of the covenant with Abimelech that "sparked off" a chain of associations focused on a chthonic cult. The accumulation of elements pointing
to underworld symbolism within a consistent overall picture favours the
first of these possibilities. The whole narrative about the covenant with
Abimelech is of later provenance. Initially, I suppose, the story contained
information only about the beginnings of the cult in Beer-sheba, that is
to say the theme of the tamarisk, the well and the lamb. The figure of
Abimelech came later, as did the association of the well's first name—
the name of the place of the cult—with the verb "to swear (an oath)" and
the number "seven" (which comes from a phonetic convergence). What
would follow from that is that the whole fragment about the conflict of
the shepherds Abraham and Isaac with the Philistine shepherds is a later
addition, as are the names of the well: "Dispute" and "Enmity." This
would accord with my supposition that the initial aetiology of Beer-
sheba was linked the story of Abraham and contained just the term באר
("well") without a proper name. The narrative concerning Isaac mentions
Abraham explicitly and complements the earlier story with the well's
names—in changed forms, I suspect—and with the whole theme of
explaining their origin.

One could, tentatively, try to explain the names of the wells, referred
to in the story about Beer-sheba (Gen 26:12-22), as a secondary text
corruption. Since both names, עשׂק and שׂטנה, differ in their meaning from
the name רחבות, they could have arisen as a result of changes in the
original forms.[113] In the case of עשׂק, the following could be proposed:

Studi semitici, NS, 12, Rome, 1994, 67-81; *idem, Note del lessicografia ebraica*,
73-78; O. Eissfeldt, *Molk als opferbegriff im punischen und hebräischen, und das
ende des gottes Moloch*, Halle, 1935.
113.   Oral communication. For a description of the methodology used to recreate
the original form of the Hebrew text and the traces indicating its changes, see in
Garbini, *Il ritorno dall'esilio babilonese*, 129-30 n. 8.

עשׁק ("dispute") ← שׁקע ("submerge")[114]

The noun עשׁק is, in the MT, a *hapax legomenon*, whereas the verb שׁקע appears several times (Num 11:2; Jer 21:64; Ezek 34:18; Amos 8:8; 9:5).

If this interpretation proves accurate then, on the basis of the symbolism associated with the aetiology of Beer-sheba, we would have to accept that next to the tamarisk (אשׁל) marking the place of contact with the underworld (שׁאול / שׁאל) was a well (באר)—the home of certain chthonic deity (?) and the entrance to the wide open mouth (רחב). This was the place of a cult of the gods of the underworld, where a sacrifice was submerged (שׁקע); this sacrifice took the place of a human and could well have been a lamb (כבשׂה).

One argument supporting the theory of the chthonic nature of the cult in Beer-sheba (though its importance should not be exaggerated) is the cult of Demeter and Persephone (Kore) there. The temple discovered there, dating from the Hellenistic era, was probably devoted to those Greek goddesses (or their local equivalents[115]) to which the terracotta figurine representing two female forms seated next to each other, generally accepted as being Demeter and Kore, testifies.[116] The weakness of this argument is that the figurine finds from this level are too modest, and do not make possible even general conclusions.[117] However, archaeologists' claims that there were underground constructions which could have been used for cult purposes in Beer-sheba may provide further evidence.[118]

Another pointer to the exceptional nature of the cult (or customs) associated with Beer-sheba might be seen in the words of Amos 8:14. In *Targum Jonathan*, in the phrase (literally) "the paths of Beer-sheba," we find, instead of the term דרך ("paths"), the term נימוסי.[119] This noun is

114.   I am indebted to Professor Giovanni Garbini for this suggestion.
115.   It has to be remembered that Greek culture, though it introduced much that was new to the Near East, often affected the form while leaving the contents of the local customs and beliefs unchanged.
116.   Z. Herzog, "Tel Beersheba," in *NEAEHL*, 1:173; S. Derfler, "A Terracotta Figurine from the Hellenistic Temple at Tel Beer-sheba," *IEJ* 31 (1981): 97-99. The closest iconographic parallel is the terracotta figurine from Melos (fifth century), reproduced in R.A. Higgins, *Catalogue of Terracottas in the Department of Greek and Roman Antiquities, The British Museum*, London, 1954, vol. 1, Pl. 610.
117.   The oldest female figurines found in Beer-sheba date from the Chalcolithic era, and the most recent to the Hellenistic era; see the illustrations in Herzog, "Tel Beersheba," 166, 171; Derfler, "A Terracotta Figurine."
118.   Derfler, *The Hellenistic Temple at Tel Beersheva*, 14-15.
119.   Instead of "paths," the LXX gives "God" here.

not a Semitic word and could be pronounced *nimosi* or *nomosi*. Yoël L. Arbeitman suggests it is derived from the Greek *nomoi* ("laws," "customs").[120] What unfortunately remains unclear is to which customs associated with Beer-sheba this actually refers.

The phrase used in the book of Amos is the basis on which J. Alberto Soggin interprets the word דרך as the name of the divinity worshipped in Beer-sheba.[121] This interpretation is supported by the LXX where in the place "the paths of Beer-sheba" we find the phrase: ζῆ ὁ θεός σου Βηρσαβεε. Unfortunately, we know nothing more about this divinity, and Soggin's theory has met with widespread criticism.

The material presented, which testifies to the link between the idea of a well and an image of the underworld, needs to be augmented by a discussion of the form the sacrifices offered there (or close to it) took. In the aetiology of Beer-sheba, written down in Gen 21, mention is made of lambs which, as has already been shown, have a peculiar status as sacrificial beasts. The archaeological material dated from the transition between the Bronze and Iron Ages and discovered by Macalister suggests, we recall, that sacrifices of animals and humans were offered in wells. So, if the lambs mentioned in the account were a substitute offering to a chthonic divinity, it is worth considering what kind of offering it was. There are two possibilities: it was either the sacrifice of the firstborn, whose form is unclear, or a child-offering of the *molk* type. This is what the book of Exodus says about the sacrifice of the firstborn:

> Do not hold back offerings from your granaries or your vats. You must give me the firstborn of your sons. Do the same with your cattle and your sheep. Let them stay with their mothers for seven days, but give them to me on the eighth day. (Exod 22:29-30)[122]

> The first offspring of every womb belongs to me, including all the firstborn males of your livestock, whether from herd or flock. Redeem the firstborn donkey with a lamb (שׂה), but if you do not redeem it, break its neck (וערפתו). Redeem all your firstborn sons. No one is to appear before me empty-handed. (Exod 34:19-20)

These passages indicate that the injunction to offer to a god the first-born encompassed animals and people alike. It was also possible to offer a surrogate sacrifice. In Exod 34:20 mention is made of redeeming a

---

120. Y.L. Arbeitman, "Detecting the God who Remained in Dan," *Henoch* 16 (1994): 9-14 (11).

121. Soggin, "Appunti per lo studio," 57-58.

122. See also Exod 13:13, which reads: "Redeem every firstborn among your sons."

donkey with a lamb,[123] and when this is not done that the donkey's neck has to be broken. The Hebrew verb ערף, "to break an animal's neck" (from the noun "neck"), is used here.[124] Both the LXX and the Vulgate omit from Exod 13:13 and from Exod 34:20 the reference to breaking the animal's neck.[125] In its verbal form this root is used in the MT in those two places and also in Deut 21:4; Isa 66:3; Hos 10:2. The mention in Hos 10:2 points to the demolishing of altars (lit. "he will break the neck of their altars"). The text of Isa 66:3 appears to contain a condemnation of religious apostates:

> But whoever sacrifices a bull is like one who kills a man, and whoever offers a lamb, like one who breaks a dog's neck; whoever makes a grain offering is like one who presents pig's blood, and whoever burns memorial incense, like one who worships an idol. They have chosen their own ways, and their souls delight in their abominations.

Undoubtedly, appropriate rituals are being contrasted with those that should be condemned. Bad religious behaviour includes: worshipping idols, spilling the blood of a pig (in other words, making blood sacrifices of an unclean animal, which may mean offering to "alien" gods), the breaking of a dog's neck, and murdering people (perhaps a reference to the sacrificing of human beings?).[126] The existence of a sacrifice based on breaking the animal's neck (or a manner of killing other than that demanded by blood offerings) is confirmed by Deuteronomy. The following text provides an important basis from which we can deduce the form and meaning of such a sacrifice:

> If a man is found slain, lying in a field in the land the Lord your God is giving you to possess, and it is not known who killed him, your elders and judges shall go out and measure the distance from the body to the neighbouring towns. Then the elders of the town nearest the body shall take a heifer that has never been worked and has never worn a yoke and lead her down to a valley that has not been ploughed or planted and where there is a flowing stream. There in the valley they are to break the heifer's neck. The priests, the sons of Levi, shall step forward, for the Lord your God has chosen them to minister and to pronounce blessings in the name of the Lord and to decide all cases of dispute and assault. Then

123.   *TDOT*, 7:43-52.

124.   The root ערף also has the meaning of "pouring, dripping, falling"; cf. the noun ערפל, "thick darkness," and also the word ערפת, "colonnade room or hall" (*KAI* 10:6, 12; 19:1; 60:5; 118:1; 122:2; 129:2).

125.   De Vaux, *Ancient Israel*, 2:443-44, to some extent excusing the authors of the Bible, writes that the tradition of offering the firstborn is archaic, and that, in time, surrogate sacrifices were introduced.

126.   R. de Vaux, *Les sacrifices de l'Ancien Testament*, Paris, 1964, 64.

all the elders of the town nearest the body shall wash their hands over the heifer whose neck was broken in the valley, and they shall declare: "Our hands did not shed this blood, nor did our eyes see it done. Accept this atonement for your people Israel, whom you have redeemed, O Lord, and do not hold your people guilty of the blood of an innocent man." And the bloodshed will be atoned for. So you will purge from yourselves the guilt of shedding innocent blood, since you have done what is right in the eyes of the Lord. (Deut 21:1-9)

The offering of a heifer (עגלה) could, according to this injunction, compensate for a murder, since the animal may take the place of an unidentified perpetrator. The elders were to make the sacrifice (priests of the tribe of Levi would only assist), after which they would have to cleanse themselves by washing their hands. This ritual took place by a stream which never dried out, away from fields where crops were planted—that is to say, in an area not possessed by any human. The rite required foreign, non-human land. It is highly probable that the sacrifice was made not on an altar but on unsanctified land and that it was a propitiatory offering to a god who ruled over a world that was alien to people—in other words, to a god of the other world. This god of Sheol was to forgive a death meted out to an innocent person.[127]

The breaking of the neck as a way of offering a sacrifice is surprising in the light of the fact that classic blood sacrifice involved the spilling of the sacrificial beast's blood. This classic form of sacrifice is expressed by the Hebrew verb זבח. This is probably the reason why references suggesting sacrificial practices associated with the cult of chthonic gods were removed from ancient translations of the Bible. The material discussed here testifies to the existence among the ancient Hebrews of a ritual involving the killing of a beast outside the "cultural" area by breaking its neck. It was an offering whose essence came down not to spilling the animal's blood, as in traditional sacrifices, but to depriving it of life. I suggest that sacrificial acts involving a heifer by a stream, the breaking of a dog's neck and the throwing of a lamb into a well were analogous, and that they all belonged to the same group of religious rituals. The sacrifice of a lamb offered before Ezra in the desert, mentioned in the Coptic *Apocryphon of Jeremiah* (34), would have performed an identical function.[128]

127. For an analogous ritual of expelling a goat intended for Azazel, see Lev 16:8-10.
128. See R.A. Kraft, "'Ezra' Materials in Judaism and Christianity," in H. Temporini and W. Haase (eds.), *Aufstieg und Niedergang der Roemischen Welt: Geschichte und Kultur Roms im Spiegel der Neueren Forschung*. II. *Principat 19.1 Religion*, Berlin, 1979, 119-36 (128).

The biblical fragments quoted above about offerings of the firstborn have been the subject of lively academic discussion concerning human sacrifice. Whereas Rainer Albertz is inclined to minimise the extent and significance of these practices,[129] many other commentators are of the opinion that they were very significant throughout Palestine.[130] For instance, Bernhard Erling[131] is of the view that this ritual differed from the *molk*, child sacrifice, type, evidence of which was found in Punic Tophet, as well as from the ordeals by fire mentioned in the book of Jeremiah and 2 Kings (16:3; 17:17; 21:6).[132] Erling considers that the discovery of pots containing the remains of children are evidence of child sacrifices (Gezer, Megiddo, Taanach),[133] but of course some of these finds could be evidence of normal burials carried out after the cremation of the remains. An analogy to these discoveries is of course Tophet in Carthage where pots containing the burnt remains of children were found under stelae. The frequent commixture of the remains of children and animals undoubtedly proves that we are dealing here with the practice of sacrificial offerings.

Bearing in mind that the majority of commentators consider the laws in Exodus to be of very archaic provenance, and remembering the *molk* type of sacrifices, it has to be said that originally the sacrifice of the firstborn had an important place in the religion of the Hebrews. The firstborn were offered not to a uranic but to a chthonic deity. As Yahweh took on more and more of the attributes of a god of heaven and Yahwism became influenced by the religion's internal evolution (for instance the reforms of Josiah), the use of surrogate sacrifices was introduced and, in time, the cult of the gods of the underworld abandoned.

Here we must move on to matters which have a direct link to chthonic sacrifices in which a well may have played a role.

Hildegarde Lewy, while searching in Palestine for traces of a cult of a god of death and the netherworld, claimed that there was probably a well

---

129.   Albertz, *A History of Israelite Religion*, 1:103 n. 62, 282.

130.   W.O.E. Oesterley, *Sacrifices in Ancient Israel: Their Origin, Purposes and Development*, London, 1937, 118-19, accepts the ritual described as the sacrifice of Isaac as probable; sacrifices of children were likely to have been frequent though not universal.

131.   B. Erling, "First-Born and Firstlings in the Covenant Code," in *Society of Biblical Literature 1986 Seminar Papers*, SBLSP 25, Atlanta, 1986, 470-78.

132.   The question of human and the *molk* type of sacrifices is too large to be analysed here, so I will limit myself to giving a few bibliographical pointers; see Bohak, "Classica et Rabbinica I"; Stager and Wolff, "Child Sacrifice at Carthage"; Garbini, *Note di lessicografia ebraica*, 1998, 73-78.

133.   Erling, "First-Born and Firstlings in the Covenant Code," 475.

in the area of the Jerusalem Temple which—just as in Mecca—served to maintain a link with the underworld.[134] The Talmud confirms the tradition whereby there was in the Holy of Holies an entrance "to the underworld stopped by a boulder."[135] Hildegarde Lewy believes that information about this "entrance" and the stopping up of the original waters of *tehom* is proof of the existence of the cult of Saturn (Nergal, Ninurt, Šalim) and what follows from that—of the offering typical of this cult (in Mecca and Byblos) of child sacrifices.[136]

Henry O. Thompson[137] drew attention to the fact that in the era of Egyptian domination there was in Beth-Shean (later Scythopolis) a cult of an underworld god in the shape of Mekal (Nergal, Seth).[138]

John Briggs Curtis has also researched the worship of chthonic gods.[139] He claims that the establishment in Jerusalem of the cult of Chemosh and Milcom (attributed to Solomon) is equivalent to the introduction of the cult of Nergal. Furthermore, some of the biblical verses referring to the Mount of Olives can be interpreted as a description of rituals devoted to this god.[140] As evidence of the cult's survival, Curtis quotes an ostracon from the fifth century BCE found in the collection of Aramaic documents discovered on the island of Elephantine in Upper Egypt.[141] In this text Nergal is listed next to other deities.

The trace of another deity, or non-Yahwistic cult, in Jerusalem has been preserved in the name of the god Salim, or Šalim,[142] known from Ugaritic texts.[143] The popularity of this deity in Palestine is indirectly confirmed by theophoric names.[144] Herbert B. Huffmon[145] drew attention

134.   H. Lewy, "Origin and Significance of the Mâgên Dâwîd: A Comparative Study in the Ancient Religions of Jerusalem and Mecca," *Archiv orientální* 18 (1950): 330-65 (344-45).

135.   *Ibid.*, 345-46.

136.   *Ibid., passim.*

137.   H.O. Thompson, *Mekal: The God of Beth-Shan*, Leiden, 1970, *passim.*

138.   It is worth noting here that in Roman times the cult of Dionysius dominated in Scythopolis—the name Scythopolis Nysa was associated with Dionysius.

139.   Curtis, "An Investigation of the Mount of Olives."

140.   *Ibid.*

141.   *Ibid.*, 153. *TADAE*, 4 D7.30.4.

142.   Cf. J. Lewy, "Les textes paléo-assyriens et l'Ancien Testament," *Revue de l'Histoire des Religions* 60 (1934): 29-65; *idem*, "The Šulmān Temple in Jerusalem," *JBL* 59 (1940): 519-22.

143.   J. Gray, *The Legacy of Canaan: The Ras Shamra Texts and their Relevance to the Old Testament*, VTSup 5, Leiden, 1957.

144.   J.H. Tigay, *You Shall Have No Other Gods: Israelite Religion in the Light of Hebrew Inscriptions*, Atlanta, 1986, 67-68, 80.

145.   H.B. Huffmon, *DDD, s.v.* "Shalem," 1428-31.

to the fact that the names of David's two sons (אבשלום / אבשלם and שלמה) contain the root שלם.[146] This element also appears in two further descriptions and contexts, namely, in the name Jerusalem (ירושלם) and also in the name of the town of "Salem" (שלם), ruled by the king-priest Melchizedek (Gen 14:18-20) and which has normally been equated with Jerusalem.[147] As in the Ugaritic texts, the deity שלם is connected to שחר, and one would be inclined to think that both—connected to the sun-rise and sun-set—could be phenomenologically equalled to Venus, as the morning, and evening star. If so, further שלם features could share similar aspects with this goddess.

Francesco Aspesi has attempted to join the well-earth image with chthonic cults.[148] Analysing the biblical passages which present the earth in an anthropomorphic manner and considering the link between Yahweh and a female chthonic divinity, he deduced that the Hebrew term אדמה— "earth," "soil"—is the name of a West Semitic goddess, a companion of Rešep. Aspersi considers the word אדמה, used to denote the earth, to be an artificial creation of the MT, with no analogy in West Semitic languages.[149] To support his theory he cites a fragment from Joel 1:10 where the word appears in a sense associated with the female god of the earth and harvest: "The fields are ruined, the ground (אדמה) is dried up; the grain is destroyed, the new wine is dried up, the oil fails."[150] According to Aspesi, the Hebrew term אדמה signifies the chthonic goddess (Mother

---

146. A more sceptical view is offered by L.K. Handy, *ABD*, s.v. "Shalom."

147. P.J. King, *ABD*, s.v. "Jerusalem," see *Jub.* 30:1 where Salem is situated close to Shechem.

148. F. Aspesi, "Precedenti Divini di *'adama*," *Studi Epigrafici e Linguistici (sul Vicino Oriente antico)* 13 (1996): 33-40.

149. *Ibid.*, 33-34.

150. *Ibid.*, 36. Cf. also Joel 2:21. A separate discussion is needed for the typical Near Eastern theme of the "Mother Earth's" mourning for the grain (דגן), grape-juice/wine (תירש/תירוש) and olives (יצהר); the common nouns could here be treated as the names of gods. On the subject of the term *tiroš*, see S. Naeh and M.P. Weitzman, "Tiroš—Wine or Grape? A Case of Metonymy," *VT* 44 (1994): 115-20; J.P. Brown, "The Mediterranean Vocabulary of the Vine," *VT* 19 (1969): 146-70; C. Rabin, "Hittite Words in Hebrew," *Orientalia* 32 (1963): 137-38 n. 20; F.C. Fensham, "The First Ugaritic Text in *Ugaritica* V and the Old Testament," *VT* 22 (1972): 296-303 (298-99); J.F. Healey, *DDD*, s.v. "Tiraš," 1642-45. See especially M. Dahood, "Ugaritic and the Old Testament," *Ephemerides Theologicae Lovenienses* 44 (1968): 35-54, esp. 53-54, where Dahood includes the following translation of Hos 7:14: "But they did not cry to me from their hearts, / But rather lamented on their beds. / They became clients of Dagon and Tirosh, they turned away from me." Dahood writes that Tirosh was a "Bacchus-like divinity" (p. 53). See also his "Hebrew–Ugaritic Lexicography XII," *Biblica* 55 (1974): 387.

Earth), strictly associated with the god of death. There would, therefore, be an analogy with Nergal and Ereshkigal or Demeter and Persephone. From this perspective the following description acquires a special significance:

> But if the Lord brings about something totally new, and the earth (אדמה) opens its mouth and swallows them, with everything that belongs to them, and they go down alive into the grave (חיים שאלה), then you will know that these men have treated the Lord with contempt… They went down alive into the grave (חיים שאלה) with everything they owned; the earth closed over them, and they perished and were gone from the community. (Num 16:30, 33)

Is there a trace of human sacrifices offered to Mother Earth? There is no doubt that the noun אדמה is used here to mean "(chthonic) goddess" and it does not seem likely that the term should always be translated neutrally, as a reference to "soil" or "plough-land."

The biblical symbolism of the earth's mouth opening allows us to present further suggestions about pairs of chthonic gods. I have already cited several passages that demonstrate the image of the well/Sheol opening and shutting its mouth. There is a further hint in the name of one of the wells mentioned in Gen 26:22—Rehoboth (from רחב, "to be wide, to be open"). The Hebrew verb פער has a very similar meaning—"to be wide open." It appears in Ps 119:131 and in Job 16:10; 29:23 in the phrase "to open the mouth wide."[151] Valuable information is also provided by Isa 5:14: "Therefore the grave (שאול) enlarges its appetite and opens its mouth (פערה פיה) without limit; into it will descend their nobles and masses with all their brawlers and revellers." Also associated with this verb is the word פער, part of the name Baal-peor,[152] a god mentioned in the Bible (Num 25:3, 5, 18; 31:16; Deut 4:3; Josh 22:17; Ps 106:28; Hos 9:10). The LXX text uses the transliteration Βεελφεγωρ[153] ("Belphegor"). Deuteronomy 3:29; 4:46; 34:6 and Josh 13:20 mention בית־פעור (Βαιθφογωρ). There is no certainty about the location of this site since Deut 4:46 points to a link with the Amorites while Deut 34:6 mentions it in the context of Moses's burial place: "They buried him [Moses] in Moab, in the valley opposite Beth-peor, but to this day no one knows where his grave is." There can be no doubt that this refers to territory in Transjordan which was given to the tribe of Reuben during the division of Canaan (Josh 13:20).

---

151. A.H. Van Zyl, *The Moabites*, Leiden, 1960, 194.
152. Doubtless this theonym is associated with the toponym "Peor."
153. The LXX also contains a transliteration of the root "Peor," Φογωρ.

The Bible presents Baal-peor as a Moabite god whose cult brought the wrath of the God Yahweh upon the Israelites. The book of Numbers states clearly what the nature of this cult was: "While Israel was staying in Shittim, the men began to indulge in sexual immorality with Moabite women, who invited them to the sacrifices to their gods. The people ate and bowed down before these gods. So Israel joined in worshiping the Baal of Peor. And the Lord's anger burned against them" (Num 25:1-3). The cult of Baal-peor is defined as a sin (Josh 22:17), and the people who participated in it "consecrated themselves to that shameful idol and became as vile as the thing they loved" (Hos 9:10). A comment in Ps 106:28 gives more details: "They yoked themselves to the Baal of Peor and ate sacrifices offered to lifeless gods."

The cult based on sexual rituals is linked here to a cult of the dead.[154] Marvin H. Pope has shown that even the rabbinical tradition associated the cult of Baal-peor not only with a sexual ritual but also (and perhaps above all) with the cult of the dead or of gods of the underworld.[155]

Archaeological materials, as well as the Bible itself, provide a lot of evidence to suggest the presence of cults of underworld gods in Palestine. Unfortunately, we are unable to establish under what names they were worshipped. Hypotheses have appeared supporting such names as: Derek, Šelim, Nergal (Ner), Baal-peor. One might also take into account such theonyms as Baal-Zebul and El Olam. The most likely hypothesis appears to be the one claiming that chthonic gods formed a pairing consisting of a god described by his name, or more accurately his title, Baal ("Lord"), and a goddess identified with Mother Earth.

The cult presented here, based on putting the sacrifices into a well or on breaking the neck of an animal, was surely not a cult of the dead. But whether these sacrifices were offered to Mother Earth, the lady of life and death, or to the god Sheol, cannot be ascertained.[156]

It is tempting to present a different etymology for the toponym "Beersheba" than the one offered by the Bible,[157] and instead of באר־שבע— "the well of the covenant"—to see the original name as באר־שבע*,

---

154.   M.H. Pope, *Song of Songs*, AB 7C, Garden City, NY, 1997, 217-18; not so Van Zyl, *The Moabites*, 194, who sees no link between the cult of Baal-peor and the cult of the dead.

155.   *Ibid.*, 217-19.

156.   Looking for analogies in the Near East one might draw attention to the Anatolian cult of an underworld divinity in which the central role was played by a spring; see M. Popko, *Wierzenia ludów starożytnej Azji Mniejszej*, Warsaw, 1989, 110, and *Religions in Asia Minor*, Warsaw, 1995, 140.

157.   I have to thank Professor Giovanni Garbini for this suggestion.

vocalised probably שְׂבַע or שָׂבַע. This small change is made by the visual similarity between the letters *š* and *ś*. Although these are separate phonemes, they were written down identically before the creation of the Masora. Reconstructed thus, the name would signify "well of plenty (satiety)" and would harmonise with the whole aetiological story.[158]

To some extent this hypothesis is confirmed by the following sentence: "the grave (שְׁאוֹל), the barren womb, land which is never satisfied (לֹא־שָׂבְעָה) with water, and fire, which never says, 'Enough!'" (Prov 30:16). Additionally to the very interesting anthropomorphic representation of the underworld, it is worth noting the image of the hungry land and the appearance of terms that are of interest to us here: "Sheol" and the verb שׂבע ("to be satiated").

Unfortunately, philological arguments can do nothing to confirm or negate this hypothesis. The Greek transcriptions in Josephus (Βηρσουβαι, Βηρσαβή, Βηρσάβη) as well as in the LXX (Βηπαβεε, -εαι, -αιε) and the testimony of *Targum Onkelos* (באר שבע),[159] *Pseudo-Jonathan* (ביר שבע)[160] and the SP (באר שבע)[161] do not allow us to draw any definitive conclusions. All we can do is carefully note that the Greek versions, which retain the vowel *a* after *sigma*, do not attest to שֶׂבַע being the original rendition. If *alpha* had been used for the Hebrew vowel *a*, then it could have been the long vowel *kametz*. In this situation, the form שָׂבַע or שָׂבְעָה seem to be more likely than שָׂבַע*. Reconstructed thus, the name באר שׂבעה* would signify "the well satiated (itself)." In constructing such a concept, we would have to accommodate the disappearance (in the written form) of the suffix –*h*, an element in the feminine conjugation of the verb. One can of course recreate the original form of the toponym without preserving the sentence structure (noun–verb), as happens in MT. Then the conjunction באר שׂבע* could be translated as "well of satiety."

If we were to accept the proposed reconstruction, the consequence would be that we would have to acknowledge that the numeral "seven" and the verb "to swear (an oath)" were later additions to the text, aimed at creating and justifying a change in the sound (and meaning) of the toponym.[162] The introduction by the editors of the Bible of such a change

158. Words originating from the root שׂבע ("to be satiated") have been attested, *inter alia*, in the Aramaic story of Ahikar (vv. 127, 129, 189) discovered in Elephantine; see A. Cowley, *Aramaic Papyri of the Fifth Century BC*, Oxford, 1923, *passim*.

159. Rosenbaum and Silbermann (eds.), *Pentateuch with Targum Onkelos*, *passim*.

160. Clarke (ed.), *Targum Pseudo-Jonathan, passim*.

161. Tal, *The Samaritan Targum, passim,* and *The Samaritan Pentateuch*, *passim*.

162. See the wordplay on שׂבע and שׁבע in Gen 41:29.

can be explained in the following way: the name "satiated well (or well of satiety)," because it attested to the existence of a chthonic cult, could have upset them, while the addition of the covenant motif would have accorded with the chief premise of the Pentateuch whose dramatic axis revolves around the theme of the promise given to the chosen people and the covenant made between it and God.[163]

So we can now attempt to reconstruct the tradition which formed the source of the narrative about the creation of a holy place in Beer-sheba. The original name (באר שבע*) was associated with the cult of a god of the underworld. Linked with that, in addition to the rituals practised there, was the motif of a well (באר), tamarisk (אשל) and a sacrificial animal—a lamb. As a result of the change in the sound of the toponym (from באר שבע* to באר שבע) it was possible (thanks to homophony) to link the proper name with the numeral "seven" (שבע) and the verb "to swear (an oath)" (שבע). The presence of both the number "seven" and the whole theme of the covenant made with Abimelech is a later version of the aetiological myth which probably referred only to the form of the cult. It was only subsequently that the political motif, relating to the covenant, was added. I contend that this was done as early as the era of the Second Temple, which obviously implies that the term "Philistine" used in this story was simply a customary description of an alien people.

We should now give separate consideration to the discussion aimed at establishing the probable date of the aetiology's text. The *terminus ante quem* is set down by the apocrypha: the book of *Jubilees* and *Liber Antiquatum Biblicarum*, and by the biblical manuscripts of Qumran.[164] We do not know the exact date of the LXX, and this makes it impossible to use the Greek translation of the Bible for dating. It is considered that the oldest manuscripts of the book of Genesis found in Qumran come from the second century BCE. The fragments that concern us here (Gen 26) are in the manuscript known as 4QpaleoGenesis^m. On the basis of palaeographical data, the publishers set the date in the middle of the second century BCE.[165] Their method, though fairly generally accepted, is not flawless since it reveals a large margin of error. This means that we need to exercise great caution when dealing with their conclusions. Regardless of how we come to date the 4QpaleoGenesis^m manuscript, it is a fact that it gives us the most reliable *terminus ante quem* of the start of the Beer-sheba tradition.

---

163. Von Rad, *Old Testament Theology*, *passim*.

164. As well as the Genesis manuscripts there is also the *Genesis Apocryphon*.

165. P. Skehan, E. Ulrich and J. Sanderson (eds.), *Discoveries in the Judaean Desert 9, 4: Qumran Cave 4—Palaeo-Hebrew and Greek Biblical Manuscripts*, Oxford, 1992, 51.

The preserved fragments of the works of Jewish historians of the Hellenistic era contain no mention of or allusions to the aetiology of Beer-sheba.[166] Such references can, however, be found in the book of *Jubilees*. This apocryphal work is frequently dated as early as the beginning of the second century BCE, but Doron Mendels offers a more persuasive argument, indicating the thirties of the second century BCE.[167] Compared with the narrative in the canonical text, the book of *Jubilees* is far more forceful in its condemnation of the Philistines, who are identified with all the antagonists in Idumea, and assesses the Edomites (Idumeaites) very harshly. The differences in assessment of neighbouring peoples could be the result of the different times of the texts' origins or of their coming from different regions (these differences manifest themselves chiefly in the emphasis placed on the degree of hostility towards neighbouring peoples). The book of *Jubilees* presents a sharp conflict between the Jews (Abraham, Jacob) and the Philistines, whereas the book of Genesis tends to emphasise the friendliness of relations.

Our knowledge of events in the region of Beer-sheba is provided by later texts. Flavius Josephus in his *Jewish Antiquities* mentions the conquest of territory in the south of Judah by Hyrcanus: "Hyrcanus also captured the Idumean cities of Adora and Marisa, and after subduing all the Idumaeans, permitted them to remain in their country so long as they had themselves circumcised and were willing to observe the law of the Jews. And so, out of attachment to the land of their fathers, they submitted to circumcision and to making their manner of life conform in all other respects to that of the Jews. And from that time on they have continued to be Jews" (*Ant* 13.9.1). Although this text does not mention Beer-sheba by name, it is certain that the lands conquered by Hyrcanus also included this town.[168]

If the biblical account claiming a religious significance for Beer-sheba does indeed refer to the times when the town played some important role, then we might have to consider the time of the divided monarchy when the town was fortified (strata I-6, I-5), rebuilt after the destruction in the

166. Cf. the work of Demetrius and Eupolemos, among others. See Albert-Marie Denis (ed.), *Fragmenta Pseudepigraphorum Quae Superunt Graeca*, Pseudepigrapha Veteris Testamenti Graece 3, Leiden, 1970; J.E. Crouch, "Demetrius the Chronographer and the Beginnings of Hellenistic Jewish Historiography," *Kwansei Gakuin University Annual Studies* 30 (1981): 1-14; Luciano Bombelli, *I Frammenti degli storici giudaico-ellenistici*, Genoa, 1986.

167. D. Mendels, *The Land of Israel as a Political Concept in Hasmonean Literature: Recourse to History in Second Century B.C. Claims to the Holy Land*, Tübingen, 1987, 57f.

168. Derfler, *The Hellenistic Temple at Tel Beersheva*, 16-17, 32-33.

tenth century and when it surely played an important role right up to its destruction towards the end of the seventh century BCE. The second period of flowering, including religious developments, coincides with the Hasmonean period. We can assume that the temple, where a cult of a syncretistic character was likely practised, might well have been rebuilt for the needs of the Yahwistic cult by Hyrcanus after he had conquered those territories between 129 and 126 BCE.[169] This would indicate that the traditions associated with Beer-sheba could be useful to the ideology of the Jewish nation. A precise assessment of the beginnings of the tradition is not possible, but we cannot ignore the fact that the Jewish centres which were instrumental in the outbreak of the Maccabean uprising probably propagated an ideology of conquest and alliances with neighbours some time before armed conflict began. In such circumstances a story about the "Jewishness" of a town lying in the far south must have been very significant. The second half of the second century BCE was a time of Judah's territorial expansion. The land of the Jews stretched "from Dan to Beer-sheba." The description of the covenant signed by Abraham and Isaac with foreigners could have mirrored the aims of the Jewish elite to make political alliances with the neighbouring peoples. Beer-sheba and its surroundings could have had a significant meaning for Hasmonean propaganda, partly because—as some scholars maintain—the name of the dynasty is derived from the toponym "Heshmon," that is to say, from the name of a place situated on the border of Judah and Negeb.[170]

Doron Mendels presents an analogous argument in his examination of the link between the book of *Jubilees* and the political events of the second century BCE.[171] For all the differences between the canonical and apocryphal texts, Mendels's reasoning can be just as readily applied to the dating of the book of Genesis.

Both the changes in the sound of the toponym "Beer-sheba" and the introduction of the covenant with Abimelech were probably made in the second half of the second century BCE, for it was then that the territories of northern Negeb became of interest to the Jews of Judah and their vital interests demanded that they regulate relations with the subject peoples. The thesis that there were two contrasting political scenarios being propagated in the second century BCE by various circles leads us to

169.   *Ibid.*, 64-65; see also Derfler, "A Terracotta Figurine"; D. Barag, "New Evidence on the Foreign Policy of John Hyrcanus I," *Israel Numismatic Journal* 12 (1992–93): 1-12.

170.   S. Weitzman, *ABD*, *s.v.* "Heshmon (place)."

171.   Mendels, *The Land of Israel.*

differentiate between the more aggressive group, whose programme finds expression in the book of *Jubilees*, and the more restrained group offering their neighbours a covenant, symbolically depicted in the book of Genesis. Of the two scenarios, that of Josephus describing the conquest and compulsory conversion of the Idumeans to Judaism, and that of the book of Genesis about a covenant between autonomous partners, the biblical account, describing the reality of the second century BCE symbolically, appears to be the more credible. Even if 4QpaleoGenesis[m] originated in the middle of the second century BCE, the above reasoning remains probable. The first decades after the Maccabean uprising could have encouraged a surge in the production of writings which not only served contemporary politics but also tidied up some older biblical material.

3.
Bethel

Archaeological Data

For more than sixty years now, researchers looking for the biblical Bethel have generally identified it as being Tell Beitin.[1] Recently, other suggestions have been proposed. According to David Livingston, it could be situated some 3 km to the south of Tell Beitin—El-Bireh.[2]

The excavations in Tell Beitin provided only fragmentary information about Bethel's supposed position.[3] It proved impossible to undertake extensive work at Tell Beitin in view of the settlements on the tell itself. In his commentary on the reports of these excavations, William G. Dever was less than flattering about their merits: the numerous publications contain more speculation and sheer guesswork than they do description of factual archaeological material.[4] Nevertheless, some description of the settlement on the tell, however superficial, can be attempted.

1. The first to suggest this identification was Edward Robinson; see W.G. Dever, *ABD, s.v.* "Beitin, Tell (place)."

2. D. Livingston, "One Last Word on Bethel and Ai—Fairness Requires No More," *BAR* 15 (1989): 11, and "Further Considerations on the Location of Bethel at El-Bireh," *PEQ* 126 (1994): 154-59.

3. The first to work on the position of Tell Beitin was William F. Albright (1927, 1934); he was followed by James L. Kelso (1954, 1957, 1960); see J.L. Kelso (ed.), *The Excavation of Bethel (1934–1960)*, AASOR 39, Cambridge, MA, 1968; further information is to be found in J.L. Kelso, "The Third Campaign at Bethel," *BASOR* 151 (1958): 3-8; "The Fourth Campaign at Bethel," *BASOR* 164 (1961): 5-19; "Bethel," in *EAEHL*, 1:190-93; "Bethel," in *NEAEHL*, 1:192-94.

4. Dever, "Beitin, Tell (place)," describes the results of the excavations published by Kelso in the following way: "There are, for example, few complete plans, no usable sections, no stratum numbers—in short, little real data... Fact and interpretation are so entangled throughout the final report that few data emerge for the archaeologist, historian, or biblical scholar."

The settlement of the Early Bronze Age IV (2200–2000 BCE) can be described as a semi-nomadic settlement. Only in the Middle Bronze Age (2000–1500 BCE) did the town develop and it was probably then that the defensive walls were built. Half-way through the second century there was a break in settlement (1500–1400 BCE). In the Late Bronze Age (1500–1200 BCE) the town apparently returned to its former splendour. This assertion, found in Kelso's publication, is not supported by any credible arguments,[5] but rather dubious evidence such as, for instance, a find which he identifies with the Canaanite cult place devoted to the god El.[6] Kelso's theory that the traces preserved in Bethel were proof of the historicity of the account of the conquest of Canaan by the Israelites has provoked much controversy.[7]

Iron Age I (1200–1000 BCE) has left traces consisting of four layers. These remains testify to a far less extensive area of settlement and a lower material culture of its inhabitants than that of the Late Bronze Age.[8] Rare finds linked with Philistine manufacture come from this period.[9] The pottery, on the other hand, is generally closer to artefacts typical of the period of Israelite settlement on Mt Ephraim.[10] It seems that settlement on the tell lasted uninterruptedly throughout the Iron Age. Tell Beitin escaped destruction during the neo-Babylonian expedition, a fact to which the very large amount of pottery dated to the sixth-century preserved there testifies. Settlement during the Persian rule is not well documented and this has given rise to disagreements about its duration. Strata associated with the Hellenistic era are dated between the fourth and second or third and second centuries BCE. Numerous numismatic finds dated between 125 BCE and 70 CE indicate how important Bethel was throughout the Hasmonean and Herodian eras. The Hellenistic era was the time of the town's great blossoming; the apogee of its development can be linked to Bacchides's investments in the mid-second century BCE.[11]

David Livingston, reassessing the accessible literary sources which had led Robertson to identify Bethel with Tell Beitin, proposed a different location for the biblical Bethel. Both Eusebius in *Onomastikon* and Jerome place Bethel twelve miles along the road from Jerusalem to

5. *Ibid.*
6. Kelso, "The Fourth Campaign at Bethel," 12-13.
7. See Lemche, *Early Israel*; *The Canaanites and their Land*; and *The Israelites in History and Tradition*.
8. Dever, "Beitin, Tell (place)."
9. Dothan, *The Philistines and their Material Culture*, 54.
10. Dever, "Beitin, Tell (place)."
11. Kelso (ed.), "The Excavation of Bethel," 47-50.

Neapolis. Tell Beitin is situated at the fourteenth milestone, whereas El-Bireh is between the eleventh and twelfth milestones.[12] Analysing the non-biblical sources, Livingston claims that Bethel should be identified with El-Bireh, and that Tell Beitin is the remnant of the biblical Beth-aven.[13] In view of the references that say that Bethel lies on the right-hand side of the road from Jerusalem to Neapolis, any identification of it with Ras et-Tahumeh must be dismissed. Livingston believes that if El-Bireh, situated alongside the Roman road, is the biblical Bethel, then Khirbet Nisya must be its neighbour Ai.[14] Unfortunately, archaeologists have not as yet carried out a thorough exploration of this area, so there is no way of confirming or disproving Livingston's hypothesis.

One other, fairly extraordinary, theme deserves mention. During excavations in Tell Beitin an inscribed stamp originating from southern Arabia was found. Palaeographic analysis of this item disclosed that the find dated from the ninth century BCE. The problem, however, is that as early as 1900 information was published about the discovery of an identical stamp in territory which is in modern-day Yemen. A lively discussion followed in the pages of *BASOR*, a discussion which attempted, on one side, to confirm the authenticity of the find and from that to show how far-reaching trade patterns of Israel and Judah were. On the other, surely more successful, side, however, efforts were made to prove that the seal does not come originally from Beitin, but was placed intentionally in the excavated site, probably by the archaeologists themselves.[15]

Biblical Information

The name Bethel (בֵּית־אֵל) appears more than sixty times in the MT.[16] It is also probable that the form בֵּית הָאֱלִי[17] in 1 Kgs 16:34 refers to Bethel.

---

12. D. Livingston, *Further Consideration*, 154-56.
13. *Ibid.*, 157-58.
14. *Ibid.*
15. G.W. Van Beek and A. Jamme, "An Inscribed South Arabian Clay Stamp from Bethel," *BASOR* 151 (1958): 9-16; A. Jamme and G.W. Van Beek, "The South-Arabian Clay Stamp from Bethel Again," *BASOR* 163 (1961): 15-18; Y. Yadin, "An Inscribed South-Arabian Clay Stamp from Bethel?," *BASOR* 196 (1969): 37-45; A. Jamme, "The Bethel Inscribed Stamp Again: A Vindication of Mrs. Theodore Bent," *BASOR* 280 (1990): 89-91.
16. Gen 12:8; 13:3; 28:19; 31:13; 35:1, 3, 6, 7, 8, 13, 15, 16; Josh 7:2; 8:9, 12, 17; 12:9, 16; 16:1, 2; 18:13, 22; Judg 1:22, 23; 4:5; 20:18, 26, 31; 21:2, 19; 1 Sam 7:16; 10:3; 13:2; 30:27; 1 Kgs 12:29, 32, 33; 13:1, 4, 10, 11, 32; 2 Kgs 2:2, 3, 23; 10:29; 17:28; 23:4, 15, 17, 19; Jer 48:13; Hos 10:15; 12:5; Amos 3:14; 4:4; 5:5, 6; 7:10, 13; Zech 7:2; 1 Chr 7:28; 2 Chr 13:19; Ezek 2:28; Neh 7:32; 11:31. The text in

The most frequently occurring form in the LXX is Βαιθηλ; only in Josh 18:22 and Neh 7:32 does the form Βηθηλ appear.[18] In Josh 2:1 Βαιθηλ equates to the Hebrew בבים, and in 15:30 to כסיל. The word כסיל there is the proper name of a place (next to Eltolad and Hormah) lying, as the context suggests, in southern Judah.[19] In other lists of towns in Judah כסיל is replaced by the names בתול (Josh 19:4) and בתואל (1 Chr 4:30). It is hard to establish whether these names indicate the toponym of some unidentified place in Judah or whether they are a simply a variant form of the name "Bethel" placed in a different context. The word כסיל (from the root כסל) has two meanings: "stupidity" (especially in the book of Proverbs) and the "Orion constellation" (Job 9:9; 38:31).

All the references in the book of Genesis come in the aetiological accounts with which I deal later. In turn, the references in the book of Joshua relate to the division of the land between the tribes of Israel; Bethel lies on the boundary point between the territory of the sons of Joseph in the north and that of the sons of Benjamin in the south. There are inconsistencies here: whereas in Josh 16:2 Bethel is said to be part of the inheritance of the sons of Joseph,[20] in Josh 18:22 it is of the sons of Benjamin (confirmed by Neh 11:31); the other inconsistency is the identification of Luz with Bethel made explicitly in Josh 18:13,[21] whereas according to Josh 16:2 the boundary stretches "from Bethel to Luz and passes along to Ataroth." Joshua 12:16 names Bethel as one of the conquered kingdoms, though this information is missing in the LXX, which might indicate its later origin. Later information about Bethel in the book of Joshua relates to a description of the localisation of Ai.

According to Judg 1:22, 23, Bethel is within the domains of the sons of Joseph. Yet we learn from Judg 4:5, in a passage about the position of the Palm of Deborah—a place of judgment (prophecy)—that the prophetess "held court under the Palm of Deborah between Ramah and Bethel in the hill country of Ephraim." The phrase "hill country of Ephraim" may indicate the position of the palm tree or only of Bethel (which would concur with Josh 16:12). Judges 20 suggests that there was an important religious and political centre in Bethel. According to this text, during an

---

1 Sam 30:27 is probably corrupted because the Hebrew word *bêt-'ēl* is the equivalent of the term Βαιθσουρ in the LXX, and from the context it is clear that it is the south of Judah that is being mentioned.

17. The LXX reads Βαιθηλίτης; the Vulgate reads *Bethel*.

18. In the LXX the name "Bethel" is missing from Gen 28:19 (Οἶκος θεοῦ; Aquila's version: Βαιθηλ); 31:13; Josh 8:12; 12:16; 18:22 (Βησανα).

19. G.A. Herion, *ABD, s.v.* "Chesil (place)."

20. This version is supported also by Judg 1:22-23 and 1 Chr 7:28.

21. Cf. Judg 1:23.

expedition against the Benjamites "[they] went up to Bethel and inquired of God. They said, 'Who of us shall go first to fight against the Benjamites?' The Lord replied, 'Judah shall go first'" (v. 18). A few verses later we find, "Then the Israelites, all the people, went up to Bethel, and there they sat weeping before the Lord. They fasted that day until evening and presented burnt offerings and fellowship offerings to the Lord" (v. 26). The reference in Judg 20:19 might simply testify to a gathering of Israel's tribes in a place lying close by the boundary of the Benjamite inheritance. However, the information relating to the questions put to God (or seeking advice from the oracle), as well as the contents of v. 26 testify to the existence of some kind of sanctuary in Bethel.[22] If the words of Judg 20:26 are taken literally, then we can assume that the mourning ritual, together with the fasting, went on till evening and that the offerings were made only "later." Does this suggest a night-time ritual of offering?

The text of Judges 20 seems to be dubious in view of the reference to the Ark of the Covenant (v. 27) and to the cult practised by Phinehas, the son of Eleazar, the son of Aaron (v. 28). Instead of acknowledging בֵּית־אֵל as a proper name, the Vulgate translates it as a common noun "domus Dei," adding also in Judg 20:18: "domum Dei hoc est in Silo." It is uncertain, therefore, whether the initial reference was to Bethel or maybe to some other sanctuary, for instance Shiloh.

Bethel's role as a religious and political centre is, however, confirmed in 1 Sam 7:15-16: "Samuel continued as judge over Israel all the days of his life. From year to year he went on a circuit from Bethel to Gilgal to Mizpah, judging Israel in all those places." Further information is provided by 1 Sam 10:3: "Then you will go on from there until you reach the great tree of Tabor. Three men going up to God at Bethel will meet you there. One will be carrying three young goats, another three loaves of bread, and another a skin of wine." This passage contains valuable information linked to the cult in Bethel. Those going to the sanctuary take with them kids, bread and wine which could signify three kinds of offering made there.

In 1 Sam 13:2 mention is made of a battle between the Israelites and the Philistines in the region of Bethel and Gibeah, and 1 Sam 30:27-31 lists the towns that David rewarded with shares of the spoils won from the Amalekites. Apart from Bethel, these are: Ramoth-Negeb, Jattir, Aroer, Siphmoth, Eshtemoa, Rachal, the cities of the Jerahmeelites, the

22. J. Blenkinsopp, "Bethel in Neo-Babylonian Period," in O. Lipschits and J. Blenkinsopp (eds.), *Judah and the Judeans in the Neo-Babylonian Period*, Winona Lake, 2003, 93-107.

Kenites, as well as those in Hormah, Bor Ashan, Athach, Hebron and "those in all the other places where David and his men had roamed." It seems that we are dealing with three kinds of towns here: (1) all those places "where David roamed," that is to say, those places that maintained his army for some time—giving them part of the spoils could signify a recompense for the costs (losses?) associated with stationing an army there; (2) Hebron, David's capital (see 2 Sam 2:1-3); (3) allied towns in various parts of Palestine. The conveying of gifts to "the elders of Judah, who were his friends" (v. 26) was probably a form of gift aimed at facilitating or strengthening covenants between allies. If this interpretation is correct, it would mean that in the story about David coming to power Palestine had only a federation of clans or even tribes, and that the centralising policy was limited to the tightening of alliances with independent leaders—the elders of Judah.

We learn from 1 Kgs 12–13, which talks of Jeroboam's funding of sanctuaries in Bethel and Dan, that: "the king made two golden calves. He said to the people, 'It is too much for you to go up to Jerusalem. Here are your gods, O Israel, who brought you up out of Egypt.' One he set up in Bethel, and the other in Dan" (1 Kgs 12:28-29).

2 Kings 2:2-6 talks about the wanderings of Elisha and Elijah before the latter's ascension. The prophets travelled to Bethel, then to Jericho, till finally they arrived at the Jordan. In both Bethel and Jericho they found "a company of the prophets" (בני־הנביאים). 2 Kings 2:23-24 relates a cruel story about Elisha who was mocked by the children of Bethel and who cursed them in the name of the Lord: "Then two bears came out of the woods and mauled forty-two of the youths."

An important clue to the kind of cult established by Jeroboam in Bethel and Dan is provided by 2 Kgs 10:29. Destroying the cult of Baal introduced by Ahab, Jehu "did not turn away from the…worship of the golden calves at Bethel and Dan." This is a powerful argument in support of the theory that the cult of calves was Yahwistic in character and its negative assessment stems not from any deviation but from the iconoclasm of the authors of the deuteronomistic collection.

2 Kings 17:24-41 relates an unusually interesting account about Assyrian settlers in Samaria. Not knowing how to worship the god there they provoked his anger: "…so he sent lions among them and they killed some of the people" (v. 25). The Assyrian king, wishing to protect the settlers from annihilation, sent a priest captured in Samaria to teach the new inhabitants how to worship the god of this land (v. 27). In the next verse we read: "So one of the priests who had been exiled from Samaria came to live in Bethel and taught them how to worship the Lord" (v. 28). Despite the priest's instruction:

each national group made its own gods in the several towns where they settled, and set them up in the shrines the people of Samaria had made at the high places. The men from Babylon made Succoth Benoth, the men from Cuthah made Nergal, and the men from Hamath made Ashima; the Avvites made Nibhaz and Tartak, and the Sepharvites burned their children in the fire as sacrifices to Adrammelech and Anammelech, the gods of Sepharvaim. (vv. 29-31)

2 Kings 23 contains a narrative about the fulfilment of a prophecy by an unnamed prophet from Judah concerning the destruction of Bethel (1 Kgs 13). Josiah, undertaking the purification of the temple in Jerusalem, commands that the vessels made for Asherah and Baal be carried and burnt, and that the ashes be taken to Bethel (v. 4) and that the non-Yahwistic—or maybe simply unorthodox—cult places be destroyed and profaned:

> Even the altar at Bethel, the high place (הבמה = τὸ ὑψηλόν) made by Jeroboam son of Nebat, who had caused Israel to sin—even that altar and high place he demolished. He burned the high place and ground it to powder, and burned the Asherah pole also (וֹשׂרף אשׁרה = κατέκαυσεν τὸ ἄλσος). Then Josiah looked around, and when he saw the tombs that were there on the hillside (בהר = ἐν τῇ πόλει), he had the bones removed from them and burned on the altar to defile it, in accordance with the word of the Lord proclaimed by the man of God who foretold these things. The king asked, "What is that tombstone (הציון = σκόπελον) I see?" The men of the city said, "It marks the tomb of the man of God who came from Judah and pronounced against the altar of Bethel the very things you have done to it." "Leave it alone," he said. "Don't let anyone disturb his bones." So they spared his bones and those of the prophet who had come from Samaria. (2 Kgs 23:15-18)[23]

This account provides an important pointer in any attempt to reconstruct the sanctuaries of ancient Palestine. The placing of graves within a holy place could be the consequence of a practice (known from many religions) aimed at ensuring that the dead are in touch with the *sacrum*. Another, albeit hypothetical, explanation would be a linkage between the activities surrounding the sanctuary—in which or in the vicinity of which graves were to be found—and a cult of a god of the underworld. This hypothesis would be supported by biblical tradition with its taboo related to the dead, the breaking of which gave rise to ritual uncleanness.

---

23. W.B. Barrick, "Burning Bones at Bethel: A Closer Look at 2 Kings 23, 16a," *SJOT* 14 (2000): 3-16. Citing the fact that this information is missing from 2 Chr 34:3-7, Barrick claims that the narrative quoted there is not about Bethel but a cemetery near Jerusalem.

2 Chronicles 13:19 gives information not present in the books of Kings. As a result of the conflict between Judah and Israel, following the incursion of the Pharaoh Shishak, Judah expanded onto Jeroboam's lands: "Abijah pursued Jeroboam and took from him the towns of Bethel, Jeshanah and Ephron, with their surrounding villages." It is hard to establish to what extent this reference in the book of Chronicles is a credible account of events that actually took place in the tenth century BCE, and to what extent it is simply a piece of editing. It does undoubtedly prove that the authors of the book of Chronicles were Judah-centred.[24] The narrative about the initiation of a royal cult in Dan and Bethel points unequivocally to the fact that Bethel was part of the northern kingdom, or Israel, whereas both the story about Josiah's religious activity (2 Kgs 23) and the reference in Jer 4:15[25] seem to testify that it is situated in the land of Judah.

Hosea 10:15 contains the prophecy against Bethel. The interpretation of this verse is not, however, clear.[26]

MT:

כְּכָה עָשָׂה לָכֶם בֵּית־אֵל מִפְּנֵי רָעַת רָעַתְכֶם בַּשַּׁחַר נִדְמֹה נִדְמָה
מֶלֶךְ יִשְׂרָאֵל

LXX:
οὕτως ποιήσω ὑμῖν οἶκος τοῦ Ισραηλ ἀπὸ προσώπου κακιῶν ὑμῶν ὄρθρου ἀπερρίφησαν ἀπερρίφη βασιλεὺς Ισραηλ.

Vulgate:
Sic fecit vobis Bethel a facie malitiae nequitiarum vestrarum.

A literal translation of the Hebrew text should probably be:

And thus shall do unto you בֵּית־אֵל because of the evil misdemeanour, your evil,[27] in the dawning (destruction) destroyed[28] will be the king of Israel.

24. M.J. Miller and J.H. Hayes, *A History of Ancient Israel and Judah*, Philadelphia, 1986, 240; they are of the view that if such a war ever did take place then it was no more than a border conflict.

25. Z. Kallai considers that the word appearing in the MT (אָוֶן) is the same as בֵּית אָוֶן (Bethel); see Z. Kallai, "Beth-El–Luz and Beth-Aven," in R. Liwak and S. Wagner (eds.), *Prophetie und geschichte Wirklichkeit im alten Israel*, Cologne, 1991, 171-88 (178).

26. The KJV translates it as "So shall Bethel do unto you because of your great wickedness: in a morning shall the king of Israel utterly be cut off"; for an account of the discussion, see D. Stuart, *Hosea–Jonah*, WBC 31, Waco, TX, 1987, *passim*.

27. The repetition of the word intensifies the expression, so this phrase denotes "great evil/your misdemeanour."

28. This juxtaposition expresses intensity and makes sense in this context: "greatly destroyed."

From this it emerges that, apart from the name of a place, "Bethel" also denotes the name or title of a god.

The references to Bethel in the book of Amos are similar; there is a juxtaposition of the condemned cult centres Bethel and Gilgal.[29] The information in Amos 3:14—"On the day I punish Israel for her sins, I will destroy the altars of Bethel; the horns of the altar will be cut off and fall to the ground"—has inclined many commentators to identify Amos with the unnamed prophet from Judah mentioned in 1 Kgs 13. Amos 5:6, just like Hos 10:15, is a passage which has caused commentators a great deal of trouble.[30]

MT:

דרשו את־יהוה וחיו פן־יצלח כאש בית יוסף ואכלה ואין־מכבה
לבית־אל

(lit.: "Seek YHWH and you shall live, or/since he will strike like fire the House of Joseph and burn [it] and there will be no-one [who] will be able to quench it in Bethel")

LXX:

ἐκζητήσατε τὸν κύριον καὶ ζήσατε ὅπως μὴ ἀναλάμψῃ ὡς πῦρ ὁ οἶκος Ιωσηφ καὶ καταφάγεται αὐτόν καὶ οὐκ ἔσται ὁ σβέσων τῷ οἴκῳ Ισραηλ.

Vulgate:
quaerite Dominum et vivite ne forte conburatur ut ignis domus Ioseph et devorabit et non erit qui extinguat Bethel.

The alteration בית־אל for בית ישׂראל follows the LXX version. If the unaltered text is applied then Bethel fulfils the role of the main sanctuary which could as *pars pro toto* denote the whole of Israel.

Amos 7:10-17 contains an account of a conflict between Amos and Amaziah, the priest of Bethel who pointedly states that Bethel is "the king's sanctuary and the temple of the kingdom" (מקדש־מלך הוא ובית ממלכה = ὅτι ἁγίασμα βασιλέως ἐστὶν καὶ οἶκος βασιλείας ἐστίν), that is to say, it is a place containing a temple of a state cult or one associated with the royal household, and doubtless that is also a royal residence.[31]

---

29. Amos 5:5 mentions Beer-sheba as well. I think, however, that this is an addition to the original text; see Chapter 2 on Beer-sheba.

30. Stuart, *Hosea–Jonah*, rejects the version preserved in the LXX and accepts the primacy of the MT with its version of "Bethel." Stuart translates the whole verse thus: "Seek Yahweh and live. Lest he progresses like a fire against the family of Joseph and consume Bethel, with no-one to quench it."

31. For an extensive discussion of the biblical tradition surrounding the sanctuary in Bethel, see in M. Bič, "Bet'el—Le sanctuaire du roi (Géographie et théologie de l'Ancient Testament)," *ArOr* 17 (1949): 46-63.

Zechariah 7:2 requires analysis if it is to be interpreted properly:[32]

MT:

וישלח בית־אל שר־אצר ורגם מלך ואנשיו לחלות את־פני יהוה

LXX:

καὶ ἐξαπέστειλεν εἰς Βαιθηλ Σαρασαρ καὶ Αρβεσεερ ὁ βασιλεὺς καὶ οἱ ἄνδρες αὐτοῦ τοῦ ἐξιλάσασθαι τὸν κύριον.

Vulgate

Et miserunt ad domum Dei Sarasar et Rogomelech et viri qui erant cum eo ad deprecandam faciem Domini.

The next verse (v. 3) is a continuation of the sentence in 7:2: "and to ask the priests of the house of the Lord of Hosts and prophets." The priests are described thus: אשר לבית־יהוה צבאות, that is, as priests "who (are) in the temple of YHWH *ṣᵊbā'ôt*." How then is the term בית־אל in Zech 7:2 to be understood? According to the LXX it is a toponym, according to the Vulgate it is a temple of God. Grammatically speaking, בית־אל could be the subject of the sentence, which would make it mean: "Bethel sent Sherezer..." This would mean that Bethel is the proper name of an otherwise unknown person. Another explanation of this convoluted verse is suggested if we accept that the whole phrase בית־אל שר־אצר is a theophoric proper name, one in which בית־אל is the name of a god.[33] With the removal of that part, the subject of the sentence becomes Zechariah (v. 1).

There is yet another interpretation of Zech 7:2. If בית־אל is taken to be a toponym introduced without a preposition, the sentence could be translated thus: "And he sent [to] Bethel Sherezer..." This resolution would be backed by the translations in both the LXX and the Vulgate.[34] In Biblical Hebrew, adverbial phrases of static place are introduced without prepositions.[35] The only analogy with Zech 7:2 might be found in Gen 35:1 where Bethel is also mentioned: "Go up to Bethel..." (קום עלה בית־אל,[36] lit. "stand, go Bethel").[37] Even if it were possible to justify

32. Stuart, *Hosea–Jonah*, translates Zech 7:2 thus: "Now Bethel sent Sharezer and Regem-melek and his men to entreat the face of Yahweh."

33. See A.P. Ross, "Jacob's Vision: The Founding of Bethel," *Bibliotheca Sacra* 142 (1985): 224-34 (236-37 n. 29, and the bibliography cited there).

34. The KJV reads: "When they had sent unto the house of God Sherezer and Regem-melech, and their men, to pray before the Lord." The use here of the plural of the verb "to send" is unjustified since in the MT this verb appears in the third person singular.

35. M. Tomal, *Język hebrajski biblijny*, Warsaw, 2000, 147-48.

36. The LXX reads: ἀναστὰς ἀνάβηθι εἰς τὸν τόπον Βαιθηλ; *Vetus Latina*: "Surge, et ascende in locum Bethel."

the last of these hypotheses there would still be a doubt as to whether בֵּית־אֵל here denotes the name of a town or, as a common noun, merely "a house of God." Nevertheless, we can make the tentative suggestion that Zech 7:2 confirms the exceptional significance of the sanctuary in Bethel in the Persian era.[38] According to Zech 7:1-3 (see the analogous 2 Chr 17:24-41), the sanctuary in Bethel was a centre of considerable authority since emissaries were sent to it to inquire about cult matters.[39] Regardless of whether the reference is to Bethel, as I suppose, or to some temple, Zech 7:3 affirms that the god worshipped in this centre was YHWH צבאות.

Nehemiah 7:32 (parallel Ezra 2:28) confirms the proximity of Ai and Bethel that the book of Joshua mentions. It is also worth noting that Nehemiah refers to "the men of Bethel and Ai," which would signify that, despite its name, Ai, which means "ruin," was not always uninhabited.

Nadav Na'aman's view is that the biblical mentions of Beth-aven (בֵּית אָוֶן, cf. Josh 7:2; 18:2; 1 Sam 13:5; 14:23; Hos 4:15; 5:8; 10:5) doubtless refer to a place called בֵּית אֶבֶן*—in other words, not a "house of weakness/idolatry" but "house of stones."[40] Na'aman believes that the term בֵּית אֶבֶן* referred to a sanctuary lying outside Bethel, just beyond the city.[41] He claims that the verse in Judg 2:1—"The angel of the Lord went up from Gilgal to Bokim and said, 'I brought you up out of Egypt and led you into the land that I swore to give to your forefathers. I said, 'I will never break my covenant with you'"—originally referred to Bethel. The secondary nature of the reading "Bokim" (הבכים) is confirmed by the LXX in which a different version has been preserved:

37. See also Gen 35:3 and 1 Sam 10:3, which read: "…three men going up to God in Bethel" (עֹלִים אֶל־הָאֱלֹהִים בֵּית־אֵל).

38. J. Blenkinsopp, "The Judaean Priesthood during the Neo-Babylonian and Achaemenid Periods: A Hypothetical Reconstruction," *CBQ* 60 (1998): 35-43 (32), where Zech 7:1-3 are translated as follows: "In the fourth year of King Darius, the word of Yahweh came to Zechariah on the fourth of the ninth month, in Chislev. Sareser, Regemmelech and his men had sent to Bethel to entreat the favor of Yahweh and to ask the priests who belonged to the house of Yahweh Sebaoth and the prophets, 'Should I mourn [weep] in the fifth month and practice abstinence as I have been doing for these many years?'" (p. 32).

39. Cf. E.A. Knauf, "Bethel: The Israelite Impact on Judean Language and Literature," in O. Lipschits and M. Oeming (eds.), *Judah and the Judeans in the Persian Period*, Winona Lake, 2006, 291-349.

40. N. Na'aman, "Beth-Aven, Bethel and Early Israelite Sanctuaries," *ZDPV* 103 (1987): 13-21.

41. *Ibid.*, 17

καὶ ἀνέβη ἄγγελος κυρίου ἀπὸ Γαλγαλ ἐπὶ τὸν Κλαυθμῶνα καὶ ἐπὶ Βαιθηλ καὶ ἐπὶ τὸν οἶκον Ισραηλ.[42]

Zechariah Kallai offers a different suggestion.[43] He considers that only in the prophetic texts does the mention of בית און refer to Bethel; elsewhere it refers to a centre situated close to Bethel. On the basis of the narrative in the book of Joshua, which describes the delineation of the boundaries between the territories of the various tribes, he asserts that בית און should be identified with Tell Maryam or Tell 'el-Askar.[44] At the same time, Kallai rejects the hypothesis that בית און is derived from בית אבן*.[45]

Developing Menahem Haran's ideas,[46] Na'aman attempts to prove that in the age of the prophets it was customary to locate sanctuaries outside towns,[47] whereas Kallai—and I think rightly—tries to demonstrate that the sanctuary at Bethel at least was within the town itself.[48] Kallai believes that the information about the altar east of Bethel does not refer to the factual position of a cult place but serves only to underline the pastoral life of the patriarchs.[49]

Yairah Amit goes one step further than Na'aman by claiming that the various obscurities in the biblical text can be properly interpreted as a hidden polemic.[50] Amit considers that the account of the migration of the Danites (Judg 17–18)[51] is this kind of text, as is Judg 2:1-5.[52]

The term "Bethel" is, therefore, both a toponym and a common noun meaning "house of god"—a temple—and it is not always clear whether the term appears with the first or second meaning. There is, in fact, a third meaning; "Bethel" is most probably the name of a god, to which the following statement testifies: "Then Moab will be ashamed of Chemosh,

---

42. *Ibid.*, 18.
43. Kallai, "Beth-El - Luz and Beth-Aven," in R. Liwak and S. Wagner (eds.), *Prophetie und geschichte Wirklichkeit im alten Israel*, Cologne, 1991, 171-88.
44. *Ibid.*, 175-76
45. *Ibid.*, 178-80.
46. Haran, *Temples and Temple-Service*, and "Temples and Cultic Open Areas as Reflected in the Bible," in Biran (ed.), *Temples and High Places*, 31-37.
47. Na'aman, "Beth-Aven."
48. Kallai, "Beth-El - Luz and Beth-Aven."
49. *Ibid.*, 182-83.
50. Y. Amit, *Hidden Polemics in Biblical Narrative*, Leiden, 2000.
51. Y. Amit, "Hidden Polemic in the Conquest of Dan: Judges 17–18," *VT* 40 (1990): 4-20. For more on this subject see the chapter on Dan.
52. Y. Amit, "Bochim, Bethel, and the Hidden Polemic (Judg 2,1-5)," in G. Galil and M. Weinfeld (eds.), *Studies in Historical Geography and Biblical Historiography: Presented to Zechariah Kallai*, VTSup 81, Leiden, 2000, 121-31.

as the house of Israel was ashamed when they trusted in Bethel" (Jer 48:13). As I have said, one of the interpretations of Zech 7:2 assumes the existence of a god Bethel. The strongest arguments for it have been provided by the Elephantine papyri,[53] the Esarhaddon inscription,[54] one Aramaic text in Demotic script[55] and the Aramaic tablet from Aleppo (c. 570 BCE).[56]

Aetiologies

Genesis 12:8-9:

> (8) From there (Shechem) he went on toward the hills east of Bethel and pitched his tent, with Bethel on the west and Ai on the east. There he built (וייבן־שם)[57] an altar (מזבח) to the Lord and called on the name of the Lord (ויקרא בשם יהוה). (9) Then Abram set out and continued toward the Negev.[58]

Genesis 13:3-4:

> (3) From the Negev he (Abram) went from place to place until he came to Bethel, to the place between Bethel and Ai where his tent had been earlier (4) and where he had first built (עשה)[59] an altar (המזבח). There Abram called on the name of the Lord.

Genesis 28:10-22:

> (10) Jacob left Beersheba and set out for Haran. (11) When he reached a certain place (מקום), he stopped for the night because the sun had set. Taking one of the stones (מאבני) there, he put it under his head and lay down to sleep. (12) He had a dream in which he saw a stairway (ladder) resting on the earth (סלם מצב ארצה),[60] with its top reaching to heaven, and the angels of God (מלאכי אלהים) were ascending and descending on it. (13) There above it stood the Lord, and he said: "I am the Lord, the

---

53. Cowley, *Aramaic Papyri*, *passim*; B. Porten and A. Yardeni, *Textbook of Aramaic documents from Ancient Egypt*, 4 vols., Jerusalem, 1986–99; see also B. Porten, *Archives from Elephantine: The Life of an Ancient Jewish Military Colony*, Berkeley, 1968.

54. *ANET*, 534.

55. W.W. Hallo (ed.), *The Context of Scripture*, Leiden, 1997, 1:314, 322.

56. J. Teixidor, *The Pagan God: Popular Religion in the Greco-Roman Near East*, Princeton, 1977, 30-31.

57. From the verb בנה, "to build."

58. Following the Vulgate, the word מזבה may be translated as "to the south."

59. Lit. "made, caused."

60. Lit.: "*sullām* placed on the ground."

God of your father Abraham and the God of Isaac. I will give you and your descendants the land on which you are lying. (14) Your descendants will be like the dust of the earth, and you will spread out to the west and to the east, to the north and to the south. All peoples on earth will be blessed through you and your offspring. (15) I am with you and will watch over you wherever you go, and I will bring you back to this land. I will not leave you until I have done what I have promised you." (16) When Jacob awoke from his sleep, he thought, "Surely the Lord is in this place, and I was not aware of it." (17) He was afraid and said, "How awesome is this place! This is none other than the house of God; this is the gate of heaven (שער השמים)." (18) Early the next morning Jacob took the stone he had placed under his head and set it up as a pillar and poured oil on top of it. (19) He called that place Bethel (בית־אל), though the city used to be called Luz. (20) Then Jacob made a vow, saying, "If God will be with me and will watch over me on this journey I am taking and will give me food to eat and clothes to wear (21) so that I return safely to my father's house, then the Lord will be my God (והיה יהוה לי לאלהים)[61] (22) and this stone that I have set up as a pillar will be God's house (יהיה בית אלהים), and of all that you give me I will give you a tenth."

Genesis 35:1-15:

(1) Then God (אלהים) said to Jacob, "Go up to Bethel and settle there, and build an altar there to God (ועשה־שם מזבח לאל), who appeared to you when you were fleeing from your brother Esau."[62] (2) So Jacob said to his household and to all who were with him, "Get rid of the foreign gods you have with you, and purify yourselves and change your clothes. (3) Then come, let us go up to Bethel, where I will build an altar to God, who answered me in the day of my distress and who has been with me wherever I have gone." (4) So they gave Jacob all the foreign gods they had and the rings in their ears, and Jacob buried them under the oak at Shechem. (5) Then they set out, and the terror of God fell upon the towns all around them so that no one pursued them. (6) Jacob and all the people with him came to Luz (that is, Bethel) in the land of Canaan. (7) There he built an altar, and he called the place El Bethel, because it was there that God revealed himself to him[63] when he was fleeing from his brother. (8) Now Deborah, Rebekah's nurse, died and was buried under the oak below Bethel. So it was named Allon Bacuth. (9) After Jacob returned from Paddan Aram, God appeared to him again and blessed him. (10) God said to him, "Your name is Jacob, but you will no longer be called Jacob; your name will be Israel." So he named him Israel.

61. LXX: ἔσται μοι κύριος εἰς θεόν.
62. This sentence, whose subject is אלהים, seems to suggest a differentiation between the god who is speaking and the god (אל) whom Jacob is to honour in Bethel.
63. In the MT the verb used here is in the plural, meaning "there the gods revealed themselves to him."

(11) And God said to him, "I am God Almighty (אל שׁדי); be fruitful and increase in number. A nation and a community of nations will come from you, and kings will come from your body. (12) The land I gave to Abraham and Isaac I also give to you, and I will give this land to your descendants after you." (13) Then God went up from him at the place where he had talked with him. (14) Jacob set up a stone pillar at the place where God had talked with him, and he poured out a drink offering on it; he also poured oil on it. (15) Jacob called the place where God had talked with him Bethel.

An analysis of the aetiological myths cited above requires us to do three things: first, to establish their interdependence; second, to discover, if possible, the order and time in which the various narratives arose; and third, to distil the elements constructing the various stories and, where possible, to examine their sources.

It is not easy to describe the relationships between the narratives dealing with Abraham and Jacob. The story of Abraham in Bethel is brief and belongs to the broader narrative of the Patriarch's itinerary, while the Jacob narrative concerning Bethel forms a separate part of his story. There are several arguments favouring the primacy of the Jacob version.[64] The first is the external evidence provided by Hos 12:4, which shows that the figure of Jacob was associated with Bethel as early as the eighth century BCE.[65] The passage in Hosea shows that in the prophet's time two myths about Jacob were current—one about his battle with the angel and another about theophany in Bethel ("He struggled with the angel and overcame him; he wept and begged for his favour. He found him at Bethel and talked with him there").[66] The second is that in the epic of Jacob the themes associating the patriarch with Bethel are the culmination, as well as a bracketing, of this patriarch's story.

Sanctuary in Bethel is located outside the town only—as was noted by Kallai—in the account about Abraham; in the prophetic books and the chronicles it is always spoken of as being an urban centre. Did this inconsistency perhaps arise as a result of interference which "relocated" the holy place to outside the town? It would be difficult to support any

64. Gunkel, *Genesis*, 167, considers that the stories about the beginnings of Bethel associated with Jacob are older than those associating the place with Abraham.

65. For more on this, see W.D. Whitt, "The Jacob Traditions in Hosea and their Relation to Genesis," *ZAW* 103 (1991): 18-43.

66. It is worth noting here that the reception of this mythical theme is not constant; in Ben Sira, Jacob is mentioned only as the one who received Isaac's blessing and gave rise to the twelve tribes of Israel (cf. Sir 44:22-23; 49:14-16).

thesis that claimed there were two different sanctuaries that were the referred to by the various biblical authors. Yet we cannot draw any definitive conclusions about the chronology of the accounts simply from this inconsistency. Nevertheless, Kallai's hypothesis about the non-urban nature of the sanctuary in Bethel as the way of tailoring the details of this narrative to the tradition of the nomadic life-style of the patriarchs does seem very likely. This would mean that the sanctuary in Bethel was indeed within the town and that the introduction in the book of Genesis of a reference suggesting its location outside the locale served to enhance Abraham's "nomadisation." Just as the ideology extolling the pastoral origins of the Israelites is a late creation, so the story of Abraham's altar outside Bethel is a re-telling of a story about Jacob establishing an urban sanctuary.

The description of Abraham's stay in Bethel consists of "standard" elements: there are repetitions of phrases about the altar of Yahweh (מזבח לאל), as well as references to calling the name of the Lord (ויקרא בשם יהוה). It is not possible to draw conclusions about the nature of the sanctuary from such references. The place of the altar is a space dedicated to "calling the name of the Lord." The impression arises that for some reason the editors of the Bible did not consider the Jacob myth to be sufficient and that they wanted to make the cult place in Bethel more credible by associating it with the person of the "ecumenical" ancestor Abraham.[67]

Describing the layers that form the literary story of Abraham, John Van Seters conceded that both Gen 12:8-9 and Gen 13:3-4 were the work of a Yahwist and that they originated in the times of the Babylonian captivity.[68]

Genesis 28 gives a detailed account of the circumstances of theophany. During his journey, Jacob reached a certain place one evening and fell asleep. The revelation he experienced there took the form of a dream vision. Genesis 35 speaks of it differently: in v. 1 we read: "Then God said to Jacob..." and in v. 9: "God appeared to him," while vv. 10-12 records the statement the deity addressed to Jacob in direct speech. There are no details of the theophany in the text; but it is clear from v. 13 that the event took place while he was awake: "Then God went up from him

67. For more on the subject of Abraham's "ecumenical" character, see A. de Pury, "Abraham: The Priestly Writer's 'Ecumenical' Ancestor," in S.L. McKenzie and T. Römer (eds.), *Rethinking the Foundations: Historiography in the Ancient World and in the Bible. Essays in Honour of John Van Seters*, BZAW 294, Berlin, 2000, 163-81.

68. Van Seters, *Abraham in History and Tradition, passim*.

at the place where he had talked with him." Even though the stories written in Gen 28 and 35 are closely related, it is impossible to resist the impression that they were written by different authors.[69]

I would be inclined to estimate that the text of Gen 35:1-15, though it is based on older themes (for example, on the description of Deborah's death or on the burial of foreign gods in Shechem), is nevertheless one of the later fragments of the book of Genesis. There are several factors supporting this. First, Gen 28:18 says that Jacob put up a stone as a pillar whereas 35:7 says he built an altar. Second, in 35:10 the theme of Jacob changing his name to Israel returns (cf. 32:28),[70] and v. 8 refers to the death of Deborah, Rebekah's nurse, and her burial in a grave beneath an oak which Jacob called "the oak of tears" (אלון בכות = Βάλανος πένθους).[71] The god revealing himself predicts good fortune for Jacob (35:11-12), which, within the structure of Jacob's pericope in Bethel, is the equivalent of Jacob's oath (28:20-21). The promise that Jacob would receive land is expressed in the sentence: "The land I gave to Abraham and Isaac I also give to you, and I will give this land to your descendants after you" (v. 12). The ideology behind this sentence is linked to the entire literature of god's promises, promises which form an extensive part of the Abraham narrative, but which are not, I think, part of the earliest layer.

The description of Jacob's second visit to Bethel (Gen 35:1-15) clearly harks back to the previous narrative. Several interesting formulations appear. Just as in the two mentions of Abraham in Bethel, so here two different verbs are used to describe the act of building an altar: עשה ("to make," "cause," v. 1 and v. 13) and בנה ("to build," v. 7). The building of an altar is what differentiates the account in Gen 35 from the description in Gen 28, where only a stone (האבן) is mentioned as a pillar/monument (מצבה). The author of Gen 35 tried to combine the earlier story of Jacob in Bethel (in which the stone with oil poured on it played a key role) and a later tradition which demanded that there be an altar present in a holy place.

69.   Speiser, *Genesis*, 269-71, believes that the fragment Gen 28:10-22 is a joint E and J version, and that Gen 35:1-15 is an E text with P additions (vv. 9-13, 15).

70.   See the chapter about the sanctuaries in Transjordan.

71.   C.T.R. Hayward, "Jacob's Second Visit to Bethel in Targum Pseudo-Jonathan," in P.R. Davies (ed.), *A Tribute to Geza Vermes*, JSOTSup 100, Sheffield, 1990, 175-92, discusses the motif, already extensively examined in the early period of rabbinical exegesis, combining the death of Deborah with the news of his mother Rebekah's death reaching Jacob.

There is also a different form of word used to describe the theophany: God simply "said to him" (vv. 1, 10, 11) and "God appeared to him again" (v. 9), and, finally, "God went up from him at the place where he had talked with him" (v. 13). None of these phrases suggests that we are dealing with a dream here. So, Jacob had direct contact with god while he was awake.

The text of Gen 35:1-4 is, apparently, a different story not dealing directly with Bethel but with the ritual burial of cult objects beneath an oak in Shechem.[72] Because of v. 5, which speaks of "the terror of God" that ensured Jacob safe passage from Shechem to Bethel, the emphasis in the understanding of Gen 35:1-4 changed. As early as the late Hellenistic period commentators accepted that the cult objects mentioned here must have come from Shechem and that they fell into the hands of Jacob's family as a consequence of Simeon's and Levi's expedition against the town (Gen 34).[73] Alberto Soggin interpreted the passage differently, namely, as a recollection of a cult burial of a god and the pilgrimage to Bethel that followed it.[74] If the topography of the district where the described events took place is accurate, then it is doubtful that such a pilgrimage, or rather a ritual funeral march, could have taken place from such an important religious centre as Shechem to Bethel, which lay some 30 km to the south. Soggin's theory appears well founded, with the exception of the conclusion he draws, on the basis of the biblical text, that Jacob travelled from Shechem to Bethel. The ritual behaviour associated with the centre in Shechem could well be the expression of a different tradition to the one in the account of Bethel.

Genesis 35:10 sees the return of the subject of Jacob's change of name to Israel. The sentences concerning us—"God said to him, 'Your name is Jacob, but you will no longer be called Jacob; your name will be Israel.' So he named him Israel"—are almost identical in form to those describing Jacob's struggle with the angel (Gen 32:28).[75] Let us compare both fragments:

---

72. For more on this subject, see the chapter about Shechem.

73. Hayward, "Jacob's Second Visit," 175-80.

74. A. Soggin, "La radice TMN—'Nascondere', 'Seppelire' in ebraico," in P. Franzaoli (ed.), *Atti del secondo congresso internazionale di linguistica Camito-Semitica. Firenze 16–19 aprile 1974*, Quaderni di Semitistica 5, Florence, 1978, 241-45; "Jacob in Shechem and in Bethel Genesis 35,1-7," in M. Fishbane and E. Tov (eds.), *Sha'arei Talmon: Studies in the Bible, Qumran, and the Ancient Near East Presented to Shemaryahu Talmon*, Winona Lake, 1992, 195-98.

75. See the chapter dealing with cult places in Transjordan.

Gen 35:10

MT:

שְׁמֶךָ וַיִּקְרָא אֶת־שְׁמוֹ יִשְׂרָאֵל וַיֹּאמֶר־לוֹ אֱלֹהִים שִׁמְךָ יַעֲקֹב לֹא־יִקָּרֵא
שִׁמְךָ עוֹד יַעֲקֹב כִּי אִם־יִשְׂרָאֵל יִהְיֶה

LXX:

καὶ εἶπεν αὐτῷ ὁ θεός τὸ ὄνομά σου Ιακωβ οὐ κληθήσεται ἔτι Ιακωβ ἀλλ᾽
Ισραηλ ἔσται τὸ ὄνομά σου

Vetus Latina:
*Et dixit ei Deus: Jam non vocabitur nomen tuum Jacob, sed Israel erit
nomen tuum. Et vocavit nomen ejus, Israel.*

Gen 32:28

MT:

וַיֹּאמֶר אֵלָיו מַה־שְּׁמֶךָ וַיֹּאמֶר יַעֲקֹב

LXX:

εἶπεν δὲ αὐτῷ οὐ κληθήσεται ἔτι τὸ ὄνομά σου Ιακωβ ἀλλὰ Ισραηλ ἔσται τὸ
ὄνομά σου

Vetus Latina:
*Et dixit ei: Non vocabitur amplius nomen tuum Jacob, sed Israel erit
nomen tuum: quia valuisti cum Deo, et cum hominibus potens es.*

Both verses—in the MT, as well as in the LXX and *Vetus Latina*—have
the same vocabulary, as well as an almost identical form and syntax.[76]

It is not possible to draw certain conclusions about the inter-rela-
tionship of these verses on the basis of their formal similarity. It is not
possible, simply from the fact that analogous vocabularies have been
deployed, to deduce which of the passages is primary and which secondary. It would be safe to assume that they both come (directly or
indirectly) from the same source. An analysis of their contexts, however,
creates the irresistible impression that there is an incoherence present in
Gen 35, whereas Gen 32 is consistent. Jacob's struggle with the angel is
an initiation myth, and this makes the change of the hero's name com-
prehensible; on the other hand, the story about Jacob's second visit to
Bethel has the appearance of being an editorial attempt to contain the
whole Jacob "epic," which actually consists of various elements drawn
from earlier stories about him, inside one framework.

A comparison of, for instance, the closing fragment of the story in Gen
35:14-15 with a fragment in Gen 28:18-19 will demonstrate that an older
tradition was used:

76. There is a greater difference in the Vulgate: "At ille nequaquam inquit Iacob
appellabitur nomen tuum sed Israhel quoniam si contra Deum fortis fuisti quanto
magis contra homines praevalebis" (Gen 32:28); "Dicens non vocaberis ultra Iacob
sed Israhel erit nomen tuum et appellavit eum Israhel" (Gen 35:10).

Gen 35:14-15:

> *Jacob* set up a *stone pillar* at the *place* where God had talked with him, and he poured out a drink offering (libation) on it (*the stone pillar*); he also poured *oil on it*. Jacob *called the place* where God had talked with him *Bethel*.

Gen 28:18-19:

> Early the next morning *Jacob* took the *stone* he had placed under his head and set it up as a pillar and poured *oil on top of it*. *He called that place Bethel*, though the city used to be called Luz.

The addition to Gen 35:14 of the term "a drink offering" (ויסך עליה נסך) indicates that this sentence is of later provenance. The only fundamental difference between the analysed sentences comes from the use of different verbs to describe the raising of the pillar. Genesis 35:14 uses the verb נצב ("to stand," "to arrange"), and Gen 28:18 the verb שׂים / שׂום ("to lay," "to place"). If my supposition that the text of Gen 28 is earlier than Gen 35 is correct, then we would expect that the use of the verb שׂים, in the meaning of raising a monument, is more archaic than נצב.

Genesis 28:10-22 talks about a theophany. What we have here is not only the aetiological myth of a holy place but also the promise of good fortune and divine protection for Jacob. Genesis 35:1-15 is both the last extensively expanded story of which Jacob is the hero, and also an account of his fulfilment of the vow he made during his first stay in Bethel. The descriptions of his visits to Bethel form a kind of bracket for the story of his stay with Laban. The primacy of Gen 28:10-22 over Gen 35:1-15 is surely demonstrated by the reference in Gen 35:1-15 to a first visit to Bethel. The use of the term "altar" (מזבח) in Gen 35, the references to Abraham and Isaac, the description of the oil offering by way of the technical term "libation" and also the exploitation of the tradition of Jacob's change of name—all this testifies to the secondary (at least compared with Gen 28:10-22), and doubtless late, nature of the narrative in this chapter. It is clear, therefore, that the passage in Gen 28:10-22 is the primary story, and that Gen 35 supplements the history of Jacob. In the epic's construction, his second visit to Bethel closes the description of the hero's deeds. There is no doubt that the author of the reference in Hos 12:5 had in mind the myth preserved in Gen 28:10-22, but did the story of Jacob fulfilling his vows exist even then?

The account in Gen 28:1-22 is a compact and, at first glance, a consistent description of a theophany. It uses terms emphasising the exceptional nature of the place itself. The word "place" (מקום = τόπος = locus)[77]

---

77. *TDOT*, s.v., מקום, 532-44.

is repeated often, and the whole narrative is systematically constructed[78] to underline the significance of the theophany and the promise that Jacob heard (vv. 13-15), and also of the vow he made to God (v. 20). The motif of the stone and the dream makes for the specificity of this narrative. Van Seters is doubtless right when he considers that it is the theme of the divine promise that links the stories of Abraham and Jacob. Although it is not strictly associated with aetiological myths it can—as in this case—appear alongside them. The revelation of the holy place takes place in a dream. The exceptional nature of the place of theophany is marked by the stone (האבן) raised as a pillar/monument (מזבח).

The story of Jacob's theophany during his visit to Bethel (Gen 28:10-22) consists of two parts: vv. 13-15 are a description *par excellence* of a theophany, with a divine proclamation, whereas vv. 11-12 is a description of an angelological vision. Verse 12 speaks of "god's angels" (מלאכי אלהים), whereas vv. 13-15 use the divine name of Yahweh. This might indicate that these fragments are of different provenance.

If this duality comes from joining different currents of a tradition or different texts, then we might be tempted to separate out its components. I suspect that the original story was the one about Jacob's arrival at "a certain place" (v. 11), the dream in which he saw angels climbing and descending a ladder (v. 12) and also the information about his fear and the assertion that this place was the gate to heaven (v. 17). The original source might have looked like this:

> (11) And when he came to a certain place (מקום) he stopped for the night, for the sun had set; and he took one of the stones (מאבני) of this place, placed it under his head and fell asleep at this place. (12) And he dreamt that there was a ladder placed on the ground (סלם מצב ארצה) whose top reached heaven and along it angels of God (מלאכי אלהים) ascended and descended. (17) He was afraid and said, "How awesome is this place! This is none other than the house of God; this is the gate of heaven." (18) Early the next morning Jacob took the stone he had placed under his head and set it up as a pillar (monument) and poured oil on top of it. (19) He called that place Bethel. Earlier this city was called Luz.[79]

---

78. See Carr, *Reading the Fractures of Genesis*, 205-208, 256-71; see also J.-M. Husser, "Les métamorphoses d'un songe. Critique littéraire de Genèse 28,10-22," *RB* 98 (1991): 321-42; G. Fleischer, "Jakob träumt. Eine Auseinandersetzung mit Erhard Blums methodischem Ansatz am Beispiel von Gen 28,10-22," *BN* 76 (1995): 82-102.

79. If one were to exclude from the original source the expression "house of God," the sentence would be: "this is none other than the gate to heaven," which makes more sense in the context of an epiphany. The reference to the house of God could have been added to explain the toponym in v. 19.

Such a segmentation would mean that the contents of v. 17, in which Jacob "said" (ויאמר) refers to the vision and not to waking reality, and that it is only in vv. 18-19 that the subject becomes events taking place after waking.

The sentence: "Jacob left Beer-sheba and set out for Haran" (v. 10), uniting larger parts of Jacob's epic, is a late addition. Verses 13-15 is the story, expanded by a Yahwist, of Jacob's angelic vision which also introduces the motif of the promise that god made to Jacob. Verse 16 speaks about the transition from the world of dream vision to the waking world, and this allows v. 17 to be added to the world "after the vision." Verses 20-21 probably refer to the divine promise of good fortune (vv. 13-15), though it is quite possible that the theme of Jacob's vows is a separate layer introduced to the narrative during a different redaction. Verse 22 seems to be the result of a final editing whose aim was to unify the older layers, and we can link it to the creation of Gen 35:1-15. Jacob's speech, formulated in the first person, links this verse to vv. 20-21, and the introduction of the words "and this stone that I have set up as a pillar will be God's house (בית אלהים)" appears to be aimed at harmonising v. 11. The second part of v. 22 is an obvious continuation of the motif of Jacob's vow (vv. 20-21).[80]

The successive stages of editing applied to the story of Jacob in Bethel were as follows:
1. Gen 28:11-12, 17-19;
2. Addition of Gen 28:13-16, 20-22;
3. Addition of Gen 28:10;
4. Composition of Gen 35:1-15;
5. Composition of Gen 13:3-4.

Unfortunately, it is not possible to establish the precise dates of the various editing insertions. The only trace of a cognisance of this myth is the mention in Hos 12:5, from which it emerges that there was already a tradition claiming that Jacob saw God in Bethel as early as the eighth

---

80. Carr, *Reading the Fractures of Genesis*, makes 28:10-12, 17-22 the basic text. However, J. Van Seters, "Divine Encounter at Bethel (Gen 28,10-22) in Recent Literary-Critical Study of Genesis," *ZAW* 110 (1998): 503-13, distinguishes the actual aetiology (28:11-12, 16aα, 17-19) from the layer associated with the divine promise (10:13-16, 20-22). See the response by D. Carr, "Genesis 28,10-22 and Transmission-Historical Method: A Reply to John Van Seters," *ZAW* 111 (1999): 399-403. My proposed identification of the primary layer of the text supports Van Seters's hypothesis except that he includes into this text also the first part of v. 16. Husser, "Les métamorphoses d'un songe," 321-42, has reached virtually diametrically opposed conclusions.

century BCE. This fragment of the book of Hosea uses the verb דבר ("to speak"). According to the hypothesis presented here, this verb appeared only in the second stage of redaction (Gen 28:13). If we argued from this premise, then it would mean that the second stage of the redaction of the Bethel myth happened before the times of Hosea. If we could establish when the story of the nomadic Abraham first appeared, a story which influenced the attempt to turn Bethel into an extra-urban sanctuary, it might allow us to calculate the date of the myth's creation. At present there is no certain answer to this question, although most researchers point to the era of Babylonian captivity.[81]

If we accept this segmentation of Gen 28:10-22, then we can consider the construction of the aetiological myth in its successive versions. According to the version that I have identified as the primary one, Gen 28:11-12, 17-19, Jacob arrives at some place and has a dream there. He dreams that "there was a ladder placed on the ground (סלם מצב רצה) whose top reached heaven and along it angels of God." The crucial mythical image, therefore, and the reason why Jacob was filled with fear is the sight of the סלם and the angels ascending and descending it.

The term מלאך אלהים ("angel of Elohim") appears several times in the Bible (Gen 21:17; 28:12; 32:2 and 1 Sam 29:9).[82] Genesis 21:17 mentions an angel of Elohim as an intermediary between Hagar and God (אלהים); Gen 32:2 mentions a vision of God's camp featuring angels of אלהים.[83] The reference in 1 Sam 29:9 precludes a deeper analysis of the concept of "angel of God" because it merely says: "Achish answered [David], 'I know that you have been as pleasing in my eyes as an angel of God…'"[84] In the LXX and the Vulgate translations, the differences between מלאך אלהים and מלאך יהוה become blurred—in both versions we find ἄγγελος τοῦ θεοῦ / κυρίου and angelus Domini / Dei.

A huge number of studies has been produced on the subject of the noun סלם, a term usually translated as "ladder."[85] סלם, which appears only once in the MT, most often is understood to derive from the verb סלל ("to raise," "to pick up"). In the LXX and the Vulgate the corresponding words are κλῖμαξ and "scala." Scholars have linked it with the

81.   *Inter alia*: J. Van Seters, *Abraham in History and Tradition*; G. Garbini, *Storia e ideologia nell'Israele Antico*, Brescia, 1986; de Pury, "Abraham."

82.   Whereas מלאך יהוה appears 65 times.

83.   For the aetiology of Mahanaim, see the chapter about the cult centre in Transjordan.

84.   The LXX omits the comparison with the angel of God, saying only "you are pleasing in my eyes, but…"

85.   Speiser, *Genesis*, translates this word as "stairway"; see also Ross, "Jacob's Vision," 228-29, with an extensive bibliography.

Akkadian word *simmiltu* and suggested that the term arose in Hebrew under the influence of the appearance of the Mesopotamian ziggurat.[86] Because of the lack of comparative material there is no way of either proving or disproving this thesis.[87]

After waking, Jacob realises that he has come upon a holy place. He associates the sight of angels moving up and down with the place where "the gate to heaven" (שער השמים) is to be found. This formulation does not appear anywhere else in the MT. The LXX translates it as πύλη τοῦ οὐρανοῦ.[88] The place where the cosmic spheres join together is the centre of the world. This is where Jacob found himself looking at the entrance to and exit from heaven. As the centre of the universe, Bethel is a holy place—and, at the same time, a terrifying one. The stone placed by Jacob is an omphalos marking the location where the heavenly and the earthly worlds meet. Nicolas Wyatt has emphasised the religious significance of the "centre of the world" where god appeared to Jacob,[89] and considers that this vision was not necessarily linked to Bethel. It could have referred to Jerusalem—the centre of the world. Wyatt, is right, in my view, to emphasise the mythological significance of the centre of the world where heaven and earth join, but his hypothesis for moving the theophany from Bethel to Jerusalem does not seem to be well-founded. We should simply acknowledge that Bethel was seen as a religious centre and in mythology was regarded as the centre of the world.

There remains the matter of whether the sight of the angels descending and ascending the סלם is interpreted as a sign that at this spot heaven touches the earth or both the earth and the underworld. The verb *yārad* ("to descend," "lead down," "drown"[90]) is of key significance here. It appears in various contexts in the Bible—for example when the subject is descending or riding down a hill (1 Sam 10:5; 25:20), when water is falling (Ezek 47:1), when the subject is travelling south (Gen 42:38; 43:20; 44:23) or drowning (Exod 15:5). The verb ירד also appears in descriptions of the underworld, which can best be illustrated by two quotations:

86. See N. Wyatt, "Where did Jacob Dream his Dream?," *SJOT* 2 (1990): 44-57 (51 and n. 23), with a further bibliography; for an extensive discussion of this hypothesis, see C. Houtman, "What did Jacob See in his Dream at Bethel? Some Remarks on Genesis 28,10-22," *VT* 27 (1977): 337-51.

87. There are three other words in Hebrew with a similar meaning: לול (1 Kgs 6:8), מעלה (e.g. 2 Kgs 9:13; Neh 3:15; Ezek 40:6) and מדרגה (Song 2:14).

88. The Vulgate: "porta caeli."

89. Wyatt, "Where did Jacob?," and *Myths of Power*, 72-74.

90. It is from this same root that the name "Jordan" (ירדן) is derived; see *DCH*, vol. 4, *s.v.*

But if the Lord brings about something totally new, and the earth opens its mouth and swallows them, with everything that belongs to them, and they go down alive into the grave (וירדו חיים שאלה), then you will know that these men have treated the Lord with contempt... They went down alive into the grave (וירדו), with everything they owned; the earth closed over them, and they perished and were gone from the community. (Num 16:30, 33)

Let death take my enemies by surprise; let them go down alive to the grave (ירדו שאול). (Ps 55:15)[91]

The verb "to descend" (ירד) is used in Isa 5:14; in Ezek 31:17; 32:21, 27 the verb is used with the meaning of "dying." It also appears in conjunction with the noun "well" (בור), which is another term for the underworld (see Ps 30:4).[92] There is no way of establishing whether the association of the verb ירד with the underworld was aimed at intensifying the tragic nature of death or whether what has been preserved is a trace of the ritual of "descending into the underworld."

On the basis of biblical evidence where the verb "to descend" was used in the context of dying, we can accept that the angels of god descending the סלם were not going down from heaven to earth but to the underworld, and that Bethel, as the centre of the world, was not a place of contact of heaven with the earth alone but with the underworld too.

The place of the angelophany is frightening not just by virtue of the vision itself but even more because of the designated holy space where the cosmic spheres touched. We read in v. 17: "He was afraid and said, 'How awesome is this place! This is none other than the house of God (בית-אלהים); this is the gate of heaven'." The MT, the LXX and the Vulgate employ the conjunction "and" in the phrase "the house of God and the gate of heaven," which logically suggests that the concepts of "house of God" and "gate of heaven" are not identical. In this instance we should deduce that the gate through which the angels come is the heavenly end of the סלם, and that the house of god is the destination to which they are going. Perhaps it was the sight of this that frightened Jacob. What was it, however, that frightened him so much? The description "house [of] *'ĕlōhîm*" could be understood as a synonym for the underworld (as the "house of the dead"), which would explain Jacob's fear. The sight of the land of the dead always awakens fear and terror.

The phrase "how awesome (מה-נורא) is this place" has its closest parallel in the wording contained in Ps 66:3: "Say to God, 'How awe-

91. See also Prov 5:5; 7:27.
92. More has been said on the symbolism of the "well" in the chapter on Beer-sheba, Chapter 2.

some (מה־נורא; lit. 'how frightening') are your deeds..." Contact with the deity or with the divine sphere evokes fear in Jacob. Fear associated with theophany is signalled also in Gen 28:13 (LXX) which uses the phrase: μὴ φοβοῦ.[93] A similar emotion, linked to not recognising an angel, is described in Judg 13. The "angel of God" (מלאך־יהוה, v. 3) bringing the annunciation of Samson's birth is taken by Manoah to be a man of God (איש האלהים, v. 8). It is only his miraculous ascension in the flame of the altar (vv. 19-20) that makes Manoah realise who the messenger was: "Manoah realised that it was the angel of the Lord (מלאך־יהוה). 'We are doomed to die!', he said to his wife. 'We have seen God!' (מות נמות כי אלהים ראינו)" (vv. 21-22). The fear for one's life after a meeting with the divinity can also be seen in the accounts of Jacob's struggle with the angel (Gen 32:30),[94] of the theophany in the burning bush (Exod 3:6) and in the revelation experienced by Gideon in Ophrah (Judg 6:22-23).[95]

The function of the stone in this story is signalled from the start with the reference to the fact that Jacob came to the place at dusk: "and [he] took one of the stones" and "put it under his head" (v. 11). When he awoke, "Jacob took the stone he had placed under his head and set it up as a pillar and poured oil on top of it" (v. 18). What we have here is information about the marking out of a holy place: the stone-pillar performs the function of an altar for libations/offerings. A development of the description of the stone pillar is to be found in v. 22: "and this stone that I have set up as a pillar will be God's house" (והאבן הזאת אשר־שמתי מצבה יהיה בית אלהים = καὶ ὁ λίθος οὗτος ὃν ἔστησα στήλην ἔσται μοι οἶκος θεοῦ).[96] This is a surprising sentence; first, because it states that the stone is to be "the house of God," which usually refers to a temple, and, second, because the construction of the pericope where v. 19 mentions the naming of the place "Bethel" does not exploit the parallelism but instead employs the expression בית אלהים. Ignoring the parallels with בית־אל in vv. 19 and 22 could be evidence of the different provenance of these verses[97] and of a significant difference between בית אלהים and בית־אל. If Gunkel is right that the word אלהים originally referred to

93. See J.W. Wevers, *Notes on the Greek Text of Genesis*, Atlanta, 1993, 166.

94. See the chapter about the cult place in Transjordan.

95. A similar phrase appears here: "Do not be afraid. You are not going to die" (אל־תירא לא תמות); see the chapter dealing with Ophrah, Chapter 6.

96. Cf. the slightly different version in the Vulgate: "et lapis iste quem erexi in titulum vocabitur Domus Dei." Instead of the phrase indicating that the stone will be "the house of god," the text suggests that the stone will be called this.

97. In both places the LXX resorts to the analogous form: Οἶκος θεοῦ. Cf. Wevers, *Notes on the Greek Text of Genesis*, 453.

the dead, these phrases would have to be translated as "house/temple of the dead" and "house/temple of God" or "of El." The construction בית אלהים appears 61 times in the MT, of which the decided majority is in later texts (1 and 2 Kings, Ezra, Nehemiah),[98] where the names of God are interchangeable, so that the compound בית אלהים there means only "the temple of God," even though originally it might have provoked an association with the house of the dead (this last meaning being completely lost in later writings).

Having erected the stone as a pillar, Jacob "poured oil on top of it (on its top)" (Gen 28:18). The term "oil" (שמן) appears again in the account of Jacob's second visit to Bethel. Oil is a substance associated with a cult as a means of anointing (see Exod 30:22-33). It was also used at offerings of food: "When someone brings a grain (food) offering to the Lord, his offering is to be of fine flour. He is to pour oil on it, put incense on it" (Lev 2:1). Oil was also used as an unction (in both religious and cosmetic contexts) and also, obviously, in lamps. Liquid offerings where oil was used are mentioned only in the narratives related to Bethel (Gen 28:18 and 35:14). Genesis 35:14 contains the phrase ויצק עליה שמן ("and he poured oil on [it]"). The yoking of the verb "to pour out" (יצק) with the noun "oil" (שמן) occurs in several other places in the Bible (Gen 28:18; 35:14; Exod 29:7; Lev 2:1, 6; 8:12; 14:15, 26; Num 5:15; 1 Sam 10:1; 2 Kgs 9:3, 6). Only twice is oil poured as an offering (Lev 2:1; Num 5:15), and in neither case do we have a libation; rather, we have the pouring of oil on food. In the remaining cases, oil is used for the anointment of priests (Exod 29:7; Lev 8:12) or a king (1 Sam 10:1; 2 Kgs 9:3, 6).[99] Anointing always consists of pouring oil onto the head (ראש). The word ראשה,[100] appearing in Gen 28:18 and 35:14 and the meaning "top" or "summit," derives from the same root as the word "head" (ראש). It is tempting, therefore, to acknowledge the activity performed by Jacob in Bethel as an echo of a cultic anointing of a priest or monarch.[101] There is no doubt that the wording of Gen 28:18 and 35:14 is very close to the wording used in fragments that describe a ritual anointment.

98.   See also Judg 17:5; 18:31; Pss 42:5; 52:10; 55:15; Eccl 4:17; Dan 1:2.

99.   The references in Lev 14:15, 26 are also to the application of oil, though not to the anointing of a priest or king. Instead, they rather refer to the cleansing of the sick.

100.   The LXX reads ἄκρος.

101.   *LAB* 59:2, instead of giving Bethlehem as the place of David's anointment as king, gives us Bethel: "Et profectus est Samuel in Bethel, et sacrificavit presbiteros, et Iesse, et filios eius."

In the Aegean world, libations of oil, though not as frequent as one of wine, were practised universally. Libations were most often performed as an offering at a crossroads, with oil being poured on to the stones or hermae.

Genesis 28:19 reads: "He called that place Bethel, though the city used to be called Luz." The Hebrew word לוז normally means "almond tree." In view of the fact that the LXX gives us its correct translation as καρυίνος (Gen 30:37), it is hard to accept that its meaning was not clear. Nevertheless, in contrast to the more frequently found transliteration of לוז in the Bible as Λουζα, the toponym in Gen 28:19 is given as Ουλαμλους. An analogous form appears in *Vetus Latina*: "Ulammaus." This reading is made up of the clause ουλαμ and the transliterated name of "Luz"—λους. Looking for the meaning of ουλαμ in such Greek words as ουλαμος ("a crowd," "a multitude" [about warriors]) or ουλος ("woolly" or "thick" [about material]) leads to a dead end.[102] It is most probable that the compound Ουλαμλους is a transliteration of two Hebrew words: אולם and לוז. An analogous mistake caused the change in the name of "Laish" to Ουλαμαις in Judg 18:29.[103]

"Luz" as the original name of "Bethel" is important to Leon Yarden's hypothesis that the tradition of the menorah and Aaron's rod derives from the sanctuary of Luz–Bethel,[104] and that the detailed description of the menorah, the decoration of which likens the candelabra to an almond-tree, is evidence of the origin of this cult object from the priests of Bethel. Developing this line of argument, Yarden also concludes that the figure of Aaron is derived from the tradition of the northern sanctuary.[105] In his work he also points to the important cult role of the almond tree (of which the representation became the menorah) as a symbol of the mother god.[106] If Yarden is right, then we would have one more argument to support the significant or even key meaning of the sanctuary in Bethel.

---

102. For all its ingenuity, we should reject the explanation whereby the compound of the word "woolly" (ουλος) with the noun "almond, almond tree" has some association with a magic practice based on the use Jacob made of wooden rods, including almond tree rods, to make sheep and goats turn the appropriate colour (Gen 30:25-43).

103. See Wevers, *Notes on the Greek Text of Genesis*, 454.

104. L. Yarden, "Aaron, Bethel, and the Priestly Menorah," *JJS* 26 (1975): 39-47.

105. *Ibid.*, 46-47; cf. Knauf, "Bethel."

106. Yarden, "Aaron, Bethel, and the Priestly Menorah," 1-42. We shall return to the subject of trees in the chapter about Hebron; see also the chapter on Beer-sheba.

Genesis 35:14 also contains information about a different kind of libation: "He poured out a drink offering on it [the stone pillar]" (וַיַּסֵּךְ עָלֶיהָ נֶסֶךְ = καὶ ἔσπεισεν ἐπ' αὐτὴν σπονδήν). The Hebrew term consists of the root נסך ("to pour out a libation," "to offer a libation") and the noun נֶסֶךְ ("libation"), which is formed from it.[107] The semantic link between נסך ("to pour") and cult objects can be seen clearly in examples from Isa 40:19; 44:10; 48:5; and Ezek 10:14, all of which speak of cast statues (פֶּסֶל נֶסֶךְ). One could propose a completely marginal hypothesis that פֶּסֶל נֶסֶךְ is not, as is generally accepted, a "cast" statue in the sense of "cast in metal," but one made for נֶסֶךְ, in other words for libation. The פֶּסֶל would then be a kind of altar in the shape of a stone pillar(?) designed for the making of drink offerings.

Apart from Gen 35:14, the combination of the verb נסך and the noun נֶסֶךְ appears only in 2 Kgs 16:13, which deals with offerings made by Ahaz: "He offered up his burnt offering and grain offering, poured out his drink offering, and sprinkled the blood of his fellowship offerings on the altar." This king "did not do what was right in the eyes of the Lord" (2 Kgs 16:2), "he walked in the ways of the kings of Israel" (v. 3). Numbers 4:7 adds further information about drink offerings by enumerating the vessels: "the plates, dishes and bowls, and the jars for drink offerings."[108] The Hebrew text gives us the following descriptors: קְעָרָה[109] (LXX: τρύβλιον), כַּף (θυίσκη), מְנַקִּית[110] (κύαθος), and קְשׂוֹת / קַשְׂוֹה[111] (σπονδεῖον). A libation, נֶסֶךְ, could be performed with wine (יַיִן, e.g. Exod 29:40; Lev 23:13), water (1 Chr 11:18) or "strong wine" (שֵׁכָר = σικερα; Num 28:7).[112] An offering of שֵׁכָר could be poured out in "a holy [place]" (בְּקֹדֶשׁ).[113]

107.   On the subject of libations and drink offerings, see P. Carstens, "The Golden Vessels and the Song of God: Drink-offering and Libation in Temple and on Altar," *SJOT* 17 (2003): 110-40.

108.   The Vulgate reads: "turibula et mortariola cyatos et crateras ad liba." For a similar list, see Exod 25:29.

109.   Also in Exod 25:29; 37:16 and 14 times in Num 7.

110.   This word is derived from the root נקה, "to be clean, to be free, to be innocent"; as a noun, the name of the vessel appears only in Exod 25:29; 37:16; Jer 52:19.

111.   Apart from that, it appears only in Exod 25:29; 37:16; 1 Chr 28:17.

112.   The Vulgate eliminates this distinction, giving "et libabitis vini"; see Num 6:3, and esp. Ps 69:12, where mention is made of those "drinking שֵׁכָר."

113.   In Num 6:3; Isa 5:11; 24:9; 29:9; 56:12; Prov 20:1; 31:4, 6, a contrast is made between "wine" and "strong drink," which suggests that these terms were used to denote different substances. In Isa 5:22 reference is made to mixing "strong drink," which could indicate a vinous origin of the potion.

Jeremiah 7:18 mentions, apart from the baking of cakes for "the queen of heaven," drink offerings for other gods.[114] Furthermore, it emerges from the text of Jer 44:17-19 that it was "the queen of heaven" who was the goddess for whom incense was burnt and libations were made. The same reference in Jer 44 talks about offerings made by the women of Judah on the roofs of houses, and the book of Ezekiel (20:28) states that the place where offerings were made, including libations, was "any high hill or any leafy tree." The book of Daniel (2:46) informs us that offerings were sometimes made to a person: "Then King Nebuchadnezzar fell prostrate before Daniel and paid him honour and ordered that an offering and incense be presented to him" (סגד ומנחה וניחחין אמר לנסכה לה, lit. "ordered that he be honoured with gifts and incense [and] said that libations [be made] to him"; the LXX reads: καὶ ἐπέταξε θυσίας καὶ σπονδὰς ποιῆσαι αὐτῷ; [Th] καὶ μαναα καὶ εὐωδίας εἶπεν σπεῖσαι αὐτῷ).

Analysing the myth of Jacob in Bethel, Cristiano Grottanelli drew attention to an analogous Phoenician practice of offering gifts in temples as thanks for a favourable return from an expedition. The offering was frequently—just as in the story of Jacob—the fulfilment of a vow made before departure on the journey.[115]

It is worth asking what kind of god appeared to the hero of this story and whether an enumeration of his characteristics is possible. Genesis 35:11 uses the description אל שדי. In the Bible this appears only in Gen 17:1; 35:11; 43:14; 48:3;[116] Exod 6:3; Ezek 10:5.[117]

Genesis 35:7 poses a problem: "There he built an altar, and he called the place El Bethel, because it was there that God revealed himself to him when he was fleeing from his brother." An analogous interpretation is to be found in *Vetus Latina*: "Et aedificavit ibi altare, et vocavit nomen loci illius, Dominus Dei: ibi enim apparuit ei Deus cum fugeret a facie fratris sui Esau." The MT gives us:

ויבן שם מזבח ויקרא למקום אל בית־אל כי שם נגלו אליו האלהים
בברחו מפני אחיו

114.   See also Jer 19:13; 32:29.

115.   C. Grottanelli, "Santuari e divinitŕ delle collonie d'occidente," in *La religione fenicia. Matrici orientali e sviluppi occidentali. Atti del Colloquio in Roma (6 marzo 1979)*, Rome, 1981, 109-37 (127-28).

116.   Gen 48:3 comprises a fragment of the blessing given to Joseph by Jacob and refers clearly to Gen 35:11.

117.   Job 8:5; 13:3; 15:25 have the analogous form of אל־שדי, though in the MT this phrase does not indicate the word "god" (אל), but the preposition אל. It is not, therefore, about El-Shaddai but only about Shaddai—"the Omnipotent." Job 35:13 uses the terms אל and שדי as synonyms, indicating: God and his attribute (name)— "Omnipotent."

The presence of the "dagesh" mark in the initial letter "mem" indicates that the word "place" (מָקוֹם) was preceded by the definite article,[118] in other words that Jacob names "[the] place אֵל בֵּית־אֵל." The LXX translates this verse somewhat differently, removing אֵל: καὶ ἐκάλεσεν τὸ ὄνομα τοῦ τόπου Βαιθηλ.[119] It is unclear how this sentence, which in fact reads, "and he called [the] place: God, House of God/God Bethel...," is to be understood. The formulation "God, House of God" makes little sense. It would be more logical to interpret אֵל בֵּית־אֵל as a combination analogous to אֵל שַׁדַּי or אֵל בְּרִית. We would then be dealing with the word "god" and its further description. The word שַׁדַּי means "omnipotent" and therefore performs the function of an adjective; בְּרִית, "covenant" is a noun with an adverbial function. It may, therefore, be that the compound אֵל בֵּית־אֵל consists of the noun אֵל ("god") and its further description, in this case the name בֵּית־אֵל. The existence of a cult of a god called "Bethel" in the West Semitic world is attested by many sources, particularly by the Aramaic papyri found in Elephantine.[120] Only two texts in the whole of the Bible—Gen 35:15 and 1 Sam 10:3—can be acknowledged with any confidence as confirmation of the honouring of a god Bethel.[121] Regardless of the interpretation of the compound אֵל בֵּית־אֵל, doubts remain about the meaning of the statement that Jacob named the place אֵל בֵּית־אֵל.

An alternative reading would be possible if the verb קָרָא, "to call," "summon"—were interpreted differently. Karel van der Toorn understands this verb in Gen 21:33 to mean not "calling on the name of the Lord" but "naming."[122] It may be that we have to do the reverse. The sentence in v. 7 would then be interpreted as: "And he built an altar there

---

118.   Wevers, *Notes on the Greek Text of Genesis*, 448, underlines that the article in the MT, which is missing in the LXX, indicates that the place under discussion is a well-known religious centre.

119.   The Vulgate reads: "et appellavit nomen loci Domus Dei."

120.   See E.R. Dalglish, *ABD*, *s.v.* "Bethel (deity)"; J.T. Milik, "Les papyrus araméens d'Hermoupolis et les cultes syro-phéniciens en Égypte perse. 2 Dieu Béthel," *Biblica* 48 (1967): 565-77; Teixidor, *The Pagan God*, 30-31; W. Rölling, *DDD*, *s.v.* "Bethel," 173-75, expresses reservations about the interpretation of the term "Herem-Bethel" as the name of a god. See also K. van der Toorn, "Herem-Betel and Elephantine Oath Procedure," *ZAW* 98 (1986): 282-85.

121.   See M.S. Smith, *The Early History of God: Yahweh and the Other Deities in Ancient Israel*, New York, 1990, 145 and 151, asserts that Jer 48:13 is proof of the existence in Palestine of the cult of Bethel, a god (according to Smith) originating in Phoenicia.

122.   Van der Toorn, *Family Religion*, 257-58 n. 94, 259; see also the chapter on Beer-sheba, Chapter 2.

and there called upon El Bethel (the god Bethel) because God appeared to him there in the time of his flight from his brother."[123] Such an explanation would demand serious interference with the MT since the Hebrew word order associates the verb קרא with the noun following the preposition ל. The evidence from the LXX, the Vulgate and the Peshitta,[124] and the analogous passage in Gen 33:20,[125] points (despite the syntactic difficulties in the Hebrew text) to the meaning, "and he called upon God in this place." This interpretation makes possible a dual meaning of the compound אל בית־אל: either it refers to a god whose name was Bethel or to a god in Bethel.[126] The second interpretation does not preclude the possibility that the name of the god revealed during the theophany is אל שדי, that is, "God from Bethel" (אל בית־אל), and that he is omnipotent (שדי).

Godfrey R. Driver has suggested one of the possible identifications of the local god in Bethel.[127] By analysing the construction of the name "Jericho" (ירחו) he concludes that "Ho founded" it. He then shows that the element חו is interchangeable with the segment "Ahi" (אחי). He also cites the information about the second founding of Jericho by Hiel of Bethel (1 Kgs 16:34). Driver says that the name Hiel (חיאל = Αχιηλ) does not mean "El lives" but "Ahi [is] El/god" (אחי [is] אל). All this would point to the existence in Bethel of a local god called חו = אחי, a deity who was worshipped also in Jericho. Unfortunately, there is nothing known of this deity's character.[128] If the conclusions Driver

---

123. Of the 13 instances of the form למקום in the MT (Gen 18:24; 21:31; 35:7; Num 13:24; Judg 15:17; 18:12; 1 Sam 23:28; 2 Sam 2:16; 6:8; 1 Chr 13:11; Neh 4:7; Jer 19:6; 19:12), support for the above interpretation comes only in Neh 4:7, where the phrase is translated "in places."

124. See comments in Wevers, *Notes on the Greek Text of Genesis*, 579-80.

125. ויצב־שם מזבח ויקרא־לו אל אלהי ישראל = καὶ ἔστησεν ἐκεῖ θυσιαστήριον καὶ ἐπεκαλέσατο τὸν θεὸν Ισραηλ = et erecto ibi altari invocavit super illud Fortissimum Deum Israhel. This sentence starts to make sense in the LXX and the Vulgate, because in the MT, if we were to follow the rules of syntax, it would need to be translated "he raised an altar there and called it (or named it) 'God the god of Israel' (or the 'God of Gods of Israel')." For more on this question, see the chapter on Shechem.

126. See the analogous formulation in the votive dedication of Zoilos of Dan in the chapter on Dan, Chapter 4.

127. G.R. Driver, "Brief Notes (Part 3): Two Gods (HW and MWT) in Proper Names," *PEQ* 77 (1945): 12-14.

128. Many proper names contain the element אחי; for example: אחטוב, אחיתפל, אחיהוד, אחיסמך, אחימן, אחירע, אחינעם, אחילוד, אחיעזר, אחיקם, אחימעץ, אחימלך. It is worth noting how numerous this type of name is among priests, particularly those of Zadok's line.

reached are correct, then, by accepting his hypothesis, we would acknowledge that חו / אחי = אל בית־אל = אל שׁדי. The omnipotent God would be the god from Bethel, and his name would be חו = אחי. Because of the lack of definitive evidence, the above exegesis has to be treated merely as a hypothesis.

The chronicles of the town of Bethel do not provide us with sufficient information to establish the date of the creation of the stories about a sanctuary there. The town existed continuously from the Late Bronze Age until the second century BCE. The biblical text proves that there was an active and doubtless important religious centre there before the Babylonian captivity (see 2 Kgs 17:28, Amos, Ezra). From the interpretation of Zech 7:1-2 presented here, we can conclude that its importance was still maintained at the turn of the sixth century BCE. The numerous references to Bethel and to its sanctuary generally reveal a negative attitude to the centre from the authors of the Bible. So the question is: How did an account of the origins of a sanctuary in Bethel, and one which was neither antipathetic to or in any way critical of it, come to be preserved in the book of Genesis?

Isaac Kalimi suggests that the contents of the book of *Jubilees*, which is so antagonistically inclined towards Bethel (32:22), have to be linked to the conflict between the Jerusalem elite and the priests of Bethel, who were still active in the second century BCE.[129] This claim allows us to postulate also the theory that the important part which the priests of Bethel or their religious heirs played in the second century BCE resulted in the sanctuary's aetiology acquiring such a prominent place in the book of Genesis. Bethel is an exceptional case. Unlike many religious centres, it drew upon itself the condemnation of the prophets and authors of the so-called Deuteronomic History (DtrH). The story of its origin is surely one of the most ancient of biblical themes. The acceptance by the editors of the Bible of Bethel's exceptional place as an important religious centre in Palestine must have influenced contemporary sacral reality. I suspect that the reason why Bethel retained its exceptional place in the Bible's description of the religious landscape of Palestine can be explained in two ways. Either the power of tradition, in other words, the narratives about the foundation of this sanctuary, were so popular and at the same time so religiously pregnant that they could not be expunged

---

129.   I. Kalimi, "Zion or Gerizim? The Association of Abraham and the Aqeda with Zion / Gerizim in Jewish and Samaritan Sources," in M. Lubetski, C. Gottlieb and S. Keller (eds.), *Boundaries of the Ancient Near Eastern World: A Tribute to Cyrus H. Gordon*, JSOTSup 273, Sheffield, 1998, 443-57 (443).

from the text, or there was a group of people—probably already active in Jerusalem—which ensured the preservation of the accounts that repre sented its local traditions. Unfortunately, it is not possible to offer anything but suppositions at this point of the discussion.

4.

Dan

Archaeological Data and Extra-Biblical Sources

Dan is situated in the far north of Israel, about 40 km north of Lake Galilee, at the foot of Mt Hermon. This ancient town has been identified with Tell el-Qadi,[1] and its original name was Laish. It is this name that is mentioned in Egyptian documents of the 18th Dynasty, in letters from Mari and in the list of towns conquered by Thutmose III.[2] In the Hellenistic era, this place, lying next to Caesarea Philippi, was given a new name: Antiochia.

The oldest settlement in the tell is linked to the Neolithic era, but its true history begins in the Early Bronze Age. There was a large and wealthy town here in the third millennium BCE. In the Middle Bronze Age a fortified town arose there whose outlines are visible to this day. Settlement in Dan–Laish lasted uninterruptedly throughout the Bronze Age. In strata dated from the twelfth century BCE, despite the lack of any signs of destruction, there are noticeable changes in the material culture of the town; these changes took place with the arrival of the Danites.[3] The development of urban-style construction can be dated from that time. Further phases of the town's construction and the reinforcement of its fortifications occurred during the tenth and ninth centuries BCE. In strata from the ninth century there are the remains of cult installations (*bamah*) with a stone altar and traces of ashes. Despite the Assyrian invasion, the town developed without hindrance until the time of the Babylonian captivity. Unfortunately, little is known about the town during the Babylonian

---

1.   A. Biran (ed.), *Dan I: A Chronicle of the Excavations, the Pottery Neolithic, the Early Bronze Age and the Middle Bronze Age Tombs*, Jerusalem, 1996; *idem* (ed.), *Dan II: A Chronicle of the Excavations and the Late Bronze Age "Mycenaean" Tomb*, Jerusalem, 2002.

2.   A. Biran, *ABD*, *s.v.* "Dan (place)."

3.   *Ibid.*

and Persian rules. There are many finds from the end of the Persian and beginnings of the Hellenistic periods associated with the area of the town's sanctuary. Among other finds there is a figurine of the god Bes, two representations of Osiris and one statuette of Astarte. Associated with the Hellenistic era is one of the most fascinating finds on the Dan tell, namely the Greek–Aramaic votive inscription: "To the God who is in Dan, Zoilos swore an oath."[4] The palaeography of this inscription indicates a dating of third or second century BCE, while Biran dates it in the middle of the second century BCE.[5] It was in this time, too, that successive edifices associated with the sanctuary were built.[6]

A fascinating inscription that has aroused the particular interest of researchers was also found in Dan.[7] It mentions the Aramaic conquests and is the first document known to us, dated by its discoverers in the ninth century BCE, which mentions ביח דוד, or "the house of David." The archaeologists' euphoria soon collided with the scepticism of scholars who proclaimed the find a fake. Giovanni Garbini, using both philological and palaeographical arguments, pronounced that what we have here is a modern counterfeit.[8]

Biblical Information

Because Dan is situated in the far north of Palestine, it often became a synonym for the ends of the country. Abraham "pursued [the kings tormenting Lot] unto Dan" (Gen 14:14).[9] Before his death, Moses saw the Promised Land because "…the Lord showed him the whole land—

---

4. A. Biran, "To the God who is in Dan," in Biran (ed.), *Temples and High Places*, 142-51, with the discussion on 148-51; D. Flusser notes that the Greek text ought to be translated as follows: "To the God who is in the district of the Danoi." Flusser underlines that it could be a trace of the memory of a people with that name; *ibid.*, 149.

5. *Ibid.*, 147.

6. *Ibid.*: "A well-built enclosure wall with the entrance from the S surrounded the sanctuary during the Hellenistic period."

7. Its first publication appears in A. Biran and J. Naveh, "An Aramaic Stele Fragment from Tel Dan," *IEJ* 43 (1993): 81-98.

8. G. Garbini, "L'iscrizione aramaica di Tel Dan," *Rendiconti della Accademia Nazionale dei Lincei* series 9, vol. 5, 1994: b. 3, 461-71; for a discussion of the doubts surrounding this discovery, see in T.L. Thompson, *The Bible in History: How Writers Create a Past*, London, 1999, 203-205, and G. Athas, *The Tel Dan Inscription: A Reappraisal and a New Interpretation*, JSOTSup 360, London, 2003.

9. The motif linking the person of Abraham with Dan is to be seen also in *Genesis Apocryphon* 22.5-8, where mention is made of his conquering the town.

from Gilead to Dan" (Deut 34:1). The name "Dan" also occurs in the popular phrase used in the Bible to denote the territory of the whole country: "from Dan to Beer-sheba" (see, e.g., Judg 20:1; 1 Sam 3:20; 2 Sam 3:10; 1 Kgs 4:25).[10] This last phrase did not necessarily refer to the extent of the country inhabited by the Hebrews but to a postulated or notional "Greater Israel."

The sanctuary in Dan became, along with Bethel, an object of disapproval to the authors of the books of Kings. One of the reproaches supposedly undermining the orthodoxy of the cult exercised in both centres was the presence, from the times of Jeroboam, of non-Levite priests there (see 1 Kgs 12:31). Jeroboam established in both Dan and Bethel a cult of calves which competed with that in Jerusalem:

> "If these people go up to offer sacrifices at the temple of the Lord in Jerusalem, they will again give their allegiance to their lord, Rehoboam king of Judah. They will kill me and return to King Rehoboam." After seeking advice, the king made two golden calves. He said to the people, "It is too much for you to go up to Jerusalem. Here are your gods, O Israel, who brought you up out of Egypt." One he set up in Bethel, and the other in Dan. And this thing became a sin; the people went even as far as Dan to worship the one there. (1 Kgs 12:27-30)

According to the books of Kings (2 Kgs 10:29), the cult in Dan was still operating in the times of Jehu—in other words, the second half of the ninth century BCE. The next biblical mention of Dan refers to the destruction of the town by the armies of Ben-Hadad of Damascus (1 Kgs 15:20; 2 Chr 16:4).

Dan is spoken of as the town in the north from which an armed threat to Judah could be expected (Jer 4:15; 8:16). From the references in Jeremiah alone it is impossible to establish whether or not Dan was a Hebrew town. It is only thanks to our knowledge of the history of northern Palestine in the period preceding the conquests of Nebuchadnezzar that we can ascertain that, in the time when the prophecies of Jeremiah were being written, Dan was in the hands of the Aramaeans from Damascus.

The book of Joshua provides the following information about the division of land among the tribes of the Danites: "The seventh lot came out for the tribe of Dan, clan by clan. The territory of their inheritance included: Zorah, Eshtaol, Ir Shemesh, Shaalabbin, Aijalon, Ithlah, Elon, Timnah, Ekron, Eltekeh, Gibbethon, Baalath, Jehud, Bene Berak, Gath Rimmon, Me Jarkon and Rakkon, with the area facing Joppa" (Josh

---

10. See above in the chapter about Beer-Sheba, Chapter 2. Cf. O. Lipschits, "'From Geba to Beersheba': A further Consideration," *RB* 111 (2004): 345-61.

19:40-46). These territories lie to the west of Jerusalem next to the Philistine Pentapolis. The continuation of this text explains the causes and circumstances of the Danites' migration: "But the Danites had difficulty taking possession of their territory, so they went up and attacked Leshem, took it, put it to the sword and occupied it. They settled in Leshem and named it Dan after their forefather" (Josh 19:47).

The book of Judges gives a slightly different reason for the Danites' migration: "The Amorites confined the Danites to the hill country, not allowing them to come down into the plain. And the Amorites were determined also to hold out in Mt Heres, Aijalon and Shaalbim" (Judg 1:34-35).

A similar distribution of the Danites—between Judea and Philistia—is confirmed by the list of towns given from their lot to the Levites (Josh 21:5, 23). According to this list it was the descendants of Kohath, son of Aaron, who lived there.

So, the biblical material provides us with two traditions: one places the Danites in Central Palestine, to the west of Judah's lot, the other locates the town of Dan in the far north of the country. Associated with the first are: the story of Samson the Danite (see Judg 13:2; 18:11), the division of the land among the Hebrew tribes (Joshua), the conflict with the Amorites and the Danites' maritime links (Judg 5:17). The other tradition, locating Dan in the north of Israel, is associated with the story of the migration of the tribe to the north (Judg 18), the expression "from Dan to Beer-sheba" (1 and 2 Kings), information from the prophets about the cult in Dan (Amos 8:14) and the location of the tribe in the north (Ezek 48:1-2), as well as the information contained in Gen 14:14. This positioning of the town of Dan in the north and of the tribe of Danites originally in Central Palestine but later in the northern extremes accords with the account of the beginnings of Dan which includes the theme of the wanderings of the descendants of Dan.

Evidence of the secondary nature of the tradition, locating Dan in the north of Palestine, comes among other things from the stories of the patriarchs. From these it is clear that both Abraham and Jacob undertook a journey, relocating from the north (Haran) to the south, and that on this journey the first significant centre was Shechem (Gen 12:6-7 and 33:18-20). Abraham and Jacob came upon it immediately upon entering Canaan. No mention is made of Dan in these accounts and yet if it had been important and an integral part of the Holy Land it would assuredly not have been overlooked by the authors or editors of the Bible. The silence over Dan could indicate that the town had not yet inscribed itself into the religious consciousness of the Hebrews as a centre needing to be associated with the figures of the patriarchs.[11] Hence the supposition that the story about the conquest of Laish, as an addition to the book of Judges, either underwent a different editorial process than did the book of Genesis, or it was written later.

A further curious fact linked to the assessment of the tribe of Dan in the Bible can be seen in the book of Chronicles. The first book talks of the twelve sons of Jacob (1 Chr 2:1-2) and then gives a list of their descendants. The genealogy, however, is missing the lineage of two tribes—that of Zebulun and Dan (see 1 Chr 2–7). The very existence of Dan is ignored to such an extent that the lands ascribed to him (namely, the possessions in the north) are given over to Manasseh: "The people of the half-tribe of Manasseh were numerous; they settled in the land from Bashan to Baal Hermon, that is, to Senir (Mt Hermon)." The Danites were ignored also in the information given about historical events being played out in the territories nominally occupied by them: "So the God of Israel stirred up the spirit of Pul king of Assyria (that is, Tiglath-pileser king of Assyria), who took the Reubenites, the Gadites and the half-tribe of Manasseh into exile. He took them to Halah, Habor, Hara and the river of Gozan, where they are to this day" (1 Chr 5:26).

The Danites (or indeed Dan) are mentioned only a few times in the books of Chronicles. We are told of Dan the son of Jacob (1 Chr 2:2); the Danites in the service of David and commanded by Azareel, son of Jeroham (1 Chr 27:22); about a certain craftsman, the son of a man of Tyre and a Danite woman (2 Chr 2:13); also the word "Dan" is given as the name of a town, not that of a tribe or a region, which was destroyed during the conquest of northern Israel by Ben-Hadad (2 Chr 16:4; paral. 1 Kgs 15:20); and in 1 Chr 21:2 and 2 Chr 30:5—in the expression familiar to us from the books of Kings "from Beer-sheba to Dan."

If we accept that the expressions in 1 Chr 21:2 and 2 Chr 30:5 are paraphrases of analogous forms of words from the books of Kings, then it is clear that the authors of the books of Chronicles have not passed on any information testifying to the presence of the tribe of Dan in northern Palestine. Indeed, it may be noted that in writing about the deeds of the sons of Jacob, they make no mention of their initial settlement in central Palestine. Only the reference to Ben-Hadad, which was also probably a paraphrase of the book of Kings (1 Kgs 15:20), gives any news about the existence of the town of Dan in northern Palestine. Taking into account also the vivid memory of the history of the town of Laish (Isa 10:30),

11. See E. Noort, "The Traditions of Ebal and Gerizim: Theological Positions in the Book of Joshua," in M. Vervenne and J. Lust (eds.), *Deuteronomy and Deuteronomic Literature*, Leuven, 1997, 161-80 (171-72).

one can conclude that the authors' conviction of the Danites' migration to the north of Palestine was not as strong as might appear at first glance.

The books of Chronicles, which are generally regarded as having been written down in the fourth century BCE, contain no information to confirm the presence of the Danites in northern Palestine. References in the prophets and in the books of Kings testify to the existence, as early as in the times of the First Temple, of the town of Laish lying at the foot of Mt Hermon. The books of Joshua and Judges provide biblical information about the journey of the Danites and about their former settlements. In any further exploration it is important to underline that during the Persian era (the time of the Chronicles' editing) the authors of the Bible were not in the least bit interested in revealing their association with the descendants of Dan. This is a characteristic of the Judah-centred aspect of the books of Chronicles, which can be seen also in the book of Nehemiah. In biblical historiography, emphasising the links between the inhabitants of Judah and the Danites made sense in the times of David and Solomon. The existence of two states probably excluded the forging of tighter links between Judah and Dan. In truth, though, one can imagine that before the Assyrian invasion, and even after Tiglath-pileser III took command over Israel, there was a sense of consanguinity between the inhabitants of Israel and those of Dan–Laish. During the Persian times, as the biblical literature of the time indicates, all ties were severed. The sense of consanguinity and interest in the tribe living in the north of Palestine (although it had long since become Aramaic) revived only during the Hellenistic times.

The existence of the town of Dan is remembered by the Jewish writers working at the end of the Hellenistic era and in the first years of Roman domination. It is mentioned in *Liber Antiquitatum Biblicarum* and also in the apocryphal book of *Enoch* (13:7): "And I went off and sat down at the waters of Dan in the land of Dan, which is south-west of Hermon."[12]

Aetiology

Judges 18:1-31:

> (1) In those days Israel had no king. And in those days the tribe of the Danites was seeking a place of their own where they might settle, because they had not yet come into an inheritance among the tribes of Israel. (2) So the Danites sent five warriors from Zorah and Eshtaol to spy out the land and explore it. These men represented all their clans. They told

12. M. Black, *The Book of Enoch or 1 Enoch: A New English Edition*, SVTP 8, Leiden, 1985.

them, "Go, explore the land." The men entered the hill country of Ephraim and came to the house of Micah, where they spent the night. (3) When they were near Micah's house, they recognised the voice of the young Levite; so they turned in there and asked him, "Who brought you here? What are you doing in this place? Why are you here?" (4) He told them what Micah had done for him, and said, "He has hired me and I am his priest." (5) Then they said to him, "Please inquire of God to learn whether our journey will be successful." (6) The priest answered them, "Go in peace. Your journey has the Lord's approval." (7) So the five men left and came to Laish (לישה = Λαισα), where they saw that the people were living in safety, like the Sidonians (צדנים), unsuspecting (שקט) and secure (ובטח). And since their land lacked nothing, they were prosperous. Also, they lived a long way from the Sidonians and had no relationship with anyone else. (8) When they returned to Zorah and Eshtaol, their brothers asked them, "How did you find things?" (9) They answered, "Come on, let's attack them! We have seen that the land is very good. Aren't you going to do something? Don't hesitate to go there and take it over. (10) When you get there, you will find an unsuspecting people and a spacious land that God has put into your hands, a land (מקום) that lacks nothing whatever." (11) Then six hundred men from the clan of the Danites, armed for battle, set out from Zorah and Eshtaol. (12) On their way they set up camp near Kiriath Jearim in Judah. This is why the place (מקום) west of Kiriath Jearim is called Mahaneh Dan[13] (מחנה־דן) to this day. (13) From there they went on to the hill country of Ephraim and came to Micah's house. (14) Then the five men who had spied out the land of Laish (ליש = Λαισα) said to their brothers, "Do you know that one of these houses has an ephod (אפוד), other household gods (תרפים), a carved image and a cast idol (פסל ומסכה)? Now you know what to do." (15) So they turned in there and went to the house of the young Levite at Micah's place and greeted him. (16) The six hundred Danites, armed for battle, stood at the entrance to the gate. (17) The five men who had spied out the land went inside and took the carved image, the ephod, the other household gods and the cast idol while the priest and the six hundred armed men stood at the entrance to the gate. (18) When these men went into Micah's house and took the carved image, the ephod, the other household gods and the cast idol, the priest said to them, "What are you doing?" (19) They answered him, "Be quiet! Don't say a word. Come

---

13. The name (camp of) Mehaneh (LXX παρεμβολὴ Δαν) also appears in Num 2:25, 31; 10:25 and Judg 13:25, except that the references in Numbers are not to the place of that name but to an army unit consisting of Danites. Judg 13:25 reads: "and the Spirit of the Lord began to stir him [Samson] while he was in Mahaneh Dan (במחנה־דן), between Zorah and Eshtaol." This indicates that Mahaneh–Dan is not a town but a territory occupied by the tribe. The difficulty lies in locating "between Zorah and Eshtaol" (Judg13:5) and "west of Kiriath Jearim" (Judg 18:12); cf. B.P. Irwin, *ABD*, *s.v.* "Mahaneh-Dan (place)." My own view is that the existence of a placed named מחנה־דן is highly doubtful.

with us, and be our father and priest. Isn't it better that you serve a tribe and clan in Israel as priest rather than just one man's household?" (20) Then the priest was glad. He took the ephod, the other household gods and the carved image and went along with the people. (21) Putting their little children, their livestock and their possessions in front of them, they turned away and left. (22) When they had gone some distance from Micah's house, the men who lived near Micah were called together and overtook the Danites. (23) As they shouted after them, the Danites turned and said to Micah, "What's the matter with you that you called out your men to fight?" (24) He replied, "You took the gods (אלהי) I made, and my priest, and went away. What else do I have? How can you ask, 'What's the matter with you?'" (25) The Danites answered, "Don't argue with us, or some hot-tempered men will attack you, and you and your family will lose your lives." (26) So the Danites went their way, and Micah, seeing that they were too strong for him, turned around and went back home. (27) Then they took what Micah had made, and his priest, and went on to Laish (ליש = Λαισα), against a peaceful (שׁקט) and unsuspecting (ובטח) people. They attacked them with the sword and burned down their city. (28) There was no one to rescue them because they lived a long way from Sidon and had no relationship with anyone else. The city was in a valley near Beth Rehob. The Danites rebuilt the city and settled there. (29) They named it Dan after their forefather Dan, who was born to Israel—though the city used to be called Laish. (30) There the Danites set up for themselves the idols (פסל), and Jonathan (יהונתן) son of Gershom (בן־גרשׁם), the son of Moses (בן־מנשׁה, lit. "grandson of Manasseh"[14]) and his sons were priests for the tribe of Dan until the time of the captivity of the land. (31) They continued to use the idols Micah had made (פסל מיכה), all the time the house of God was in Shiloh.

Allusions to a historical reality which might have influenced the emergence of a tradition of a Danite migration from central to northern Palestine remain very uncertain.[15] Some scholars see in this story traces of events unfolding during the migration of the Sea Peoples and in the Danites they see one of the migrating groups of the times—the Denyen.[16]

14.   This is a well-known place because of a strange error: the LXX follows the MT and gives Μανασση, while the Vulgate gives "Filii Mosi." There is no doubt that the Gershom mentioned here is the son of Moses (מֹשֶׁה), and not of Manasseh (מנשׁה) (see Exod 2:22); nevertheless, this error is intriguing and makes us reflect on the text since it is hard to imagine that a copyist could have overlooked such an inconsistency. The preservation in the LXX of the reading "Manasseh" reveals a strongly rooted reading of this text. Cf. Haran, *Temples and Temple Service*, 77, esp. n. 26; S. Weitzman, "Reopening the Case of the Suspiciously Suspended Nun in Judges 18:30," *CBQ* 61 (1999): 448-60, sees the trace of a Samaritan tradition in this verse.

15.   Cf. D.W. Manor, *ABD*, *s.v.* "Laish"; Biran, "Dan."

16.   Garbini, *I Filistei*, 65-67; Arbeitman, "Detecting the God," 12-13, sees in "the god from Dan" the Luvian god ᴰtiwat, and in the tribe of Dan, the Indo-European

A reference in Judg 5:17 gives weight to this hypothesis: "Dan [...] lingered by the ships." The use of ships by apparently nomadic Israelite tribes does appear to be most unlikely however, and less so if applied to the descendants of the Sea Peoples. Archaeological finds reveal that during the Iron Age, along with the arrival of new settlers in territories ascribed to the tribe of Dan, there was a development in metallurgy.[17] Trude Dothan writes about the cultural achievements of the Sea Peoples and their influence on other societies, though without reaching definite conclusions.[18] One often comes across claims that the migration of the Danites corresponded to the historical reality of the great migrations of the end of the Bronze Age. Scholars are also inclined to identify the Danites with the perpetrators of the destruction on the tell of Dan.[19] Other opinions appear, too, suggesting that this narrative be kept separate from historical reality.[20]

Regardless of whether or not the migration of the Danites was a historical fact, one can posit that—in the consciousness of the ancient Israelites—the tribe of Dan occupied the area of the town bearing their name. In the history of Palestine one can point to just two periods when this territory was within the boundaries of the Hebrew state.[21] The first occurred from the arrival of the Sea Peoples and the commingling of settlements at the turn of the thirteenth and twelfth centuries BCE[22] until the disintegration of the united kingdom[23] or the collapse of the northern

Adana people; F.A. Spina, "The Dan Story Historically Reconsidered," *JSOT* 4 (1977): 60-71 (62-63, 68); A.B. Cooke, *Zeus: A Study in Ancient Religion*, Cambridge, 1940, 3:354 n. 6, follows L.B. Hollandem in claiming the Denyens and the Danites were one and the same people.

17. Biran, "Dan."

18. Dothan, *The Philistines and their Material Culture*, 83-84, 296.

19. R.G. Boling, *Judges: Introduction, Translation, and Commentary*, AB 6A, Garden City, NY, 1975, 266-67.

20. Cf. U.F.W. Bauer, "A Metaphorical Etiology in Judges 18:12," *Journal of Hebrew Scripture* 3 (2001), online at http://www.arts.ualberts.ca/jhs/.

21. Unfortunately, archaeology cannot furnish any information which might settle this question; see Biran, "Dan."

22. The Iron Age did not start at the same time as the arrival of the Hebrews but we can assume that the memory of events which occurred in Palestine remained independent of changes in settlement.

23. I am ignoring the extensive and very lively discussion on the historicity of the kingdom of Solomon, preferring simply to direct readers to Fritz and Davies (eds.), *The Origins of the Ancient Israelite States*; Davies, *In Search of "Ancient Israel"*; *Convegno sul tema: Le origini di Israele, Roma, 10–11, II, 1986*, Rome, 1987.

kingdom (722 BCE). The second period takes place during the late Hasmonean era and the rule of the Herodian dynasty. The claim, suggested in some works and based on the text of 2 Kgs 23:19,[24] that during his reign Josiah also took over territories at the farthest northern point of Israel, does not have sufficient support in the source materials.[25]

The Danites are consistently referred to as one of the twelve tribes of Israel (Gen 30:6; 49:16-17; Josh 20:40-48; Judg 5:17). Some scholars point to the possibility that the inclusion of Dan, Gad and Asher to the tribe of Jacob was a later addition, to which the status of their mothers would testify—Bilhah and Zilpah were concubines in the house of Jacob.[26]

Yoël Arbeitman attempted to show a link between three texts: Jacob's blessing of Dan (Gen 49:16), a sentence in the book of Amos (8:14) and the votive inscription of Zoilos (second century BCE).[27] He accepted that Jacob's statement that "Dan will provide justice for his people as one of the tribes of Israel," emphasising that Dan was to be "as one of the tribes of Israel," is evidence that the Danites were late joining the group of tribes of Israel. The phrase in the book of Amos—"who swear...or say, 'As surely as your god lives, O Dan'"—is analogous to the two-language inscription of Zoilos.[28] On the basis of the *Pseudo-Jonathan Targum* to Gen 30:5-6, Arbeitman also claimed that the phrase explaining the name of the son of Bilhah can be interpreted as: (1) "God judged me" or (2) "God is Danite/Adanan."[29] If this interpretation is accurate, then we would have to conclude that the Bible has preserved a trace of a sense of the Danites' ethnic separateness. It is not known how long this separateness lasted, but all the biblical evidence points to a late acceptance by the Israelites of an association with the Danites.

There is, then, a tradition in the Bible of the late accession of Dan, Gad and Asher to the collection of the tribes of Israel. The *terminus ante quem* of this process is marked by the Song of Deborah (Judg 5), a text naming both Asher and Dan as Israelite tribes which did not participate in the battle against the Philistines. For Dan "lingered by the ships" and Asher "remained on the coast and stayed in his coves" (v. 17). Maybe

24. See Josephus, *Ant* 10.1.4.

25. Cf. T.C. Mitchell, "Judah until the Fall of Jerusalem (c.700–586 B.C.)," *CAH* 3.2:390-91.

26. G.W. Ahlström, "Was Gad the God of Tell Ed-Duweir?," *PEQ* 115 (1983): 47-48.

27. Arbeitman, "Detecting the God."

28. *Ibid.*

29. *Ibid.*, 13.

Giovanni Garbini is right to see in these tribes groups that were part of the Sea Peoples.[30] This would mean that the Song of Deborah came into being when the tribes of the first phase of settlement by the Sea Peoples were already sufficiently assimilated with the native Semitic element to feel related to, but not sufficiently to break off links with, the Philistines. This still vivid sense of consanguinity between peoples of Indo-European origin would explain the passivity of the Danites and the Asherites in the battle against Sisera. Establishing the time of the creation of the *Song of Deborah*, if it were possible, would also show the period when the intensive process of assimilating the Semites' former conquerors in the territory of Canaan was taking place.

There are several allusions in the Bible to the links between the Danites and the non-Hebrew population. The territories occupied by the descendants of Dan in the maritime region of central Palestine were probably inhabited by the Sea Peoples, and in time this became an area of Phoenician settlement. The northward migration was associated with the capture of Laish—a Sidonian town. Samson (שמשון), the most famous member of the Danite tribe, was closely linked to the Philistines. Commentators have fairly generally associated this hero, on the basis, among other factors, of the name meaning "sunny" (שמשון, from שמש, meaning "sun"), with a Philistine tradition of a solar hero.[31]

Several other tropes allow us to link the Danites with the Sea Peoples (or the remnants of them) and with the Phoenician world. In Exod 31:6; 38:23 and in 2 Chr 2:12-13, mention is made of craftsmen of the tribe of Dan; in the book of Exodus it is Aholiab, son of Ahisamach, and in 2 Chr 2:12-13 reference is made to "a wise son, endowed with intelligence and discernment [...] Huram-Abi, a man of great skill," "whose mother was from Dan and whose father was from Tyre. He is trained to work in gold and silver, bronze and iron, stone and wood, and with purple and blue and crimson yarn and fine linen. He is experienced in all kinds of engraving and can execute any design given to him. He will work with your craftsmen and with those of my Lord, David your father." The MT (2 Chr 2:12) gives the name as חורם אבי,[32] and the following verse gives further information about him: בן־אשה מן־בנות דן, which means "Huram-Abi, son of a woman of the daughters of Dan." In this place the LXX reads: καὶ νῦν ἀπέσταλκά σοι ἄνδρα σοφὸν καὶ εἰδότα σύνεσιν τὸν Χιραμ τὸν πατέρα μου ἡ μήτηρ αὐτοῦ ἀπὸ θυγατέρων Δαν καὶ ὁ πατὴρ αὐτοῦ ἀνὴρ Τύριος. The term חורם אבי should not—as in the NIV—be understood as

30. Garbini, *I Filistei*.
31. Spina, "The Dan Story Historically Reconsidered," 62.
32. See BDB, *s.v.*, and *DCH*, *s.v.*, which do not give the name חורם אבי.

a complex proper name, but following the LXX it should be accepted that the craftsman sent to Solomon is unnamed and that לחורם אבי signifies "belonging to my son Huram," in other words, to the renowned Hiram of Tyre (see 1 Kgs 7:13). Regardless of the difficulties associated with interpreting 2 Chr 2:12-13, we can accept that the Danites were in some way associated with craftsmanship and metallurgy.

All the information about the Danites and about the town of Dan inclines us to accept the interpretation of those scholars who identify this tribe with that of the Denyen—one of the groups belonging to the Sea Peoples. Placing the Danites in two regions of Palestine can be explained in one of two ways. Either the narrative about their migration is real, which would make it echo events that happened in about the twelfth century BCE, or the biblical authors remembered that this people lived in two different parts of Canaan (much as the Greek tribes lived in Greece proper and on the shores of Asia Minor). In the latter case, the story of the migration would merely serve as an attempt to give a mythic explanation for this state of affairs.

Yairah Amit, presenting his theory of the existence in the Bible of so-called hidden polemics, did so on the example of a fragment of the book of Judges (chs. 17–18).[33] In his view, the story of the journey of the Danites alongside explicitly worded opinions smuggled in elements of propaganda, the direct object of this attack being not the sanctuary in Dan, but the one much closer to Judah, namely, the sanctuary in Bethel.[34] Reconstructing the circumstances of the origin of this hidden polemic, Amit claims that the blatant disapproval of the sanctuary in Bethel came about with the book of Amos and the body of DtrH (that is, its earlier version). In the period between the fall of Israel (722 BCE) and the rule of Josiah (622 BCE—the traditional date for the so-called reforms of Josiah), the sanctuary in Bethel was a clear rival to Jerusalem and it is in this period that Amit places the writing of Judg 17–18, saying that after 622 the critical opinion of Bethel could have been expressed openly and not concealed within a different extended motif.[35]

If the text of Judg 18 came into being during united kingdom times, then one would have to accept the conservative scholars' view that there was a lively writing centre at the courts of Kings David and Solomon.[36]

---

33. Amit, *Hidden Polemics*, esp. 99-129, and "Hidden Polemic in the Conquest of Dan." Cf. also Amit's "Bochim, Bethel."

34. Amit, *Hidden Polemics*, 110-18, 125-29.

35. *Ibid.*, 117-18, 128-29.

36. A critique of this assumption has been made most forcefully in Van Seters, *In Search of History*; Edelman (ed.), *The Fabric of History*; Thompson, *Early History*

If, however, it occurred during the northern kingdom times, then one would need to explain the critical notes aimed at fellow tribesmen who comprised one part of the state organism. In such a case, Amit's theory would be helpful, as would the conviction of many authors that there was a continuous Israelite literary tradition on the territory of Judah in existence after 722 BCE.[37] After the fall of Samaria, Israel's elite were supposed to have moved to the territory of the southern kingdom and tried to consolidate their traditions there. It is likely that the myths and stories found in the book of Judges about the heroes of the north (not necessarily in the form we have them today), as well as in part of the Psalms, were written down in the territory of Judah after Israel's disaster in 722 BCE. This, for example, is the view taken by Robert Boling,[38] who comes down on the side of the theory of a three-stage redaction of the book of Judges. The oldest collection was supposed to have been created in the eighth century, the seventh century brought the Deuteronomic redaction (associated with the creation of Deuteronomy), while the sixth century brought the deuteronomistic part (the creation of the collection of Deuteronomy–2 Kings).[39] According to him, ch. 18 was added to the book of Judges as a consequence of the Deuteronomic redaction.[40] Boling is right that this fragment has been added to an earlier whole. In this he is following Julius Wellhausen, who wrote: "the Levites…occur only in the two appendices to the book of Judges (chaps. xvii., xviii., and xix., xx.), of which, however, the second is unhistorical and late, and only the first is certainly pre-exilic."[41] While we can apply the chronology suggested by Boling to the majority of the text of the book of Judges, the motif of the Danite migration still requires explanation: Why write a polemical history when the subject of the criticism is no longer in the authors' sphere of influence or even interest? In the seventh century BCE the sanctuary in Dan was no kind of threat to the dominant role of the centres in Judah.

---

of the Israelite People; Lester L. Grabbe (ed.), *Can a 'History of Israel' Be Written?*, JSOTSup 245, Sheffield, 1997.

37. Cf. M.D. Goulder, *The Psalms of Asaph and the Pentateuch: Studies in the Psalter, III*, JSOTSup 233, Sheffield, 1996.

38. Boling, *Judges*, 23, 29-38.

39. *Ibid.*, 30.

40. For a discussion of the hypotheses associated with the place of Judg 17–21 in the body of DtrH, see M.A. O'Brien, *The Deuteronomistic History Hypothesis: A Reassessment*, OBO 92, Göttingen, 1989, 97-98.

41. Wellhausen, *Prolegomena*, 141-42. See also G. von Rad, *Old Testament Theology*, 332 n. 9; where the author claims that "Chs. xvii–xxi are only a later addition to the Deuteronomistic Book of Judges."

Assuming that the history in Judg 18 has something to do with events that occurred at the beginning of the Iron Age, it might be worth asking when and why this narrative was added to the biblical book. As I have endeavoured to show, neither the times of Josiah nor the Persian era favoured the propagation of the idea of consanguinity with the Danites, if only because such ties were not felt then. Regardless of whether the migration described in Judg 18 was a historical fact or a literary fiction, we have to uncover in what circumstances this narrative made its way into the Bible.

Robert G. Boling admits that the chronology in the book of Judges is totally improbable and asserts that it came into being as a result of the composition of a large historiographic deuteronomistic body of work in the seventh century BCE.[42] Some scholars move the time of its creation from the time of Josiah to that of the Babylonian captivity.[43] Recently, Philip R. Davies has set out to prove that the book of Deuteronomy, on which the whole historiographic body is dependent, came into being in the fifth century BCE.[44]

It has been known for some time that biblical chronology in the MT makes use of cycles and that the last of these ends in 164 BCE, that is, the date of the re-dedication of the Temple in Jerusalem by the Maccabeans.[45] Since the biblical chronology was established no earlier than the middle of the second century BCE, and since it was the difficulties associated with that which provided Boling with the idea of moving the dating of the text, one might posit the hypothesis that the text of Judg 18—in its present form—was created during the Hasmonean dynasty. The next step would be to show the circumstances that persuaded the authors or the editors of the Bible to write, or expand, or maybe merely preserve the older story about the migration of the Danites and the origins of the town of Dan.

The first attempt in over four hundred years to dispense with Judah's isolationism came during the Hasmonean period. This opening out onto

42. Boling, *Judges*, 23.

43. Cf. Vervenne and Lust (eds.), *Deuteronomy and Deuteronomic Literature*; A. de Pury, T. Römer and J.-D. Macchi (eds.), *Israel Constructs its History*, JSOTSup 306, Sheffield: Sheffield Academic Press.

44. P.R. Davies, "Josiah and the Lawbook," a paper presented during the European Seminar on Historical Methodology, Berlin, July, 2002; *idem*, "The Place of Deuteronomy in the Development of Judean Society and Religion," in *Recenti tendenze nella ricostruzione della storia antica d'Israele. Roma, Convegno internazionale, 6–7 Marzo 2003*, Rome, 2005, 139-55.

45. Miller and Hayes, *A History of Ancient Israel and Judah*, 58-59; Thompson, *The Bible in History*, 73-75.

the world brought territorial expansion. Doubtless it was then that conditions favoured the remembrance of stories relating almost identical occurrences. As a result of successive conquests, the Hasmoneans gradually extended the boundaries of their state in all directions. One can assume that before they marched into the territories of Galilee and of Idumea with their armies, Jewish propaganda referred to these territories. During the first phase of the Maccabean revolt, Simon went armed into Galilee but did not incorporate it into the Hasmonean state (1 Macc 5:9-23; *Ant* 12.8.2). These first expeditions—though the sources favourable to the Hasmoneans describe them as liberation of their threatened countrymen and bringing them into Judah—could well have been exercises in pillaging. During the reign of Jonathan (160–143 BCE), the brother of Judas Maccabeus, as a result of martial expeditions and diplomatic activity, the territory of the Jewish state was extended. It is not known precisely how far it did extend,[46] and the references in 1 Macc 10–11 (esp. 1 Macc 11:28) as well as Josephus's text (*Ant* 13.8) do not allow us to make any definitive assessment of where its final northern boundary ran.[47]

The land around Dan could have been annexed to the Hasmonean state as a result of the expeditions of John Hyrcanus (135/4–104 BCE) or of Aristobulus known as the Philhellene (104–103 BCE).[48] In that case the Hasmonean armies would have conquered the districts around Dan, following the same tracks as those ascribed to the Danites. This ambivalent view of the Danites from the contemporary temporal perspective might well be explicable in the light of Hasmonean politics. We could explain their determinedly conservative attitude by the need to call on the tradition of the twelve tribes, while the need to construct and maintain a powerful, centralised state would, in turn, explain the unfavourable attitude to that tradition which acknowledged Dan as an important religious centre.

46.   Flavius Josephus (*Ant* 13.5.8) writes that Jonathan ruled Judea, Joppa (Jaffa) and Samaria; Demetrius joined incorporated into Judea districts previously belonging to Samaria: Aphairema, Lydd and Ramathaim.

47.   1 Macc 11:28: "Then Jonathan desired the king, that he would make Judea free from tribute as also the three governments, with the country of Samaria"; *Ant* 13.125: "When Jonathan turned to him with the request that for the whole of Judea and the three toparchies of Samaria, Joppa and Galilee he could pay three hundred talents"; cf. P. Schäfer, *The History of the Jews in Antiquity: The Jews of Palestine from Alexander the Great to the Arab Conquest*, Luxemburg, 1995, 54-56.

48.   1 Macc 11–12; on the subject of Aristobulus, see also Flavius Josephus, *Ant* 13.10.2.

Being unable to establish a date for the beginnings of the aetiology of Dan, I would like to offer my personal conviction that the second century BCE, with all its political and ideological circumstances, favoured the creation of such a text rather than the period before the Babylonian captivity or the Persian era when the conditions for the creation of such a large literary work, and particularly this story, had not arisen.

Another argument in support of this conclusion is the rather startling coincidence that Hasmoneus, ordained as an archpriest in 152 BCE, had the name Jonathan (Ιωναθαν).[49] This was the same name as that of the Levite from the line of Gershom (Ιωναθαμ = יהונתן, Judg 18:30),[50] abducted from Micah!

Any reconstruction of the process by which the Sea Peoples settled in the territory of Palestine is, unfortunately, largely speculative. There are, however, several aspects which indicate the important role played in this process by the peoples who settled in Canaan towards the end of the Bronze Age. Danites were probably Danunians, one of the peoples who formed the ethnic mix which gave rise to the Jewish nation. Whether or not they really did stop on their journey in central Palestine only to settle ultimately at its northern extremes is unknown. The only source giving this sequence of events is the Bible. If we accept that these were historical events we would have to consider also the historicity of the details described in the Bible. The next crucial question relates to the situation of the population of Palestine: at which moment could the story of the Danites appeal to the Bible's editors? It is my view that even if an ancient story of the conquest of Laish did exist, its antiquity alone would not be enough to have it included in the book of Judges. Other factors would be decisive in that. It could be that an ancient account of the conquest of distant towns was useful in the new politics of the Jewish state, conducted by the Hasmoneans, propagating as they did the idea of expansion. The political situation in the middle of the second century BCE assuredly assisted in underlining links with the Danites and reminding

49. For the argument that the Maccabees descended from the line of Aaron and not of Zadok, see D.W. Rooke, "Kingship as Priesthood: The Relationship between the High Priesthood and the Monarchy," in J. Day (ed.), *King and Messiah in Israel and the Ancient Near East: Proceedings of the Oxford Old Testament Seminar*, JSOTSup 270, Sheffield, 1998, 187-208 (206-208), and, recently, A. Schofield and J.C. VanderKam, "Were the Hasmoneans Zadokites?," *JBL* 124 (2005): 73-88.

50. According to R. Zadok, *The Pre-hellenistic Israelite Anthroponomy and Prosopography*, Leuven, 1988, the use of the name "Jonathan" in pre-Hellenistic times is found only in the Bible; on a Samarian ostracon (45.3), dated from the eighth century BCE, the name is written in the shortened version: *ywntn*; cf. A.R. Millard, "YH and YHW Names," *VT* 30 (1980): 208-12 (210).

people of their great triumphs. The fact that the Danites of the second century BCE differed slightly from the people of Judah meant that certain references in the text point out that they were susceptible to evil cults (hence the inclusion of the theme of the temple of Micah in the story of the migration). One can deduce that religious differences accompanied the sense of ethnic affiliation.

Of particular significance is the fact that in *Jewish Antiquities* Josephus mentions the journey of the Danites merely as an aside (*Ant* 5.3.1) and leaves out the motif of the capture of the Levite. In his account the Danites were not aggressors but refugees, and they did not capture Laish but established a new town—Dan (Δάνα).[51]

A further argument supporting the thesis that the origin of the formation of the town of Dan is a late creation is provided by *Seper Ha-Yamim*,[52] the Samaritan equivalent of the Bible's collection of the books of Joshua–2 Kings. There is not even a trace of a story about the journey of the Danites there. For some reason, the Samaritans did not accept this tradition as canonical or considered it quite simply superfluous.

Manuscripts found in Qumran provide no evidence that would allow us to discount the possibility that the theme of the conquest of Dan was a late addition to the book of Judges. There are only a few and tiny fragments of the book there, and ch. 18, which contains the description of the conquest of Dan, is missing.[53]

Abraham Malamat has pointed to the similarities between the narrative concerning the migration of the Danites and the story of the exodus from Egypt and the conquest of Canaan.[54] He is inclined to accept that the story of Moses came first; this would support the reconstruction being proposed here. I do not, however, believe it is possible to resolve whether what we are dealing with here is mutual influence of the two stories, nor which story influenced which; it is, after all, quite possible that they were both constructed following a similar narrative pattern. It needs great care to establish the veracity of a story which has been created using a known literary model. There is always the possibility that what we are dealing with is not a description of reality but a literary topos. If Malamat is right and the description of the Danite migration really was influenced by the exodus of the Israelites from Egypt (which

---

51. In *Ant* 1.10.1 "Dan" appears as the name of a spring, while it is the name of a town in 5.3.1 and 8.8.4.

52. MacDonald (ed.), *The Samaritan Chronicle*.

53. Corrado Martone, *The Judaean Desert Bible: An Index*, Turin, 2001.

54. A. Malamat, "The Danite Migration and the Pan-Israelite Exodus–Conquest: A Biblical Narrative Pattern," *Biblica* 51 (1970): 1-16.

does not preclude the historicity of the first of these events), then we would be able to conclude that it occurred after the shaping of the narrative in the book of Exodus.

The question of the name of the town captured by the Danites is a puzzling one. The LXX consistently uses the name Λαισα, whereas the MT uses: ליש / לישה. The disparity in the way the proper name is written in Josh 19:47, where reference is made to the capture by the Danites of Leshem / Lakish (MT: לשם; LXX: Λαχις[55]), could be the result of a scribe's error.[56] There is also the possibility that alongside "Dan" the old toponym of "Laish" was used. This is supported by the reference in Isa 10:30: "Cry out, O Daughter of Gallim! Listen, O Laishah (לישה = Λαισα)! Poor Anathoth!" Bearing in mind the number of biblical instances where the town (or region) of Dan is mentioned, one has to assert that it is probable that both names were in use contemporaneously.

The aetiology of Dan talks of the carefree nature and happiness of the inhabitants of Laish; this could be evidence of the magnificence of the conquered territories, as well as a mirroring of some kind of mythical thinking. We have the description of "a peaceful and unsuspecting people" (עם שקט ובטח, Judg 18:7, 27). The analogous expression (השקט ובטח) can be found only in Isa 32:17: "The fruit of righteousness will be peace; the effect of righteousness will be *quietness and confidence* forever." This is a description of the situation after "the Spirit is poured upon [the people] from on high," thanks to which "the desert becomes a fertile field, and the fertile field seems like a forest. Justice will dwell in the desert and righteousness live in the fertile field" (Isa 32:15-16).

A similar "paradisal" tradition is to be found in the apocryphal text *Liber Antiquitatum Biblicarum*. When Phinehas (Pinchas?) died, god said to him: "Et nunc exurge et vade hinc, et habita in Danaben, in monte, et inhabita ibi annis pluribus, et mandabo ego aquile mee, et nutriet te ibi, et non descendes ad homines, iam quousque perveniat tempus ut probcris in tempore, et tu claudas celum tunc, et in ore tuo aperitur..." (*LAB* 48.1).[57] The name "Danaben" is probably the conjunction *Dan-'Aben* ("stone/cliff Dan"), and may well signify the hill of Dan, that is Mt Hermon, a "place which lacks none of the things that are on earth."

Dan, originally Laish, is a symbol of happiness. Its inhabitants lead a contented life untroubled by any concerns. It is also a paradisal place in the vision of Pinchas who was fed by an eagle sent to him by God. This

55. The Greek Λαχις is generally equivalent to the Hebrew לכיש.

56. Malamat, "The Danite Migration," 15 n. 3.

57. Trans. by D. Harrington in *OTP*, vol. 2. G. Kisch (*LAB*, *passim*) draws attention to the analogy of this passage with 1 Kgs 17:4.

view of it could have several sources. The most likely seems to be that Dan, being synonymous with the idea of "the north," acquired its paradisal connotations from its very geographical situation. To the Hebrews, the south was associated with the Negev desert (both the name of the desert and the direction is given by the same word—בגנ), whereas the north is associated with fertility and plenty, the best example of which is the name "Lebanon," used in the Bible as a synonym for fertility and wealth. There are many springs at the foot of Mt Hermon and it is there that the River Jordan starts. It is no surprise, therefore, that for the inhabitants of the dry and semi-desert Judah the district of Dan should become a symbol of fertility and happiness.

If this paradisal picture of Dan arose in the consciousness of the inhabitants of Judah, then it is possible that the account of the Danite migration and the occupation of Laish could have been formed there, too. If this were indeed so, then we would gain another argument in favour of a Judah or even Hasmonean origin for the text of Judg 18.

The information that Laish was a Sidonian town (v. 7) does not add much to a study of the local cult. Unfortunately, we know little about Sidon, one of the most important of Phoenician towns. The town's chief god was Eshmun, identified with Aesculapius.[58] Apart from him, Ashtarte–Aphrodite was also worshipped there.[59] 1 Kings 11:5 talks of Ashtaret as the goddess of the Sidonians (see also 1 Kgs 11:33; 2 Kgs 23:13). It was from Sidon that Jezebel, daughter of King Etbaal, who became Ahab's wife, came. 1 Kings 16:31-32 links the spread of the cult of Baal in Samaria with her person.[60] Judges 10:6 mentions, among others, Sidonian gods whom the Israelites served. 2 Samuel 24:6 testifies to the existence of a link, or at least communication, between Dan and Sidon. Though the Sidonians are mentioned as being excellent craftsmen, they—according to our extra-biblical knowledge—were renowned mainly for their seafaring prowess (see Isa 23:2-4, 12). The fact that the Graeco-Roman tradition links the origins and flowering of Sidon with the arrival of the Sea Peoples is also of importance here.[61]

The note that Laish was originally inhabited by the Sidonians is a very important pointer enabling us to date the account in Judg 18. If we accept

---

58. J. Teixidor, *The Pagan God: Popular Religion in the Greco-Roman Near East*, Princeton, 1977, 34.

59. *Ibid.*, 37.

60. For a discussion of the probable role of Jezebel in the cult of Baal-Eshmun, see in G.A. Yee, *ABD*, *s.v.* "Jezebel."

61. Cf. P.C. Schmitz, *ABD*, *s.v.* "Sidon (place)"; Garbini, *I Filistei. Gli Antagonisti di Israele, passim.*

that the name "Sidonians" is used in Judg 18 not as a description of the inhabitants (or their descendants) of a specific Phoenician town, but of the peoples who had originally inhabited the foot of Mt Hermon, then, since Middle Eastern sources testify to the existence of Sidon as early as the fourteenth century BCE,[62] it would not be possible to state precisely when the narrative about the Danites was created. We can, however, accept that the term "Sidonians" denotes not only the indigenous inhabitants of Laish, but also the actual population known to the authors of the Bible. The Bible documents links between northern Palestine and Sidon. It is, therefore, quite feasible that in times very distant from the migration of the thirteenth century BCE the population of Dan admitted to certain links with Sidon. It may be no coincidence that a statue of Aphrodite from the second century BCE was found in Dan;[63] the goddess is identified with Astarte, the object of particular reverence in Sidon.

A separate study would need to be devoted to the cult practised in the sanctuary in Dan during the Hellenistic period. Suffice it to mention here the dual-language (Greek and Aramaic) inscription found in Dan:

(1)   ΘΕΩΙ

(2)   [Τ]ΩΙ ΕΝ ΔΑΝΟΙΣ

(3)   [?]ΩΙΛΟΣΕΥΧΗΝ

(4)   [? נדר זילס עלן].[64]

Bearing in mind both the distance and the ambivalent not to say hostile attitude of the Bible editors to the cult in Dan, we can dismiss the possibility that the local god was Yahweh. Arbeitman believed that the god worshipped in Dan evolved from the Luvian cult of ᴰTiwat-, evidenced in an inscription from Karatepe. Its name is etymologically linked to the Greek word "Zeus" and signifies a male uranic god.[65]

The Dan aetiology provides few pointers to the identity of the divinity worshipped in the place. In Judg 18:31 the term פסל מיכה is used, which translates as "statue of god [belonging to] Micah," and in 2 Kgs 21:7 we find פסל האשרה—"a statue of Astarte." Hebrew syntax allows פסל מיכה to be translated not as a "statue [belonging to] Micah" but "statue of Micah." The name of this man from Judg 17–18 has been written down in two ways: מיכה or מיכיהו. The second of these forms is a Yahwistic name and means "who [is] like Yehu." An analogous construction can be found in the angelic name "Michael" (מיכאל)—"who [is] like god." The shorter form, deriving from the construction מי – כ, or "who [such/is]

62. Schmitz, "Sidon (place)."
63. Biran, "To the God who is in Dan," 145-47.
64. Arbeitman, "Detecting the God," 11-12.
65. *Ibid.*, 12.

like" may be an abbreviated form of a theophoric name in which the god's name has been omitted. We could, however, look for a different etymology for the word מיכה. There is evidence of a cult in Palestine of the god Mekal, identified with Seth and Nergal.[66] Unfortunately, there are no data to help us make anything more of this hypothesis linking the name of the person mentioned in Judg 18 with this god than mere speculation.

The description of the origins of the holy place in Dan (Jud 18) resorts to terminology applicable to the formalisation and good organisation of a temple cult. So, mention is made here of a holy place or "God's house," as well as of specific cult objects found there, and also of a priest who officiates over it. Our attention is drawn to the tension between the negative and positive assessments of the Danites' sanctuary. There is no doubt that the editors and the audience of the Bible viewed the fact that the function of the priestly role was devolved upon a Levite in a positive light, as they did the migration itself and the occupation of the territories. The objects of the cult, however, are viewed negatively. These include "an ephod (אפוד), other household gods (תרפים), a carved image and a cast idol (פסל ומסכה)" (v. 14).[67] The fact that they had previously been used in Micah's household sanctuary intensifies their negative connotations since the shekels of silver used in making them came from robbery (Judg 17:1-4), and Micah initially installed one of his sons to serve in his sanctuary (Judg 17:5), taking on a Levite only later (Judg 17:9-10).[68]

The three items found in the sanctuary in Dan belong to various categories. פסל is a statue probably representing a god. It is this term that is used in biblical formulations forbidding the creation of images of God (e.g. Exod 20:4; Lev 26:1; Deut 4:16, 23, 25). The meaning of the word תרפים is not entirely clear. This term appears, among others, in the description of the flight of Jacob from Laban as the name of the objects which Rachel took from her father's house and then concealed. Scholars consider that it could refer to figures associated with the cult of the dead (images?) and used for divination.[69] The term אפוד is one of those words in the Bible which have several meanings. So, for instance, in Exod 28:27-31 it signifies an item of a priest's dress, in Judg 8:27 and 1 Sam

---

66. H.O. Thompson, *Mekal: The God of Beth-Shan*, Leiden, 1970.

67. Cf. Haran, *Temples and Temple Service*, 28, considers that the Danites took a statue of YHWH from the house of Micah.

68. De Vaux, *Ancient Israel*, 2:307–308.

69. K. van der Toorn, "The Nature of the Biblical Teraphim in the Light of the Cuneiform Evidence," *CBQ* 52 (1990): 203-22; see also J. Huehnergard, "Biblical Notes on Some New Akkadian Texts from Emar (Syria)," *CBQ* 47 (1985): 428-34.

21:9 it is a metal cult object, while in 1 Sam 23:6-12 it is an essential item when asking for advice from an oracle. In the LXX it is transcribed as εφωδ (Judg 17–18) or εφουδ. There is no doubt that both פסל, and the terms תרפים and אפוד, associated with fortune-telling, would, in the mind of a rigorous Yahwist, be related with negative religious practices.

The account of Dan's history underlines the Levite origins of the priests there, which is in contrast to the Deuteronomic account in 1 Kgs 12:31 where the author, critically inclined towards Dan, draws attention to their unsuitability as being "all sorts of people." At the same time this account points to the Mosaic descent of the priests in Dan which contrasts with the dominant version of the biblical tradition linking the chief priests with the descendants of Aaron.[70] Judges 18:30 notes that the priestly line coming down from Jonathan, son of Gershom, lasted "until the time of the captivity," and therefore till either 722/721 BCE,[71] or the time of the Babylonian exile (597–587 BCE).

There is an astonishing inconsistency in the information about the Levite taken on by Micah. We read that: "A young Levite from Bethlehem in Judah, who had been living within the clan of Judah, left that town in search of some other place to stay" (Judg 17:7-8). How could a Levite at the same time be a member of the tribe of Judah? The phrase ממשפחת יהודה clearly points to affiliation to a tribe. The publishers of *BHS* consider that what we are dealing with here is a gloss. Regardless of the interpretation of and reasons for the inconsistency, the provenance of the Levite mentioned is dubious.

The story of the priest from the line of Gershon/om in the north of Palestine is consistent with the information in the book of Joshua since— as the list of Levite towns shows—the descendants of Gershom were allocated property within the lots of Issachar, Asher, Naphthali and Manasseh (Josh 21:6, 27-33).

The Levite officiating at the cult in Dan is undoubtedly a curious figure, to which his uncertain origins in Bethlehem and the surprising "error" in his genealogy (Moses–Manasseh) testify. 1 Chronicles 6:17 mentions only two sons of Gershom, son of Levi: Libni and Shimei (a continuation of the genealogy in 1 Chr 6:5-6). They received lots in the north of Palestine: "The descendants of Gershon, clan by clan, were allotted thirteen towns from the tribes of Issachar, Asher and Naphtali, and from the part of the tribe of Manasseh that is in Bashan" (1 Chr 6:62), and "the Gershonites received the following: From the clan of the

---

70. See F.M. Cross, *Canaanite Myth and Hebrew Epic: Essays in the History of the Religion of Israel*, Cambridge, MA, 1973, 195-215 (195-206).

71. J.M. Berridge, *ABD*, *s.v.* "Jonathan (person)."

half-tribe of Manasseh they received Golan in Bashan and also Ash-
taroth, together with their pasturelands" (1 Chr 6:71). Here it is worth
noting that the description in the book of Chronicles of the distribution of
the priestly tribes and the territories allocated to the Gershomites omits
Dan.

It must surely be allowed that the figure of Gershon, son of Moses,[72] is
based on that of Gershom, son of Levi.[73] What is not clear, unfortunately,
is what purpose this multiplication of priestly tribes served. One of the
theories explaining these complications states that at the time when these
tribal genealogies were being constructed there were many conflicts
between the clans.[74] The descendants of Aaron, the descendants of Zadok
and the descendants of Moses were three different priestly groups calling
upon different origins. The differences in genealogy could signify that
these priests came from various parts of Palestine where their influence
still held sway. The reference to the association with Dan of a Levite
from the tribe of Moses (a Mushite?), a Gershonite, could hint at the
existence in the north of Palestine of a priestly clan, knowledge of which
we have to thank the antagonistic polemical attitude towards it of the
priests in Jerusalem.

72. Mentioned also in 1 Chr 23:16; 26:24 as the father of Shebuel.
73. Following Wellhausen, this is the view of Cross, *Canaanite Myth*, 197-98.
74. Compare, for example, with the conflict between the Oniads, priests at the
temple in Leontopolis, and the representatives of the Hasmonean dynasty in Jerusalem.

5.

Hebron, Mamre

Archaeological Data and Information from Extra-Biblical Sources

Writing about the archaeology of Hebron, Avi Ofer expresses regret that it is impossible to carry out fundamental excavations in the town and its vicinity, particularly as there are no publications of the results of earlier archaeological works.[1] Ofer identifies the biblical town of Hebron[2] with Tell Hebron, and considers that Haram el-Khalil (including the cave of Machpelah) is the remnant of a construction developed during the Second Temple, while the contemporary town of Hebron was a settlement also originating in the time of the Second Temple. Furthermore, Jebel Nimra and Haram Ramath el-Khalil (researchers do not agree on this) are identified with Mamre.

The excavations in Tell Hebron uncovered remains dating from the Early Bronze Age. In the stratum from the Middle Bronze Age (in the S region), cuneiform script containing proper names and the number of sheep and goats (maybe a count of sacrificial beasts) was found on clay tablets, as was the imprint of a scarab dated from the 12th Dynasty. Also discovered were ashes and the bones of sheep and goats.[3] Ofer contends that during the middle Bronze period Hebron was the capital of a kingdom and that the names on the tablets are evidence of the western Semitic (Amorite) origin of the people, as well as of the presence of a Huritic minority.[4] During the Bronze Age the town's importance

---

1. A. Ofer, "Hebron," in *NEAEHL*, 2:606-609 (607).
2. It is, unfortunately, difficult to ascertain what Ofer understands by the word "biblical." What he probably means are the times of the united monarchy, but just the mere fact that the archaeological terminology has been mixed with the biblical indicates how far the archaeology of Palestine is presently subject to ideologisation.
3. Ofer, "Hebron."
4. *Ibid.*, 608.

diminished. The chief remains from that period are caves used as graves and domiciles.[5]

Discussing the subsequent settlement in Hebron in the Iron Age, Avi Ofer claims that the apogee of this process came at the turn of the tenth century BCE, that is to say, in the times of David. During the Persian period the tell was abandoned, and the beginnings of the settlement in the area of today's town (in the valley) are not known.[6]

In the Persian period, Hebron found itself outside the administrative district of the Jewish province of Yehud.[7] Some scholars claim that the Edomite/Idumean settlement started there as early as the times of Nebuchadnezzar.[8] According to Charles Carter, it was only in the later Persian period that the area around the town became part of the province.[9] Scholars considered that the information in 1 Macc 4–5 was proof of the Edomites' presence in these regions, especially as Jewish tradition located the grave of Esau around Hebron.[10] The discovery close to Hebron of an altar with a dedication to the god Qos supports the accuracy of this claim.[11]

In extra-biblical material, the oldest mention of Hebron is to be found in ostraca from the eighth century BCE.[12]

The Deirel-Arba'in building found on the tell is associated in popular tradition with the burial chamber of Ruth and Jesse (the father of David).[13]

Mamre is identified with the Arab Haram el-Khalil, 3 km north of Hebron.[14] The excavations of 1926–28 and 1984–86 discovered a wall enclosing an area of some three thousand square metres (approx. 50 × 65 metres), and inside it a Byzantine church which performed sacral functions as late as the time of the Crusades. Shimon Applebaum claims

---

5.   *Ibid.*, 609.

6.   *Ibid.* Cf. C.E. Carter, *The Emergence of Yehud in the Persian Period: A Social and Demographic Study*, JSOTSup 294, Sheffield, 1999, 100 and 111.

7.   *Ibid.*, 82-83.

8.   P.W. Ferris, Jr, *ABD*, *s.v.* "Hebron (place)."

9.   Carter, *The Emergence of Yehud*, 98.

10.   N. Kokkinos, *The Herodian Dynasty: Origins, Role in Society and Eclipse*, JSPSup 30, Sheffield, 1998, 38, cites *Jub.* 38:8 and *T. Jud.* 9.

11.   Carter, *The Emergence of Yehud*, expresses no definite opinion about the presence of the Edomites during the Persian period in the vicinity of Hebron; see 82, 98-99, 111.

12.   *EJ*, *s.v.* "Hebron," 8:227; Ofer, "Hebron."

13.   It is curious that though the Bible often underlines David's origins in Bethlehem, Jesse was supposed to have been buried in Hebron; I say more about this matter in the chapter dealing with Ophrah.

14.   I. Magen, "Mamre," in *NEAEHL*, 3:939-42.

that this place was a *temenos* as early as the ninth to seventh centuries BCE. The remnants in Ramat el-Khalil testify to the fact that there was building work done in this area in the Hasmonean reign, probably under John Hyrcanus (c. 128 BCE).[15]

Itzhak Magen's view is that, because of the similarity of the masonry on the temple mound and the buildings around the Cave of Machpelah in Hebron, the remnants examined by him in Mamre should be dated in the times of the Second Temple. Magen writes: "The excavators believe, therefore, that King Herod built the site for Edomites, who had inhabited the area since the destruction of the First Temple. Following the destruction of the First Temple, the site became a pagan cult site, one of the main ones of its kind in the Hebron Hills, where annual celebrations were held in the gods' honor."[16] This would mean that the construction at Haram el-Khalil originated in the times of Herod the Great.[17] Additional archaeological information comes from discoveries which include objects from Roman and Byzantine times: many coins, a marble statue of Dionysius and also an altar with a dedication to the Edomite god Qos.[18]

F. Nigel Hepper and Shimon Gibson[19] have suggested a different location for the biblical Mamre; they identify it with the modern 'Ain Sabta, which lies north-west of Hebron and where a holy tree was worshipped as late as the end of the nineteenth century. This fact suggested to the authors a link with the place where the tree of Abraham was supposed to have grown. Their theory appears to be erroneous if only because the practice of ascribing ancient origins to cult places—in this case associating a holy tree with the tree of Abraham—is widespread and there is no basis to suppose that this modern holy place has existed there since ancient times.

Excavations prove that Mamre has a special character as early as the time of the Second Temple. Flavius Josephus mentions the holy place and the tree that grew there twice. In *Antiquities* (1.10.4), when he writes

15. S. Applebaum, *ABD*, *s.v.* "Ramat el-Khalil."

16. Magen, "Mamre," 942.

17. For a discussion of the similarities between the remains in Haram el-Khalil, the sanctuary of Machpelah and the temple in Jerusalem, see D.M. Jacobson, "The Plan of the Ancient Haram el-Khalil in Hebron," *PEQ* 113 (1981): 73-80.

18. Magen, "Mamre," 941; for more on the subject of the nature of Qos as "Lord of the Beasts" and a god responsible for natural phenomena, see E.A. Knauf, *DDD*, *s.v.* "Qos," 1272-78; other dedications in his honour are analysed by I. Beit-Arieh, "The Edomite Shrine at Horvat At Qitmit in the Judean Negev: Preliminary Excavation Report," *Tel Aviv* 18 (1991): 93-116.

19. F.N. Hepper, and S. Gibson, "Abraham's Oak of Mamre: The Story of a Venerable Tree," *PEQ* 126 (1994): 94-105.

about the deeds of Abraham, he talks of "the oak called Ogyges" (Ὠγύγην καλουμένην δρῦν), and in the *War of the Jews* (4.9.7) he mentions that at a distance of six furlongs from Hebron there stands "a huge terebinth-tree" (τερέβινθος μεγίστη), one "which is said to have stood there ever since the creation."[20]

Jerome twice mentions the markets that took place there, writing: "alii uero, quod ultima captitate sub Hadriano, quando et urbs subuersa est Hierusalem, innumerabilis populus diuersae aetatis et utriusque sexus in mercato Terebinthi uenundatus sit" (*In Hieremiam* VI.18.6),[21] "Legamus ueteres historias, et plangentium traditiones Iudaeorum, quod in tabernaculo Abrahae—ubi nunc per annos singulos mercatus celeberrimus exercetur—post ultimam euersionem, quam sustinuerunt ab Hadriano..." (*In Zachariam* III.11.4-5).[22] The story of the Jewish prisoners brought by Hadrian to the market beneath the terebinth is also repeated in *Chronicon Paschale* (*Patrologia Greca* 92. col. 613).[23]

In turn Eusebius of Caesarea mentions an altar in Hebron (*Vita Constantini* III.53.100; *Onomasticon* 6.12-14; 76.1-3), and the existence in that area of a holy oak (or terebinth) and the annual ceremony (market) that took place there is also mentioned by Sozomenus (*Ecclesiastic History* II.4).[24]

Biblical Information

When it talks about Hebron, the Bible creates the image of an important administrative centre, especially in the early history of the state. The town has a Hittite past (Gen 23);[25] before its conquest it had its own king (Josh 10:3, 23), called the Amorite (Josh 10:5; see also Judg 1:10). After the conquest it became a Levite town (Josh 21:11) as well as one of the towns of shelter (Josh 20:7). We have to remember that the towns mentioned in Josh 20 and 21 were a late addition; however, at the time

20. Josephus, *The Jewish War*, trans. H.S.J. Thackeray, LCL, Harvard, MA, 1997.
21. *Corpus Christianorum. Series Latina*, 74:307.
22. *Ibid.*, 76 A:851.
23. Magen, "Mamre."
24. Cf. D. Sperber, *The City in Roman Palestine*, New York, 1998, 30-31 n. 21, accepts the identification of the place Butnah with the place indicated by Sozomen in the vicinity of Hebron also known as אילה (Τερέβινθος). Citing Talmudic texts forbidding the Jews taking part in these markets (in view of their pagan nature), Sperber writes that of course the Jews did participate in them.
25. There is the question here of whether the references in the Bible to the Hittites really do mean that people or, for instance, whether they mean all non-Jews residing in Palestine.

that the text was created (probably in the second century BCE), they must have been of special significance.

According to biblical tradition, Hebron fell to the lot of Caleb and his descendants (Num 13; Josh 14:6-15; 15:13; Judg 1:20). It is generally associated with the deeds of the patriarchs. The sanctuary found in the supposed burial chamber of Machpelah was created no later than the times of Herod.[26]

It is with Hebron that the Bible links the beginnings of the history of David as monarch (2 Sam 2:11; 5:1-5). The biblical text has left suggestions that a cult place existed there as early as the united kingdom. The oath which Absolom made and the promise of its fulfilment is evidently associated with Hebron:

> At the end of four years, Absalom said to the king, "Let me go to Hebron and fulfil a vow I made to the Lord. While your servant was living at Geshur in Aram, I made this vow: If the Lord takes me back to Jerusalem, I will worship the Lord in Hebron..." While Absalom was offering sacrifices, he also sent for Ahithophel... (2 Sam 15:7-8, 12)

That last reference is proof positive of the existence of some kind of sanctuary in Hebron.[27] Rainer Albertz describes the oath made by Absalom as part of a *zebah* type of offering, typical of a family sanctuary.[28] Further verses prove that Hebron was not just a religious but also an administrative centre (a capital?): "Then Absalom sent secret messengers throughout the tribes of Israel to say, 'As soon as you hear the sound of the trumpets, then say, "Absalom is king in Hebron"'" (2 Sam 15:10).

In the age of the divided kingdom, Hebron is mentioned only once, namely as one of the fortified cities of Judah strengthened by King Rehoboam (2 Chr 11:10), which would indicate that at the beginning of the history of the divided kingdom, that is, in the tenth century BCE, it was within Judah.

We can distinguish several periods in the history of Hebron as a border town, lying at the place of contact between the Hebrew and Edomite Arabic cultures, during which stories about the origin and development of holy places there could have arisen. These periods would certainly include the time of the Judah monarchy up to the fall of the state (597–587 BCE). A negative attitude towards the Edomites dominated this era,

26. Jacobson, "The Plan of the Ancient Haram el-Khalil."
27. Cf. Ofer, "Hebron," 607.
28. Albertz, *A History of Israelite Religions*, 1:101 n. 56. Albertz points to the similarity of the activity performed by Absalom and the evidence found in Kuntillet 'Ajrud, particularly in the expression "YHWH from Samaria," which appears on vessels found there (1:282).

as Bert Dicou demonstrated, and this found expression in attributing joint blame to them for the fall of Jerusalem (see especially Jer 49, Obadiah, Ezek 35–36).[29] John R. Bartlett offered a different concept, claiming that there was a sense of a bonding (brotherhood?) between the Jews and the Edomites from time immemorial.[30]

The Hebrews' characteristic turning away from southern Judah during the Persian period could be indicated—as J.M. Myers noted—by a lack of anti-Edomite accents in Nehemiah and Ezra.[31] Myers's argument is correct as long as it is not applied exclusively to the fifth century but includes also the Hellenistic times.[32] Evidence of the presence of the Edomites in the region of Hebron is provided by numerous finds associated with Edomite craftsmanship, as well as votive offerings naming their god Qos.[33]

Bible scholars assume that the story about the grave of the patriarchs in Hebron was known as early as the Persian period and, following on from that, they envisage pilgrimages to this sanctuary.[34] This is understandable, assuming that stories about the patriarchs existed in their present (or not very different) form as early as First Temple times. Yet if we accept, after Van Seters,[35] Thompson[36] and Garbini,[37] that the figure of Abraham was created during the Babylonian captivity, then it is hard to comprehend why it should be associated with a place situated on the border, or even beyond the border, and not within the state. There is no doubt that the story linking David with Hebron arose from before the captivity, but the thesis linking Abraham with Hebron during the times of captivity still requires proof. Pilgrimages to the grave of the patriarchs during the Persian period have been deduced from circumstantial clues. One of these is the text in Amos 5:5: "Do not seek Bethel, do not go to Gilgal, do not journey to Beersheba…" The first thing to be said here is that this verse does not mention Hebron at all, the second—that the reality of the times of Amos might not have reflected the reality of the period of the Second Temple.

29. Dicou, *Edom, Israel's Brother and Antagonist*, 171-81.
30. Bartlett, *Edom and the Edomites*.
31. Myers, "Edom and Judah," 385-86 n. 32.
32. Cf. Garbini, *Il ritorno dell'esilio babilonese*, 173-216.
33. Magen, "Mamre," 939-42. For more on the subject of the extent of the Hebrew province of Yehud, see Carter, *The Emergence of Yehud.*
34. De Pury, "Abraham," esp. 177. Cf. de Vaux, *Ancient Israel*, 292, who claims that pilgrimages to Mamre are reported from the first century CE.
35. Van Seters, *Abraham in History and Tradition*.
36. Thompson, *The Historicity of the Patriarchal Narrative*.
37. Garbini, *Storia e ideologia*, 111-23.

What the references to Hebron in the Pentateuch (Gen 37:14; 53:27) underline most strongly is the association of Isaac with the town. In the books of Joshua (14:13-14; 15:13) and Judges (1:20; cf. 1 Chr 2:42), there is talk of Canaanite inhabitants of Hebron and of giving this town to Caleb. The tradition linking Hebron and its vicinity with Caleb and the Calebites is very strong. The book of Numbers (chs. 13–14) tells of spies sent to Canaan and of the tribe of Judah, assessing only Caleb favourably:[38] "But because my servant Caleb has a different spirit and follows me wholeheartedly, I will bring him into the land he went to, and his descendants will inherit it" (Num 14:24). The strongly emphasised presence in Hebron and its surroundings of the tribe of Caleb[39] is laid on top of the simultaneous picture of Hebron as the town of the Hittites.

The Bible offers further information about Hebron in 1 Macc 5:65: "Then Judas and his brothers went out and fought the descendants of Esau in the land to the south. He struck Hebron and its villages and tore down its strongholds and burned its towers on all sides."

The book of *Jubilees* inflates the significance of Hebron considerably; in it Abraham finds himself in Hebron on his way to Egypt (13:10-12), after which he makes a covenant with God in Mamre-Hebron (14:1-19).[40] It is also in Mamre that the prophecy of Isaac's birth is announced (16:1-4),[41] and it is there that Sarah is buried (19:1-19). Abraham, it seems, lives in Hebron permanently. Here, along with Isaac, Ishmael and Jacob [*sic*][42] he celebrates the Feast of Weeks (the feast of the first fruits of the harvest) (22:1-9). Finally, he is also buried at Mamre (23:1-7). The book of *Jubilees* also talks of the burial in Machpelah, next to Sarah, of both Rebecca and Leah (36:21-24). *Jubilees* also locates the beginnings of the conflict between Jacob and Esau in Hebron (37:14-15). This is where we learn that Jacob was buried in the family grave (45:13-15), where the bones of his descendants were also laid (46:9-10).[43]

---

38. Joshua is also assessed positively (see Num 14:36-38), but the tradition associated with him is regarded as being of later date, see M.J. Fretz and R.I. Panitz, *ABD*, *s.v.* "Caleb (person)."

39. The name "Caleb" means "dog" which does rather complicate the matter of distinguishing proper names from common nouns. For more on this question, see *ibid.*

40. In the biblical version of Gen 15 the place of this covenant is not specified.

41. Cf. Gen 18:1-15.

42. See Abraham's extended blessing of Jacob in *Jub.* 22:10-30.

43. The book of *Jubilees* describes this theme at greater length than does the book of Genesis. However, like Genesis, *Jubilees* does not mention the burial of Joseph in Hebron (*Jub.* 46:9).

Archaeology provides evidence that Hebron and its surroundings really were in the Hasmonean sphere of influence. Finds of coins minted by the Hasmoneans[44] support the theory, as do the remains in Rameth-el-Halil of an edifice which, it is supposed, guarded the holy area of Mamre; its beginnings are dated in the times of Herod the Great and are associated (in view of the similarities in masonry) with the building activities of that king.[45] There are no data letting us state whether (as 1 Macc 5:65 describes) the Hasmoneans occupied this territory only as a result of conquests or (as Neh 11:25 claims) the Jews were living there before then.[46]

The name "Mamre," which appears in the Bible ten times, but only in the book of Genesis (in this respect there is a certain consistency between the MT and the LXX), occurs in two separate, though closely linked, meanings: as the name of a place "the oaks of Mamre" (Gen 13:18; 18:1) and as the name of a person (Gen 14:13, 24). The oak grove of Mamre (אלני ממרא) serves as a point of reference for the position of the cave of Machpelah (Hebron): "Machpelah, before Mamre" (Gen 23:17, 19; 25:9), or, more precisely, "to the east of Mamre" (Gen 49:30; 50:13).[47]

Genesis 35:27 might support the identification of Mamre with Hebron: "Jacob came home to his father Isaac in Mamre, unto the city of Arbah which is Hebron, where Abraham and Isaac had stayed" (cf. Gen 23:19). If it is true that Mamre and Hebron are separate places, then this pericope can be interpreted as a mental short-cut or proof of the blurring of the differences in the localisation of the two places. Whatever the reasons for it, the passage in Gen 35:27 reveals a tradition separate from that of the rest of Genesis. This could be a symptom of the fact that it comes from the story of Jacob which is more closely associated with centres in the north of Palestine (Bethel, Gilead) than the sanctuaries in the south (Hebron, Beer-sheba).

In the Qumran manuscripts, Mamre appears in only two texts: in the so-called 4QAges of Creation fragment, 4Q180 (fr. 2-4 col. 2.4), and in a short snatch of text marked as 4Q482 (1.3) or 4QpapJub[1?]. The first text, 4QAges of Creation, is a paraphrase of the biblical story of Abraham and the epiphany of the three men in Mamre. The text specifies:

44.   Y. Baruch, "Hebron, ed-Deir," *Excavations and Surveys in Israel* 14 (1994): 121-22.

45.   Jacobson, "The Plan"; for a documentation of the excavations, see E. Mader, *Mambre. Die Ergebnisse der Ausgrabungen im heiligen Bezirk Ramet el-Halil in Südpalästina 1926–1928*, vols. 1–2, Freiburg, 1957.

46.   See Ferris, "Hebron."

47.   See de Vaux, *Ancient Israel*, 292.

"The three men [who] appear[ed to Abraha]m in the oak wood of Mamre are angels."[48]

The person named as Mamre, mentioned in Gen 14:13 and 14:24, who went with Eshcol (אשכל)[49] and Aner (ענר),[50] was an Amorite. References to him have made commentators suggest that the name of the sanctuary comes from his name.[51] These three sons of Anak, confederates of Abraham, are analogous to the mythic Anakites, giants inhabiting the district of Hebron: "And there we saw the giants, the sons of Anak, which come of the giants…" (Num 13:33).[52]

The reference to the Anakites in Num 13:22 gives us names different from those provided by the story of Abraham (Gen 13:14), namely, Ahiman (אחימן = Αχιμαν), Sheshai (ששי = Σεσσι) and Talmai (תלמי = Θελαμιν), descendants of Anak (ענק = Εναχ).[53] Biblical tradition describes the Anakites as giants, the best testimony of this being the sentence in Deut 1:28: "Our brothers have made us lose heart. They say, 'The people are stronger and taller than we are; the cities are large, with walls up to the sky. We even saw the Anakites there.'" The physical stature of the Anakites is also mentioned in Deut 9:2: "The people are strong and tall—Anakites! You know about them and have heard it said: 'Who can stand up against the Anakites?'" The Bible is unequivocal in setting their presence in the district of Hebron. The information in Josh 11:22 makes the giants' ethnicity implicit: "No Anakites were left in Israelite territory; only in Gaza, Gath and Ashdod did any survive." Since some Anakites were to be found in Gaza, Gath and Ashdod, in other words in Philistine towns, it means that the Jews regarded the Anakites of Hebron as Philistines, too. Assuredly, the terms "Amorites" and "Hittites" were used as equivalents of the term "Philistine(s)" in the Bible.[54]

Thus, the Bible contains two traditions regarding the Anakites. One, naming the giants Ahiman, Sheshai and Talmai, is recorded in Num 13:22; Josh 14:4 and Judg 10. The other talks about the Anakites Eshcol, Mamre and Aner, and is found only in Gen 13–14. The name "Sheshai"

---

48. García Martínez and Tigchelaar (eds.), *The Dead Sea Scrolls Study Edition.*

49. Gen 14:13, 24; this noun, signifying "grape-vine," also appears in Gen 27:35; Num 13:23; Deut 1:24; Song 1:14 and in a different form in Gen 40:10; Deut 32:32; Song 7:8, 9.

50. Gen 14:13, 24; 1 Chr 6:55 mentions the name "Aner" in the context of information about the settlement of the Levites.

51. M. Liverani, "Le Chêne de Sherdanu," *VT* 27 (1977): 212-26 (213).

52. E. Lipiński, "'Anaq–Kiryat 'Arba'–Hebron et ses Sanctuaires tribaux," *VT* 24 (1974): 41-55 (43).

53. See also references to these Anakites in Josh 15:13-14 and Judg 1:20.

54. Cf. K.E. Lowery, *ABD*, s.v. "Sheshai (person)."

is derived from the Hurrian language;[55] the etymology of the other brothers' names is uncertain. The names of the Anakites in the story about Abraham are also the names of places; this could signify that originally the three sons of Anak had the names given in Num 13:22 and only in time were they changed by resorting to the names of places in the region of Hebron. There is, therefore, no doubt that the story contained in Gen 13–14 is later than that about the spies sent into Canaan.

In any analysis of myths related to the beginnings of sanctuaries, the etymologies and meanings of proper names are crucial.

The term "Hebron" (חברון) comes from the root חבר, "to unite," "to join."

The name "Mamre" (ממרא) is usually associated with the root מרא, "to be fruitful," "plump," "full," although its etymology is uncertain.[56]

In the name "Kiriath-Arba," קרית signifies "town," with the part ארבע, derived from the root רבע, "foursome," and everything that is four-part.[57]

Yoël Arbeitman has presented a theory in which the word ארבע should be associated with the Indo-European root *ar-*, being a literal equivalent of the Hebrew verb חבר, because it signifies "to join," "to make a covenant," and the like.[58] This semantic identity has also been noted by M. O'Conner, who remarked that in both cases the meanings are close to the concept of "friendship" contained also in the Arabic name el-Khalil.[59] According to Arbeitman and O'Conner, the same semantic value can be seen in the name "Mamre," which is associated with the Hittite *miu-mar*, signifying "friendship," "alliance."[60]

---

55. *Ibid.*

56. *DCH* does not give the original root (see 5:333); BDB gives two roots for מרא, (I) "to beat the air," "flap the wings"; (II) "to be well-fed," "fat."

57. Rashi derives the name "Kiriath Arba" ("the town of four") from the place inhabited by the four giants, Aciman, Sheshai, Talmai and their father Anak, or of the place of burial of four couples (Adam and Eve, Abraham and Sarah, Isaac and Rebecca, and Jacob and Leah).

58. Y.L. Arbeitman, "The Hittite is thy Mother: An Anatolian Approach to Genesis 23," in Y. Arbeitman and A. Bomhard (eds.), *Bono Homini Donum: Essays in Historical Linguistics in Memory of J. Alexander Kerns*, Amsterdam, 1981, 889-1026; *idem*, "Minōs, the Ὀαριστής of Great Zeus, ἀ, ἀ, and ὀ-Copulative, the Knossan Royal Titulary and the Hellenization of Crete," in Y. Arbeitman (ed.), *A Linguistic Happening in Memory of Ben Schwartz*, Louvain-la-Neuve, 1988, 411-62.

59. M. O'Conner, "The Etymologies of Tadmor and Palmyra," in Arbeitman (ed.), *A Linguistic Happening*, 235-54 (244).

60. Arbeitman, *The Hittite is Thy Mother*, 959-1002; see also Arbeitman's synthesis in *ABD*, *s.v.* "Mamre." See also E.A. Knauf, *ABD*, *s.v.* "Toponyms and Toponymy."

The idea of a union or an alliance as a constituent of the Hebron tradition has been explored most fully by Edward Lipiński.[61] He drew attention to the feasibility of explaining the name Kiriath-Arba by positing the federal character of Hebron. Since its name contains the element of "foursome," it could be that its genesis stems from the existence of four communities represented by the Amorites Mamre, Eshcol and Aner (Gen 14:13, 24) and their ally Abraham. Each of these tribes had its own sanctuary which would mean that the burgeoning alliance was based on the equality of four religious centres which would be, according to Lipiński: (1) the valley of Eshcol, (2) the temple of 'Anat-Rum, (3) the plain of Mamre and (4) the grave of Abraham (the cave of Machpelah).[62] This same fourfold character of Hebron can be seen in the theme dealing with the Calebites living in the town (1 Chr 2:18-19), since mention is made of the four parts (clans) of Caleb (see the four sons of Hebron in 1 Chr 2:43).[63]

One of the heroes—founders of the federation—was of course supposed to be Abraham, and the religious centre associated with him was the cave of Machpelah. The names of the other heroes are associated with those of cult centres, for what we have here are proper names that are identical with toponyms: the Amorite whose name is Mamre relates to the grove of Mamre, and Eshcol (Gen 14) relates to the brook or valley of Eshcol (Num 13:23-24; 32:9; Deut 1:24). The situation with Aner is far more complex; his name has an equivalent only in the name of the town allotted to the sons of Kohath, of Aaron's line from the lot of Manasseh (1 Chr 6:55).[64] According to Lipiński, there was a sanctuary in the vicinity of Hebron which was associated with the Aner tradition and dedicated to Anath-Rum. This would be identified with the place Ainon (Αἰνών) mentioned in John's Gospel (3:23).[65]

Lipiński reconstructs the name of the sanctuary Anat-Rum, on the basis of Canaanite–Phoenician linguistic analogy and the variations in the text in the SP, in such a way that he comes to a form close to the biblical form—ענר. This reconstruction would allow us to recreate the form: ענ>ת<רם*, in other words a form analogous to that found in the Sidonian inscription in Delos: Ανατραμ.[66] Lipiński believes that the place

---

61. Lipiński, "'Anaq–Kiryat 'Arba'–Hebron."

62. *Ibid.*, 54-55.

63. *Ibid.*

64. Josh 21:25, parallel to the passage in 1 Chr 6:55, speaks of Taanach; see M.C. Astour, *ABD*, s.v. "Aner (person)"; M. Hunt, *ABD*, s.v. "Aner (place)."

65. Lipiński, "'Anaq–Kiryat 'Arba'–Hebron," 52-54.

66. *Ibid.*, 53.

Ainon (Αινών) to which John 3:23 testifies is the same as the town Beth-Anoth (בית־ענות; LXX: [B] Βαιθαναμ, [A] Βαιθανωθ), mentioned in Josh 15:59. The precise location of this centre is known to have been about 3 km from Mamre[67] and 6 km from Hebron.[68]

We can say something more about the holy place which the valley of Eshcol was supposed to be. Its name is derived from the common name אשכל, signifying a "grape-vine."[69] In the book of Numbers we read:

> They [the Israelite spies] went up through the Negev and came to Hebron, where Ahiman, Sheshai and Talmai, the descendants of Anak, lived. (Hebron had been built seven years before Zoan in Egypt.) When they reached the Valley of Eshcol, they cut off a branch bearing a single cluster of grapes. Two of them carried it on a pole between them, along with some pomegranates and figs. That place was called the Valley of Eshcol because of the cluster of grapes (אשכל) the Israelites cut off there. At the end of forty days they returned from exploring the land. (Num 13:22-25)

Although this valley has not been precisely located, the description, emphasising the discovery of the grape-vines, fits in with the reality of the region north of Hebron.[70]

The accuracy of the hypothesis about the federal nature of Hebron is supported by the etymologies that Arbeitman proposes. We can accept that the proper names Hebron and Kiriath Arba derive from a real or mythical alliance. What is less clear is whether or not the idea suggesting the existence of four confederated sanctuaries is based on sufficiently strong testimonies.[71] A much simpler hypothesis is one that suggests the existence of a town with an urban sanctuary, and of a cult place of a different nature outside its walls. Lipiński bases his hypothesis only partly on a reconstruction of religious realities. Its weakness stems from a lack of archaeological evidence confirming the existence of a sanctuary

---

67. According to Eusebius *Bethanin* lay some 2 miles north of Terebinth; see. S.E. McGarry, *ABD*, *s.v.* "Beth-Anoth (place)"; Lipiński, "'Anaq–Kiryat 'Arba'–Hebron," 52-53; F.-M. Abel, *Géographie de la Palestine*. Vol. 1. *Géographie physique et historique*, Paris, 1933, 403-404.

68. F.-M. Abel, *Géographie de la Palestine*. Vol. 2. *Géographie politique. Les villes*, Paris, 1938, 267.

69. Gen 40:10; Num 13:23, 24; Deut 32:32; Isa 65:8; Mic 7:1; Song 1:14; 7:8, 9. See F.-M. Abel, *Géographie de la Palestine*, 1:403-404.

70. Cf. W.I. Toews, *ABD*, *s.v.* "Eshcol (place)"; Carter, *The Emergence of Yehud*, 255-56; C.E. Walsh, *The Fruit of the Wine: Viticulture in Ancient Israel*, Harvard Semitic Monographs 60, Winona Lake, 2000.

71. The subject is treated with restraint by C. Grottanelli, "The Ogygian Oak at Mamre and the Holy Town of Hebron," *Vicino Oriente* 2 (1979): 39-63.

at Anath-Rum and any kind of identification of the valley of Eschcol. There is an additional difficulty posed by the late origin of the construction in Mamre. An important argument against Lipiński's hypothesis is the primary tradition relating to the Anakites. If we were to accept his hypothesis we would also have to accept that the tradition came into being after the birth of the new Anakites. Later I will present a thesis which will significantly alter the date of the story concerning the patriarchs' grave in Hebron. Accepting that will necessitate the moving of the existence of a real federation of sanctuaries as far forward as the second century BCE.

The biblical text, the later history, the archaeological excavations and Arbeitman's theory based on an analysis of toponyms all suggest that Hebron and Kiriath-Arbah are the same place. Even though it lies close by, Mamre is a separate place.[72]

Aetiologies

Genesis 13:18:

> So Abram moved his tents and went to live near the great trees of Mamre at Hebron, where he built an altar to the Lord (ויבן־שם מזבח ליהוה).

Genesis 23:1-20:

> (1) Sarah lived to be a hundred and twenty-seven years old. (2) She died at Kiriath Arba (that is, Hebron) in the land of Canaan, and Abraham went to mourn for Sarah and to weep over her. (3) Then Abraham rose from beside his dead wife and spoke to the Hittites. He said, (4) "I am an alien and a stranger among you. Sell me some property for a burial site here so I can bury my dead." (5) The Hittites replied to Abraham, (6) "Sir, listen to us. You are a mighty prince among us. Bury your dead in the choicest of our tombs. None of us will refuse you his tomb for burying your dead." (7) Then Abraham rose and bowed down before the people of the land, the Hittites. (8) He said to them, "If you are willing to let me bury my dead, then listen to me and intercede with Ephron son of Zohar on my behalf (9) so he will sell me the cave of Machpelah, which belongs to him and is at the end of his field. Ask him to sell it to me for the full price as a burial site among you." (10) Ephron the Hittite was sitting among his people and he replied to Abraham in the hearing of all the Hittites who had come to the gate of his city. (11) "No, my lord," he said. "Listen to me; I give you the field, and I give you the cave that is in it. I give it to you in the presence of my people. Bury your dead." (12) Again Abraham bowed down before the people of the land (13) and

---

72. Magen, "Mamre," 939-42.

he said to Ephron in their hearing, "Listen to me, if you will. I will pay the price of the field. Accept it from me so I can bury my dead there." (14) Ephron answered Abraham, (15) "Listen to me, my lord; the land is worth four hundred shekels of silver, but what is that between me and you? Bury your dead." (16) Abraham agreed to Ephron's terms and weighed out for him the price he had named in the hearing of the Hittites: four hundred shekels of silver, according to the weight current among the merchants. (17) So Ephron's field in Machpelah near Mamre—both the field and the cave in it, and all the trees within the borders of the field— was deeded (18) to Abraham as his property in the presence of all the Hittites who had come to the gate of the city. (19) Afterward Abraham buried his wife Sarah in the cave in the field of Machpelah near Mamre (which is at Hebron) in the land of Canaan. (20) So the field and the cave in it were deeded to Abraham by the Hittites as a burial site.

The distinguishing feature in this story of the mythical origins of the holy place in Mamre is the mention of the building of an altar in the valley (of the great trees). In turn, what is said about Hebron is that the cave of Machpelah was in a field.[73] Therefore, Hebron became a holy place because the patriarchs were buried there.

I suspect that one could assert that there was an older and more important religious centre in Mamre near Hebron. Roland de Vaux admits that priestly circles were negatively inclined towards that cult and maintains that it was by their hands that the Bible was edited, hence the silence in the MT over that cult.[74] What indicates the older origins and the greater importance of the sanctuary in Mamre compared with the urban centre in Hebron (Machpelah) is the originality of the story about Mamre and the derivative nature of the story about the grave of the patriarchs. An ideology unfavourable to the centre in Mamre has obscured its religious weight, elevating the neighbouring urban sanctuary in Hebron—the grotto of Machpelah. The extended story of the purchase of the land and the setting up of the patriarchs' grave, as well as the entire introductory narrative—can be evidence of the late origins of this history. In the MT only Gen 13:18 includes a direct trace of the significance attached to the holy place in the grove of Mamre, or rather by the oak of Mamre.

There is a continuation of the history of the cave of Machpelah in accounts dealing with the burial of successive patriarchs: Abraham (Gen 25:7-10), Isaac (35:27-29) and Jacob (49:29-33). Tradition has it that this place became the burial place of three patriarchal couples: Sarah and

73. The other difference is that Mamre (oak grove) is also a place of habitation (Gen 13:18; 14:13) whereas Machpelah is a grave; for more on the subject of sepulchral connotations, see Liverani, "Le Chêne de Sherdanu," 213.

74. De Vaux, *Ancient Israel*, 293.

Abraham, Rebecca and Isaac, and Leah and Jacob. The story of the patriarchs' grave is recorded in the vibrant biblical tradition stating that the best grave for a person is their father's tomb. Examples characterising this attitude are found in Judg 8:32; 2 Sam 2:32; 17:23; 19:37; 21:14; 2 Kgs 22:20; 2 Chr 34:28. It is a legal transaction that authorises Jewish ownership in Hebron: notably, Abraham does not accept the cave as a gift but pays for it (Gen 23:20).[75] It is a purely commercial transaction: the goods, the price, the act of purchase. The Jewish right to Hebron is based on a legal commercial agreement. The extended narrative (Gen 23) about the buying of a plot for a family grave, and also the emphasis on the land's and whole town's earlier affiliation to the Hittites, plays a crucial part in the aetiology of a holy place in Hebron.

The name of the cave, "Machpelah" (מכפלה), is derived from the root כפל, signifying "to double," "to be double." In the MT it appears in Gen 23:9, 19; 25:9; 49:30; 50:13—always with the definite article; in the LXX it is rendered as: σπήλαιον τὸ διπλοῦν[76] and in the Vulgate, which follows the LXX here, it is given as *spelunca duplex*, which is justified by the presence of the definite article applied to a common noun and not to a proper name. It would seem evident that we are dealing here with a "double (or two-part)" cave which, as tradition has it, contains the graves of the patriarchs. Trying to uncover a link between the meaning of this term and the fact that six people were buried in the cave, commentators have suggested, for instance, the following: since three patriarchal couples were buried there it is possible that the cave was divided into two parts—one given over to the burial of the men, the other to the burial of the women. This kind of speculation is reminiscent of artificial theories created to rationalise biblical accounts. I suspect that it is enough to confine ourselves to the statement that biblical tradition located in Hebron some kind of "two-part" cave.

This story about the grave of the patriarchs is not the only one. A trace of another one is preserved in the Acts of the Apostles: "Then Jacob went down to Egypt, where he and our fathers died. Their bodies were brought back to Shechem and placed in the tomb that Abraham had bought from the sons of Hamor at Shechem for a certain sum of money" (Acts 7:15-16). The theme of buying land has been preserved but the place has been moved from Hebron to Shechem. It seems unlikely that it refers to the grave of Joseph even though the information about his burial really is similar: "And Joseph's bones, which the Israelites had brought up from Egypt, were buried at Shechem in the tract of land that Jacob

75. Cf. Golka, "Aetiologies," 40-41.
76. Only at Gen 49:30 does the LXX confine itself to σπήλαιον παρὰ Εφρων.

bought for a hundred pieces of silver from the sons of Hamor, the father of Shechem. This became the inheritance of Joseph's descendants" (Josh 24:32). However, the land where the grave is situated was bought by Jacob, not Abraham. The LXX gives the name "Hamor" as Αμορραίος, or "Amorite." According to Acts 7:16, the owner of the land in Shechem was Ἐμμώρ, nevertheless the text in Acts 7:16 is decidedly not consistent with the text in Gen 23. The Vulgate mentions the name Emmor three times (Josh 24:32; Judg 9:28; Acts 7:16). In each case it refers to Emmor, the father of Shechem. We can, therefore, accept that the Amorite from Shechem and Emmor from Shechem are the same person.

In the available information about graves, versions that give an alternative to, or disagree with, the version in Gen 23 are: the mention of Joseph's grave in Shechem (Josh 24:32), Esau's in the vicinity of Hebron (*Jub.* 38:8), Ruth's and Jesse's in Hebron (modern popular tradition) as well as Jacob's and "our fathers" in Shechem (Acts 7:16). The following sentence, which is ascribed to Joseph, also suggests that Shechem was the place of Jacob's burial: "My father made me swear an oath and said, 'I am about to die; bury me in the tomb I dug for myself in the land of Canaan'" (Gen 50:5).[77]

Taking all this into account, the following hypothesis can be proposed: the story about the purchase of the land for the patriarchs' grave was initially associated with Shechem.[78] This is supported by the mention made of the location of Joseph's grave there as well as the text in the Acts of the Apostles (7:16). Hebron, as his royal city, was originally associated with David and his family,[79] but it was also associated with the Anakites and the Calebites. The Bible's story was changed when these territories were taken over, or maybe during the Jewish–Idumean conflict over the right to rule them. Whatever the reason, the patriarchs' grave was "relocated" from Shechem in the north to Hebron in the south. The Idumean–Jewish conflict could have coincided chronologically with a deterioration of relations between the Jews and the Samaritans, an expression of which would be the Jews' efforts to minimise Shechem's religious importance.

77. This is the interpretation presented by E. Bloch-Smith, *Judahite Burial Practices and Beliefs about the Dead*, JSOTSup 123, Sheffield, 1992, 114 n. 1; see also S.E. Loewenstamm, "The Death of the Patriarchs in Genesis," in B. Uffenheimer (ed.), *Bible and Jewish History: Studies Dedicated to the Memory of J. Liver*, Tel Aviv, 1971, 110-13, 119 (Hebr.), *non vidi*; after Na'aman, "Beth-aven," 18 n. 34.

78. I write more on this subject in the chapter dealing with Shechem, Chapter 7.

79. It is quite feasible that the monarchic tradition of David in Hebron is Hittite in origin or—even more likely—Philistine. In other words, this is a non-Semitic tradition.

The meaning of the story about the burial cave in Hebron is unusually easy to decipher: the people who had traditionally located the grave of the mythical ancestors of Israel in Hebron gave tongue to their rights to this territory. It is, however, harder to establish a date for the start of this tradition: did it take shape as early as the period of the First Temple when Hebron was one of the towns of Judah, or after the Babylonian captivity as an expression of this region's striving to belong to Judah? In contrast to the history of David—king of Hebron—the aetiology discussed here gives the impression of being a later creation. It takes on a specific significance when set alongside the fact that there was a gradual growth in the number of non-Jewish peoples in these territories after the sixth century BCE. The only biblical mention of the continuity of Jewish settlement in the vicinity of Hebron is to be found in the book of Nehemiah (11:25). And yet, archaeological evidence points to the fact that right up until the Hasmonean expansion (particularly under the leadership of John Hyrcanus) there was a Jewish population—as has already been mentioned—living in the vicinity of Hebron among the dominant Idumean society. It is only within the context of the conquest of these territories by the Jewish state and its taking control of them that the expanded histories of Hebron's "proto-Jewishness" begin to make obvious sense. The mass presence of Idumeans in this region led to conflict, and if we also take into account the Jews' memory of Hebron as the capital of David, then the propaganda importance of "proving the Jewishness" of Hebron becomes apparent.

If we accept this hypothesis, it would allow us to define with some precision the date of the creation (in its present form) of this story of the double burial cave in Hebron—namely, to the years of Hasmonean rule. This would accord with the archaeologists' deductions, for they date the oldest objects found in the vicinity of the holy place near the patriarchs' grave to that very time. Another indication is the fact that biblical references to Hebron comprise two sets: the first contains information about the monarchic (Canaanite, Amorite, Davidic) origins of the town, while the second contains information which comes from comparatively late texts and proving it belonged to Judah.

The story about the origins of the holy place in Hebron, apart from the reference to the patriarchs' grave—included in the Bible, as seems likely, only as late as the second century BCE—gives no details about the nature of the cult practised there. There was a sanctuary in the capital of David, where Absalom still reigned, but the god worshipped there and the form which the cult took remain unknown. Of the various hypotheses on the subject, particularly noteworthy is E.G.H. Kraeling's theory about the existence at Hebron of a solar cult associated with the figure of Samson.[80] Our ignorance on this matter is almost total. There are only two traces suggesting the nature of the cult at Hebron. The first is the town's presence as a capital, a factor which brings with it a whole layer of ritual concentrated on the person of the ruler. The other is the sanctuaries found close by. One of them was most certainly Mamre.

The fundamental distinguishing feature of the aetiological myth, apart from the laconic reference to Mamre, is the statement that Abram built an altar "in the great trees of Mamre (באלני ממרא) near Hebron (אשר בחברון)." What is important here is the proper name "Mamre" and the attribute or determinant of the holy place—"the great trees" (אלני). In the MT, only the plural form is used (אלני), whereas in the LXX translation there is talk of only one δρῦς: Αβραμ ἐλθὼν κατῴκησεν παρὰ τὴν δρῦν τὴν Μαμβρη (Gen 13:18).[81]

As Roland de Vaux writes, there was a syncretic cult in the vicinity of Hebron in Roman times which was focused on the Ogygian oak; the tree was supposed to have grown there since the beginning of the world.[82] The proper name of the tree is given by Flavius Josephus, who writes "Now Abram dwelt near the oak called Ogyges—the place belongs to Canaan, not far from the city of Hebron" (*Ant* 1.1.4). The acknowledgment that the oak of Ogyges has existed since ancient times is implied by the following claim: "Hebron had been built seven years before Zoan in Egypt" (Num 13:22).[83] Mythical thinking linked the concept of a tree's ancient origin to imagining it as the centre of the world: a tree growing since the times before the Jews had even settled in Canaan was a cosmic tree, the mark of the centre of the world and *axis mundi*.

Following to the testimonies of the LXX, Vulgate, Peshitta, and of Josephus, and in later times of Jerome and Sozomen, we can accept that originally the biblical text spoke of just one tree. The introduction of the plural form in the MT was aimed at diminishing the role of the sanctuary and above all at erasing the memory of its function as a holy tree.[84]

The Bible provides a lot of information about trees associated with cults. An analysis of the part played by groves, oaks or trees in general

---

80. E.G.H. Kraeling, "The Early Cult of Hebron and Judg. 16,1-3," *The American Journal of Semitic Languages and Literatures* 41 (1924–25): 174-78 (here referring to 16:3).

81. The Vulgate omits the reference to a tree and translates: "venit et habitavit iuxta convallem Mambre quod est in Hebron."

82. De Vaux, *Ancient Israel*, 2:292-93.

83. Grottanelli, "The Ogygian Oak," 42-45.

84. Arbeitman, "Mamre."

can help us to illuminate the religious connotations of the aetiology of Mamre.[85]

In Gen 13:18 we find the term "grove," the name of the tree in the plural form בּאֵלֹנֵי, i.e., "in אֵלֹנֵי" or "in אֵלֹנֵי." Dictionaries include this word in the form אֵלוֹן.[86] According to Clines, אֵלוֹן, with the vocalisation *sere*, signifies "terebinth," whereas when written with *patah*, as in אַלוֹן, it signifies "oak."[87] This distinction applies only to the MT since the earlier manuscript, without diacritic signs, presents both words in the same form. It is therefore not clear whether Gen 13:18 is speaking about an oak or a terebinth.

The matter becomes even more complicated when we compare the Hebrew text with its ancient translations. In the LXX the Hebrew form אלה (e.g. Judg 6:11, 19) or אלון (e.g. Gen 12:6; 13:18; Judg 4:11) appears as the noun δρῦς[88] or, on several occasions, βάλανος.[89] Inconsistently, the LXX applies the name "terebinth" (τερέβινθος), occasionally using it for the Hebrew word אלה (Isa 1:30; Ezek 6:13; but not in Gen 13:18).

The following pericopes are examples of the problems associated with identifying Hebrew and Greek names of trees:

Isaiah 6:13 reads: "And though a tenth remains in the land, it will again be laid waste. But as the terebinth and oak leave stumps when they are cut down so the holy seed will be the stump in the land" (καὶ ἔτι ἐπ' αὐτῆς ἔστιν τὸ ἐπιδέκατον καὶ πάλιν ἔσται εἰς προνομὴν ὡς τερέβινθος καὶ ὡς βάλανος ὅταν ἐκπέσῃ ἀπὸ τῆς θήκης αὐτῆς). In this pericope, τερέβινθος represents אלה, and βάλανος represents אלון.

At Hos 4:13 we read: "They sacrifice on the mountaintops and burn offerings on the hills, under oak, poplar and terebinth, where the shade is pleasant. Therefore your daughters turn to prostitution and your daughters-in-law to adultery" (ἐπὶ τὰς κορυφὰς τῶν ὀρέων ἐθυσίαζον καὶ ἐπὶ τοὺς βουνοὺς ἔθυον ὑποκάτω δρυὸς καὶ λεύκης καὶ δένδρου συσκιάζοντος ὅτι καλὸν σκέπη διὰ τοῦτο ἐκπορνεύσουσιν αἱ θυγατέρες ὑμῶν καὶ αἱ νύμφαι ὑμῶν μοιχεύσουσιν). In this sentence, δρῦς represents אלון, λεύκη represents לבנה, and δένδρον represents אלה.

---

85. See the chapter dealing with Beer-sheba and the information on the subject of the tamarisk there.

86. *DCH*, 1:288, 296, and also 212 with the entries referring to the names of people and places.

87. *Ibid.*, 288; cf. Koehler-Baumgartner, *s.v.*

88. Gen 12:6; 13:18; 14:13; 18:1; Deut 11:30; Judg^A 4:11; 6:11, 19; 9:37; 1 Sam 10:3; 2 Sam 18:9, 10, 14; 1 Chr 10:12; 13:14; Hos 4:13 and Amos 2:9.

89. Gen 35:8; Judg 9:6; Isa 2:13; 6:13.

The Occurrence of the Nouns אַלּוֹן, אֵלוֹן
and their Versions in the LXX and Vulgate

אֵלוֹן[90]			אַלּוֹן[91]		
Gen 35:8	Βάλανον	*Quercus Fletus*	Gen 12:6	Δρῦς	*Convalle*
1 Chr 4:37	Αλλων	*Allon*	Gen 13:18	Δρῦς	*Convalle*
Isa 2:13	Δένδρον βαλάνου Βασαν	*Quercus Basan*	Gen 14:13	Δρῦς	*Convalle*
Isa 6:13	Βάλανος	*Quercus*	Gen 18:1	Δρῦς	*Convalle*
Isa 44:14	Δρυμου ὁ εφύτευσεν κύριος	*Quercus*	Gen 46:14	Αλλων	*Helon*
Ezek 27:6	Βασανίτιδος	*Quercus Basan*	Num 26:26	Αλλων	*Helon*
Hos 4:13	Δρῦς	*Quercus*	Deut 11:30	Δρῦς	*Valle*
Amos 2:9	Δρῦς	*Quercus*	Josh 19:30	Μωλα	*Helon*
Zech 11:2	Δρύες της Βασανίτιδος	*Quercus Basan*	Judg 4:11	Δρῦς	*Valle sennim*
			Judg 9:6	Βαλάνω	*Quercus*
			Judg 9:37	Ηλωνμαωνενιμ	*Quercus*
			Judg 12:12	Αιλωμ	*Ahialon*
			1 Sam 10:3	Δρῦς	*Quercus*

We can also see the extent of the complications associated with Hebrew tree names and their equivalents in ancient translations by showing what forms were translated as "terebinthus" in the Vulgate:

"Terebinth" in the Vulgate

Gen 35:4	הָאֵלָה	Τερέμινθον τὴν ἐν Σικιμοις
Gen 43:11	בָּטְנִים	Τερέμινθος
1 Sam 17:2	בְּעֵמֶק הָאֵלָה	Κοιλάδι αὐτοὶ Παρατάσσονται
1 Sam 17:19	בְּעֵמֶק הָאֵלָה	(none)
1 Sam 21:9	בְּעֵמֶק הָאֵלָה	Κοιλάδι Ηλα
1 Kgs 13:14	הָאֵלָה	Δρῦς
Sir 24:22	(none)	Τερέμινθος (Sir 24:16)
Hos 4:13	אֵלָה	Δένδρον
Isa 6:13	אֵלָה	Τερέμινθος

90. *DCH*, 1:288, translates this as "oak."

91. *DCH*, 1:288, translates this as "terebinth." *DCH* supplies a separate entry for the proper name—Elon, son of Zebulon (Gen 46:14; Num 26:26; Judg 12:11, 12). In Josh 19:33 it is written variously, depending on the manuscript.

The testimony of the LXX and the differences in the words signifying "terebinth" and "oak," which, as just noted, stem from the application of different diacritic signs, makes it plausible that the contrast between the two types of tree is merely a problem created by contemporary scholars.[92] I suspect that there is no way of establishing which of these trees the authors of the biblical texts had in mind. That is why it is acceptable to treat both forms as textual variants. The comparison of Hos 4:13 and Isa 6:13, where the term אלון appears coupled with אלה, as well as the confusion of the descriptions in the LXX allows us to acknowledge that both names belong within the same semantic field denoting "a holy tree." The use of different names results from a consistent adoption of MT whereas the original biblical text may not have contained any such distinction.[93]

During my discussion of the aetiology of Beer-sheba I drew attention to the significance of tamarisk (אשל, Gen 21:33). The story about the origins of Mamre provides further material giving us food for thought about the religious significance of trees and the symbolism associated with them. Genesis 13:18 mentions that Abraham went to live in the "oak grove" (באלני)[94] of Mamre. The oak grove is also a place of theophany (Gen 18:1). The noun אלון in the sense of "oak" appears also in Gen 12:6 and Judg 9:6 in association with the name of the place Shechem; in Judg 9:37 as the "diviner's oak" (אלון מעוננים); in Gen 35:8 as "the oak of weeping" (אלון בכות), the place of Deborah's burial in the vicinity of Bethel; in Judg 4:11 as the "Oak of Zaanannim" (אלון בצענים [בצעננים]), associated with the Kenites and in 1 Sam 10:3 as "the oak of Tabor" (אלון תבור), next to which Saul was to meet three men. As this shows, in biblical tradition trees mark places of burial and holy places where altars, for example, are found. Trees are also associated with soothsaying and divination. There are several descriptions of theophanies beneath trees. The act of theophany experienced by Abraham completes the picture of Mamre:

> The Lord appeared again to Abraham while he was camped near the oak grove belonging to Mamre. One day about noon, as Abraham was sitting at the entrance to his tent, he suddenly noticed three men standing nearby. He got up and ran to meet them, welcoming them by bowing low to the ground. "My lord," he said, "if it pleases you, stop here for a while." (Gen 18:1-3)

---

92. Cf. Frazer, *Folk-Lore*, 3:51 n. 3; the author contends that one should follow the ancient translations and in the places where doubt exist render it as "oak."

93. U. Cassuto, *A Commentary on the Book of Genesis*, Jerusalem, 1964, 2:325-26.

94. See Gen 14:13.

This fragment has proved very troublesome to commentators since vv. 1 and 3 leave no doubt that we are dealing with one person, whereas v. 2 explicitly speaks of three men (שְׁלֹשָׁה אֲנָשִׁים). Basing his view on a later tradition, Frazer accepts the epiphany of a god in three persons.[95]

Later in the story of Abraham's visitation by the three men there is mention of a meal prepared for them. We have, then, a picture of Mamre with an altar built by Abraham and a feast shared with three men who are identified with god.[96] The story of the three אֲנָשִׁים invited to a feast by Abraham is described also in the *Genesis Apocryphon* (21:21-22). The following sentence appears just after a fragment which is the equivalent of Gen 13:18: "and I sent an invitation to Mamre, Arnem, and Eshcol, the three Amorite brothers, (who were) my friends; and they ate together with me and drank with me."[97] It emerges from this text that Abraham raised an altar, thereby sanctifying the place, and afterwards invited his friends to a feast whose nature is not known, though one may assume that a certain ritual is involved. The apocryphal text, apart from the reference to the friendship between the Anakites and Abraham, emphasises their participation in an event that explains the circumstances of the creation of a cult place (*Genesis Apocryphon* 22:5-8). The canonical biblical book informs us only that Mamre, Eshcol and Aner were friends of Abraham (Gen 14:13, 24). Unfortunately, it is impossible to establish whether the original story talked of the Anakites or of supernatural creatures. I would be inclined to accept the primary nature of the apocryphal text. In such a case, the feast belongs to the ritual associated with raising an altar (in other words, marking out a holy place).[98] I suspect that it was only later that the two motifs were conflated: that of the theophany (hence the divine person) and that of the feast with the participation of the three guests.

Mamre, being an ancient town with a sacred tree growing there that symbolised the *axis mundi*, was an image of the centre of the world where the cosmic spheres—heaven, earth and the underworld—met, and where, so it was believed, visions of a divinity could be seen. We need, therefore, to consider whether the theophany described in Gen 18:1-5

95. Frazer, *Folk-Lore*, 3:58.

96. Cf. P. Xella, "L'Episode de Dnil et Kothar (*KTU* 1. 17 [= *CTA* 17] v 1-31) et Gen. XVIII 1-6," *VT* 28 (1978): 483-88, who tries to show an analogy between the Ugaritic text and the Bible story; the hosting and provision of a meal to a god is, according to him, a common Mediterranean mythic motif (484-85).

97. J.A. Fitzmyer, *The Genesis Apocryphon of Qumran Cave I: A Commentary*, Rome, 1966, 71.

98. An analogy can be found in the story of Jacob and Laban in Galeed (Gen 31:54); see the section dealing with Galeed.

was of a uranic or a chthonic nature since the space around the cosmic axis could be a place of visitation by gods of heaven and gods of the underworld equally.

To resolve this question, it is essential first and foremost to establish the function ascribed to trees in the Bible. Mario Liverani claims that the burials of Deborah and Rachel beneath trees have something to do with necromancy.[99] As has already been stated, trees have indeed often been determinants of burial places. Furthermore, the association of trees with the practices mentioned earlier could also indicate the existence there of a cult of gods of the underworld since Sheol—the land of the dead—is their domain. We can therefore assume that necromancy is associated with a cult of a chthonic nature whose occurrence is also indicated by the symbolism of the tamarisk. We also have to remember that the custom, described by Sozomen, of throwing sacrifices into a well in Mamre is unequivocal evidence of the persistence of a chthonic cult at this location.

The cult of El was also associated with a holy tree, a fact which is indicated by the etymological colligation—אל and אלון—and also by the explicitly expressed relationship of this god with sanctuaries near holy trees (El-Shaddai in Hebron, El-Berith in Shechem).[100]

The Bible also links the presence of trees with divination: the Palm of Deborah (Judg 4:5) and "diviners' oak" (Judg 9:37) are the best evidence of this. Unfortunately, we know too little about the divinatory practices of the ancient Hebrews to state authoritatively what character they had.[101] The episode of the woman from En-dor summoning the spirit of Samuel confirms the existence of necromantic practices (1 Sam 28:3-25).[102] Roland de Vaux mentions the function performed in mystery cults by Ogyges—a figure from Greek mythology—whose name, we may recall, was used by Josephus in naming the tree in Mamre.[103]

---

99.   Liverani, "Le Chêne de Sherdanu," 213.

100.   *Ibid.*, 216.

101.   Giovanni Garbini is of the view that oracles, closely associated with judging, were an institution emanating from the cult of the powers of the world of the dead; see Garbini, *Note di lessicografia ebraica*, 130-35, 152-63.

102.   B.B. Schmidt, "The 'Witch' of En-Dor, 1 Sam. 28, and Ancient Near Eastern Necromancy," in M. Meyer and P. Mirecki (eds.), *Ancient Magic and Ritual Power*, Leiden, 1995, 111-29; *idem, Israel's Beneficent Dead: Ancestor Cult and Necromancy in Ancient Israelite Religion and Tradition*, Tübingen, 1994; cf. a somewhat different appraisal of necromancy and of the text of 1 Sam 28 in F. Cryer, *Divination in Ancient Israel and its Near Eastern Environment: A Socio-Historical Investigation*, JSOTSup 142, Sheffield, 1994, 230.

103.   De Vaux, *Ancient Israel*, 2:292-93.

My own view is that all the available data relating to religious practices and the symbolism of trees point to their association with the
underworld rather than the celestial sphere. It can be supposed that both
the theophanies near trees and the predictions associated with trees reveal
a belief in the sacral nature of the underworld. Chthonic gods, then,
appeared near oaks and questions were asked to the dead during divination. If that really is the case, then it was surely the chthonic nature of
the cult in Mamre that became a factor spurring on the editors of the
Bible in their efforts to marginalise the significance of this centre.

The considerations set out above justify, in my opinion, the need to
find an etymology for the name "Mamre" other than the one hitherto
proposed. The divinatory nature of trees, and particularly the acknowledgment that a holy tree was a place of contact with a god and, consequently, of a theophany beneath the trees—all this may suggest the
name "Mamre" is derived not from the root מרא, but from the root ראה,
"to see," "to look," and the noun formed from it. If this were the case,
מראה would refer to a "vision."[104] The tree of Mamre would, then, be
thoroughly divinatory,[105] and the theophanies occurring beneath it would
be ascribed to it by definition.

The discovery at Hebron of traces of a Dionysian cult and the obvious
etymological/semantic link of the toponym "Eshkol" with the word
"wine" lead us to consider the circumstances in which worship of the
Greek god assuredly began there. If the Hellenistic period saw a development of the local religiousness merely dressed in Greek robes, then we
could attempt to describe the original form of the cult in Mamre on the
basis of Dionysian cult practised there. The cult of Dionysus, the nature
of which was often mystical, contained all the elements which the biblical tradition ascribes to trees: the presence of an oracle, the sanctification of wine, evident chthonic connotations (the god who went down
to Hades). Several not mutually exclusive causes probably defined its
particular place in the religion of Hebron during the Hellenistic period.[106]
The mere fact that this area was an important centre of wine-making was
sufficient reason for the cult of the god of wine to flourish there during
the Hellenistic period. It is probable that the original cult in Mamre had
further elements in common with the Dionysian cult, evidence of which

104.   Cf., e.g., Num 12:6; Ezek 11:24.
105.   Corresponding to this name is the "diviners' oak" (אלון מעוננים), near
Shechem, mentioned in Judg 9:37.
106.   The rather modest archaeological finds do not allow us to form an unequivocal view.

would be the name of the tree supplied by Flavius mentioned earlier—Ogyges—which just happens to be the name of the father of Cadmos, grandfather of Dionysius. The naming of the oak "Ogyges"—insofar as it was not accidental—allows us to deduce that we are dealing here with traces of a mystery ceremony or the existence of an oracle. The people of Hebron could also discover in Dionysius some traits of the Idumean god Qos who was worshipped there.[107]

Another important element of the Hebron mythology is linked to its role as a capital—the town being David's first headquarters. According to Eduard Nielsen, the Mamrc oak fulfilled a religious function at the enthronement of David (2 Sam 2:1-4) and the oath made to him by the Israelite elders (2 Sam 5:3).[108] The mythical and ritual complex of concepts associated with Hebron-Mamre, and especially the crucial role of the tree, may be explained (or complemented) by a strange story in 2 Samuel. Most significant is the following fragment:

> Now Absalom happened to meet David's men. He was riding his mule, and as the mule went under the thick branches of a large oak, Absalom's head got caught in the tree. He was left hanging in midair (lit. between heaven and earth), while the mule he was riding kept on going. When one of the men saw this, he told Joab, "I just saw Absalom hanging in an oak tree." Joab said to the man who had told him this, "What! You saw him? Why didn't you strike him to the ground right there? Then I would have had to give you ten shekels of silver and a warrior's belt." But the man replied, "Even if a thousand shekels were weighed out into my hands, I would not lift my hand against the king's son. In our hearing the king commanded you and Abishai and Ittai, 'Protect the young man Absalom for my sake.' And if I had put my life in jeopardy—and nothing is hidden from the king—you would have kept your distance from me." Joab said, "I'm not going to wait like this for you." So he took three javelins in his hand and plunged them into Absalom's heart while Absalom was still alive in the oak tree. And ten of Joab's armour-bearers surrounded Absalom, struck him and killed him. (2 Sam 18:9-15)

This puzzling fragment conceals, it seems, certain information associated with a cult and with mythic imaginings. Absalom dies at the hands of ten servants—which is consonant with the whole story. And yet, earlier, when hanging in the tree, he receives three javelin blows to his heart. He dies, therefore, in two ways which cannot be reconciled in one story. This whole story can be interpreted literally, as the description of a

---

107. One shared attribute, for example, was command over the animal kingdom.
108. E. Nielsen, *Shechem: A Traditio-Historical Investigation*, Copenhagen, 1955, 221-22.

battle and the factual circumstances of Absalom's death, or it can tempt one to offer a different explanation. Suspended "between heaven and earth," the king's son dies from three blows to the heart. The tiny probability of such a scene being played out in circumstances of reality conflicts with its popularity in the world of myth. Jesus, suspended "between heaven and earth," dies for humankind.[109] By analogy to the passion of Jesus, the description of Absalom's death can be interpreted as a remnant of a mythical motif presenting a dying god/king. This explanation seems even more likely when we realise that the name of the king's son who is dying on the tree is Absalom (אבשלום), which means "[his] father [is] Shalim." So, what we have here is the death of a god's son.[110]

The holy tree—the axis of the cosmos located in the middle of the world—could have suggested to the Hebrews' mythical thinking a transference of esoteric knowledge accessible only by means of revelation or initiation. Following this track, we discover the complexity of the cult practised in Mamre. The tree that grew there not only illustrated the cosmic axis, but also symbolised a source of knowledge accessible to a very few, exclusively by way of initiations into the mystery.

The myths associated with the sanctuary in Mamre reveal various beliefs and rituals linked with it. The holy tree marks the central spot where the various cosmic spheres touch, thanks to which a theophany is possible. The biblical account of the epiphany of the three men in Mamre contains the trace of a sacral feast and the experience of a theophany associated with necromancy. In the myth about the genesis of the holy place, the demarcation of a sacred area is established by building an altar and providing a feast to honour a divinity. The symbolism of the trees and the proximity of the graves of the patriarchs indicate that the god worshipped in Mamre was undoubtedly associated with the underworld. The vitality of the chthonic cult, we may recall, has been evidenced as late by Sozomen in his *Ecclesiastic History* (II.4).

---

109.   It is not out of place to mention here the piercing of Jesus' side with a spear; see Eliade, *Patterns in Comparative Religion*, 276-78, 292-94.

110.   For more about the god Shelim/Shalim, see the chapter about Ophrah, Chapter 6.

6.
Ophrah

The location of Ophrah is not known.[1] The book of Joshua (18:23) mentions a place of that name among the towns belonging to the tribe of Benjamin; it could apply to the present-day town of et-Taiyebeh, north-east of Bethcl. Another possibility suggests the place situated in the territories belonging to Manasseh—in the valley of Jezreel between Megiddo and Mt Tabor. An attempt has also been made to locate Gideonite Ophrah in present-day 'Affuleh in the valley of Jezreel.[2] Ernst Axel Knauf, in turn, has suggested that the biblical Ophrah is Jinsâfût.[3]

The Bible provides only very modest snippets of information concerning Ophrah (עפרה). Apart from the book of Judges (to be discussed shortly), we read about Ophrah in Josh 18:23 and 1 Sam 13:17. The Ophrah mentioned in these two verses is usually identified with the already mentioned et-Taiyibeh, which lies some 7 km north-east of Bethel. This would mean that its location was between the territories occupied by the tribes of Benjamin and of Ephraim.[4] That would make it different to the place mentioned in the story of Gideon. 1 Chronicles 4:14 uses the term "Ophrah" (עפרה) to denote the proper name of a person from the generation of Judah.[5] Another biblical reference which could help to extend our knowledge of Ophrah's whereabouts is Mic 1:10: "Tell it not in Gath; weep not at all. In Beth Ophrah (בית לע פרה) roll in the dust." The LXX text does not make it any easier to resolve whether or not this means Ophrah when it says: οἱ ἐν Γεθ, μὴ μεγαλύνεσθε, οἱ ἐν

1. J. Simons, *The Geographical and Topographical Texts of the Old Testament*, Leiden, 1959, 291, §561.
2. J.M. Hamilton, *ABD*, *s.v.* "Ophra."
3. E.A. Knauf, "Eglon and Ophrah: Two Toponymic Notes on the Book of Judges," *JSOT* 51 (1991): 25-44 (34-39).
4. Driver, *Notes on the Hebrew Text*, 102.
5. According to the genealogy in 1 Chr 4:1-14, עפרה was the grandson of Othniel, son of Kenaz, descendant of Caleb, also mentioned in Judg 3:7-11.

Ακιμ, μὴ ἀνοικοδομεῖτε ἐξ οἴκου κατὰ γέλωτα, γῆν καταπάσασθε κατὰ γέλωτα ὑμῶν. The section Mic 1:10-16 is considered the most opaque and the most corrupted text of the whole book; its Hebrew version is very poorly preserved.[6] It is noteworthy that this passage uses the noun עפר, signifying "dust"—in other words, the noun used derives from the same root as the proper name "Ophrah." Regardless of the textual difficulties, we must remember that Mic 1:10 is part of the prophecies directed against the towns of Judah. Biblical references to Ophrah point to three different parts of Palestine: the aetiological story of the altar—as we shall see—points to the lands of Manasseh; Josh 18:23 and 1 Sam 13:17 suggest some place in Benjamin's purlieu (et-Taiyibeh?); 1 Chr 4:14 and assuredly Mic 1:10 link the name with Judah.

Aetiology

Judges 6:11-32:[7]

> (11) The angel of the Lord (מלאך יהוה)[8] came and sat down under the oak in Ophrah that belonged to Joash the Abiezrite, where his son Gideon was threshing wheat in a wine press to keep it from the Midianites. (12) When the angel of the Lord appeared to Gideon, he said, "The Lord is with you,[9] mighty warrior." (13) "But sir," Gideon replied, "if the Lord is with us, why has all this happened to us? Where are all his wonders that our fathers told us about when they said, 'Did not the Lord bring us up out of Egypt?' But now the Lord has abandoned us and put us into the hand of Midian." (14) The Lord turned to him and said, "Go in the strength you have and save Israel out of Midian's hand. Am I not sending you?" (15) "But Lord (אדני)," Gideon asked, "how can I save Israel? My clan is the weakest in Manasseh, and I am the least in my family." (16) The Lord answered, "I will be with you, and you will strike down all the Midianites together." (17) Gideon replied, "If now I have found favour in your eyes, give me a sign that it is really you talking to me. (18) Please do not go away until I come back and bring my offering (מנחה), and set it before you." And the Lord said, "I will wait until you return." (19) Gideon went in, prepared a

6. D.R. Hillers, *ABD*, *s.v.* "Micah, Book of."

7. The italicised fragments in vv. 25-32 follow the original text in the version suggested by A. de Pury, "Le raid de Gédéon (Juges 6,25-32) et l'histoire de l'exclusivisme yahwiste," in T. Römer (ed.), *Lectio Difficilior Probabilior? L'exegèse comme expérience de décloisonnement. Mélanges offerts à Françoise Smyth-Florentin*, Heidelberg, 1991, 181.

8. Cross, *Canaanite Myth*, 252 is of the view that the term "angel of Yahweh" is a typical deuteronomistic turn of phrase.

9. The LXX reads κύριος μετὰ σοῦ. This is analogous to Gen 26:28; 1 Sam 17:37; 20:13; 2 Sam 7:3; 1 Chr 22:16, and also in the annunciation scene in Luke 1:28.

young goat, and from an ephah of flour he made bread without yeast.
Putting the meat in a basket and its broth in a pot, he brought them out and
offered them to him under the oak. (20) The angel of God (מלאך האלהים)
said to him, "Take the meat and the unleavened bread, place them on this
rock, and pour out the broth." And Gideon did so. (21) With the tip of the
staff that was in his hand, the angel of the Lord touched the meat and the
unleavened bread. Fire flared from the rock, consuming the meat and the
bread. And the angel of the Lord disappeared. (22) When Gideon realised
that it was the angel of the Lord, he exclaimed, "Ah, Sovereign Lord
(אדני יהוה)! I have seen the angel of the Lord face to face (פנים
אל־פנים)!"[10] (23) But the Lord said to him, "Peace![11] Do not be afraid.
You are not going to die." (24) So Gideon built an altar to the Lord there
and called it The Lord is Peace. To this day it stands in Ophrah of the
Abiezrites. (25) *That same night the Lord said to him, "Take a bull from
your father's herd*, and a second that is seven years old.[12] *Tear down your
father's altar to Baal* and cut down the Asherah pole (האשרה) beside it.
(26) Then build a proper kind of altar to the Lord your God (ליהוה
אלהיך)[13] on the top of this height (האשרה).[14] Using the wood of the
Asherah pole that you cut down, offer the second bull as a burnt offering."
(27) *So Gideon took ten men from among his servants and did as the* LORD
*told him. But because he was afraid of his father's household family and
the citizens of the town, he did it at night rather than in the daytime.* (28)
*In the morning when the citizens of the town got up, there was Baal's
altar, demolished*, with the pole beside it cut down and the second bull
sacrificed on the newly built altar! (29) *They asked each other, "Who did
this?" When they carefully investigated, they said, "Gideon son of Joash
did it."* (30) *Then the citizen of the town demanded of Joash, "Bring out
your son. He must die, because he has broken down Baal's altar* and cut
down the pole (האשרה) beside it." (31) *But Joash replied to those who*

10. A similar conjunction appears in Gen 32:31; Exod 33:11; Deut 34:10; Ezek
20:35.

11. The LXX reads εἰρήνη σοι, as does the greeting at the end of 3 John (1:15).
See also the LXX versions of Judg 19:20; 1 Sam 20:21; 1 Chr 12:19; 2 Chr 4:26; Dan
10:19.

12. The information about the second bull has created difficulties for interpreters;
see D. Rudman, "The Second Bull in Judges 6: 25-28," *Journal of Northwest Semitic
Languages* 26 (2000): 97-103, where he concludes that the sacrifice of the second
bull was one of asking forgiveness for committed sins.

13. A turn of phrase which is typical of Deuteronomy. In the whole of the
Hebrew Bible it appears 259 times: 198 times in Deuteronomy, nine times in Exodus
(chiefly in chs. 20 and 34), four times in Joshua (chs. 1 and 9), eleven times in 1 and
2 Samuel, eight times in 1 and 2 Kings, five times in 1 and 2 Chronicles, eight times
in Isaiah, seven times in Jeremiah, three times in Hosea, and once each in Genesis,
Judges, Psalms, Amos, Micah, Song of Songs.

14. This phrase's equivalent in the LXX is ἐπὶ κορυφὴ ν τοῦ Μαουεκ τούτου. LXX[A]
reads ἐπὶ τῆς κορυφῆς τοῦ ὄρους Μαωζ.

> *stood round him, "Are you going to fight for Baal or are you trying to save him?* Whoever fights for him shall be put to death by morning! *If Baal really is a god, let him fight for himself for it is his altar that has been broken."* (32) *So that day they called Gideon "Jerub-Baal* (ירבעל), *" saying, "Let Baal contend with him* (ירב בו הבעל), *because he demolished Baal's altar.*

The construction of the entire aetiological myth is clearly made up of two parts: vv. 11-24 form a story about a theophany and the building of an altar to Yahweh, and vv. 25-32 constitute a separate narrative partially reprising the previous one.[15]

The narrative written down in Judg 6:11-24 uses only the name Gideon. The "angel of the Lord" appears to the hero beneath the oak in Ophrah. This experience motivates him to build an altar, in other words to mark out a sanctified place.

The story contained within Judg 6:25-32 includes not only the founding myth which tells us about the erection of an altar to Yahweh, but also about the origins of the name "Jerubbaal." Judges 6:25 emphasises that the epiphany took place at night. Similar epiphanies are described in Gen 26:24 (Isaac); Judg 7:9 (Gideon); 2 Sam 7:4 (Nathan); 2 Chr 7:12 (Solomon). We can categorise all nocturnal experiences of "the word of God" as epiphanies during sleep.[16] The story under discussion has brought together two traditional currents, and hence the theme of a waking epiphany (Judg 6:11) and the sleeping epiphany (Judg 6:25); hence also v. 24 talks of erecting an altar beneath an oak and straight afterwards tells colourfully of the destruction of the altar to Baal and the building of a fresh one, along with a sacrifice, to Yahweh.

Herbert Haag has posited the hypothesis that, initially, there was a story about Ophrah (Judg 6:11-24). Its hero was Gideon. In time, a second story arose, and its hero was Jerubbaal; this story took place in a place whose name is not mentioned. Finally, the history of Gideon was joined to the themes of the story about Jerubbaal and Abimelech.[17] Though critical of this theory, Emerson admits that the Judg 6:25-32 fragment does not mention the name "Ophrah," only the term "town."[18] Haag sees in the Judg 6–9 section the coming together of the story of Gideon, founder of the holy place in Ophrah and hammer of the Midianites, with the story of Jerubbaal and Abimelech, strongly linked with

---

15. Cf. C.F. Whitley, "The Sources of the Gideon Stories," *VT* 7 (1957): 157-64 (158); de Vaux, *Ancient Israel*, 2:306; de Pury, "Le raid de Gédéon," 173-205.

16. Cryer, *Divination in Ancient Israel*, 263-72.

17. H. Haag, "Gideon—Jerubbaal—Abimelek," *ZAW* 79 (1967): 305-14.

18. J.A. Emerson, "Gideon and Jerubbaal," *JTS* NS 27 (1976): 292-93.

Shechem. Emerton rejects the theory of two heroes and claims that there is insufficient evidence for the arguments claiming the separateness of the figures of Gideon and Jerubbaal.[19]

A brief summary of the appearance of the names of these four figures will allow us to draw certain conclusions. Gideon and Joash appear alongside one another in five places (Judg 6:11, 29; 7:14; 8:13, 32); Jerubbaal and Joash appear once only (Judg 8:29);[20] and Jerubbaal and Abimelech appear five times (Judg 9:1, 16, 19, 24, 28). Not once is there a mention of the pairing of Gideon–Abimelech.[21]

Taking the above into account as well as the fact that the identification of the figure of Jerubbaal with Gideon is expressed explicitly only in Judg 7:1 and 8:35, in other words in places which bear traces of later editing,[22] we can agree with Haag that the story contained in Judg 6–9 is a compilation of at least two collections of stories related to different figures and almost certainly different places: Gideon, son of Joash, linked with Ophrah,[23] and Jerubbaal and his son Abimelech, acclaimed the king of Shechem.

Researchers have tried to indicate not only that Joash had royal power but also that Gideon-Jerubbaal was a king.[24] Accepting that Gideon was a king whose power extended also into Shechem would explain the story about anointing Abimelech king of Shechem (Judg 9).

We can, then, accept that Judg 6:11-24 is a narrative about the calling of Gideon and the erection of an altar in Ophrah, whereas vv. 25-32 relate to Jerubbaal and events that explain not so much the origins of the Yahweh altar as the genesis of the name "Jerubbaal."

The basic problem, however, is how to establish the location of Ophrah, the place where this whole history of Gideon was supposed to have been played out.

The Hebrew name "Ophrah" (עפרה) is conveyed by the LXX as Εφραθα and Γοφερα (1 Sam 13:17). The term Εφραθα corresponds not

---

19. *Ibid.*, 309-10.

20. "Jerub-Baal son of Joash went back home to live"; there is no mention of Jerubbaal living in Ophrah.

21. Only in Judg 8:30-32 is their relationship mentioned, though the mention of Abimelech (v. 31) appears to be an interpolation.

22. Emerton, "Gideon," admits that the use of these two very different names is the strongest argument in favour of distinguishing the two figures from each other.

23. Haag, "Gideon," is prepared to reject any link between Gideon and Ophrah, claiming that information on it is a later interpolation; see the discussion of this hypothesis in Emerton, "Gideon," 303 and 310-11.

24. For an extended analysis and statement of Gideon's royal powers, see *ibid.*, 295-99.

only to the name "Ophrah" but also to "Ephrath(ah)," אפרת(ה) (Gen
35:16, 19; 48:7; Ruth 4:11; Ps [131]132:6; 1 Chr 2:24, 50; Mic 5:1). The
text of Josh 15:59 is more extensive in the LXX than in the MT, and there
are in Josh 18:23 two traditions of writing the name: Εφραθα and Αφρα.
Obadiah 20 presents a different version; the Greek name Εφραθα corresponds to the Hebrew *hapax legomenon* ספרד,²⁵ which is rendered in the
Vulgate as "Bosphor." Instead of the name "Ophrah" in Judg 8:27, LXXᴬ
puts "Ephraim."²⁶ The original text of the aetiology of Ophrah, reconstructed by de Pury, contains no topographical references or any information about Gideon's tribal affiliation.

The only indications linking Gideon and Ophrah with Manasseh are to
be found in Judg 6:15 and in references to Gideon's descent from Joash,
son of Abiezer.

Robert Boling unequivocally concludes that the formulations emphasising Gideon's descent from Abiezer—"that belonged to Joash the
Abiezrite" (v. 11),²⁷ "to this day it stands in Ophrah of the Abiezrites"
(v. 24)—were later interpolations.²⁸ The figure of Abiezer of the tribe of
Manasseh does not have deep roots in the Bible. There are two people in
the Bible bearing that name: Abiezer, son of Gilead and descendant of
Machir (Josh 17:2; 1 Chr 7:18), and the Benjaminite from Anathoth, one
of David' warriors (2 Sam 23:27; 1 Chr 11:28; 27:12).²⁹ The former is
mentioned in late books (Joshua and 1 Chronicles), whereas the latter in
a much earlier one. Originally, therefore, there must have existed a history of the Benjaminite Abiezer, of his son Joash and grandson Gideon;
the identification of Abiezer, grandfather of Gideon, with a descendant of
Manasseh came only later. It is possible that the Benjaminite Abiezer
was linked to an Ophrah located in territories belonging to the tribe of
Benjamin.

In the aetiology itself only the text of Judg 6:15 suggests a link
between Gideon and Manasseh: "My clan is the weakest in Manasseh,
and I am the least in my family." In the whole story of the deeds of
Gideon it is also noted in Judg 6:35 and 7:23.³⁰ Yet only v. 15 contains
an evident genealogical suggestion describing Gideon's tribal affiliation.

25. BDB, *s.v.*
26. Cf. Boling, *Judges*, 160.
27. Emerton ("Gideon," 310) drew attention to the fact that in v. 11 it is not
Ophrah which is linked to Abiezer but only Joash.
28. Boling, *Judges*, 134.
29. Cf. D.G. Schley, *ABD*, *s.v.* "Abiezer."
30. Judg 6:35 names the descendants of Manasseh, Asher, Zebulun and Naphthali, and Judg 7:23 names those of Naphthali, Asher and Manasseh.

The phrase about the youngest son in this verse could be evidence of an interpolation.

In the MT the name Gideon appears only in the book of Judges. The Hebrew form corresponds to the Greek Γεδεων and the Latin *Gedeon*. The Vulgate records the name of the father of Abidan (אבידן) in this very way in Num 1:11; 2:22; 7:60, 65; 10:24. The Gideon mentioned in the book of Numbers comes from the tribe of Benjamin. In the MT we have the phrase "son of Gideon" (בן־גדעוני), the name being given as Γαδεωνι in the LXX. The name of his son, the Benjaminite Abidan, signifies "my father [is a] judge."[31] It is not possible to establish whether or not it originally referred to the same figure. If it did, then it would be another clue linking Gideon with the tribe of Benjamin.

Γεδεων / Gideon appears in the genealogy of Judith (Jdt 8:1) as a Simeonite; he is also mentioned in the Epistle to the Hebrews (Heb 11:32).

The name "Joash" (יואש – Ιωας = Ioas) is given to eight people in the Bible: the father of Gideon, one king of Judah (ninth century BCE) and one king of Israel (eighth century BCE), the son of Ahab, king of Israel (ninth century BCE), a servant of David and also one descendant of Judah (1 Chr 4:22) and two Benjaminites (1 Chr 7:8; 12:3). A statistical analysis would reveal that this name appeared most frequently in the south of Palestine.

It is not possible, however, to draw any conclusions about the origin or tribal affiliation of Gideon on the basis of the context in which this name, as also the names Joash and Abiezer, appear in the Bible. This means that proclaiming Gideon as a Manassehite and locating Ophrah in the territories occupied by that tribe is done on the basis of the contents of just one verse.

In my view, it is possible to show that the toponym "Ophrah" (עפרה), describing the scene of the story about the building by Gideon of an altar to Yahweh, is an artificial creation, one that is not a factual indication that the settlement existed in territories belonging to Manasseh. If the details of the location of the story's action had been real, then Ophrah would have had to have been a large town with a fortress inside the walls or rather just next to the city-walls. The truth is, however, that none of the remains discovered in the area belonging to the tribe of Manasseh meet such conditions. Therefore, the search of Gideon's Ophrah should be concentrated outside the territories of Manasseh. Taking into account the likelihood of profound interference in the text written down in the book of Judges and the conflation resulting from it of the figures of

31. D.F. Laundeville, *ABD*, *s.v.* "Gideoni (person)."

Jerubbaal and Gideon, we can posit the hypothesis that Gideon's Ophrah is identical with the place Ephrathah, or Bethlehem.[32]

In the Hebrew text the difference between the name עפרה and אפרתה comes down to just the first letter. This discrepancy can be explained on philological grounds. The name אפרתה probably derives from the noun אפר, signifying "ash," "dust."[33] The root אפר is not found in the Bible. The name עפרה is derived from the reconstructed root עפר II: the root עפר I signifies "sprinkling with ash," and the noun עפר derived from it has the meanings "ash," "dust," "earth." There is, therefore, a complete semantic correlation of the roots עפר and אפר. What we cannot clarify is whether these roots functioned interchangeably, hence the differences in toponym. In Mishnaic Hebrew, an exchange of the first root letter *aleph* and *ayin* can be seen. We should assume that this difference in the toponyms' written forms, while retaining their similarity, resulted from editorial intent and not a phonetic phenomenon.

A further argument in favour of such a thesis is the identical transliteration of these names into Greek. The LXX gives Εφραθα for both עפרה and אפרתה, which indicates not only the link between toponyms, but also the dating of the editorial interference in the MT which caused their differentiation.

Josephus in *Antiquities* omits the motif of the building of an altar to Yahweh by Gideon and, in describing his wars with the Midianites, mentions the name of the family place: Ἐφρὰν (5.229-32). He uses the same term as a variant of the name Ephraim (2.180; 5.83, 130, 136, 267), and also to indicate the town founded by one of the sons of Abraham and Keturah (1.15.1).

Sefer ha-Yamim omits the entire aetiology of Ophrah and gives only the information (without a mention of Jerubbaal) that Gideon, bearing the title of king, met God's angel, conquered the Midianites and ruled for seven years.[34] After the successful battle he returned to אלון מורה—the oak of Moreh near Shechem, regarded by the Samaritans as the most important religious centre in Israel, and where his son Abimelech was king (Judg 9:1-6). As we can see, this is a more consistent story than the one written down in the book of Judges. A later tradition associated with Gideon brings no detailed information. *Liber Antiquitatum Biblicarum* contains the motif of the appearance of the angel of God who called on

---

32. That is the view of G. von Rad, *Genesis: A Commentary*, London, 1956. Cf. my article presenting the identification of Ophrah with Ephrata, based on this chapter: "Where to Look for Gideon's Ophra?," *Biblica* 86 (2005): 478-93.

33. Cf., e.g., Num 19:9, 10; 2 Sam 13:19; Job 13:12; Ps 102:10; Isa 44:20.

34. Macdonald (ed.), *The Samaritan Chronicle*, 104 (*39).

Gideon to fight the Midianites. The only reference associated with the aetiology of Ophrah is found in the summation of ch. 36, wherein v. 4 relates Gideon as saying that he had destroyed the altar to Baal. There is, however, no name given to the place.

Linguistic evidence allows us to accept the hypothesis of the close association, or even identity, of the places named "Ophrah" and "Ephrathah."

Ephrathah, on the road to which Rachel died (Gen 35:16, 19; 48:7) and where Ruth settled (Ruth 4:11), has been linked to Bethlehem.[35] This is explicitly expressed by two texts: "So Rachel died and was buried on the way to Ephrathah (that is, Bethlehem)" (Gen 35:19), and "But you, Bethlehem Ephrathah (בית־לחם אפרתה), though you are small among the clans of Judah, out of you will come for me one who will be ruler over Israel..." (Mic 5:2). The testimony of 1 Chr 2:19 supports locating Ephrathah in Judah. This is a fragment of the genealogy of the descendants of Judah which names Ephrath as the wife of Caleb who is strongly associated with the territories of southern Judah.[36] Psalm 132:6 points to the proximity of Ephrathah to Kiriat-Jearim, that is to say the boundary of the territories of Judah and Benjamin.[37] The association of Ephrathah with Judah, or the boundaries of Judah and Benjamin, is linked to the relocation of the grave of Rachel; this was originally situated within the territories of Benjamin and later moved deep into those of Judah.

The biblical text confirms the existence of some sort of sanctuary in Bethlehem. Arriving there to anoint David as king, Samuel says: "I have come to sacrifice to the Lord. Consecrate yourselves and come to the sacrifice with me" (1 Sam 16:5). Menahem Haran's view is that there was a familial sanctuary there.[38] He bases his thesis on an interpretation of two texts—Judg 19:18 and 1 Sam 20:6. The mention of a Levite travelling to Bethlehem is a weak argument, but the information in 1 Samuel provides sufficient material: "David earnestly asked my permission to hurry to Bethlehem, his home town, because an annual sacrifice is being made there for his whole clan" (1 Sam 20:6). The same information is repeated in 1 Sam 20:28-29: "David earnestly asked me for permission to go to Bethlehem. He said, 'Let me go, because our family is observing a sacrifice (זבח משפחה) in the town and my brother has ordered me to be

---

35. Cf. J. Briend, "Bethléem-Ephrata," *Le Monde de la Bible* 30 (1983): 29.

36. See also 1 Chr 4:14 and the mention of the Judahite Ophrah.

37. L.M. Luker, *ABD*, *s.v.* "Ephrathah," identifies Kiriat-Jearim with Tell el-Acher, which is situated some 10 km north of Jerusalem; cf. J.M. Hamilton, *ABD*, *s.v.* "Kiriat-Jearim (place)."

38. Haran, *Temples and Temple Service*, 34, 307-309.

there.'" Such annual sacrifices demanded, it would seem, a separate cult place, and though they were familial by nature, they took place in a marked sanctuary (compare the story of Elkanah and the sacrifices offered in Shiloh; 1 Sam 1). The biblical text, therefore, provides no arguments to make impossible the identification of Ophrah with Ephrathah/Bethlehem.

The phrases that identify Ephrathah with Bethlehem relate to the location of Rachel's tomb. The biblical story of her death and the birth of Benjamin reads as follows:

> Then they moved on from Bethel. While they were still some distance[39] from Ephrath, Rachel began to give birth and had great difficulty. And as she was having great difficulty in childbirth, the midwife said to her, "Don't be afraid, for you have another son." As she breathed her last—for she was dying—she named her son Ben-Oni. But his father named him Benjamin. So Rachel died and was buried on the way to Ephrath (that is, Bethlehem).[40] Over her tomb Jacob set up a pillar,[41] and to this day that pillar marks Rachel's tomb. Israel moved on again and pitched his tent beyond Migdal Eder. (Gen 35:16-21)

The location of Rachel's tomb is by no means obvious.[42] The place generally regarded as being the site of her burial is Ramat Rahel,[43] a place situated between Jerusalem and Bethlehem, in the territory of Judah. That, however, conflicts with the assumption that the place of Benjamin's birth should be on land belonging to that tribe, in other words, north of Jerusalem.

Conflicting with the account in Gen 35:16-21 are the testimonies provided by 1 Sam 10:2 and Jer 31:15, which locate Rachel's tomb in the land of Benjamin. Her tomb, within the territory of Benjamin or, more precisely, on its boundary, has been located in, among other places, the

---

39.   The word כברה used here is included by Tov, *The Greek and Hebrew Bible*, 509, in the group of words of unknown meaning; G. Garbini takes a different view and shows that this term is derived from the word ברה*, signifying a length of road travelled in the course of a two-day march; see Garbini, *Note di lessicografia ebraica*, 34-39.

40.   An analogous placement in Gen 48:7.

41.   MT: מצבה, LXX: στήλη, Vulgate: "titulus," *Vetus Latina*: "columna"; see also "column" in *Jubilees*.

42.   Simons, *Geographical and Topographical Texts*, 291, §383 and §§666-68.

43.   For reports on the excavations carried out at Ramat Rahel, see S. Moscati, A. Ciasca and G. Garbini, *Il Colle di Rachele (Ramat Rahel). Missione Archeologica nel Vicino Oriente*, Rome, 1960; Y. Aharoni *et al.*, *Excavations at Ramat Rahel: Seasons 1959 and 1960*, Rome, 1962; *Excavations at Ramat Rahel: Seasons 1961 and 1962*, Rome, 1964; see also R.W. Younker, *ABD*, *s.v.* "Ramat Rahel."

vicinity of Kirbet-Jearim;[44] this would appear logical in view of the fact that Rachel's death took place at Benjamin's place of birth. It would be strange if the eponymous hero was not born on territory that later belonged to his descendants but in some other area.

The way this contradiction is most often resolved is by resorting to the theory of a "relocation" of Rachel's tomb within the biblical texts.[45] To begin with, it was located in the vicinity of Mizpah. However, when Judah's importance grew, it was "relocated" south, closer to Bethlehem, supposedly associated with building up the Davidic tradition.[46] Matitiahu Tsevet believes that the literary operation of "relocating" Rachel's tomb from the vicinity of Kiriat-Jearim to Bethlehem was associated with the process of the integration of the tribes of Israel.[47] From the fall of the northern state onward, Judah played an increasing role which also entailed the taking over of the north's mythical traditions and expanding them around figures associated with the tribe of Judah and its territory.[48] Zecharia Kallai believes that the story in the book of Genesis about Rachel's tomb and the lack of clarity about its location should be regarded as belonging to the category not of topographical imprecision but that of literary phenomena stemming from the needs of biblical historiography.[49] It is Kallai's view that the narrative of Gen 35 is an expression of the domination of the tribe of Judah over the other descendants of Israel.[50] He also concludes that the ideology which expanded the greatness of "the house of David" was a decisive factor in the creation of a "southern" location for Rachel's tomb.[51]

Giovanni Garbini tried to explain the moving of the grave not only in terms of ideological reasons, but also by resorting to philological arguments. He decided that the term כברת־הארץ,[52] which appears in Gen

44. M. Tsevet, "Studies in the Book of Samuel, II," *HUCA* 33 (1962): 107-18.

45. There is no information on the subject of Rachel's tomb as an existing cult place from before the Roman era.

46. Bloch-Smith, *Judahite Burial Practices*, 114 n. 4.

47. Tsevet, "Studies in the Book of Samuel, II," 115.

48. Not S.M. Langston, *Cultic Sites in the Tribe of Beniamin: Beniaminite Prominence in the Religion of Israel*, Frankfurt, 1998, who believes in a specific place occupied by Benjamin. Cf. Knauf, "Bethel."

49. Z. Kallai, "Rachel's Tomb: A Historiographical Review," in J.A. Loader and H.U. Kieweler (eds.), *Vielseitigkeit des Alten Testaments. Festschrift für Georg Sauer zum 70. Gebertstag*, Frankfurt, 1999, 215-23.

50. *Ibid.*, 220-21.

51. *Ibid.*, 221-22.

52. See the transliteration in the LXX: Χαβραθα. *Vetus Latina* reads "Chabratha in terra Chanaan."

35:16 (and also in Gen 48:7; 2 Kgs 5:19), derives from the word ברה*, signifying the length of road travelled during a two-hour march, or, in his view, about 11 km.[53] This is equal to the distance separating Ramah in the land of Benjamin from contemporary Ramat Rahel. This thesis, in my view, is a valid one, one that makes an important contribution to the debates about the dating of biblical texts. Accounts giving two different locations for Rachel's tomb could not have arisen at the same time. As Kallai and Garbini have shown, the process of "relocating" Rachel's tomb only makes sense if one accepts that initially the grave was placed in the vicinity of Ramah, in Benjamin's purlieu, and later that holy place was commandeered and moved south to Bethlehem-Ephrathah. If that is so, the passages testifying to the "northern" tradition (1 Sam 10:2 and Jer 31:15) are earlier than the story in the book of Genesis, which places the tomb in territory inhabited by Judah.

The first settlements in Ramat Rahel arose at the turn of the ninth century BCE. At that time a citadel was erected there.[54] During the divided kingdom, the importance of Ramat Rahel grew. A large number of *lmlk*-type stamps found there is evidence of the site's importance in the royal administration of Judah.[55] The citadel, reconstructed as a royal residence,[56] was destroyed during Nebuchadnezzar's expedition or during the Babylonian captivity.[57] The Persian period is synchronous with intensive civilian settlement, evidence of which are, among others, the numerous *yhd/yhwd* type stamps. Between the fifth and third centuries BCE there was a construction in Ramat Rahel described by Yohanan Aharoni as a Persian fortress.[58] There are astonishingly few finds from the Hellenistic period which could be evidence, for instance, of the destruction of the centre by Antiochus III in 199 BCE.[59] There are no precisely dated finds from a later period until the coins of Alexander Janneus (103–76 BCE).[60] Aharoni identifies Ramat Rahel with the biblical Beth-haccerem (Jer 6:1; Neh 3:14).[61] This name signifies "the house of

---

53. Garbini, *Note di lessicografia*, 35.

54. Aharoni *et al.*, *Seasons 1961 and 1962*, 119-20; see also Y. Aharoni, "Excavation at Ramat Rahel," *BA* 24 (1961): 98-118; *idem*, "The Citadel of Ramat Rahel," *Archaeology* 18 (1965): 15-25; "Ramat Rahel," in *NEAEHL*, 3:1261-67.

55. Aharoni *et al.*, *Seasons 1961 and 1962*, 119.

56. *Ibid.*, 120.

57. *Ibid.*; a later date for the destruction of the citadel is suggested by the discovery there of a stamp of King Jehoiakin (stratum VA).

58. Aharoni, *The Citadel*, 16.

59. Aharoni *et al.*, *Seasons 1961 and 1962*, 121.

60. *Ibid.*

61. *Ibid.*, 122; cf. R.W. Younker, *ABD*, *s.v.* "Beth-Haccerem."

the vineyard,"[62] which is confirmed by archaeological evidence: a substantial wine-making centre existed in Ramat Rahel. Aharoni also considers that Jer 22:13-19, which talks of the building of a house for Jehoiakim (608–597) outside the walls of Jerusalem, refers to Ramat Rahel.[63]

The term "Beth-haccerem" also appears in the *Genesis Apocryphon* (22:13-15). The valley of שׁוא, which is the royal valley (עמק מלכא) also known as בית כרמא, is where Abraham stopped and was met by Melchizedek.[64] According to the route of Abraham's journey, this place lies to the south of Jerusalem.

The existence of Rachel's tomb close to Bethlehem is confirmed by: Eusebius, the so-called *Guide to Jerusalem* (a copy of which was preserved in the Cairo genizah), Benjamin of Toledo (c. 1170) and numerous later testimonies establishing the continuity of this tradition from the Middle Ages to the present day.[65]

My remarks about the association of the names Ophrah and Ephrathah are confirmed by the establishment of the original name of Ramat Rahel. Giovanni Garbini rejects any identification of Ramat Rahel with Beth-haccerem and proposes a different solution.[66] On the basis of data from the Georgian calendar (tenth century CE), Garbini reconstructs the name *Beto'er / Betebrey / Betebre* as בית חפר or בית עפרה.[67] The latter possibility strengthens the thesis supporting the existence of the tomb of Rachel in the vicinity of Bethlehem, that is, Beth Ephrathah or—according to the version in Mic 1:10—Beth-Leaphrah (בית לעפרה). Garbini's reconstruction shows the equivalence of names linked with the root עפר and אפר.

Micah 5:2 reads: "But you, Bethlehem Ephrathah, though you are small among the clans of Judah, out of you will come for me one who will be ruler over Israel, whose origins are from of old, from ancient times." This Messianic mention of Bethlehem-Ephrathah appears to be linked to the story of Gideon; this can be seen in the use of a similar phrase in the LXX: ἰδοὺ ἡ χιλιάς μου ἠσθένησεν ἐν Μανασση (Judg 6:15); Εφραθα ὀλιγοστὸ ϛ εἶ τοῦ εἶναι ἐν χιλιάσιν Ιουδα (Mic 5:2). The MT has preserved a trace of this analogy. The equivalent of the Greek χιλιάς in

62. See the use of the term כרם in Deut 22:9; Isa 3:14; Song 8:11.
63. Aharoni *et al.*, *Seasons 1961 and 1962*, 122-23.
64. Fitzmyer, *The Genesis Apocryphon, passim*.
65. See *EJ* 13:1489-90.
66. G. Garbini, "Sul nome antico di Ramat Rahel," *Rivista degli Studi Orientali* 16 (1961): 199-205.
67. It has to be emphasised that the version reconstructed by Garbini contains *ayin*, not *aleph*.

Mic 5:2 is the Hebrew אלף. In Judg 6:15, the same word is used: אלף.
Gideon says of himself, הנה אלפי הדל במנשה (lit.: "lo [I am] a weak
thousands-man in Manasseh," ἰδοὺ ἡ χιλιάς μου ἠσθένησεν ἐν Μανασση),
while Mic 5:1 writes of Bethlehem: בית־לחם אפרתה צעיר[68] להיות באלפי
יהודה (lit.: "Bethlehem-Ephrathah weak since you are in the thousands of
Judah," καὶ σύ Βηθλεεμ οἶκος τοῦ Εφραθα ὀλιγοστὸς εἶ τοῦ εἶναι ἐν
χιλιάσιν Ιουδα).

DCH gives the word אלף as coming from the root אלף III, meaning not
"a thousand" but "a clan." According to Clines, this phrase appears
thirteen times in the MT, namely (apart from Judg 6:15), in Num 1:16
(χιλίαρχος); Num 10:4 (ἄρχοντες ἀρχηγοὶ); Num 31:5 (χιλιάς); Josh
22:14 (χιλίαρχος); Josh 22:21 (χιλίαρχος); Josh 22:30 (πάντες οἱ
ἄρχοντες); 1 Sam 10:19 (φυλή); 1 Sam 23:23 (χιλιάς); 1 Chr 12:21
(ἀρχηγοὶ χιλιάδων; *principes milium*); Zech 12:5, 6 (χιλίαρχος). This
term refers to Judah four times, to Israel six times, twice to Manasseh
(Judg 6:15; 1 Chr 12:21), while on one occasion (1 Sam 10:19) it does
not refer to any specific tribe. This distribution of words derived from
אלף III, and their Greek counterparts, reveals that Clines's decision is
somewhat arbitrary.[69] His suggestion that there is a separate root signifying "clan" is understandable in view of the context, but the Greek term
φυλη appears only in 1 Sam 10:19 (in other words, the only places it is
separate from a specific tribe or people). In all other places, the LXX
translates it either as a "thousand" or a "thousandman."[70]

It does seem, therefore, that there is a link between the sentence in
Mic 5:2 and Judg 6:15, though it is difficult to establish now the
direction of the influence. Nevertheless, this does confirm the hypothesis
that Gideon's Ophrah is the same place that Micah calls Ephrathah—in
other words, another name for Bethlehem.

Chapter 20 of the *Testament of Joseph* contains details about the
location of Rachel's tomb, but unfortunately these are not enough to help
us decide which biblical tradition the text is based on: "And carry up
Zilpah your mother and bury her close to Bilhah, by the Hippodrome,
near Rachel" (*T. Jos.* 20.3).[71] The reference to a hippodrome, which also

---

68. *BHS* suggests a change of reading to אפרת הצעיר.
69. Mandelkern and BDB do not distinguish between the roots אלף II and III.
70. What sometimes differentiates the person of the head of a thousand and the
thousand itself is the context (cf. Josh 22:14).
71. H.W. Hollander and M. de Jong, *The Testaments of the Twelve Patriarchs:
A Commentary*, SVTP 8, Leiden, 1985, 409. Cf. The translation by H.C. Kee ("Take
Asenath, your mother, and bury her by the hippodrome, near Rachel, your grand-
mother") in *OTP*, vol. 1.

may be found in LXX Gen 48:7, could relate to a construction erected in the vicinity of Jerusalem by Herod the Great.

In ch. 32 of the book of *Jubilees* the birth of Benjamin is mentioned twice: "At that time [i.e. during her stay in Bethel] Rachel became pregnant with her son Benjamin…" (*Jub.* 32:3); and:

> During the night Rachel gave birth to a son. She named him Son of my Pain because she had difficulty when she was giving birth to him. But his father named him Benjamin on the eleventh of the eighth month, during the first year of the sixth week of this jubilee. Rachel died there and was buried in the country of Ephrathah, that is, Bethlehem. Jacob built a pillar at Rachel's grave—on the road above her grave. (*Jub.* 32:33-34)

This repetition of a reference to the birth of Benjamin could be the trace of two traditions related to the place of birth and also the grave of Rachel. Initially, this event was located in the north (the vicinity of Bethel according to *Jub.* 32:3), and later in the land of Ephrathah, that is, Bethlehem.

The phrase "in the country of Ephrathah" (*Jub.* 32:34) is a rather unusual combination bearing in mind that the word "country" or "land" (אֶרֶץ, γῆ, *terra*)[72] is normally used to describe larger territories, a region inhabited by a tribe, an area and so on, rather than a town. The only parallel turn of phrase, though it is not completely analogous, is found in the Gospel of Matthew (2:6): "And you, Bethlehem, in the land of Judah." The term "land" has been used to describe Judah, but in juxtaposition with the name "Bethlehem." This could be evidence that, at least in the time when the book of *Jubilees* came into being, the toponym "Ephrathah" was a term describing a larger territory and not a synonymous name of the town of Bethlehem.

The place in question could have had two names simultaneously. The form "Bethlehem" (בֵּית לֶחֶם), or "house of bread," could have been the description of a "serving domicile." Aaron Demsky has shown how proper names of places were derived from the name of the goods supplied or produced in them.[73] It is possible that the name "Bethlehem" was used alongside the name "Ephrathah" and that, in time, the former name came to dominate over the latter in biblical tradition.

There is another explanation for the "Bethlehem-Ephrathah" conjunction. If the mention of "the land of Ephrathah" in *Jub.* 32:34 is not accidental, then it could testify to the fact that Bethlehem was a town

---

72. VanderKam (trans.), *The Book of Jubilees*, 287, where Latin "in terra eufrata" is shown.

73. A. Demsky, "House of Achzib: A Critical Note on Micah 1:14b," *IEJ* 16 (1966): 211-15.

situated within the borders of an area called Ephrathah. It is, however, not possible to ascertain whether this was the name of a region or of a tribe living there.

The LXX translation retained the original Hebrew version of the text of the story of Gideon in which the name Ophrah does not feature but Ephrathah does. If we are to accept that "Ophrah" is an artificial creation which was to supplant the term "Ephrathah-Bethlehem,"[74] we would still have to establish why such a change took place and when. The key to the answer lies, in my view, in the royal ideology which, based on the Davidic tradition, exploited the exceptional significance of the town of David. Gideon, who also came from a royal town (let us remember that in *Seper ha-Yamim* he is called a king), became, in mythic-historic terms, a rival of the only great king born in Bethlehem—David. We can, there-fore, detect here an attempt to weaken Gideon's position and to erase his links with Bethlehem, which would be a way of strengthening the myth of David. That would also be the purpose of Gideon's proclamation after his victory over the Midianites (Judg 8:22-23), when he refused to accept the title of king: "But Gideon told them, 'I will not rule over you, nor will my son rule over you. The Lord will rule over you.'"

Tradition linked the person of David not only with Bethlehem—as has been stated already—but also with Hebron. David's road to kingship in Hebron began by accepting the ascendancy of the Philistines. According to this tradition, he was strongly associated with the Philistines and his family headquarters were in Hebron and not Bethlehem.[75] This inter-pretation accords with the thesis of the non-Semitic origin of the name דויד / דוד.[76] We might venture the claim that the association of the mon-arch with Bethlehem was borrowed from the story of Gideon and trans-posed to David. This king's artificial genealogy, the reiterated emphasis on his origins in Bethlehem, together with considerable restraint in proving his allegiance to one of the tribes of Israel all point to such a conclusion. It would also explain both Gideon's royal connections and the attempt to erase his links with Bethlehem by creating a fictional urban entity in the shape of Ophrah.

An argument in support of this thesis is the motif of the battle between David and Goliath. 1 Samuel 17 talks of David overcoming the Philistine

74. Cf. H. Cazelles, *ABD, s.v.* "Bethlehem"; the conjunction of the names "Bethlehem and "Ephratah" to describe the same place is also found in the historian Demetrius from the third century BCE (fr. 2:10).

75. See the motif of Absalom making his way to the familial sanctuary in Hebron.

76. According to some theories, "David" is not a proper name but a throne name. This does not alter the fact that there is no certain etymology of this word based on the Hebrew language; see D.M. Howard, *ABD, s.v.* "David (person)."

Goliath while, a few chapters later, we find the following information:
"In another battle with the Philistines at Gob, Elhanan son of Jaare-
Oregim the Bethlehemite killed Goliath the Gittite, who had a spear with
a shaft like a weaver's rod" (2 Sam 21:19; cf. 1 Chr 20:5). The conqueror
of Goliath, then, is not David but Elhanan of Bethlehem. Sirach 47:4-5
lays down an evident *terminus ante quem* for ascribing the victory to
David: "Did not he kill the giant, and take away reproach from his
people? In lifting up his hand, with the stone in the sling he beat down
the boasting of Goliath." The figure of Elhanan (אלחנן) mentioned in
2 Samuel is also to be found in the list of David's warriors (2 Sam 23:24;
1 Chr 11:26), with the additional information that he came from Bethlehem. Various explanations have been suggested for this discrepancy.
First, some (notably Driver) have attempted to identify Elhanan son of
Jair (1 Chr 20:5) with Elhanan son of Jaare-oregim (2 Sam 21:19) on the
basis that the book of Chronicles has preserved the father's original
name, the form "Jaare-oregim" of 2 Samuel being seen as a distortion
resulting from conflating the name "Jaar" with the word ארגים, "weaver's
rod" (from ארג, "to weave"), which appears in the same verse.[77] Second,
in trying to eliminate the discrepancy arising from ascribing the same
deed to two people to see in Elhanan the figure of David himself. This
thesis requires an acceptance that the name "David" is a throne name.
What makes this theory probable is the appearance in texts from Mari of
the royal title *davidum*, though it is not consonant with the mention in
1 Chr 20:5, which ascribes to Elhanan the killing of Goliath's brother.
Regardless of which hypothesis to explain this inconsistency in the
biblical text we accept, it is clear that what we are dealing with here is an
attempt by the Bible's authors to combine David with some hero coming
from Bethlehem renowned for deeds of war.[78]

Although this matter will not, I suspect, find a final resolution, I am
inclined to see in Elhanan the model for a brave warrior from Bethlehem
whose deeds were adduced, in a two-stage process, to David. In the first
stage (in 2 Sam 23:24),[79] Elhanan was made the son of Dodo (דדו), that
is to say, of David (דוד),[80] while in the second stage, the killing of a
different Philistine was ascribed to him.[81]

---

77. Driver, *Notes on the Hebrew Text*, 354-55.

78. S.G. Dempster, *ABD*, s.v. "Elhanan."

79. 1 Chr 11:26 talks of the father of Elhananan as being דודי = Δωδω.

80. Evidence of this could be the original form of the name preserved in the
LXX—Δουδί—whereas the name of David is rendered as Δαυιδ.

81. The matter is complicated by the mention in Judg 10:1 of the rule of Tola, the
son of Puah and grandson of Dodo (דודו).

This example of the relationship between the figures of David and Elhanan is evidence of the practice aimed at enlarging the heroic myth of David at the expense of other heroes. A similar fate to that met by Elhanan could have befallen Gideon, who was not removed from the Bible, but whose fame was ascribed to David. The difference between Gideon and Elhanan stems from the fact that the memory of the former's achievements was so strong that it would have been too risky to deprive him of his significance; accordingly, the only adjustment introduced was applied to his origins. The mythical motif of Gideon was preserved but the editors of the Bible introduced corrections to erase the similarity of the judge with David.

The altar which god commanded Gideon to destroy (Judg 6:26) is to be found on the "top of the fortress" (ראש המעוז). The noun מעוז signifies "fortress," "stronghold,"[82] and is translated (e.g. in Ps 31:3) in the LXX οἶκος καταφυγῆς, and in the Vulgate as *domus refugii*.

If Judg 6:26 really does refer to some fortification then it would make it possible to identify it and thereby to locate Ophrah. The LXX translation (ἐπὶ κορυφὴν τοῦ Μαουεκ) does not make locating the position of the "fortress" any easier. The *Codex Alexandrinus* has a transliteration of the Hebrew term, reading Μαωζ. Unfortunately, the word Μαουεκ appears only once in the LXX. The difference in the forms (Μαωζ and Μαουεκ) is probably not the result of a copyist's error. The form Μαουεκ does not derive from any Greek word and is probably a transliteration of the Hebrew term used in the LXX as a proper name. If it were possible to establish which Hebrew word was the basis of this transliteration, then it may enrich our knowledge of the fortress in Ophrah.[83] The Vulgate attempts to eliminate the text's obscurities by limiting itself to rendering it as "in summitate petrae." Biblical evidence does not, therefore, allow us to establish what the word Μαουεκ signifies nor what its etymology is.

Even if we accept that Ophrah and Bethlehem-Ephrathah is the same place, we still need to show that the finds in Ramat Rahel confirm that that was where the action of the story of Gideon was located. The key to this would be the discovery of the fortress where Gideon was said to have built his altar. Archaeology tells us that there were fortifications in Ramat Rahel and that they were there from the turn of the ninth/eighth centuries BCE to the beginnings of the sixth century BCE, and also during the Persian period (fifth to third centuries BCE). If the hypothesis is

82. See also Pss 28:8; 31:3; Isa 23:4; Ezek 30:15; Dan 11:7, 31.

83. The noun מלך, "king," a form of the name (מעוך) from 1 Sam 27:2, or the verb מעך, "to press," "to squeeze out," "to squeeze" (cf. 1 Sam 26:7), can also be taken into account.

correct, then the most probable date for the beginnings of the story about the building of an altar to Yahweh would be the years during which there was a royal citadel in Ramat Rahel.

If it was situated in Bethlehem, the fortress (מעוז) in the story about Gideon brings to mind Migdal Eder, or the tower (מגדל) mentioned in the story of the death of Rachel in Gen 35:21. There mention is made of מגדל־עדר, "tower of the flock."[84] Unfortunately, we do not know whether this term offers a description of the tower or whether it is a compound proper name. We also do not know where precisely such a tower would be located. Assuming that Gideon's fortress (מעוז) and "the towers of the flock" are one and the same, a further unclear biblical term could be introduced here, namely בית מלוא / ביתמלא/מלוא, a form of words used in a context indicating an edifice in the vicinity of Jerusalem (2 Sam 5:9; 1 Kgs 9:15, 24; 11:27; 2 Kgs 12:21; 1 Chr 11:7-8; 2 Chr 32:5). This same term refers to an object found not far from Shechem: "Then all the citizens of Shechem and Beth Millo (MT: וכל־בית מלוא; LXX: οἶκος Βηθμααλων) gathered beside the great tree at the pillar in Shechem to crown Abimelech king" (Judg 9:6);[85] "[…] let fire come out from Abimelech and consume you, citizens of Shechem and Beth Millo (MT: וכל־בית מלוא; LXX: οἶκος Βηθμααλων),[86] and let fire come out from you, citizens of Shechem and Beth Millo, and consume Abimelech!" (Judg 9:20).[87]

Scholars admit to there being considerable difficulty in identifying both the term and the place it denotes.[88] The use of the word "Millo" with reference to both Jerusalem (or its suburbs) and to Shechem may indicate that it is not a proper name but a technical term. The etymology of the word מלוא, derived almost certainly from the root מלא, "to fill," opens up several reconstructions: "beth-Millo" could, for instance, signify a "house full (of wheat)," or a barn, or a "house full (of people)," and if the people are armed then we are dealing with a fortress. This interpretation is supported by the six-fold use of the מלוא / מלא with the definite article,[89] as well as the LXX translation. The Greek text uses the transliteration οἶκος

---

84. This name appears also in Mic 4:8 in association with Jerusalem.

85. If Ophrah and Bethlehem are one and the same, then the mention in Judg 9:5 of the murder of the sons of Jerubbaal assumes particular significance. The analogy with the "massacre of the innocents," described in the New Testament (Mt 2:16-18), may be not accidental.

86. *Codex Alexandrinus* reads οἶκος Μααλλων.

87. In Lev 5:12 and Judg 6:38 the form מלוא appears not as a proper name but a term denoting "full."

88. M. Görg, *ABD*, *s.v.* "Beth-Millo (place)"; W.H. Mare, *ABD*, *s.v.* "Millo."

89. 2 Sam 5:9; 1 Kgs 9:15, 24; 11:27; 1 Chr 11:8; 2 Chr 32:5.

Βηθμααλ(λ)ων / Μααλλων in Judg 9:6, 20 and οἶκος Μαλλω in 2 Kgs 12:21. In 2 Sam 5:9 and 1 Kgs 11:27 the Greek equivalent of the Hebrew מלא is the word ἄκρα.

Trying to establish the location of beth-Millo in Jerusalem, Richard C. Steiner concludes that that was the name given to the construction lying against the city walls.[90] This, however, does not explain what the term "beth-Millo" meant in relation to the construction in the vicinity of Shechem. I think that a better explanation would be to accept that the term "beth-Millo" was a technical term denoting some construction of a defensive nature located outside the city walls.

In this context the passage in 2 Kgs 12:20 is important: "And his servants arose, and made a conspiracy, and slew Joash in the house of Millo (LXX: οἶκος Μαλλω), which goeth down to Silla." If "the house of Millo" really was a construction lying against the city walls, then the killing of Joash took place in Jerusalem and it would be there that one would need to look for that "descent to Silla" (MT: סלא היורד, Vulgate: "in descensu Sela," the LXX somewhat differently: οἴκῳ Μαλλω τῷ ἐν Γααλλα[91]).

Greek Γααλλα and Hebrew סלא are used only in this verse of the Bible, and the only word which could be linked to the Hebrew סלא is the name Sallu mentioned in Neh 11:7 belonging to a certain Benjaminite. The vocalisation of this name seems to have been changed, since the LXX gives it in the form of Σηλω, while the Vulgate gives "Sellum."[92]

The meaning of the word סלא remains uncertain. It is true that commentators claimed that "Silla" was the name of a street or a district in Jerusalem.[93] This, however, is an arbitrary thesis unsupported by any proofs. Nor is it certain that Sella and the "house of Millo" standing close by really were to be found in Jerusalem, nor that they adjoined the city walls, nor that they were some distance from them. The term בית מלוא is as I suppose a technical description of a fortress or a stronghold, and that is why looking for such a construction outside the walls does not take into consideration the principles of constructing city defences. If a מלוא / ἄκρα was built, then it would be done within the walls, as the last point of resistance, or well away from them as a *domus refugii*. And if בית מלוא was outside the city walls, then it could be the same fortress (מעוז = Μαουεκ) mentioned in the book of Judges (6:26). Maybe it is

90. R.C. Steiner, "New Light on the Biblical Millo from Hatran Inscriptions," *BASOR* 276 (1989): 15-23.

91. Some manuscripts give σελλα.

92. Cf. F.W. Schmidt, *ABD*, s.v. "Sallu (person)."

93. D.C. Liid, *ABD*, s.v. "Silla (place)."

identical with מגדל־עדר, marking out the road from Jerusalem to Bethlehem. Unfortunately, we have no evidence to decide whether or not such an identification is correct.

A further argument in favour of the view that the action of the Gideon story was moved from Ephrathah-Bethlehem to a made-up Ophrah could be the identity of the god appearing there.

In view of the fact that Judg 6:22 speaks of an angel (מלאך), the phrase, "The Lord said to him: 'Peace be with you'" (ויאמר לו יהוה שלום לך, v. 23), can also be translated as "said to him: Yahweh-Peace (יהוה שלום) be with you," which resonates with the following verse: "and called it [the altar] the Lord is Peace" (ויקרא־לו יהוה שלום; lit. "and called it: Yahweh-Peace").[94] The LXX translates it respectively: κύριος εἰρήνη (v. 23) and Εἰρήνη κυρίου (v. 24). We would, then, be dealing with a god (Šalom/Šelim), which would be linked with Yahweh. In his commentary, Robert Boling[95] omits the Yahweh-Shalem/Shalim variant, while Herbert B. Hoffmann acknowledges this possibility.[96] The existence on the territory of Palestine of a cult of a god named Shalim/Shalem,[97] known from Ugaritic texts,[98] is confirmed by, among other things, theophoric names.[99]

If we accept that the contents of v. 24 show a trace of a cult of Shalim/Shalem, then we should follow that track by analyzing the aetiology of Ophrah and the figure of Gideon.

Huffmon points out[100] that the two sons of David—Absalom (אבשלום) and Solomon (שלמה)—both have names which contain the element שלם.[101] The same element also appears in two different (?) contexts, namely, in the name Jerusalem (ירושלם) and "Salem" (שלם)—the place where the king-priest Melchizedek ruled (Gen 14:18-20). Normally Salem, when associated with this person, is identified with Jerusalem.[102] If, then, the town of David was associated with the cult of a non-Yahwist god, the motives driving the authors of the Bible to change the location of the altar of the god Shalim become comprehendible. Gideon was a hero associated with Ephrathah and with the cult of Shalim. And David, too, was linked with this god.

94. Cf. de Pury, "Le raid de Gédéon," 176.
95. Boling, *Judges, passim.*
96. Huffmon, "Shalem."
97. Lewy, "Les textes paléo-assyriens"; *idem,* "The Šulmân Temple."
98. Gray, *The Legacy of Canaan.*
99. Tigay, *You Shall Have No Other Gods,* 67-68, 80; Driver, "Brief Notes," 12-13.
100. Huffmon, "Shalem," 1430.
101. Handy, "Shalem," represents a sceptical approach to this.
102. King, "Jerusalem."

The tradition which recognised Jerusalem as a centre of the cult of a god named Shalim/Shalem persisted until the second century BCE. Eupolemos (F 2 [34:13-14]) speaks of the temple there being dedicated to the god Selim (Σηλώμ), to whom Solomon made a sacrifice of a thousand oxen.[103]

The identity of the god appearing in the aetiology of Ophrah is unclear also because of the form of the name Baal used: it appears in four places (Judg 6:25, 28, 30, 32), and each time it is preceded by the definite article. The form הבעל appears 29 times in the whole Bible,[104] and the form בעל as many as 58.[105] In the book of Judges, not counting ch. 6, the word "Baal" appears without an article also in Judg 3:3; 8:33; 9:4; 19:22, 23, and each time it is complemented by an addition, for example: בעל הבית, בעל ברית, בעל חרמון. It is not clear whether this really does refer to a god worshipped under the name of Baal, or to some other god called "Lord." Bearing in mind that the second part of the story (in which the form הבעל appears) explains the derivation of the name Jerubbaal, it may be doubtful whether originally it really did refer to Baal. To explain the derivation of the name "Jerubbaal" it was essential to use the name "Baal," but maybe the word did not denote the name of a god here, just the noun "lord," which was used to describe some other god.

An assessment of a sanctuary in Ophrah, whose beginnings are linked with Jerubbaal-Gideon, is not unequivocal since, after the aetiological text (a positive one from Yahwism's point of view), the following passage, deuteronomistic in spirit, appears: "Gideon made the gold [ear-rings captured during the war with the Midianites] into an ephod (אפוד),[106] which he placed in Ophrah, his town. All Israel prostituted themselves by worshipping it there, and it became a snare to Gideon and his family" (Judg 8:27).

Gideon was to have built in the designated place "an altar on a layer of stones." The Hebrew text mentions only the building of an altar: מזבח [...] הזה במערכה (Judg 6:26). The literal translation of this phrase should read: "an altar [built] according to the proper rules" because the

103.   It appears that Mendels, *The Land of Israel*, 45, erroneously equates Σηλώμ with Shiloh.

104.   Apart from in Judg 6, the form הבעל also appears 21 times in 1 and 2 Kings, and in 2 Chr 23:17; Jer 19:5; 32:35; Zeph 1:4.

105.   The form בעל appears in the Pentateuch, Joshua, Chronicles, Ezra and also in the Prophets; see also 2 Sam 5:20, "Baal-Perasim" (בעל פרצים), and 2 Kgs 1:8, "hairy man" (איש בעל שער).

106.   The use of the word "ephod" to denote a cult object connects this fragment with Judg 18, but conflicts with the word's most frequent usage as a term for a priestly robe (e.g. Exod 25:7; 1 Sam 2:18).

adverbial phrase במערכה refers to the verb "to build" and not to the noun "altar." An altar built on proper principles was one which the translators of the King James Version regarded as one built of unhewn stones (see Exod 20:25), but there is no evidence for this hypothesis in the text.[107]

The text points to the presence of אשרה within the *temenos* in Ophrah.[108] Verse 25, according to the MT, reads: ואת־האשרה אשר־עליו תכרת (lit. "...and cut down the asherah which [is] there"); LXX reads: καὶ τὸ ἄλσος τὸ ἐπ' αὐτὸ ὀλεθρεύσεις; and the Vulgate reads: "et nemus quod circa aram est succide." The term אשרה corresponds to the Greek ἄλσος, "grove." The sense of this term as a "tree" or a "grove" is confirmed in a later part of the narrative where this instruction appears: "...Using the wood of the Asherah pole that you cut down, offer the second bull as a burnt offering" (v. 26). The MT reads והעלית עולה בעצי האשרה אשר תכרת; the LXX reads: καὶ ἀνοίσεις ὁλοκαύτωμα ἐν τοῖς ξύλοις τοῦ ἄλσους οὗ ἐξολεθρεύσεις; the Vulgate reads "et offeres holocaustum super lignorum struem quae de nemore succideris." So, there is no doubt that אשרה is a wooden object, though we cannot state with any certainty that it is a pole or a growing tree. The biblical injunction against its planting (נטע; φυτεύσεω; *plantare*) suggests that we are dealing with a tree: "You shall not plant for yourself any tree, as a wooden image, near the altar which you build for yourself to the Lord your God" (Deut 16:21 NKJV). 2 Kings 21:3 mentions "preparing" (עשה) an asherah, and 2 Kgs 23:15 its "burning" (שרף).[109] As this suggests, the term אשרה denotes a tree growing in a sacred place. But this was not its only meaning. The term אשרה (a feminine noun) was also used to describe a goddess; this is shown, for instance, by its use in the plural in both its masculine[110] and feminine[111] forms. It would, then, be not only the name of a wooden cult object, but also the name of a divinity.[112] The wooden object called אשרה most probably contained the image of a goddess of that name.[113]

107. Cf. R.D. Haak, *ABD, s.v.* "Altars."

108. In the MT this noun, with the definite article, appears in Judg 3:7; 6:25, 26, 30; 1 Kgs 16:33; 18:19; 2 Kgs 13:6; 18:4; 21:7; 23:6, 14; 2 Chr 14:2; 17:6; 19:3; 24:18; 31:1; 33:19; 34:7; and without an article in Deut 16:21; 2 Kgs 21:3; 23:15; 2 Chr 33:3.

109. See also 1 Kgs 16:33; 18:19; 2 Kgs 13:6; 18:4; 21:7; 23:6, and particularly 2 Chr 33:3.

110. 2 Kgs 23:14; 2 Chr 14:2; 17:6; 24:18; 31:1; 33:19; 34:7; Isa 27:9; Ezek 27:6.

111. Judg 3:7; 2 Chr 19:3; 33:3.

112. W.G. Dever, "Archaeology and the Ancient Israelite Cult: How the Kh. El-Qom and Kuntillet 'Arjud 'Asherah' texts have changed the Picture," *Eretz Israel* 26 (1999): 9-15; Ackerman, *Under Every Green Tree*, 55-66; S.A. Wiggins, *A*

There is disagreement among scholars about the extent, nature and popularity of the cult of Asherah. Here we will concentrate only on the function of the goddess's image, or symbol, in the shape, unknown to us, of a wooden object. Enough has already been written about the role and nature of the goddess, so suffice it now to assert that her cult extended quite far[114] and that its status was officially endorsed (or at least acknowledged by the state).[115]

A wooden pole described as an אשרה was a common element of the landscape of ancient Palestine.[116] The period of the First Temple, as emerges from comments by the prophets and the books of Kings, was the time of Asherah's great popularity. We may suppose that in the cult of sacred trees—even without the name אשרה—elements stemming from the cult of this goddess have been preserved. The so-called asherot—wooden poles, or rather sacred trees growing within holy places (במות)—comprised, next to an altar, an essential item furnishing a cult place. As the book of Judges (ch. 6) demonstrates, the cult of Asherah intermingled with the cult of Baal. Biblical literature presents a consistent picture of the religion of Palestine, frequently called Canaanite, which was condemned by Yahwism. At the same time, on the basis of archaeological data, chiefly from inscriptions from Kuntillet Ajrud and Khirbet el-Qom, we can see that Asherah was not associated in any particular way with Baal since a goddess of that name is presented in these inscriptions as a companion of Yahweh.[117] Despite the existence of these few epigraphic

Reassessment of "Asherah": A Study According to the Textual Sources of the First Two Millennia B. C. E., AOAT 235, Neukirchen–Vluyn, 1993; Binger, *Asherah*; J.M. Hadley, *The Cult of Asherah in Ancient Israel and Judah: Evidence for a Hebrew Goddess*, Cambridge, 2000.

113.   See W. Robertson Smith, *The Religion of the Semites: The Fundamental Institutions*, New York, 1959 (repr. from the edition of 1894), 193-97.

114.   Ackerman, *Under Every Green Tree*.

115.   S.M. Olyan, *Asherah and the Cult of Yahweh in Israel*, Atlanta, 1988, esp. 23-37.

116.   Ackerman, *Under Every Green Tree*, 60.

117.   W.G. Dever, "Iron Age Epigraphic Material from the Area of Khirbet el-Kom," *HUCA* 40–41 (1969–70): 139-204; *idem*, "Asherah, Consort of Yahweh? New Evidence from Kuntillet 'Ajrûd," *BASOR* 255 (1984): 21-35; Z. Meshel, *Kuntillet 'Ajrut: A Religious Center from the Time of the Judean Monarchy on the Border of Sinai*, Jerusalem, 1978; *idem*, "Did Yahweh Have a Consort?," *BAR* 5 (1979): 24-35; J. Day, "Asherah in the Hebrew Bible and Northwest Semitic Literature," *JBL* 105 (1986): 385-408; J.A. Emerton, "New Light on Israelite Religion: The Implications of the Inscriptions from Kuntillet 'Arjud," *ZAW* 94 (1982): 2-20; *idem*, "Yahweh and his Asherah: The Goddess or Her Symbol?," *VT* 49 (1999): 315-37; A. Lemaire, "Les inscriptions de Khirbet el-Qom et l'Asherah

remains, the cult of Asherah is reconstructed mainly on the basis of biblical texts containing the descriptions and condemnations of non-Yahwistic religions.[118]

André Lemaire claims that asherot are exclusively trees which grow around sacred places (במות).[119] Edward Lipiński, who considers that it signified a cult place, probably a holy grove, reached a similar conclusion on the basis of an analysis of the word אשרת / אשרה.[120] This interpretation excludes the existence of a goddess named אשרה, but it does explain the link between that word and a cult place with trees.[121] The weakness of this hypothesis is that it does not explain the images visible on pots found in Kuntillet Ajrud depicting two male and one (seated) female figure with the inscription: "For Yhw and his Asherah." Furthermore, this theory would require a reinterpretation of the biblical passages which mention the prophets of Asherah. For example: "Now summon the people from all over Israel to meet me on Mt Carmel. And bring the four hundred and fifty prophets of Baal and the four hundred prophets of Asherah, who eat at Jezebel's table" (1 Kgs 18:19).[122]

Lipiński's and Lemaire's theories attempt to make the concept of אשרה fit into a picture of a monotheistic Yahwist cult. This creates the impression that the denial of the existence of a goddess of that name is, in part, the result of an ideological conviction about the "purity" of the ancient religion of the Hebrews.

The aetiological narrative concerning Ophrah contains evident elements of cultish activities.[123] The theophany beneath the tree is accompanied by a sacrifice (מנחה) and its miraculous burning before the face of the divinity. Gideon behaves before the god just as he would have done before its image. He makes a sacrifice and its acceptance is synonymous with its burning on the altar (see Gen 4:3-5). The divinity burns the

de Yhwh," *RB* 84 (1977): 595-608; J.M. Hadley, "The Khirbet el-Qom Inscription," *VT* 37 (1987): 50-62; *idem*, "Some Drawings and Inscriptions on Two Pithoi from Kuntillet Ajrud," *VT* 37 (1987): 180-213.

118.   Archaeological material to reconstruct the cult of Asherah is used by R. Hesrin, "A Note on the 'Lion Bowls' and Asherah," *Israel Museum Journal* 7 (1988): 115-18.

119.   A. Lemaire, "Who or What was Yahweh's Asherah? Starling New Inscriptions from Two Different Sites Reopen the Debate about the Meaning of Asherah," *BAR* 10.6 (1984): 42-51.

120.   Professor Edward Lipiński's gave a lecture on this subject at the University of Warsaw on 29 November 2001.

121.   The LXX most often translates the term אשרה as αλσος.

122.   See also 2 Chr 24:18 where Hebrew אשרה is given by the LXX as ᾽Αστάρτα.

123.   De Vaux, *Ancient Israel*, 2:306.

offering placed on the rock (הסלע), using a staff for this purpose (Judg 6:20-21), in a way similar to Moses getting water from a rock (הסלע) (Num 20:7-11).

This myth contains certain elements that we have seen in the aetiological themes discussed earlier. It has, for instance, a theophany beneath a sacred oak (האלה), one which, by the way, is reminiscent of the epiphany of the three men described in Gen 18:1-15, where the announcement of Isaac's birth is accompanied—just as in this story—by a confusion of the people speaking: three men (v. 2) with Yahweh (v. 13), and the angel of the Lord (v. 11) with Yahweh (v. 14).[124] It also has the motif of erecting an altar (v. 24) and a change of the hero's name (v. 32). Verse 32 is a classic example of the mythological genesis of a name. The name "Jerubbaal" derives from ירב בו הבעל, "to fight with Baal." Unlike the case of, for example, "Beer-sheba," the translation of v. 32 in the LXX does not take into account the play on words arising from the conjunction of the verb ירב and the name ירבעל. It is likely that the etymology of the name "Jerubbaal" (presented in Judg 6:32), conflating the name ירבעל with the phrase ירב בו הבעל, is, from a linguistic point of view, erroneous. It derives the name of the hero from the root ריב, "to argue," "to dispute," "to resist," "to stand against," whereas its theophoric name derives from the root ירה, "to throw," "to cast," "to arrange," which would give the meaning of "Baal establishes/resolves" (by analogy with ירואל in 2 Chr 20:16), or from the root רבב signifying "greatness," giving: "Let Baal reveal his greatness."[125]

Events associated with the influence of supernatural powers (hence the epiphany of the angel and the miraculous burnt offering) and the activity of one man, Gideon, who starts the celebration of the cult (hence the building of the altar and the first sacrifice), are decisive in establishing a holy place in Ophrah.

Verse 17 is interesting; it tells of the story's hero's demands for a sign which would prove the divinity of the "apparition." What we have here is a cluster of the word "sign" (אות) with the verb "to do," "to cause" (עשׂה). The theophany itself is not enough for Gideon to acknowledge the power of the divinity. That is why he asks for a sign in the shape a sacrifice being burnt with the help of the rod.[126] The theophany is completed only

124. Von Rad, *Genesis*, 227-28, believes that the angel Yahweh is in this story identical with god.

125. Emerton, "Gideon and Jerubbaal," 290.

126. The term "rod" or "staff" (משׁענת, from שׁען, "to support oneself") appears to denote a simple stick (e.g. reed) in Exod 21:19; 2 Kgs 18:21; Isa 36:6; Ezek 29:6; Zech 8:4; while in 2 Kgs 4:29-31 it denotes a magical tool with the help of which Gehazi, the servant of Elisha, tries to revive a dead boy.

by a cratophany. Using the same process, the angel of the Lord (מלאך
יהוה) proves his divinity when he foretells the birth of Samson. "As the
flame blazed up from the altar towards heaven, the angel of the Lord
ascended in the flame. Seeing this, Manoah and his wife fell with their
faces to the ground" (Judg 13:20). In this story (v. 19) the words "sacrifice" (המנחה) and "rock" (הצור; cf. Judg 6:21) also appear, but not
"altar," as well as the phrase "the Lord did an amazing thing" (ומפלא
לעשות;[127] lit. "he did unusual/strange things"). The most striking evidence
of the reality of god and his power revealing itself in the sending down
of fire is the scene of the "duel" between the prophet Elijah and the
prophets of Baal: "Then the fire of the Lord fell and burned up the sacrifice, the wood, the stones and the soil, and also licked up the water in the
trench" (1 Kgs 18:38). Fire, and control over it, is a manifestation of
divinity and power.

The story of Gideon contains various repetitions, as for instance the
motif of "testing" god and his will. Before setting off against the Midianites, having destroyed the altar of Baal, Gideon will put god's patience to
another test:

> Gideon said to God, "If you will save Israel by my hand as you have
> promised, look, I will place a wool fleece on the threshing-floor. If there
> is dew only on the fleece and all the ground is dry, then I will know that
> you will save Israel by my hand, as you said." And that is what happened.
> Gideon rose early the next day; he squeezed the fleece and wrung out the
> dew—a bowlful of water. Then Gideon said to God, "Do not be angry
> with me. Let me make just one more request. Allow me one more test
> (אנסה, from נסה) with the fleece." This time make the fleece dry and the
> ground covered with dew. That night God did so. Only the fleece was
> dry; all the ground was covered with dew. (Judg 6:36-40)

It is not possible to establish whether this fragment was originally part
of the story of Gideon or of Jerubbaal. The repetition of the scene in
which the hero waits for a supernatural creature to give him a sign
confirming its divinity could be an integral element in the construction
of the myth or it could be the result of the overlaying of different
traditions

The references to Egypt (Judg 6:13), the allusions to the calling of
Moses, and also the parallelisms indicate an association between this text
and the book of Exodus.[128] It is impossible to show whether the direction

---

127. See Exod 15:11; Pss 77:15; 78:12; 88:11; Isa 25:1; Job 37:5.
128. B.G. Webb, *The Book of the Judges: An Integrated Reading*, JSOTSup 46,
Sheffield, 1987, 147-49.

of the influence was from the book of Exodus to the book of Judges, or the reverse.[129]

Gideon is called "Jerubbaal," a name which also appears in an altered form—ירבשת (2 Sam 11:21). This duplicate form is a result, according to scholars, of a change in the sound of the name Jerubbaal.[130] The part בֶּשֶׁת derives from the word בֹּשֶׁת, signifying "shame," "disgrace." If we accept that, after the victory of Yahwism over Baalism, the name Jerubbaal (Judg 6:32) was changed to Jerubesheth (2 Sam 11:21), then we might establish a chronology of the texts. "Jerubbaal," the old form, changes to "Jerubesheth" in a later text. The question of when the process of eliminating the theophoric element "baal" from proper names appearing in the Bible started remains.

Matitiahu Tsevet presents a theory whereby the changes in non-Yahwistic theophoric names do not correspond to biblical practice. In his view, "Jerubesheth" is an alternative form for the hero's name and not the result of editorial interference inspired by religious orthodoxy.[131]

A. Graeme Auld has proposed an important argument.[132] Examining the late origins of the theme of the aggression of the Midianites,[133] he reaches the conclusion that vv. 7-10, preceding the aetiology under discussion (Judg 6), were an interpolation,[134] and that the figure of Gideon is secondary in relation to Jerubbaal.[135] Auld shows the influence of the books of Chronicles on the vocabulary of the story of Gideon,[136] and then concludes that the entire history of Gideon was a secondary, very revised version of the earlier story of Jerubbaal, and also an adaptation of the motif of Jacob's change of name (to Israel) in Penuel (Gen 32:27-31).[137] Auld does not guess at a date for the text's origin. He confines himself to the statement that among the later interpolations in the book of Judges, chs. 17–21, which most commentators reckon are late additions, are even

---

129.   Cross, *Canaanite Myth and Hebrew Epic*, 253, considers that the phrase "bring from Egypt" is characteristic of deuteronomistic literature.

130.   K.E. Lowery, *ABD*, *s.v.* "Jerubbaal"; R.C. Bailey, *ABD*, *s.v.* "Jerubbešet."

131.   M. Tsevet, "Ishboshet and Congeners: The Names and their Study," *HUCA* 46 (1975): 71-87 (83-87).

132.   A.G. Auld, "Gideon: Hacking at the Heart of the Old Testament," *VT* 39 (1989): 257-67.

133.   *Ibid.*, 258-59.

134.   *Ibid.*, 263. Cf. the analogous statement in M. Abegg, P. Flint and E. Ulrich, *The Dead Sea Scrolls Bible*, New York, 1999, 209.

135.   Auld, "Gideon," 264.

136.   *Ibid.*, 264-65.

137.   *Ibid.*, 267.

older than chs. 6 and 7.[138] Although the linguistic similarities of the story of Gideon and of Chronicles narrow the probable time of this tradition's beginnings, it allows us to date the text only superficially. Indicating the close linguistic associations and—which follows from it—looking for a common author will help us to decide the date of the redaction only and not of the origins of the tradition itself. I agree that the narrative about Gideon contains traces of many revisions, but the beginnings of this story of the hero's deeds are very ancient.

The theory presented by Auld is part of a wave of scholarship revising the findings of older biblical scholarship. The material found in the book of Judges has long been seen as a collage of texts of various provenance. The discussion revolved—and continues to revolve—around the nature of these earlier sources. Were they written documents, or oral accounts? This question was raised when the theory about the existence in the Pentateuch of several documents—allegedly also present in the book of Judges—started to be eroded.[139] Initially, it was considered that oral accounts contributed only slightly to the book of Judges,[140] though in time it was accepted that the role of this form of transmission had been underestimated.[141]

It appears impossible (and it certainly is here) to resolve the dilemma posed by the presence in the Bible of relics of an oral tradition. Bearing in mind Auld's argument, it is worth considering where and when the story of Gideon and of his building of an altar in Ophrah could have begun. The place where the events took place and the figure of the hero himself are of fundamental significance, as is his association with the ideology of kingship.

The scrolls containing fragments of the book of Judges found in Qumran and containing fragments of the book of Judges do not comprise the text in its final form.[142] Eugene Ulrich reconstructed the story of interest to us here. Ulrich based it on Judg 6:2-6, 11-13, 20-22, found in

---

138. By contrast G.A. Yee, "Ideological Criticism: Judges 17–21 and the Dismembered Body," in *Judges and Method: New Approaches in Biblical Studies*, Minneapolis, 1995, 146-70 (167), claims that chs. 17–21 come from the time of Joshua.

139. See Whitley, *The Sources*, 158-59, and the bibliography there.

140. *Ibid.*

141. D.M. Gunn, "Narrative Patterns and Oral Tradition in Judges and Samuel," *VT* 24 (1974): 296-317; on the subject of research on the presence of an oral tradition in the Bible see my article: "Stan badań nad historią i religią starożytnej Palestyny," *Przegląd Historyczny* 91 (2000): 435-49 (443-44).

142. See 4QJudg[a] and 1QJudg in Abegg, Flint and Ulrich, *The Dead Sea Scrolls Bible*, 208; see also Martone, *The Judaean Desert Bible*.

Qumran. After v. 13 and after v. 22 the text is considerably damaged. The entire reconstruction performed by Ulrich consists, to a large extent, of editorial additions. The papyrus text does not contain either the mention of Egypt (v. 13) or the name Ophrah (reconstructed in v. 11).[143]

It seems impossible to establish a precise date for the origin of the story which relates the founding of a holy place whose hero is Gideon. Various biblical references to the victory over the Midianites (Isa 9:3; 10:26; Ps 83:9-12) give some indication, but they do not speak directly about Gideon or the sanctuary he founded.[144] If the place of the action is indeed Ramat Rahel, then the date of the citadel's construction there decides the *terminus post quem* of the story's origin, that is, the end of the ninth and beginning of the eighth century BCE. The change of location of Rachel's grave, which must have occurred no earlier than the second half of the sixth century, provides no information that allows us to date precisely the aetiology of a holy place in Ophrah-Ephrathah since the stories of Gideon and Rachel's tomb could have arisen independently of each other. The examples of aetiological motifs discussed above show that there were often graves of ancestors in the vicinity of holy places. The story of Ophrah does not mention the existence of any grave and this may suggest that the story of Rachel's tomb derives from a separate tradition.

If, however, we accept that the existence of the graves of important people was a fundamental element of a holy place (or at least of the myth of its origin), then we would surely show an interdependence between the stories of Gideon and Rachel. Accepting such a premise, I am inclined to say that the story of Gideon originated in the eighth or seventh century BCE, and the editorial intervention leading to the removal of Rachel's grave (sixth or fifth century BCE) to a place known to be a religious centre founded by Gideon ensured the essential element which is the presence of a tomb for that sanctuary's aetiology. Following Auld's suggestion, the model of the fortress in Ophrah would not be the citadel dating from the eighth or seventh century BCE, but the fortifications from the Persian period. But this dating would be inconsistent with the time needed to complete the process of marginalising the role of Gideon and building up the tradition of David.

---

143.   The name Ophrah is also reconstructed in Judg 9:5.

144.   The *terminus ante quem* of the history of the conflict with the Midianites is marked by Proto-Isaiah (second half of the eighth century) and the creation of Ps 83 (sometimes dated in the eighth century but sometimes even in the second century). For more on Ps 83, see Goulder, *The Psalms of Asaph*, 166-73.

Another process undergone by the story of Gideon was one in which its hero was made into a descendant of Manasseh. If the erasure of his associations with Ephrathah-Bethlehem was partly attributable to the tendency to inflate the Davidic tradition, then this process, especially the interpolation proclaiming directly that Gideon belonged to the tribe of Manasseh, should be linked in time to the growth of the Messianic idea of a redeemer who will emerge from the house of David. The final move was to change the name of the proper name "Ephrathah" to "Ophrah." Taking into account the version of the text contained in the LXX and Josephus, we can accept that this change was introduced no earlier than the first century CE.

7.

Shechem and Gilgal

Shechem

Archaeological Data and Extra-Biblical Sources

It is believed that biblical Shechem should be located in Tell Balâtah, situated some 65 km north of Jerusalem.[1] Excavations were started there in 1912 (E. Sellin) and continued in the years 1914, 1926–1927, 1932 and 1934 (H. Steckeweh), and again in 1956–64 (G.E. Wright). The oldest traces of settlement there come from the Chalcolithic period. Shechem was settled again in the Middle Bronze Age (the period of the Middle Bronze Age IIA is generally dated from 1850 to 1750 BCE). Egyptian sources dated in the eighteenth century BCE mention *skmm*, interpreted as the name "Shechem." The IIB stratum (1750–1650 BCE) is where the oldest remains of city walls have been found. The same period dates the remains of constructions which served sacral purposes (analogous with those of Beth-Shean in stratum IX).[2] Shechem was settled continuously during the period of the Hyxoses. One suggestion is that the inhabitants of that time were of Indo-European origin.[3] The temple built in the middle of the second millennium has been described by archaeologists as a "massive fortress-temple (*migdal*)."[4] The dimensions of the building, dated from the seventeenth or sixteenth century BCE, allow us to suppose that at that time the town was the capital of the entire region (from Megiddo to Gezer).[5] Traces of previous destruction have been

1. E.F. Campbell, *Shechem II: Portrait of a Hill Country Vale. The Shechem Regional Survey*, Atlanta, 1991; E.F. Campbell and G.R.H. Wright, *Shechem III: The Stratigraphy and Architecture of Shechem/Tell Balâtah*. Vol. 1, *Text*. Vol. 2, *Illustrations*, Boston, 2002.
2. G.E. Wright, "Shechem," in *EAEHL*, 4:1083-94 (1086-88).
3. G.E. Wright, *Shechem: The Biography of a Biblical City*, New York, 1965, 94-95.
4. Wright, "Shechem," 1089.
5. *Ibid.*, 1090.

preserved in strata of the Middle Bronze Age. These signs of destruction are likely to be evidence of Egyptian conquests carried out by Ahmose I (1570–1546 BCE) and Amenhotep I (1546–1526 BCE). After the second of these invasions, the town underwent a crisis, though in the period documented by texts from el-Amarna the town was already dominating the region again. During the reign of the Pharaoh Amenhotep III (1417–1379 BCE), the ruler of Shechem was someone called Lab'ayu (letters from Tell el-Amarna, *EA* 242-46, 25-54).[6]

The city walls and the temple were rebuilt in the Late Bronze Age, though they were not restored to the dimensions of its predecessor. Dated from this period is the find denoted as a *massebah* ("well decorated stone column of large proportions").[7]

The town was destroyed towards the end of the Bronze Age. Strata XI–XII record the times of the united kingdom during which Shechem developed and, as archaeologists claim, played a significant role in Solomon's system of regal administration. The end of the tenth century BCE brought with it further destruction probably. This was the result of the campaign of the Pharaoh Shishak (or Shoshenq I) (918 BCE).[8] Remains of a small temple have been discovered in stratum XI and the traces of the restoration following the destruction towards the end of tenth century BCE in stratum X. The next stratum (IX-b) testifies to the existence of a robust town which could have been destroyed as a result of an earthquake or of wars (possibly the invasion of Ben-hadad 960–953 BCE).[9] The town from the time of stratum IX-a was probably destroyed by Hazael (c. 910 BCE). Stratum VIII proves that until the middle of the eighth century BCE, Shechem functioned in peace, though its importance diminished as that of neighbouring Samaria, expanding under the Omri dynasty's rulers of Israel, grew. Up until the eighth century BCE, Shechem remained an administrative centre to which taxes from the neighbouring regions were paid.[10] The constructions in stratum VII were destroyed at the same time as was Samaria (about 724–722 BCE). During Samaria's domination, Shechem could have continued to function as an important religious centre.[11] Originating from the period of the kingdom of Israel is the cuneiform text of a hymn in praise of the god Shamash.[12]

6. *Ibid.*
7. *Ibid.*, 1090-92.
8. *Ibid.*, 1093.
9. *Ibid.*
10. *Ibid.*
11. Wright, *Shechem: The Biography*, 144.
12. Smith, *Palestinian Parties*, 25, gives ninth–eighth century BCE.

Found in stratum VI was a modest settlement from Assyrian times bearing traces of dual destruction in the seventh century BCE. No particularly characteristic architectural finds have been encountered in strata VI and V, but numerous imports of Greek ceramics dated from between 525 and 475 BCE testify to the fact that the centre existed uninterruptedly. Over the next one hundred and fifty years (i.e. up until about 330 BCE), Shechem was abandoned. Four strata have been classified from the Hellenistic period: IV and III from the reign of the Ptolemy's, II and I from the domination of the Seleucids.[13]

There have been numerous coins from the Hellenistic period found in Shechem, minted between the end of fourth and the end of the second century BCE. The end of the tell's settlement is probably linked to the expedition of John Hyrcanus (107 BCE).[14] There is a dispute among scholars regarding the assessment of Jewish-Samaritan relations—was the final abandonment of Shechem caused by the fall of Samaria (107 BCE) or the destruction of the temple on Mt Gerizim (128 BCE)?[15] The numismatic finds, the latest of which are coins from Antioch (112–111 BCE) and also those minted by Alexander II Zabinas (128–123 BCE) and by Antiochus VIII Grypus (121–120 BCE), indicate unequivocally that 128 BCE did not mean the end of settlement in Shechem.[16]

In any discussion of the town's history it is impossible to omit the finds on the hills situated in its vicinity: Gerizim[17] and Ebal.[18] The absolute difference in levels calculated from the foot of the hills where Shechem is located to their peaks is 280 metres (Gerizim) and 340 metres (Ebal).[19]

Adam Zetal conducted the excavations on Mt Ebal and he guessed that the traces of the constructions found there were relics of cult buildings,[20] pointing to the presence of a large platform (7×9 m) with a special ramp leading up to it. The discovery of animal bones and votive vessels discovered at this location confirmed, for Zetal, the cultic nature of this structure. There have been no traces of residential settlements found in

---

13. G.E. Wright, "The Samaritans at Shechem," *HTR* 55 (1962): 357-60. Cf. anonymous, "Chronique Archéologique—Sichem," *RB* 69 (1962): 257-66.

14. Wright, "Shechem," 1093-94.

15. E.F. Campbell, "Shechem, Tell Balatah," in *NEAEHL*, 4:1354, opts for the former.

16. Wright, "Samaritans," 358.

17. I. Magen, "Garizim, Mount," in *NEAEHL*, 2:484-93.

18. A. Zertal, "Ebal, Mount," in *NEAEHL*, 1:375-77.

19. For a discussion of the geography and biblical traditions of Ebal and Gerizim, see Noort, "The Traditions of Ebal and Gerizim."

20. A. Zertal, *ABD*, *s.v.* "Ebal, Mount (place)."

these constructions. According to Zertal, the altar arose at the beginning of the Iron Age (thirteenth century BCE) and was used for a short time, more or less till the middle of the twelfth century BCE.[21] He admits that the cult nature of this find is not universally accepted; other scholars regard the excavated architectural elements as the remains of a defensive tower.[22]

Finds on the tell raise similar doubts: for example, the construction which Wright regards as a temple (of El Berit) was, according to other researchers, a large household building.[23]

Biblical Information

There are a total of 63 references to the name "Shechem" (שכם) in the Bible. As the proper name of the son of Hamor it is mentioned in Gen 33:19 and another ten times in Gen 34. A different Shechem, a descendant of Manasseh, the son of Joseph, is mentioned in Num 26:31; Josh 17:2; 1 Chr 7:19. As the name of a town, "Shechem" appears in Gen 35:4; 37:12, 13, 14; Josh 17:7; 20:7; 21:21; Judg 9:1, 2, 3, 6, 7, 18, 20, 23, 24, 25, 26, 28, 31, 34, 39, 46, 47, 49, 57; 21:19; 1 Kgs 12:1, 25; Pss 60:8; 108:8; Hos 6:9; Jer 41:5; 1 Chr 6:52; 7:28; 2 Chr 10:1.

Genesis 35:4 speaks of the burial by Jacob "of the foreign gods and the rings in their ears" under an oak in the vicinity of Shechem. This activity is part of a cleansing carried out on the road to Bethel.

The reference in Gen 37:12-14 is part of a story about Joseph: Jacob, living in the valley of Hebron (v. 14) sends Joseph to his brothers who are tending their flocks in Shechem (v. 13).

Shechem was part of the lot of the tribe of Manasseh (Josh 17:7) and was marked out as one of the towns of shelter: "So they set apart Kedesh in Galilee in the hill country of Naphtali, Shechem in the hill country of Ephraim, and Kiriath Arba (that is, Hebron) in the hill country of Judah" (Josh 20:7). In the listing of Levitical towns, it figures—next to Gerer, Kibzaim and Beth-horon—as belonging to the tribe of Ephraim (Josh 21:20-22; 1 Chr 6:52); this is confirmed also by 1 Chr 7:28 (where Bethel, Naaran, Gezer and Ayyah are also mentioned).

---

21. *Ibid.*
22. Zertal, "Ebal, Mount," 1:376-77; for an account of the discussion of Zertal's theory, see Noort, "The Traditions of Ebal and Gerizim," 168-70 n. 34.
23. J.D. Currid, "A Note on the Function of Building 5900 at Shechem—Again," *ZDPV* 105 (1989): 42-46; cf. M.D. Fowler, "A Closer Look at the 'Temple of El-Berith' at Shechem," *PEQ* 115 (1983): 49-53.

An extensive fragment in Judg 9 concerns Abimelech, proclaimed king in Shechem.[24] His association with the town can be explained both by virtue of Shechem belonging to the lot of Manasseh, and by his own family ties: his mother was a woman of Shechem (cf. Judg 8:11):

> Abimelech son of Jerub-Baal went to his mother's brothers in Shechem and said to them and to all his mother's clan, ask all the citizens of Shechem, "Which is better for you: to have all seventy of Jerub-Baal's sons rule over you, or just one man?" Remember, I am your flesh and blood. When the brothers repeated all this to the citizens of Shechem, they were inclined to follow Abimelech, for they said "He is our brother." (Judg 9:1-3)

Presumably as early as the times of Solomon Shechem was a centre of power since it was to there that his son Rehoboam went: "Rehoboam went to Shechem, for all the Israelites had gone there to make him king" (1 Kgs 12:1).[25] The first ruler of the northern state, Jeroboam, moved his capital from Shechem to Penuel (1 Kgs 12:25).

The book of Psalms mentions Shechem together with Succoth, Gilead and the territories of Manasseh, Ephraim and Judah (Pss 60:6-7; 108:8). The book of Jeremiah (41:5), while talking of the killing of Gedaliah and his people, mentions that "eighty men who had shaved off their beards, torn their clothes and cut themselves came from Shechem, Shiloh and Samaria, bringing grain offerings and incense with them to the house of the Lord."[26]

In the book of Hosea, the name Shechem occurs in the context of the prophet's rebukes and the descriptions of the misdemeanours committed by the dwellers of Judah and Ephraim:

> Gilead is a city of wicked men, stained with footprints of blood. As marauders lie in ambush for a man, so do bands of priests; they murder on the road to Shechem, committing shameful crimes. I have seen a horrible thing in the house of Israel. There Ephraim is given to prostitution and Israel is defiled. Also for you, Judah, a harvest is appointed. (Hos 6:8-11)

---

24. See the chapter on Ophrah and in it the arguments about the separateness of the traditions concerning Gideon and Abimelech.

25. See also 2 Chr 10:1.

26. N. Na'aman believes that this passage proves the significant religious role played by Shechem in the times of Jeremiah; see "The Law of the Altar in Deuteronomy and the Cultic Site Near Shechem," in McKenzie and Römer (eds.), *Rethinking the Foundations*, 141-61 (157 n. 45).

Shechem is also mentioned as a point of orientation in the topography of Palestine in a passage containing an unusually interesting description of a woman's ritual associated with the sanctuary of Shiloh, which lies "to the north of Bethel, and east of the road that goes from Bethel to Shechem, and to the south of Lebonah" (Judg 21:19).

As already mentioned, according to the Bible there are two important hills close to Shechem—Gerizim (גרזים) and Ebal (עיבל). The former, which became a religious centre for the Samaritans, is mentioned in Deut 11:29; 27:12; Josh 8:33 and Judg 9:7. The latter appears in Deut 11:29; 27:4, 13; Josh 8:30, 33, and also—as the name of several people—in Gen 36:23 and 1 Chr 1:40. Both these names frequently appear together, so it can be assumed that the hills comprised an integral part of the holy territory around Shechem. To cite a relevant fragment of biblical text:

> When the Lord your God has brought you into the land you are entering to possess, you are to proclaim on Mt Gerizim the blessings, and on Mt Ebal the curses. (Deut 11:29).

> When you have crossed the Jordan into the land the Lord your God is giving you, set up some large stones and coat them with plaster. Write on them all the words of this law when you have crossed over to enter the land the Lord your God is giving you, a land flowing with milk and honey, just as the Lord, the God of your fathers, promised you. And when you have crossed the Jordan, set up these stones on Mt Ebal, as I command you today, and coat them with plaster. Build there an altar to the Lord your God, an altar of stones. Do not use any iron tool upon them. Build the altar of the Lord your God with stones from the field and offer burnt offerings on it to the Lord your God. Sacrifice fellowship offerings there, eating them and rejoicing in the presence of the Lord your God. And you shall write very clearly all the words of this law on these stones you have set up. Then Moses and the priests, who are Levites, said to all Israel, Be silent, O Israel, and listen! You have now become the people of the Lord your God. Obey the Lord your God and follow his commands and decrees that I give you today. On the same day Moses commanded the people: When you have crossed the Jordan, these tribes shall stand on Mt Gerizim to bless the people: Simeon, Levi, Judah, Issachar, Joseph and Benjamin. And these tribes shall stand on Mt Ebal to pronounce curses: Reuben, Gad, Asher, Zebulon, Dan and Naphtali. (Deut 27:2-13)

This story is embellished with fresh details in a fragment from the book of Joshua, describing the fulfilment of the above prediction:

> Then Joshua built on Mt Ebal an altar to the Lord, the God of Israel, as Moses the servant of the Lord had commanded the Israelites. He built it according to what is written in the Book of the Law of Moses—an altar of uncut stones, on which no iron tool had been used. On it they offered to the Lord burnt offerings and sacrificed fellowship offerings. There, in the

presence of the Israelites, Joshua copied on stones the law of Moses,
which he had written. All Israel, aliens and citizens alike, with their elders,
officials and judges, were standing on both sides of the ark of the covenant
of the Lord, facing those who carried it—the priests, who were Levites.
Half of the people stood in front of Mt Gerizim and half of them in front
of Mt Ebal, as Moses the servant of the Lord had formerly commanded
when he gave instructions to bless the people of Israel. (Josh 8:30-33)

The proximity of Gerizim and Shechem is confirmed by a note like the
following in the book of Judges: "When Jotham was told about this, he
climbed up on the top of Mt Gerizim and shouted to them, Listen to me,
citizens of Shechem, so that God may listen to you" (Judg 9:7).

Aetiologies

Genesis 12:4-7:

> (4) So Abram left, as the Lord had told him; and Lot went with him.
> Abram was seventy-five years old when he set out from Haran. (5) He
> took his wife Sarai, his nephew Lot, all the possessions they had accu-
> mulated and the people they had acquired in Haran, and they set out for
> the land of Canaan, and they arrived there. (6) Abram travelled through
> the land as far as the site of the great tree of Moreh (עד אלון מורה) at
> Shechem (עד מקום שכם[27]). At that time the Canaanites were in the land.
> (7) The Lord appeared to Abram and said, "To your offspring I will give
> this land." So he built an altar there to the Lord, who had appeared to him
> (ויבן שם מזבח ליהוה הנראה אליו).[28]

Genesis 33:18-20:

> (18) After Jacob came from Paddan Aram, he arrived safely[29] at the city of
> Shechem in Canaan and camped within sight of the city. (19) For a
> hundred pieces of silver, he bought from the sons of Hamor, the father of
> Shechem, the plot of ground (חלקת השדה) where he pitched his tent.[30]
> (20) There he set up an altar (ויצב־שם מזבח) and called it El Elohe Israel
> (אל אלהי ישראל).

27. Lit. "to the place Shechem."

28. Van Seters, *Abraham in History and Tradition*, considers that the text of
Gen 12:4a, 6a and 7 belongs to the first layer (the so-called pre-J), and therefore
originates before the Babylonian captivity.

29. The MT uses the word שלם here (cf. LXX: εἰς Σαλημ πόλιν Σικιμων; Vulgate:
"transivitque in Salem urbem Sycimorum"), which could be a pronoun or a noun;
see the extensive discussion on this subject in Nielsen, *Shechem*, 223-24.

30. Lit. "He bought a flat field, [where] he pitched a tent, from the hand [of] the
sons of Hamor, father of Shechem, for a hundred קשיטה."

Joshua 24:1-4, 13-28:

> (1) Then Joshua assembled all the tribes of Israel at Shechem. He summoned the elders, leaders, judges and officials of Israel, and they presented themselves before God. (2) Joshua said to all the people, "This is what the Lord, the God of Israel, says: Long ago your forefathers, including Terah the father of Abraham and Nahor, lived beyond the River and worshipped other gods. (3) But I took your father Abraham from the land beyond the River and led him throughout Canaan and gave him many descendants. I gave him Isaac, (4) and to Isaac I gave Jacob and Esau. I assigned the hill country of Seir to Esau, but Jacob and his sons went down to Egypt." [...] (13) So I gave you a land on which you did not toil and cities you did not build; and you live in them and eat from vineyards and olive groves that you did not plant.
>
> (14) "Now fear the Lord and serve him with all faithfulness. Throw away the gods your forefathers worshipped beyond the River and in Egypt, and serve the Lord. (15) But if serving the Lord seems undesirable to you, then choose for yourselves this day whom you will serve, whether the gods your forefathers served beyond the River, or the gods of the Amorites, in whose land you are living. But as for me and my household, we will serve the Lord." (16) Then the people answered, "Far be it from us to forsake the Lord to serve other gods! (17) It was the Lord our God himself who brought us and our fathers up out of Egypt, from that land of slavery, and performed those great signs before our eyes. He protected us on our entire journey and among all the nations through which we travelled. (18) And the Lord drove out before us all the nations, including the Amorites, who lived in the land. We too will serve the Lord, because he is our God."
>
> (19) Joshua said to the people, "You are not able to serve the Lord. He is a holy God; he is a jealous God. He will not forgive your rebellion and your sins. (20) If you forsake the Lord and serve foreign gods, he will turn and bring disaster on you and make an end of you, after he has been good to you." (21) But the people said to Joshua, "No! We will serve the Lord." (22) Then Joshua said, "You are witnesses against yourselves that you have chosen to serve the Lord." "Yes, we are witnesses," they replied. (23) "Now then," said Joshua, "throw away the foreign gods that are among you and yield your hearts to the Lord, the God of Israel." (24) And the people said to Joshua, "We will serve the Lord our God and obey him." (25) On that day Joshua made a covenant for the people, and there at Shechem he drew up for them decrees and laws. (26) And Joshua recorded these things in the Book of the Law of God. Then he took a large stone (ויקח אבן גדולה) and set it up there under the oak (שם ויקימה תחת האלה) near the holy place of the Lord (אשר במקרש יהוה). (27) "See!," he said to all the people, "his stone will be a witness (לעדה) against us. It has heard all the words the Lord has said to us. It will be a witness (לעדה) against you if you are untrue to your God." (28) Then Joshua sent the people away, each to his own inheritance.

Joshua 24:32:

> And Joseph's bones, which the Israelites had brought up from Egypt, were buried (קברו) at Shechem (בשכם) in the tract of land (בחלקת השדה) that Jacob bought for a hundred pieces of silver from the sons of Hamor, the father of Shechem. This became the inheritance of Joseph's descendants.

Shechem must have been of great religious importance to the Hebrews since its aetiology is associated with two patriarchs as well as with Joshua.

The stories about the patriarchs with aetiological references to the holy place in Shechem show certain similarities. Abraham travels from Haran to Bethel, merely stopping at Shechem. Similarly, Jacob travels the road—though in truth not a straight one—from Paddan Aram. The book of Genesis (chs. 31–33) contains a description of the journey from the north to Galeed (31:43-55), then through Penuel along the Jabbok (32:22-32) and Succoth (33:17) to Shechem, but its ultimate destination is Bethel (35:1-15).

Reaching Shechem, both patriarchs stop outside the town—Abraham "under an oak" and Jacob "on a plot of ground"—and both build an altar there. However, the vocabulary used to describe the constructing of the altar is different in the two stories: of Abraham it is said "so he built an altar to the Lord" (ויבן־שם מזבח ליהוה, deriving from בנה, "to build"), and of Jacob that "he set up an altar" (ויצב־שם מזבח, deriving from נצב, "to raise," "to set up"). Eduard Nielsen considers that the noun "altar" (מזבח) replaced the older form "pillar" (מצבה).[31] The use of different verbs is significant in that the phrase "build an altar" occurs exceptionally frequently in the Bible;[32] the wording ויבן־שם מזבח occurs six times (Gen 12:7, 8; 13:18; 26:25; 35:7; 1 Sam 7:17), whereas the combination of the noun מזבח with the verb נצב appears just once (Gen 33:20).

Another, immediately apparent, difference is the employment of different names of god: Abraham dedicated his altar to "Yahweh," whereas Jacob "called it El Elohe Israel (אל אלהי ישראל)." We come across the combination אל אלהי in the MT also in Num 16:22: "God of the spirits of all flesh (אל אלהי הרוחת לכל־בשׂר)."[33]

The phrase "he called it [the altar] El Elohe Israel" (Gen 33:20) demands comment. The verb קרא means not only "to call" or "name,"

---

31. Nielsen, *Shechem*, 225.

32. Cf., e.g., Exod 20:25; Num 23:1; Deut 27:6; Josh 8:30; 1 Kgs 9:25; 18:32; 2 Kgs 21:4; 1 Chr 21:22; 2 Chr 8:12; 33:4, 15.

33. In 2 Chr 32:19 and Neh 2:4, though the consonants are analogous, אל performs the function of a particle and not of a proper noun.

but also "to call upon" or "summon," "call for," "call to." The Hebrew sentence, containing the particle ל, indicates unambiguously that it involves the act of name-giving. The KJV and the NIV translations are in conflict with both the text of the LXX (καὶ ἔστησεν ἐκεῖ θυσιαστήριον καὶ ἐπεκαλέσατο τὸν θεὸν Ισραηλ[34]) and the Vulgate version ("et erecto ibi altari invocavit super illud Fortissimum Deum Israhel"). Both these translations indicate a calling on God and not, as in MT, a naming of the altar "the God of Israel" or "God is the God of Israel."[35] The Greek text, and especially the later Latin translation of Jerome, indicate that the original fragment could have read: "There he raised an altar and called upon the God of Israel" (ויקרא אל אלהי ישראל*, a reading that would be analogous to the Hebrew version of Sir 46:5; 47:5, which reads קרא אל אל עליון).[36]

Both the use of the atypical noun and the rare description of god suggest that the text of Gen 33:20, very isolated in biblical material, represents an old editorial layer. On the other hand, the reference in Gen 12:6 to the stay in the land of the Canaanites and the promise to give it to Abraham and his descendants indicates its late origins.[37] We may suppose that the narrative linking the figure of Abraham with Shechem (Gen 12:6-7) was influenced by the motif of Jacob in Shechem (Gen 33:18-20).[38]

The story of the building of an altar by Abraham provides information about the topography of the holy place: the altar is located under the oak of Moreh (אלון מורה). In its translation of this verse (Gen 12:6), the LXX mentions an oak, but gives it a different name: καὶ διώδευσεν Αβραμ τὴν γῆν εἰς τὸ μῆκος αὐτῆς ἕως τοῦ τόπου Συχεμ ἐπὶ τὴν δρῦν τὴν ὑψηλήν οἱ δὲ Χαναναῖοι τότε κατῴκουν τὴν γῆν. In the Vulgate, the specification "oak" disappears: "pertransivit Abram terram usque ad locum Sychem usque ad convallem Inlustrem Chananeus autem tunc erat in terra."

---

34. Other appearances of the verb ἐπικαλέω in the form ἐπεκαλέσατο confirm its meaning of calling on God or calling the name of God (Gen 12:8; 13:4; 21:33; 26:25; 33:20; 1 Sam 12:18; 1 Kgs 17:21; 1 Chr 4:10; 2 Macc 15:21; Sir 2:10; 46:5, 16; 47:5). In 2 Kgs 23:17 the verb is not used in reference to God. In the preserved fragments of the Hebrew text of the Wisdom of Sirach (46:5; 47:5) we have: "he called upon the Most High," כי קרא אל אל עליון ("Because he called on the Most High [El Eliyon]"); see P.C. Beentijes (ed.), *The Book of Ben Sira in Hebrew: A Text Edition of all Extant Hebrew Manuscripts and a Synopsis of all Parallel Hebrew Ben Sira Texts*, VTSup 68, Leiden, 1997, *passim*.

35. Analogous with Gen 35:7.

36. The RSV reads: "He called upon the Most High, the Mighty One" and "he appealed to the Lord, the Most High"; cf., e.g., Judg 15:18: ויקרא אל־יהוה.

37. Nielsen, *Shechem*, 213-14.

38. *Ibid.*, 215.

The phrase ἐπὶ τὴν δρῦν τὴν ὑψηλήν can be translated as "to the oak, the tall one / to be found high up." The word מורה itself is derived from the root ירה, "to throw," "to shoot" (in the conjugation *hiphil*, "to teach"), and signifies "teacher," "diviner."[39] In the MT we come across one other mention of the oak of Moreh,[40] namely, in the description of the location of the hills of Gerizim and Ebal: "As you know, these mountains are across the Jordan, west of the road, towards the setting sun, near the great trees of Moreh (אצל אלוני מרה = πλησίον τῆς δρυὸς τῆς ὑψηλῆς), in the territory of those Canaanites living in the Arabah in the vicinity of Gilgal" (Deut 11:30).

Otto Eissfeldt drew attention to the discrepancy in the location of the oak of Moreh. One time the story says that it grows near to Shechem, another time that it is opposite Gilgal.[41] Comparing several texts (Deut 11:29-32; 27:1-8, 11-13, and Josh 8:30-35), Eissfeldt concluded that initially they referred to Shechem and that the information referring to Gilgal is secondary.[42] In Deut 11:30 Eissfeldt corrects the MT (in my opinion justly, as evidenced by the LXX) and uses the singular form: the oak of Moreh.[43]

Information about a tree growing close to Shechem runs through the biblical text repeatedly, though the name Moreh is not used.

The oak, beneath which so much was supposed to happen, was, as its very name suggests, linked with divination.[44] What is interesting is whether the "diviner's oak" (אלון מעונינים = Ηλωνμαωνενιμ) mentioned in Judg 9:37 is some other tree growing in the vicinity of Shechem, or the same tree differently named. Regardless of the reply to such a question, the act of theophany described as happening by the oak confirms our conviction of the tree's sacral nature, and the large number of similar descriptions in the Bible is evidence of a deeply rooted tradition ascribing a divinatory nature to sacred trees.

Additional information about a holy place in Shechem is provided by the important description of purification and by Jacob's journey to Bethel:

39. M. Hunt, *ABD, s.v.* "Moreh (place)," de Vaux, *Ancient Israel*, 2:289, considers as probable translations "Oak of the Teacher," "Oak of the Diviner."

40. Nielsen, *Shechem*, 222.

41. O. Eissfeldt, "Gilgal or Shechem?," in J.I. Durham and J.R. Porter (eds.), *Proclamation and Presence: Old Testament Essays in Honour of Gwynne Henton Davies*, London, 1970, 90-101; see also the section dealing with Gilgal and the thesis that Gilgal was located in the vicinity of Shechem below, pp. 206-15.

42. *Ibid.*, 97-100.

43. *Ibid.*, 92 and n. 5.

44. Nielsen, *Shechem*, 216-22.

Then God said to Jacob, "Go up to Bethel and settle there, and build an altar there to God, who appeared to you when you were fleeing from your brother Esau." So Jacob said to his household and to all who were with him: "Get rid of the foreign gods you have with you, and purify yourselves and change your clothes. Then come, let us go up to Bethel, where I will build an altar to God, who answered me in the day of my distress and who has been with me wherever I have gone." So they gave Jacob all the foreign gods they had (כל־אלהי הנכר בידם) and the rings in their ears (ואת־הנזמים אשר באזניהם), and Jacob buried them under the oak at Shechem (ויטמן אתם יעקב תחת האלה אשר עם־שכם). (Gen 35:1-4)[45]

Jan Alberto Soggin drew attention to the unusual application in this passage of the verb טמן,[46] which was also used in the Punic inscription on the golden Pyrgi tablets in the context of the burial of a god.[47] Despite the fact that in Hebrew the act of digging and burial is expressed by the verb קבר, Soggin showed that the verb טמן could be used with a similar meaning. He claims that although the biblical sentence (even translated as "Jacob buried them beneath the oak") speaks only of denying foreign gods, its sub-text contains the suggestion of a ritual involving the burial of a dead god.[48]

In any discussion of the cult connotations of the verb טמן, which appears in Gen 35:1-4, it is impossible to ignore the role of the objects which the members of Jacob's family renounce; as we read in v. 4, "they gave Jacob all the foreign gods they had and the rings in their ears." So we have here אלהי הנכר, "foreign gods," and הנזמים, "earrings."

The noun נזם, frequently translated as "earrings," appears 16 times in the MT (Gen 24:22, 30, 47; 35:4; Exod 32:2, 3; 35:22; Judg 8:24, 25, 26; Job 42:11; Prov 11:22; 25:12; Isa 3:21; Ezek 16:12; Hos 2:15). It is derived from the reconstructed root נזם*. Genesis 24:47; Isa 3:21 and Ezek 16:12 speak of the wearing of נזם in the nostrils, while Gen 35:4 and Exod 32:2-3 refer to this being in the ears. Genesis 24:22, 30, 47; Exod 35:22; Judg 8:24-26; Job 42:11; Prov 11:22[49] and 25:12 emphasise that the נזם are made of gold.

---

45. The LXX supplements v. 4 with καὶ ἀπώλεσεν αὐτὰ ἕως τῆς σήμερον ἡμέρας. Cf. the *Vetus Latina* version: "Et tradiderunt Jacob deos alienos qui erant in manibus eorum, et inaures quae erant in auriculis eorum: et abscondit ea Jacob subter terebinthum, quae est in Sichimis, et perdidit ea usque in hodiernum diem."

46. Soggin, "La radice TMN."

47. For more on this subject, see J.A. Soggin, "'La sepultura della Divinità' nell'iscrizione di Pyrgi (Lim.8-9) e motivi paralleli nell'Antico Testamento," *Rivista degli Studi Orienatli* 45 (1970): 245-52.

48. Soggin, "La radice TMN," 244-45.

49. "Like a gold ring in a pig's snout is a beautiful woman who shows no discretion."

In the book of Hosea the wearing of ornaments is linked with the cult of Baal:

> I will punish her for the days she burned incense to the Baals; she decked herself with rings and jewellery, and went after her lovers, but me she forgot, declares the Lord. (Hos 2:13)

Perhaps it was about נזם that the passage a few verses earlier speaks:

> Rebuke your mother, rebuke her, for she is not my wife, and I am not her husband. Let her remove the adulterous look from her face[50] and the unfaithfulness[51] from between her breasts. (Hos 2:2)

The phrase "let her remove זנוניה from her face" is given by the LXX as ἐξαρῶ τὴν πορνείαν αὐτῆς ἐκ προσώπου μου, whereas the formulation "ונאפופיה from between her breasts" reads καὶ τὴν μοιχείαν αὐτῆς ἐκ μέσου μαστῶν αὐτῆς. The Vulgate translates it fairly faithfully: "auferat fornicationes suas a facie sua et adulteria sua de medio uberum suorum." The Hebrew noun זנונים is the equivalent of the Greek noun πορνεία, and the word נאפום is the word μοιχεία.[52]

Judges 8:24 contains an interesting pointer by linking the wearing of נזם with allegiance to the Ishmaelites: "It was the custom of the Ishmaelites to wear gold ear-rings."

It is worth asking whether the ornaments which Jacob buried (Gen 34:5), from which Gideon made an ephod (Judg 8:24-27) and from which Aaron cast a golden calf in the desert (Exod 32:2-4), were simply a source of metal or whether they had a specific religious meaning. The passage from the book of Hosea cited earlier gives one indication. If golden ornaments worn in the nostrils were a sign of cult prostitution, then their condemnation by Yahwism is understandable, and their place near *teraphim* justified.

Victor Avigdor Hurwitz rejected the earlier translations of the term הנזמים as "amulets" or "images of gods."[53] In his view, the earrings' religious function depends on the interpretation of the pronoun "their"

---

50. Lit. "let her remove the adultery from her face." The word זנוניה is derived from the root זנה, "to commit adultery." The nominal form זנונים, "prostitution," "adultery," it appears in twelve places.

51. The noun נאפופיה, "adultery," is a *hapax legomenon*, and derives from the verb נאף, which appears in the MT a total of 31 times, including in the commandment: "Do not commit adultery" (Exod 20:14; Deut 5:18).

52. Cf. Hos 4:2; Jer 13:27.

53. V.A. Hurwitz, "Who Lost an Earring? Genesis 35:4 Reconsidered," *CBQ* 62 (2000): 28-32, together with a bibliography and a summary of the discussions to date.

(הם-), in the formulation "in their ears" (באזניהם). According to Hurwitz, earrings served to decorate the images of foreign gods and this naturally condemned them to the same fate as the images themselves.[54] The lack of biblical evidence to confirm the custom of decorating the images of gods somewhat weakens this argument. A further weakness comes from the incomprehensible behaviour of the members of Jacob's family: since they were going to bury the gods, why did they first take off the earrings only to bury them, too?

Genesis 33:19 mentions the buying a field: "For a hundred pieces of silver, he bought from the sons of Hamor, the father of Shechem, the plot of ground where he pitched his tent." The MT contains the unclear term, במאה קשיטה, "a hundred קשיטה."[55] This turn of phrase recurs in Josh 24:32 and Job 42:11: "and each one gave him a piece of silver (קשיטה) and a gold ring (נזם זהב)." The LXX gives δὲ αὐτῷ ἕκαστος ἀμνάδα μίαν καὶ τετράδραχμον χρυσοῦν ἄσημον, while the Vulgate translates it as "et dederunt ei unusquisque ovem unam et inaurem auream unam." The indication in the LXX that the term קשיטה was linked to the word for "sheep" is not supported by Hebrew etymology.[56] The term קשיטה is derived from the root קשט*, while "sheep," "lamb" is כבשה in Hebrew. The fact is that both the word for "sheep" (כבשה) used in Gen 21:28-30; Lev 5:6; Num 6:14; 2 Sam 12:4-6, and קשיטה is conveyed by the Greek term, ἀμνάδα.[57]

Appearing alongside the problematic קשיטה is the noun נזם, the same one which figured in the story of the burial of ornaments and foreign gods under the oak in Shechem. By drawing on the discussions about the likely forms of a chthonic cult and the role of a lamb in it,[58] we could put forward a hypothesis linking the idea of קשיטה with the word "lamb" (כבשה). In this case, the evidence of the LXX is a strong argument in favour of equating these two terms.

G.R.H. Wright[59] went even further in his reconstruction. Basing his work on the mythical picture of Shechem in the Bible, and particularly on the analogies between Shechem and Delphi, he showed that in the belief system of the inhabitants of Palestine, Shechem was regarded as

---

54. *Ibid.*

55. Cf. Nielsen, *Shechem*, 224-25.

56. BDB, *s.v.* "unit of (unknown) value, perh. weight."

57. Altogether the word ἀμνάδα appears in 21 times: Gen 21:28-30; Lev 5:6; Num 6:14; 2 Sam 12:4-6, and thirteen times in the seventh chapter of the book of Leviticus.

58. For more on this subject, see the chapter on Beer-sheba, Chapter 2.

59. G.R.H. Wright, "The Mythology of Pre-Israelite Shechem," *VT* 20 (1970): 75-82.

the centre of the world. The following text is of crucial importance to Wright's concept: "But Gaal spoke up again: Look, people are coming down from the centre of the land (טבור הארץ = ὀμφαλοῦ τῆς γῆς), and a company is coming from the direction of the soothsayers' tree" (Judg 9:37). Wright ascribes to Shechem all the features which characterise the exceptional nature of the centre of the world: the presence of an *axis mundi* in the form of a holy tree and/or a cosmic hill, life-giving water (the source called Jacob's well in New Testament times; see John 4:5-15) and a tomb (Joseph's). Shechem's central location is a factor which merely complements the mythical picture of this town.

The burial of Joseph's remains is mentioned in the book of Joshua (24:32). Cristiano Grottanelli pointed out that the figure of Joseph is similar in many respects to that of a dying god.[60] Like Adonis (Tammuz), Joseph is distinguished by his exceptional beauty.[61] Furthermore, if we accept a structuralist analysis of the text, his deeds are a series of symbolic deaths: the casting into a well has the characteristic of an initiation[62] (Gen 37:12-24)—*nota bene*, Joseph's brothers tended their flocks in the vicinity of Shechem[63]—as does the imprisonment (Gen 39).

Commentators have drawn attention to the cultic nature of the activities taking place beneath the oak in Shechem. Jan Alberto Soggin concluded that the book of Genesis (35:1-4) presents evidence of the performance of a ritual cleansing preceding the undertaking of a pilgrimage to a sanctuary;[64] this kind of practice could take place—according to Soggin—at a time following the final triumph of Yahwism.[65] According to Soggin's theory, the pilgrimage theme was taken from the narrative in which Jacob was to make his way to Bethel. It is possible that the activity described by the verb "to go" in the text might have been applied to, for instance, a procession performed in the sanctuary at Shechem itself. The conjunction of this ritual with the sanctuary in Bethel might have been the result of later editorial processes.

According to Soggin's and Grottanelli's idea, this initial rite would have looked like this: in a sanctuary located in the middle of the world, a ritual was performed aimed at recalling or "replaying" the scene of the

---

60. C. Grottanelli, "Spunti comparativi per la storia biblica di Giuseppe," *Oriens Antiquus* 15 (1976): 115-40.

61. *Ibid.*, 138-39.

62. For more on this subject, see the chapter on Beer-sheba, Chapter 2.

63. Though it is true that Gen 37:17 says that Joseph's brothers moved, with their flocks, to Dothan.

64. Soggin, "Jacob in Shechem," and "La sepultura della Divinità," 250.

65. Soggin, "Jacob in Shechem," 198.

death of a god of vegetation; this ritual was accompanied by lamentation (hence the divesting of ornaments) and a procession. It is hard to say to what extent this was linked, as Nielsen believes, to the sacral functions of a king, but there is no doubt that strong associations existed between this institution and Shechem (Abimelech, Judg 9; Rehoboam, 1 Kgs 12:1).

If we were to accept that such a ritual really did take place in Shechem (regardless of the period), then we would have to admit that its most obvious analogy is the ritual of repeating the death of Baal described in Ugaritic texts.

It may be no coincidence that it was in Shechem, the supposed central sanctuary where rituals associated with the cult of the death and resurrection of the god of vegetation was situated, that the Bible located the tomb of Joseph.[66]

Commentators are not, however, of one mind on this question. Some place the tomb in the vicinity of the settlement of 'Askar, others at the foot of Mt Ebal or close to the village of Salim.[67] The first of these suggestions is considered to be the most likely, though this settlement was inhabited only in the Hellenistic period.[68] This would mean that the biblical descriptions placing the grave of Joseph in Shechem would need to be dated no earlier than the Hellenistic period.

The theme of the death of the young god of vegetation is mirrored in the biblical story of Joseph's symbolic death as he is thrown into a well (Gen 37:20-34):[69]

> "...Come now, let us kill him and throw him into one of these cisterns (הברות = εἰς ἕνα τῶν λάκκων) and say that a ferocious animal (חיה רעה = θηρίον πονηρόν) devoured him. Then we shall see what comes of his dreams." When Reuben heard this, he tried to rescue him from their hands. "Let us not take his life," he said. "Do not shed any blood. Throw him into this cistern (הבור = εἰς τὸν λάκκον τοῦτον) here in the desert (אשר במדבר = τὸν ἐν τῇ ἐρήμῳ), but do not lay a hand on him." Reuben said this to rescue him from them and take him back to his father. So when Joseph came to his brothers, they stripped him of his robe—the richly ornamented robe he was wearing—and they took him and threw him into the cistern. Now the cistern was empty; there was no water in it.

66. For more on traces of an older tradition locating the graves of other patriarchs in Shechem, see the chapter dealing with Hebron, Chapter 5.

67. On this subject, cf. Na'aman, "The Law of the Altar," 156 n. 44.

68. *Ibid.*

69. In the chapter on Beer-sheba I cited and discussed the same text, while concentrating there on the meaning which the well (cistern) had among symbols of death.

As they sat down to eat their meal, they looked up and saw a caravan of Ishmaelites coming from Gilead. Their camels were loaded with spices, balm and myrrh, and they were on their way to take them down to Egypt. Judah said to his brothers, "What will we gain if we kill our brother and cover up his blood? Come, let's sell him to the Ishmaelites and not lay our hands on him; after all, he is our brother, our own flesh and blood." His brothers agreed. So when the Midianite merchants came by, his brothers pulled Joseph up out of the cistern and sold him for twenty shekels of silver to the Ishmaelites, who took him to Egypt. When Reuben returned to the cistern and saw that Joseph was not there, he tore his clothes. He went back to his brothers and said, "The boy (הילד = παιδάριον) is not there! Where can I turn now?" Then they got Joseph's robe, slaughtered a goat (שעיר עזים = ἔριφον αἰγῶν) and dipped the robe in the blood. They took the ornamented robe back to their father and said, "We found this." Examine it to see whether it is your son's robe. He recognised it and said, "It is my son's robe! Some ferocious animal (חיה רעה = θηρίον πονηρόν) has devoured him. Joseph has surely been torn to pieces (טרף טרף יוסף = θηρίον ἥρπασεν τὸν Ιωσηφ)." Then Jacob tore his clothes, put on sackcloth and mourned for his son many days. (Gen 37:20-34)

Several elements of this story suggest links with the myth of a dying god of vegetation and several others point to an analogy between Joseph and Dionysus.[70] Casting into the cistern could be symbolic of death or could be reflecting some specific ritual. Certain matters deserve particular attention: the description of Joseph as a "boy" (הילד = παιδάριον),[71] the role of the goat and its blood, the motif of the hero being torn to pieces by a wild animal (חיה רעה; lit. "wild creatures, beings") and the implied association with fragrances and aromas (Gen 37:25). It is probable that the robe worn by him (כתנת הפסים = τὸν χιτῶνα τὸν ποικίλον)[72] is particularly significant. The term כתנת הפסים, which was already unclear to translators of ancient times (hence the discrepancy in versions),[73] occurs again only in the narrative concerning Tamar's

70. Cf. Wright, "Joseph's Grave."

71. In this context, see W. Lengauer, "Dionysos dimorphos," *Kwartalnik Historii Kultury Materialnej* 1-2 (1998): 87-92; the author writes about the feminine quality of Dionysus.

72. See Garbini, *Note di lessicografia ebraica*, 111-15; the author considers that the term פסים used to describe the robe is linked not to the length of the robe itself, or its sleeves, but to the material, probably linen; it is, therefore, derived not from the root פסס, but from פשת and the noun פֵּשֶׁת.

73. A comparison of all the ancient versions and a discussion of the hypotheses associated with the etymology of this word can be found in Garbini, *Note di lessicografia ebraica*.

defilement: "She was wearing a richly ornamented robe (כתנת פסים = χιτὼν καρπωτός = *talaris tunica*), for this was the kind of garment the virgin daughters of the king wore" (2 Sam 13:18). Without being sure what the term פסים denotes, one can only draw attention to the fact that Joseph wore the kind of robe worn by "the virgin daughters of the king."

G.R.H. Wright noted that the analogies between the figures of Joseph and Dionysus come down to three key mythical themes: (1) miraculous birth, (2) death at a young age, (3) rebirth.[74] Virtually every element in the story of Joseph and his brothers has an equivalent in the Dionysian myths. The symbolic death of Joseph is linked with the killing of a goat (שעיר עזים), which was closely linked to Dionysus.[75] Jacob concludes that his son was torn to pieces, which is analogous to the Dionysian σπαραγμός; Joseph (by virtue of a new Egyptian name[76] and his courtly function) becomes the giver and, simultaneously, the lord of the crops which recalls Dionysus as the god of the harvest and gifts of the earth. The fertility and plenty associated with the figure of Joseph are expressed in Jacob's blessing: "Joseph is a fruitful vine (בן פרת), a fruitful vine near a spring, whose branches climb over a wall" (Gen 49:22). The circumstances of Joseph's birth are also important:

> During wheat harvest, Reuben went out into the fields and found some mandrake plants (וימצא דודאים בשדה = εὗρεν μῆλα μανδραγόρου ἐν τῷ ἀγρῷ), which he brought to his mother Leah. Rachel said to Leah: "Please give me some of your son's mandrakes." [...] Then God remembered Rachel; he listened to her and opened her womb. She became pregnant and gave birth to a son. (Gen 30:14, 22-23)

Mandragora, or mandrake (*Atropa belladonna*), was a plant to which powerful magic and healing properties were ascribed and which was often used as an aphrodisiac.[77] It is not without significance, according to Wright, that the conception and birth of Joseph occur thanks to the openly expressed will of God, which, indirectly, makes Joseph the son of God.[78]

Joseph as a hero of a biblical "romance" is characterised by one other important faculty—he can interpret dreams (Gen 37:1-11; 40; 41). He

---

74. Wright, "Joseph's Grave," 479.

75. On the links between Dionysus and a goat, see W. Lengauer, "Dionizos rogaty," in *Nunc de Svebis dicendum est. Studia archaeologica et historica Georgio Kolendo ab amicis et discipulis dicata*, Warsaw, 1995, 157-60.

76. Cf. Wright, "Joseph's Grave," 483, translates Joseph's new name— צפנת־פענח (Gen 41:45)—as "He who gives life-giving food."

77. *Ibid.*, 481.

78. *Ibid.*

is, therefore, a soothsayer or diviner.[79] Hence the association of this figure with a sacred tree, a place of divination *par excellence*, is highly probable.

The *Testament of Joseph* mentions Joseph's exceptional beauty; it talks of the lust he inspired in the wife of Potiphar. The following sentence appears there: "And I fasted in those seven years, and I appeared to the Egyptian as one who lives luxuriously; for those who fast for God's sake receive beauty of face" (*T. Jos.* 3.4). And further on: "And he [God] gave me also beauty as a flower, beyond the beautiful ones of Israel; and he preserved me unto old age in strength and in beauty, for I was like Jacob in all things" (*T. Jos.* 18.4).[80]

The Quranic tradition has expanded the theme of the lust of Potiphar's wife (Gen 39) and has ascribed to Joseph the power of attracting women: "Go back to your lord and ask him, what is the case of the women who cut their hands... He said: How was your affair when you sought Yusuf to yield himself (to you)? They said: Remote is Allah (from imperfection), we knew of no evil on his part" (Q 12:50-51).[81] The same *sura* talks of one more attribute testifying to Joseph's unusual power, namely, the gift of healing: "Take this my shirt and cast it on my father's face, he will (again) be able to see... So when the bearer of good news came he cast it on his face, so forthwith he regained his sight" (Q 12:93, 96).

The fact that in the description of Joseph's "death" the Bible mentions "spices, balm and myrrh" (Gen 37:25) points to an analogy with the myth of Adonis, a god who died young, and was strongly associated with various fragrances.[82]

Wright also drew attention to Ps 22:13-19, which can be interpreted as a description of behaviour comparable to the Greek σπαραγμός:[83]

> Many bulls surround me; strong bulls of Bashan encircle me. Roaring lions tearing their prey open their mouths wide against me. I am poured out like water, and all my bones are out of joint. My heart has turned to wax; it has melted away within me. My strength is dried up like a potsherd,

79. *Ibid.*, 476-86.

80. Hollander and de Jong, *The Testaments of the Twelve Patriarchs*.

81. This and other fragments of the Quran are quoted in the translation by M.H. Shakir, New York, 1983. Cf. Wright, "Joseph's Grave," 484.

82. There is an extensive bibliography on the subject of Adonisin S. Ribichini, *Adonis. Aspetti 'orientali' di un mito greco*, Rome, 1981; *idem, Adonis. Relazioni del colloquio in Roma 22–23 maggio 1981*, Rome, 1984. In the latter volume, see especially D. Sabbatucci, "Il problema storico-religioso di Adonis: confronto tra il momento frazeriano e il moderno," 17-24; O. Loretz, "ADN come epiteto di Baal e i suoi raporti con Adonis e Adonaj," 25-33.

83. Wright, "Joseph's Grave," 482.

and my tongue sticks to the roof of my mouth; you lay me in the dust of death. Dogs have surrounded me; a hand of evil men (עדת מרעים / συναγωγὴ πονηρευομένων[84]) has encircled me, they have pierced my hands and my feet. I can count all my bones; people stare and gloat over me. They divide my garments among them and cast lots for my clothing.

The best evidence of the existence of a ritual or even just the memory of the custom commemorating the "death" of Joseph is to be found in the book of *Jubilees*:

> For this reason, it has been ordained regarding the Israelites that they should be distressed on the tenth of the seventh month—on the day when (the news) which made (him) lament Joseph reached his father Jacob—in order to make atonement for themselves on it with a kid—on the tenth of the seventh month, once a year—for their sins. For they had saddened their father's (feeling of) affection for his son Joseph. This day has been ordained so that they may be saddened on it for their sins, all their transgressions, and all their errors; so that they may purify themselves on this day once a year. (*Jub.* 34:18-19)

If the mention of the day of mourning refers to a reality which the author experienced, then it follows that what we have here is confirmation of the existence of a ritual associated with a dying god. Particularly notable is the mention of the tenth day of the seventh month, that is, the month of Tishri (September–October).[85] In the Jewish ritual calendar this day is the same as the feast of Yom Kippur, during which a sacrifice has to be made for one's sins. Only on that one day, once a year, did the priest walk through the curtain to the Holy of Holies. Chapter 16 of the book of Leviticus[86] contains the canonical description of the day of Atonement. One of the ritual requirements imposed on the priest relates to his dress: "This is how Aaron is to enter the sanctuary area [...] He is to put on the sacred linen tunic, with linen undergarments next to his body; he is to tie the linen sash around him and put on the linen turban. These are sacred garments" (Lev 16:3-4). On the day of mourning the dead Joseph is set down for the whole of Israel on the tenth day of the month of Tishri, and it is on that day that the Jews celebrate the Day of Atonement, and the priest in the Temple puts on holy robes similar to those worn by the patriarch (god?) who is being remembered. When "dying" in the cistern or by dint of wild animals, Joseph was wearing a characteristic robe, assuredly linen,[87] which was supposed to protect the

84. Both the MT and LXX use the same expressions, which appear in Gen 37:33.
85. De Vaux, *Ancient Israel*, 1:185-86.
86. See de Vaux, *Ancient Israel*, 2:507-10, notes that Lev 16 is one of the most reworked and comparatively late fragments of that book.
87. Garbini, *Note di lessicografia ebraica*, 111-15.

priest entering the Holiest place in the Temple from death.[88] On the Day of Atonement, a sacrifice was made in the Temple of a calf and a goat. The singularity of this act lay in the use of the blood to sprinkle the ark and the corners of the altar (Lev 16:15, 18).

The Day of Atonement is also the time when the goat is sacrificed to Azazel (Lev 16:8-10).[89] When an animal is banished to the desert it undoubtedly indicates that it is being offered to a god connected with the world of the dead. We should note that in both this case and the case of Joseph's feigned death at the well (Gen 37:31), a goat (שעיר) was killed. What the priest has to do with the goat for Azazel is important:

> He is to lay both hands on the head of the live goat and confess over it all the wickedness and rebellion of the Israelites-all their sins-and put them on the goat's head. He shall send the goat away into the desert in the care of a man appointed for the task. The goat will carry on itself all their sins to a solitary place; and the man shall release it in the desert. (Lev 16:21-22)

The message of this feast-day is as follows: "on this day atonement will be made for you, to cleanse you. Then, before the Lord, you will be clean from all your sins" (Lev 16:30).

There is an almost total analogy between the symbolism of the Day of Atonement, and its associated rituals, and the concepts connected with a god who dies for sins. The death of a god, generally associated with a god of vegetation, is a form of cleansing. It is a sacrifice of redemption thanks to which the society can continue to function. The death of a god gives life to people. This motif, which is universally present in Middle Eastern belief systems, can also be found in the story of the redemptive death of Jesus.

There is a sufficient basis to accept the fact that mourning rituals in Israel were practised at a time coinciding with the ceremonies of the Day of Atonement (the tenth day of the month of Tishri). The location of Joseph's grave—that of the incarnation of a dying god—in Shechem indicates that festivities for a dying god were held there, and it may have been there that the centre of a cult devoted to him was found. Both the act of cleansing and the pilgrimage, or rather procession, could have been part of the rituals associated with this festival. The god worshipped in Shechem had a feast day devoted to it on the tenth day of the month of Tishri and it was on this feast day that the rituals mentioned in the deeds of Jacob may have been performed.

---

88. Cf. Lev 10:1-5.

89. On the subject of sacrifices to Azazel, see M. Münnich, "Azazel—nowe interpretacje," *Ruch Biblijny i Liturgiczny* 55.2 (2002): 89-108.

The Bible uses the term "the house of Joseph" (בית יוסף) in relation to the tribes of Manasseh and Ephraim. This form can be found in Josh 17:17; 18:5; Judg 1:22, 23, 35; 2 Sam 19:21; 1 Kgs 11:28; Amos 5:6; Zech 10:6 and Obad 18.[90] When describing the conquest of Canaan, the book of Joshua treats the tribes of Ephraim and Manasseh jointly, whereas the book of Judges separates them: it mentions the settlement of the Manassehites in the vicinity of Beth-shean, Taanach, Dor, Ibleam, Megiddo, and of the Ephraimites in Gezer, and also emphasises the fact that the lives of the populace of Canaan were spared (Judg 1:22-29). In 2 Sam 19:20 "the house of Joseph" is mentioned in a way that is usually limited to depicting a tribe and 1 Kgs 11:29 names "the house of Joseph" as a separate administrative unit in the division of Solomon's kingdom. So, the differentiation between Ephraimites and Manassehites is lost.[91] Amos 5:6 uses the terms "house of Joseph" and "Israel" interchangeably, and Zech 10:6 places "the house of Joseph" and "the house of Judah" side by side (Ephraim is mentioned in the next verse). The separation of Ephraim and the subjectivity of "the house of Joseph" can be seen most clearly in Obad 18-19:

> The house of Jacob will be a fire and the house of Joseph a flame; the house of Esau will be stubble, and they will set it on fire and consume it. There will be no survivors from the house of Esau. The Lord has spoken. People from the Negev will occupy the mountains of Esau, and people from the foothills will possess the land of the Philistines. They will occupy the fields of Ephraim and Samaria, and Benjamin will possess Gilead.

The longevity of the tradition connecting Joseph with Shechem is seen in the New Testament: "So he came to a town in Samaria called Sychar, near the plot of ground Jacob had given to his son Joseph" (John 4:5).

Joseph is the eponymous patron of the district of Shechem to which a remark by Flavius Josephus in *Jewish Antiquities* testifies:

> When the Jews are in difficulties, they [the Samaritans] deny that they have any kinship with them, thereby indeed admitting the truth, but whenever they see some splendid bit of good fortune come to them, they suddenly grasp at the connection with them, saying that they are related to them and tracing their line back to Ephraim and Manasseh, the descendants of Joseph. (*Ant* 11.8.6)[92]

---

90. Cf. Gen 43:18, 19; 50:8, where the form בית יוסף does not refer to Joseph's descendants but literally to his house.

91. For an analogous treatment of the phrase "house of Joseph," see Rev 7:8.

92. Wright, "The Samaritans at Shechem," 362-63, emphasises that this passage comes from the most anti-Samaritan source that Flavius Josephus used.

The biblical tradition that emphasises the affiliation of the region of Shechem to the heritage of Manasseh and Ephraim—sons of Joseph—is further proof of Joseph's strong link with this town.

Eduard Nielsen attempted to combine the ritual described in Gen 35:1-4 with kingship rituals. He pointed to the analogies between the burial (destruction) of foreign gods with other valuable objects and similar Egyptian and Mesopotamian customs.[93] In considering the likely circumstances of such a magical practice he concluded that it was performed to protect the king—the chief figure in the ritual performed close to the sacred oak.[94]

The tree is also mentioned in the narrative of the proclamation of Abimelech as king: "Then all the citizens of Shechem and Beth Millo gathered beside the great tree [oak] (אלון) at the pillar (מצב) in Shechem to crown Abimelech king" (Judg 9:6). The LXX translates the end of v. 6 as πρὸς τῇ βαλάνῳ τῇ εὑρετῇ τῆς στάσεως τῆς ἐν Σικιμοις, while the Vulgate has "iuxta quercum quae stabat in Sychem." Neither the Greek translation nor the Vulgate mentions the pillar. The noun מצב is derived from the verb נצב, "to stand," "to place." Words deriving from this root denote a cult object mentioned many times in the Bible (note, e.g., the מצבה placed by Jacob in Bethel, when making a covenant with Laban, and over the grave of Rachel). In 2 Kgs 10:26-27 the word מצבות denotes objects found in the temple of Baal. The LXX gives στήλα τοῦ Βααλ, while the Vulgate gives "statua de fano Baal." What this shows is that the noun מצב denotes some cult object. It is, however, possible that there has been an error in translation and that the sentence in Judg 9:6 has a slightly different meaning, "by the standing oak which [is] in Shechem," which would indicate the sacred nature of the tree, not a pillar.

Undoubtedly, a pillar did play some part in the coronation ritual (or proclamation of kingship).[95] Evidence for this is found in the story of the coming to power of Joash and the suppression of Athaliah:

> She looked and there was the king, standing by the pillar (על־העמוד = ἐπὶ τοῦ στύλου = *super tribunal*), as the custom was (כמשפט = κατὰ τὸ κρίμα). The officers and the trumpeters were beside the king, and all the people of the land were rejoicing and blowing trumpets. Then Athaliah tore her robes and called out, Treason! Treason! (2 Kgs 11:14)

Note also a passage about Josiah: "The king stood by the pillar (על־העמוד = πρὸς τὸν στύλον) and renewed the covenant in the presence of the Lord" (2 Kgs 23:3). The Vulgate does not mention a pillar

---

93. E. Nielsen, "The Burial of the Foreign Gods," *StTh* 8 (1955): 103-22.
94. *Ibid.*, 121-22.
95. Cf. de Vaux, *Ancient Israel*, 1:102-103.

(column) here, interpreting the text as being about steps: "stetitque rex super gradum." The pillar mentioned in connection with certain kingship rituals in Jerusalem is a different pillar from the one mentioned in Judg 9:6. The Hebrew word עמוד is also used to denote a pillar (column) of fire or smoke (Exod 13:22; 14:19; 33:9-10; Deut 31:15; Judg 20:40;[96] Neh 9:19) as well as elements of the Jerusalem Temple (1 Kgs 7:15, 21; 2 Kgs 25:17). If Roland de Vaux[97] is right in regarding העמוד as one of the elements of the decoration of the Temple, then this object would be stone whereas the coronation of Abimelech undoubtedly takes place beneath a sacred tree.

Ed Noort put forward a theory to explain the evolution and mutual influence of the texts in the books of Deuteronomy and Joshua concerning the hills of Ebal and Gerizim.[98] He took the text of Deut 27:4, 8 to be the first layer, the two originally contiguous verses later being split by the interpolation of vv. 5-7. The text of Deut 27:4-8 influenced the final form of Josh 8:30-32. Noort believes that the ritual described in Josh 8:30-32 originally took place in the vicinity of Jordan, in other words, in Gilgal-Jericho.[99] Although the reconstruction of the history of the text's transmission suggested by Noort seems to be true, his proposition that Gilgal came before Shechem is arbitrary and, in my view, erroneous.

Researchers generally agree that the references to Shechem, Ebal and Gerizim in Deut 11:26-30; 27 and Josh 8:30-35; 24 are late additions.[100] Nadav Na'aman concluded that the verses in question, both in the book of Deuteronomy and in the book of Joshua, came about as a late addition to an already existing deuteronomistic collection.[101] He agreed that the narrative about the building of an altar on newly settled ground contains many references to Greek customs. If Greek rituals influenced the Hebrew literary tradition, then it must have occurred in the sixth or fifth century BCE.[102] In his conclusions, Na'aman strives to date the texts concerning the beginnings of a sanctuary in Shechem found in Deuteronomy and Joshua to the period after the destruction of the Temple in Jerusalem and before its restoration. His reconstruction would mean that the fragments in question should be described as "proto-Samaritan" because the idea of the exceptional nature of Jerusalem is replaced by the idea of

---

96. Here without any sacral connotations.
97. De Vaux, *Ancient Israel*, 1:102-103.
98. Noort, "The Traditions of Ebal and Gerizim," 176-80.
99. *Ibid.*, 176.
100. Na'aman, *The Law of the Altar*, 141-42.
101. *Ibid.*, 157-58.
102. *Ibid.*, 159.

the exceptional nature of Shechem.[103] This theory, though it explains the genesis of the references in question, does not explain why they have been preserved in the Bible. For if the aim was indeed as Na'aman claims then, after the reconstruction of the Jerusalem Temple, the first thing the representatives of the revived priestly élite would have done would have been to remove these embarrassing writings. Na'aman's explanation that later editors attempted to minimise or to erase the sense and meaning of the text appears to be unconvincing.[104]

A discussion of the function of the narrative in the book of Joshua (ch. 24) requires a separate study.[105] Undoubtedly the key theme of this story is that of the making of the covenant and the significance attached to the law which is to be read out. The traditional understanding is that the covenant made in Shechem is an accord between Israel and God. My view, however, is that this theme is an expression of a secondary theology based on the idea of an accord between the chosen nation and its God, and that to begin with the agreement was between people and that God was a party overseeing the covenant. The agreement was made "before God" who—as the highest religious authority—became the guarantor of its validity.

From epigraphic material documenting religious customs in ancient Palestine, Jeffrey H. Tigay distinguished the inscriptions dealing with oaths and promises.[106] What emerges from all the documents Tigay names, and from the extensive comparative available material from Mesopotamia,[107] is that the god performed the role only of a guarantor, in other words an authority called upon to act as witness to, or punish the one guilty of breaking, the oath. The oath, or promise—in other words, an agreement of a legal nature—demands religious sanction to ensure its legal enactment before God.

Chapter 24 of the book of Joshua contains an expanded version of the story of the covenant described in the book of Deuteronomy (11:26-32 and 27:1-26), one in which the role of Moses as the law-giver is emphasised. In truth, this is not an agreement between the chosen people and God, but between the chosen people and Moses, the law-giver. This is best seen in the following sentence: "Moses and the elders of Israel commanded the people: Keep all these commands that I give you today"

---

103.   Cf. Noort, "The Traditions of Ebal and Gerizim," 167-68, demonstrates that there was a tendency towards ascribing more importance to Mt Gerizim than to Mt Ebal.

104.   Na'aman, "The Law of the Altar," 159-61.

105.   Nielsen, *Shechem*, 86-141.

106.   Tigay, *You Shall Have No Other Gods*, esp. 33-34 and 36.

107.   Van der Toorn, *Family Religion, passim.*

(Deut 27:1). Among the actions forbidden in ch. 27 and deserving of condemnation (curse) are: carving or casting of images of gods (v. 15), lack of honour for one's parents (v. 16), trespass or theft (v. 17), not obeying the laws of hospitality and the rights appertaining to orphans and widows (v. 19), adultery (v. 20), sodomy (v. 21), incest (vv. 22-23), murder (vv. 24-25). These injunctions derive from the Decalogue, but in point of fact they relate to the whole area of humankind's relationship with God. Only to a small extent do they set down rules for religious behaviour. The majority of these are regulations taken from civil or criminal law.[108] The original story of the covenant in Shechem, contained in the book of Deuteronomy, attached great weight to the introduction and sanctioning of legal principles. Moses laid down the law for the Israelites and they swore to respect it. The presence and role of the god of Israel in this act coincides with what we know on the basis of oath-taking rituals in the Middle East: a person undertakes something (in this instance to obey the law), and the divine being guarantees that the person will keep his word. If the person breaks his oath, then God will send punishment down on him.

The authors of the narrative in Josh 24 interpreted the covenant in Shechem very differently: Joshua speaks to the Israelites in the name of God (vv. 2-13), and God becomes a party to the agreement made. The people promise fidelity to the real God. The actual content of the covenant in Shechem becomes a declaration of belief in Yahweh and the abandoning of other deities.

A comparison with the version in the book of Deuteronomy shows that the details accompanying the making of the covenant are different, too. Deuteronomy 27:4-8 mentions the setting up of stones covered in plaster and the creating an altar of stones untouched by any metal tool. Burnt offerings are to be accompanied by feasts ("…eating them and rejoicing in the presence of the Lord your God," Deut 27:7). The account in Josh 24 is decidedly more ascetic. There is no mention of either eating or rejoicing before the Lord. Verse 26 speaks of writing the law in a book (!) and setting a great stone under an oak which was "near the holy place of the Lord." This stone becomes a witness to the Israelites' declaration of loyalty. The mention of topographic details (stone, oak, holy place of the Lord) shows that the text's authors had in mind an actual image of a holy place in Shechem, where there was one standing stone, and not—as Deut 27 states—several stones.[109] The announcement of the covenant in Deuteronomy contains no mention of the oak or the holy

---

108.   Of course, this distinction was not known in ancient times.
109.   For more, see the section on Gilgal below, pp. 206-15.

place. The authors of Josh 24 did, however, know about the appearance of the *temenos* in Shechem and did not hesitate to introduce details showing evidence of it.

There is no doubt in my mind that in the old account of the covenant in Shechem (in Deuteronomy) the subject was an agreement made between people and guaranteed by God, whereas in the book of Joshua (ch. 24) what we are dealing with is a late tradition of a decidedly different vision of a covenant from a theological point of view. Here a new relationship appears—between God and the chosen people. This revolution in the approach to the covenant has left a troublesome element when it comes to the description's coherence. A covenant must have a witness. Since it cannot be God, because God is one of the parties to the agreement, this function is performed by the people itself and by the stone.[110] From a religious standpoint, the covenant described in Josh 24 is closer to the covenant made by Ezra (Neh 8–9; cf., e.g., the significance of the book) than to its original model in the book of Deuteronomy.

John Van Seters argued against the thesis that ch. 24 of the book of Joshua was part of the Deuteronomistic work and, on the basis of analysis, included this fragment in the Yahwistic literature of the Babylonian captivity.[111] His argument is persuasive except for the assertion that for an author writing in exile, Shechem's religious authority was sufficient reason to place an event like the making of a covenant there.[112]

S. David Sperling challenged Van Seters's conclusions. He determined that the author of Josh 24 did not need to draw on older traditions and he therefore argued that the story originated in the eighth century BCE.[113] In this discussion, however, Van Seters has presented the stronger arguments. It appears well justified to accept that this text is a later addition to the body of deuteronomistic corpus.[114]

The ritual on Mt Ebal and in Shechem is linked to the codification of the Torah ("Law of Moses"), for there is a clear mention of writing the

110.   For more on the subject of the role of the stone as a witness, see Chapter 8, the section on Galeed, pp. 218-34.

111.   J. Van Seters, "Joshua 24 and the Problem of Tradition in the Old Testament," in W. Boyd Barrick and J.R. Spencer (eds.), *In the Shelter of Elyon: Essays on Ancient Palestinian Life and Literature in Honor of G.W. Ahlström*, JSOTSup 31, Sheffield, 1984, 139-58.

112.   *Ibid.*, 153.

113.   S.D. Sperling, "Joshua 24 Re-examined," *HUCA* 58 (1987): 119-36.

114.   Supporting Van Seters's theory is, *inter alia*, Yair Hoffman's thesis, propounded in the course of the analysis of a different text, that extensive narratives rich in detail are highly likely to be later additions; see Y. Hoffman, "Aetiology, Redaction and Historicity in Jeremiah XXXVI," *VT* 46 (1996): 179-89 (182-83).

words of the Torah on stones.[115] Even if we understand that "the Book of the Torah of Moses" (ספר תורת משה) relates only to certain fragments of the Pentateuch (e.g. the so-called Law [Codex] of Holiness, Lev 17–26) the fact that there is an emphasis on the role of the writing and on the status of the Torah indicates that these verses are of late origin. In Van Seters's view, it was the period of the Babylonian captivity or the beginning of the Persian period. This dating, analogous to the theory of Pentateuch sources and their dating, is based on the author's arbitrary choices. The only certainty, in my view, is that the story in the book of Joshua is secondary in relation to the text in the book of Deuteronomy. I believe that it is impossible to set a precise date for this tradition's origins, although the emphasis on the part played by writing and the decided novelty of making God one of the parties agreeing to the covenant point to a fairly late time. But there is no way of saying whether that is the Persian or the Hellenistic period. The details in the description showing evidence of the existence in Shechem of some sacred buildings when the text came into being are a significant pointer. It has to be remembered that there was a break in settlement there during the Persian period. If, then, the archaeological data are interpreted correctly, the existence of the sanctuary described in Josh 24:26 marks the time of the text's creation. It could not have been the Persian period. We are dealing here with either an account of a reality from before the sixth century BCE, which seems unlikely in light of the innovative presentation of the covenant's structure, or—more likely—with a description of reality in the Hellenistic period. There is no doubt that there was a sanctuary in Shechem at that time. Although this is pure speculation, I would be inclined to suspect that the text of Josh 24 (or the tradition which lies at its beginnings) came into being in the Hellenistic period. A more precise dating for the writing of this text would depend on a consideration of the prevalence of tensions between the Samaritans and the Jews and the establishment of their causes.

There can be no doubt that the Bible (especially the New Testament) and Flavius Josephus confirm the existence of such a conflict—one which, if it really had grown to the levels suggested by Josephus, would be an indication of the *terminus ante quem* of the story of the covenant in Shechem. In that case we would have to acknowledge that this narrative represents a proto-Samaritan branch of the tradition; that, in turn, would require an explanation of why such a text should have been preserved in the Hebrew Bible. Josephus's testimony is greatly exaggerated, and the conflict between the Jews and the Samaritans in the Hellenistic period

---

115. Cf. Noort, "The Traditions of Ebal and Gerizim," 178-80.

was not as sharp as is generally supposed. Taking this into account, I would be inclined to date the fragment of the book of Joshua in question, ch. 24, in the third century BCE.

The popular belief in the existence of a mutual antagonism between the Jews and the Samaritans is a result of taking the biblical information and Josephus's comments at face value. The truth, however, appears to be a little more complicated. The New Testament parable of the Good Samaritan (Luke 10:29-37), the scene with the Samaritan woman at the well (John 4) and the reference to the Samaritans' lack of hospitality (Luke 9:51-56) do not necessarily fully reflect the relationship between the two sides. There is no doubt that Flavius Josephus is decidedly anti-Samaritan so his account cannot be taken as objective. Nevertheless, the conflict certainly did exist.

The following quotation testifies to the fact that, in the eyes of the Jews, the Shechemites were ethnically alien: "There are two nations which my soul abhorreth: and the third is no nation. They that sit on Mt Seir, and the Philistines, and the foolish people that dwell in Shechem" (Sir 50:25-26).[116] The same is also true of Josephus's *Jewish Antiquities*: "they said that they were Hebrews, but were called the Sidonians of Shechem" (*Ant* 11.8.6). According to the most extreme view, preserved in 2 Kgs 17:24-41, the inhabitants of Samaria were descended from the people settled there by the Assyrians.

The account that Josephus gives of the building of the sanctuary on Mt Gerizim is somewhat hazy, since he writes:

> [Sanballat] said that he would build a temple similar to that in Jerusalem on Mt Garizein—this is the highest of the mountains near Samaria –, and undertook to do these things with the consent of King Darius. (*Ant* 11.8.2)

A little further on, he says:

> [Hyrcanus] captured Samoga and its environs, and, in addition to these, Shechem and Garizein and the Cuthaean nation, which lives near the temple built after the model of the sanctuary at Jerusalem, which Alexander permitted their governor Sanaballetes to build for the sake of his son-in-law Manasseh, the brother of the high priest Jaddua. (*Ant* 13.9.1)

Archaeological finds tend to confirm the second of these versions since they provide evidence of a settlement at Tell er-Râs "which Alexander permitted."[117] It is not only the numismatic and ceramic finds that

116. The LXX gives v. 27 as: οἱ καθήμενοι ἐν ὄρει Σαμαρείας καὶ Φυλιστιιμ καὶ ὁ λαὸς ὁ μωρὸς ὁ κατοικῶν ἐν Σικιμοις.

117. E.F. Campbell, "Jewish Shrines of the Hellenistic and Persian Period," in F.M. Cross (ed.), *Symposia Celebrating the Seventy-fifth Anniversary of the*

support, this but also the architecture which suggests Greek influences. This indicates not only the beginnings of settlement there after 332–331 BCE but also a significant Greek population. The Greek presence in Shechem is mentioned by Eusebius, Jerome and Synkellos. On his return from Egypt, Alexander was supposed to have pacified the town (where a hostage sent by him had been burned) and to have left a detachment of his soldiers there.[118]

The history of Shechem, or rather the mythology associated with this place, became a source of dispute between the Jews and the Samaritans. The issue was the location of the hill in Moriah—the place where Isaac was offered in sacrifice (Gen 22:1-18), as also where Abraham met Melchizedek (Gen 14:17-20).[119] Both Samaritans and Jews tried to prove that important events in the mythical deeds of the patriarchs were played out in their holy places. The argument put forward by Kalimi, taken from the Jewish historiography of the Hellenistic period, indicates that not all literary testimonies were created on an *ad hoc* basis, for immediate propaganda purposes. The passage in question is ascribed to Pseudo-Eupolemos (Eusebius, *Praep. Ev.* 9.17.5-6): "He was made welcome in the town which lies in the holy place of Agragizim and received gifts from Melchizedek, the priest of God and the king."[120] This passage reveals clearly a favourable attitude to Gerizim and confirms the sanctity of the place. This has inclined commentators to assess it as being Pseudo-Eupolem. Meanwhile, Giovanni Garbini has shown that there is nothing to stand in the way of dismissing the separation of the work into that of Eupolemos and Pseudo-Eupolemos.[121] Looking for a dislike of Samaritans and their sanctuary in the work of a historian who lived in the second century BCE appears to be misguided. This is because it is only on the basis of an assumption that Eupolemos, a Jew closely associated with the Maccabees, must have harboured a hatred of the inhabitants of Samaria that the separation of fragments ascribed to Eupolemos and those traditionally ascribed to Pseudo-Eupolemos is made. Eupolemos

Founding of the American Schools of Oriental Research (1900–1975), Cambridge, 1979, 159-61.

118. Wright, "Samaritans," 363-65.

119. For an extensive discussion of this question and the bibliography, see Kalimi, "Zion or Gerizim?," and also I. Hjelm, *Jerusalem's Rise to Sovereignty in History and Tradition*, JSOTSup 404, London, 2004.

120. Jacoby, *FGrHist* 724 F1; A.-M. Denis, *Fragmenta Pseudepigraphorum Quae Supersunt Graeca*, Leiden, 1970, 197-98.

121. G. Garbini, "Eupolemo storico giudeo," *Atti della Accademia Nazionale dei Lincei, Rendiconti* 9/9, fasc. 4, (1998): 613-34 (613-16); see also R. Doran, "Jewish Hellenistic Historians before Josephus," *ANRW* 20.1: 264.

was active before 128 BCE, that is to say, *before* the destruction of the Samaritan temple by John Hyrcanus, and the fragments of his work testify merely to the existence of a different current of tradition to the one which came to be included in the biblical canon. The fact that a Jewish historian closely associated with Judas Maccabaeus should write this unequivocally excludes any pro-Samaritan bias. What we have here is a tradition which was adopted by the Samaritans but rejected by the Jews.

We can, then, accept that up until the destruction of the temple on Mt Gerizim in 128 BCE, relations between the Jews and the Samaritans were not as strained as has been generally supposed, and there was certainly no conflict of a religious nature. Indicative of this is the example of Sanballat, the governor of Samaria, mentioned in the book of Nehemiah: his opposition to Nehemiah is the result of a conflict based on material interests and probably stemming from a fear of a loss of income, and not a conflict of a religious nature. As late as the second century BCE, Samaritans lived in the same centres as the Jews in harmony. There is evidence of this in the inscriptions at Delos which mention the Israelites making offerings to the god of Shechem.[122] The sense of commonality existed as late as the first century CE, an indication of which was the participation of the Samaritans in the Jewish uprising against the Romans (66–70 CE).

The description in Gen 33 of the purchase of land by Jacob has, it seems, its source in the tradition recounting the existence of a tomb of the patriarchs in the vicinity of Shechem. An indirect proof of this could be the reference to the burial of Jacob: "My father made me swear an oath and said, 'I am about to die; bury me in the tomb I dug for myself in the land of Canaan'" (Gen 50:5).[123] This motif was expunged from the Hebrew Bible, but was preserved in the Acts of the Apostles: "Then Jacob went down to Egypt, where he and our fathers died. Their bodies were brought back to Shechem and placed in the tomb that Abraham had bought from the sons of Hamor at Shechem for a certain sum of money" (Acts 7:15-16).[124] This is part of a speech by Stephen which should rather not be linked to a Samaritan tradition.[125] It is a trace of a Jewish tradition

122.   P. Bruneau, "'Les Israélites de Délos' et la juiverie délienne," *Bulletin de Correspondance Hellénique* 106 (1982): 465-504. Cf. A.D. Crown, "Redating the Schism between the Judaeans and the Samaritans," *JQR* 82.1–2 (1991): 17-59.

123.   Cf. Bloch-Smith, *Judahite Burial Practices*, 114 n. 1.

124.   For more on this subject see the chapter on Hebron.

125.   C.H.H. Scobie, "The Origins and Development of Samaritan Christianity," *NTS* 19 (1973): 390-414; "The Use of Source Material in the Speeches of Acts III and VII," *NTS* 25 (1979): 399-421.

which has been omitted in the canonical text of the Hebrew Bible. Acknowledgment that two parallel accounts existed locating the tomb of the patriarchs in Shechem and in Hebron (or maybe even that there was an older account relating to Shechem[126]) is an important factor in the analysis of the history of the Bible. The fact is that as late as the second century CE there were interpolations in the text of the Bible and these interpolations must have been serious since the resting place of the patriarchs was "moved" and all traces of the patriarchs' burial in Shechem were erased. It does not seem that the story of Shechem was erased earlier than the middle of the second century. This is, first, because the Jews had no reasons before then to minimise the sanctity of this place, and secondly, because even the rejected and denied tradition was still alive in the time when the Acts of the Apostles were written.

Lately—and quite rightly, in my view—the date of the destruction of the temple on Mt Gerizim has ceased to be regarded as the point at which the paths of the Jews and the Samaritans parted.[127] Alan D. Crown has shown how various Samaritans and Jews used testimonies about the patriarchs to prove that the rightful religious centre was—respectively— either in Shechem or Jerusalem. What is interesting is the exacerbation of this dispute culminating in the interfering in the biblical text that occurred only in the second–third century CE.[128]

What is puzzling, however, is why the covenant was made in the vicinity of Shechem. Later disputes between the Samaritans and the Jews regarding the supremacy of Jerusalem or Gerizim reveal the controversial part played by Shechem subsequently. However, for some important reasons the editors of the Bible did not remove from the text the information that such an important event took place in Shechem, nor did they "move" it to Jerusalem. My view is that we need to look for the reason for this in the nature of the god worshipped in both centres.

Jerusalem saw the development of the cult of Yahweh, regarded as a tribal or national divinity to whom the attributes of other gods, primarily Shelim, an evidently chthonic god, were ascribed. This chthonic facet of the Yahweh cult appeared in such rituals as the *molk* ritual or in the existence of *tophet* in Jerusalem (see 2 Kgs 16:3; 17:17; 21:6; 23:10).[129]

It is not clear what cult was practised in Shechem. As I have tried to indicate earlier, the tradition linking Joseph to this place and the locating

126. See the chapter dealing with Hebron, Chapter 5.
127. Crown, "Redating the Schism," 17-50; see also the state of research in Hjelm, *The Samaritans*.
128. Crown, "Redating the Schism."
129. On the subject of *molk* ritual, see Garbini, *Note di lessicografia ebraica*, 73-78.

of his grave there is evidence of the existence of a cult of a god who
"dies young." The cult of Baal Berith (בעל ברית = Βααλ διαθήκην /
Βααλβεριθ[130]), even if Baal may be seen as the young dying-god, might
have been of a different kind. The cult is mentioned by the book of
Judges (8:33 and 9:4). Then again, in another part of the book (Judg
9:46) there is talk of El Berith (בעל אל ברית / Βαιθηλβεριθ). In the LXX,
the name Βαιθηλβεριθ also appears in Judg 9:50. It can, therefore, be
supposed that we are dealing with one of the incarnations of Baal, a
popular god in the Ancient Near East, namely, "Baal of the Covenant."
On the other hand, the fact that the Israelites made the covenant in
Shechem would indicate that the name אל ברית should be understood to
mean "Lord of the Covenant" and also "Guardian of the Covenant." The
origins of this god and its nature are not clear. It is supposed that the cult
of Baal took many forms and was practised in many ways throughout
Palestine. One indication could be the information about a specific Baal
brought to the territories of Israel from outside. This event is mentioned
in 1 Kings:

> Ahab son of Omri did more evil in the eyes of the Lord than any of those
> before him. He not only considered it trivial to commit the sins of
> Jeroboam son of Nebat, but he also married Jezebel daughter of Ethbaal
> king of the Sidonians, and began to serve Baal and worship him. He set
> up an altar for Baal in the temple of Baal that he built in Samaria. Ahab
> also made an Asherah pole and did more to provoke the Lord, the God of
> Israel, to anger than did all the kings of Israel before him. In Ahab's time,
> Hiel of Bethel rebuilt Jericho. He laid its foundations at the cost of his
> firstborn son Abiram, and he set up its gates at the cost of his youngest
> son Segub, in accordance with the word of the Lord spoken by Joshua son
> of Nun. (1 Kgs 16:30-34)

The sins and wickedness of Ahab far exceed the "sin of Jeroboam"
who worshipped the calves placed in the sanctuaries of Dan and Bethel.
What was Ahab's grievous fault? He took as his wife Jezebel, the
daughter of the King of Sidon, and introduced the cult of the Sidonian
Baal, most probably Baal Shamim, "Lord of the Heavens," worshipped
by both the Phoenicians and the Aramaeans.[131] The cult of the god of the
heavens could have existed in Palestine before the times of Ahab, but the
above mention could be an indication of the part played by this ruler in

---

130.   The Vulgate, following the LXX, gives: "Baal foedus" and "Baalberith."
131.   There is an enormous bibliography on the subject of this divinity; R.
Pettazzoni, *Wszechwiedza bogów*, Warsaw, 1967, p. 87 n. 24, for example, asserts
that the Baal worshipped on Mt Carmel is identical with the Phoenician Baal
Shamim.

the propagation of the cult. The Bible does indirectly point to the vitality of the Uranian cult, which is preserved in Yahwistic terminology. Of the numerous descriptions of God in conjunction with the noun "heaven," the majority is to be found in late texts or could be associated with traditions originating in the northern kingdom. The expression יהוה שמים appears in Pss 11:4; 14:2; 36:6; 102:20; 103:19; Isa 66:1; Num 3:50. The expression אלהים / אלהי השמים appears in Gen 24:3, 7; Deut 4:39; 10:14; Josh 2:11; 1 Kgs 8:23; 2 Chr 6:11; 20:6; 36:23; Ezra 1:2; Neh 1:4, 5; 2:4, 20; Pss 53:3; 115:3; Eccl 5:1; Jonah 1:9. Particular attention should be paid to Deut 3:24; Ps 136:26 and Lam 3:41, where the conjunction אל השמים appears. It would seem that the same divinity that was worshipped in the temple on Mt Gerizim took the name, during the Maccabean revolts, of Olympian Zeus (Διὸς Ὀλυμπίος = Διὸς Ξενίος, 2 Macc 6:2), and that it was this that became the "abomination of desolation" (βδέλυγμα ἐρημώσεως) mentioned in 1 Macc 1:54. As Tcherikover asserted, the "abomination of desolation" was none other than Baal Shamim.[132] If this hypothesis is true, then the installation by Antiochus IV of the cult of an Uranian god in Jerusalem undoubtedly caused increased tension between the Jews and the Samaritans.

The cult of a god of heaven introduced by Ahab was decidedly antagonistic to the Yahwistic cult. This could be because of the likely chthonic nature of the Hebrews' tribal god. If the religion of the "Lord of Heaven" spread over the whole area of the northern kingdom, then it reached Shechem, too.

We can explain setting the story of such an important event as the making of a covenant in the hills surrounding Shechem in one of two ways. Either we are dealing with a tradition reaching back to the period of the early kingdom, expanding the myth in Israel about the exodus from Egypt,[133] or with such a strong manifestation of a sense of separateness of the divinity worshipped in Shechem that the authors regarded it as obvious that the making of a national-founding covenant should be done before the face of that divinity.[134]

132. Cf. J. Scurlock, "167 BCE: Hellenism or Reform?," *JSJ* 31 (2000): 125-61; E.J. Bickerman, "The Altars of Gentiles: A Note on the Jewish 'Ius Sacrum'," in *Studies in Jewish and Christian History*, Leiden, 1980, 2:324-46.

133. On the subject of the Exodus from the northern kingdom, see in Y. Hoffman, "A North Israelite Typological Myth and a Judaean Historical Tradition: The Exodus in Hosea and Amos," *VT* 39 (1989): 169-82; Goulder, *The Psalms of Asaph*; Cross, *Canaanite Myth and Hebrew Epic, passim*.

134. See the information about Galeed in the chapter devoted to the sanctuaries in Transjordan, Chapter 8.

Gilgal

Archaeological Data and Extra-Biblical Sources

The name Gilgal comes from the root גלל and signifies a ring or circle, by implication a ring of stones.[135] It is a rare instance of a place which is not mentioned in the book of Genesis; its aetiology is given only by the book of Joshua. Hitherto, archaeologists have found no traces of it.[136] Some scholars believe that there could have been several centres of that name.[137] A fundamental problem arises when we set the aetiological narrative locating Gilgal opposite Jericho on the banks of the Jordan, alongside this passage: "As you know, these mountains [Ebal and Gerizim] are across the Jordan, west of the road, towards the setting sun, near the great trees of Moreh, in the territory of those Canaanites living in the Arabah in the vicinity of Gilgal" (Deut 11:30).

The LXX conveys the name "Gilgal" by using two terms: Γαλγαλ / Γαλγαλα. These names appear in 40 places.[138] In the MT the term "Gilgal" appears in 39 places. There are several differences between the uses of this name in the MT and LXX. The term Γαλγαλ / Γαλγαλα in Josh 13:5 is the equivalent of the Hebrew בעל גד, in Josh 22:10, while Josh 24:31 and 1 Sam 15:4 have no equivalents in the MT. The Hebrew forms (ה)גלגלה

135.   Wade R. Kotter, *ABD*, *s.v.* "Gilgal (place)."

136.   Bouce M. Bennett, Jr, "The Search for Israelite Gilgal," *PEQ* 104 (1972): 111-22; Tamar Noy, "Gilgal," in *NEAEHL*, 2:517-18. Other accounts suggest various hypotheses concerning the location of Gilgal; the finds in the place traditionally described as the biblical Gilgal point only to a settlement from early Neolithic times (eighth millennium) and after the Arab conquests; see Otto Bächli, "Zur Lage des alten Gilgal," *ZDPV* 83 (1967): 64-71; Tamar Noy, "Ten Years of Research in the Area of Gilgal, Lower Jordan Valley," *The Israel Museum Journal* 4 (1985): 13-16, and "Gilgal I—An Early Village in the Lower Jordan Valley. Preliminary Report of the 1987 Winter Season," *The Israel Museum Journal* 7 (1988): 113-14; H.-J. Kraus, "Gilgal. Ein Beitrag zur Kulturgeschichte Israels," *VT* 1 (1951): 181-91; G.M. Landes, "Report on an Archaeological 'Rescue Operation' at Suwwanet eth-Thaniya in the Jordan Valley North of Jericho," *BASORSup* 21 (1975): 1-22; J. Muilenburg, "The Site of Ancient Gilgal," *BASOR* 140 (1955): 11-27. Gilgal is usually located on the east side of the Jordan, but there is also a hypothesis identifying it with Deir 'Alla; see S. Kloppenborg, "Joshua 22: The Priestly Editing of an Ancient Tradition," *Biblica* 62 (1981): 347-71 (348 n. 7). An older bibliography is recorded by F. Langlamet, *Gilgal et les Récits de la Traversée du Jourdain (Jos., III-IV)*, Cahiers de la Revue Biblique 11, Paris, 1969, 13 n. 1.

137.   Kotter, "Gilgal (place)"; Haran, *Temples and Temple Service*, 31-32.

138.   Josh 4:19, 20; 5:9; 9:6; 10:6, 7, 9; 13:5; 14:6; 15:7; 22:10; 24:31; Judg 2:1; 3:19; 1 Sam 7:16; 10:8; 11:14, 15; 13:4, 7, 8, 12, 15; 15:4, 12, 21, 33; 2 Sam 19:16, 41; 2 Kgs 2:1; 4:38; 1 Macc 9:2; Hos 4:15; 9:15; 12:12; Amos 4:4; 5:5; Mic 6:5.

and גלילות in Josh 4:10; 10:15, 43 have no equivalent in the LXX. Deuteronomy 11:30 uses the form Γολγολ. The most significant difference appears in Josh 12:23 where in the Hebrew text we have the sentence: מלך־גוים לגלגל ("the king of the nations of Gilgal") while the Greek is: βασιλέα Γωιμ τῆς Γαλιλαίας. According to the LXX, then, the subject is not Gilgal but Galilee. The explanation of this confusion is not apparent bearing in mind the list of conquered kings (Josh 12:7-24) has the names of the towns, not the territories, next to the kings' names; this would suggest that the MT version is correct. Nevertheless, this inconsistency causes complications in the translation of those fragments where the name "Gilgal" appears. The terms Γαλγαλ / Γαλγαλα found in LXX contains the vowel "a," which is confirmed by the Vulgate which uses the form "Galgal." This suggests that the later change of the name's notation to "Gilgal" was done by the Masoretes. According to the vocalisation to which the LXX, the Vulgate and *LAB* testify, its original pronunciation was **galgal*.

We do not know if "the idols (מן־הפסילים) near Gilgal" which Judg 3:19 mentions are supposed to refer to the objects whose raising was linked with Joshua. The references in Josh 9:6; 10:7, 9 confirm the importance of Gilgal in the Joshua tradition because they indicate that that was the location of his armies' camp.[139] According to the biblical account there was also an important religious centre there (cf. the association of Saul with Gilgal described in 1 Sam 11–13, as well as the critical assessments by the prophets in Ezra 4:15 and Amos 4:4; 5:5 of the sanctuary there). The evidence for the existence of a sanctuary there is given by 1 Sam 15:33 (KJV): "…And Samuel hewed Agag in pieces before the Lord in Gilgal" (see also 1 Sam 15:21). Mention is also made in Neh 12:29 of "the house of Gilgal" (בית הגלגל).

1 Samuel 7:16 mentions Gilgal, Bethel and Mizpah together—three places where Samuel meted out justice over Israel. The oldest biblical mention suggesting the existence of a story about the Israelites crossing the Jordan in the vicinity of Gilgal is the following fragment of the book of Micah: "My people, remember what Balak king of Moab counselled and what Balaam son of Beor answered. Remember your journey from Shittim to Gilgal, that you may know the righteous acts of the Lord" (6:5).[140] Its author is surely referring to the motif in Num 22–23, but shows no familiarity with the details contained in Josh 4:1-5, 12.

---

139. See 2 Sam 19:16, which mentions the gathering of the people by David.
140. See also Josh 24:9: "When Balak son of Zippor, the king of Moab, prepared to fight against Israel, he sent for Balaam son of Beor to put a curse on you." Here the dependence on Mic 6:5 is evident.

Aetiology

Joshua 4:1–5:12:

(1) When the whole nation had finished crossing the Jordan, the Lord said to Joshua, (2) "Choose twelve men from among the people, one from each tribe, (3) and tell them to take up twelve stones from the middle of the Jordan from right where the priests stood and to carry them over with you and put them down at the place where you stay tonight." (4) So Joshua called together the twelve men he had appointed from the Israelites, one from each tribe, (5) and said to them, "Go over before the ark of the Lord your God into the middle of the Jordan. Each of you is to take up a stone on his shoulder, according to the number of the tribes of the Israelites, (6) to serve as a sign among you. In the future, when your children ask you, 'What do these stones mean?' (7) tell them that the flow of the Jordan was cut off before the ark of the covenant of the Lord. When it crossed the Jordan, the waters of the Jordan were cut off. These stones are to be a memorial to the people of Israel for ever." (8) So the Israelites did as Joshua commanded them. They took twelve stones from the middle of the Jordan, according to the number of the tribes of the Israelites, as the Lord had told Joshua; and they carried them over with them to their camp, where they put them down. (9) Joshua set up the twelve stones that had been in the middle of the Jordan at the spot where the priests who carried the ark of the covenant had stood. And they are there to this day. (10) Now the priests who carried the ark remained standing in the middle of the Jordan until everything the Lord had commanded Joshua was done by the people, just as Moses had directed Joshua. The people hurried over, (11) and as soon as all of them had crossed, the ark of the Lord and the priests came to the other side while the people watched. (12) The men of Reuben, Gad and the half-tribe of Manasseh crossed over, armed, in front of the Israelites, as Moses had directed them. (13) About forty thousand armed for battle crossed over before the Lord to the plains of Jericho for war. (14) That day the Lord exalted Joshua in the sight of all Israel; and they revered him all the days of his life, just as they had revered Moses. (15) Then the Lord said to Joshua, (16) "Command the priests carrying the ark of the Testimony to come up out of the Jordan." (17) So Joshua commanded the priests, "Come up out of the Jordan." (18) And the priests came up out of the river carrying the ark of the covenant of the Lord. No sooner had they set their feet on the dry ground than the waters of the Jordan returned to their place and ran in flood as before. (19) On the tenth day of the first month the people went up from the Jordan and camped at Gilgal on the eastern border of Jericho. (20) And Joshua set up at Gilgal the twelve stones they had taken out of the Jordan. (21) He said to the Israelites, "In the future when your descendants ask their fathers, 'What do these stones mean?' (22) tell them, 'Israel crossed the Jordan on dry ground'. (23) For the Lord your God dried up the Jordan before you until you had crossed over.

The Lord your God did to the Jordan just what he had done to the Red Sea when he dried it up before us until we had crossed over. (24) He did this so that all the peoples of the earth might know that the hand of the Lord is powerful and so that you might always fear the Lord your God."

(5:1) Now when all the Amorite kings west of the Jordan and all the Canaanite kings along the coast heard how the Lord had dried up the Jordan before the Israelites until we had crossed over, their hearts sank and they no longer had the courage to face the Israelites. (2) At that time the Lord said to Joshua, "Make flint knives and circumcise the Israelites again." (3) So Joshua made flint knives and circumcised the Israelites at Gibeath Haaraloth.[141] (4) Now this is why he did so: All those who came out of Egypt—all the men of military age—died in the desert on the way after leaving Egypt. (5) All the people that came out had been circumcised, but all the people born in the desert during the journey from Egypt had not. (6) The Israelites had moved about in the desert forty years until all the men who were of military age when they left Egypt had died, since they had not obeyed the Lord. For the Lord had sworn to them that they would not see the land that he had solemnly promised their fathers to give us, a land flowing with milk and honey. (7) So he raised up their sons in their place, and these were the ones Joshua circumcised. They were still uncircumcised because they had not been circumcised on the way. (8) And after the whole nation had been circumcised, they remained where they were in camp until they were healed. (9) Then the Lord said to Joshua, "Today I have rolled away the reproach of Egypt from you." So the place has been called Gilgal to this day. (10) On the evening of the fourteenth day of the month, while camped at Gilgal on the plains of Jericho, the Israelites celebrated the Passover. (11) The day after the Passover, that very day, they ate some of the produce of the land: unleavened bread and roasted grain. (12) The manna stopped the day after they ate this food from the land; there was no longer any manna for the Israelites, but that year they ate of the produce of Canaan.

The aetiology of Gilgal as part of the effective story of the conquest of Canaan by Joshua demanded a special formulation because it involved the place of first contact of "the sons of Israel" with the Promised Land after they had crossed the Jordan and set up a religious sanctuary. That is why, apart from the scene revealing divine power (the stopping of the waters of Jordan—a motif echoing the description of the crossing of the Red Sea[142]), as a result of which the foreign kings were terrified, three other mythical images are shown: the setting of the twelve stones as a sign (אות) (4:6) and memorial (לזכרון), the ritual circumcision with the

---

141. הערלות from the root ערל, "to circumcise," and the noun ערלה, "foreskin," "uncircumcision."

142. Thomas B. Dozeman, "The yam-sup in the Exodus and the Crossing of the Jordan River," *CBQ* 58 (1996): 407-16.

use of flint knives (חרבות צרים[143]); and the celebration of Passover. It seems that the text of Josh 5:10 forms the logical ending of the story whose culmination is the circumcision scene, whereas v. 9, which presents the etymology of the name Gilgal, comprises the conclusion.[144]

The information about the use of flint knives (Josh 5:2) in circumcision suggests the artificial attempt to show how archaic this practice was, whereas, in fact, this detail is so improbable that it is evidence not of the archaic nature of the circumcision but of an attempt to accentuate its ancient origins. This emphasis on the use of flint tools betrays the fact that the author was trying to make the reality he described appear ancient.

The raising of twelve stones in Gilgal expresses the idea of Israel being a nation comprising twelve tribes. This reference, however, cannot serve as an indication of the date of this narrative since the consciousness of the existence of a union of twelve tribes as a constituent factor in the history of the Israelites is a comparatively old phenomenon, appearing throughout ancient history. Undoubtedly, as Thomas L. Thompson noted, for historiography and biblical theology, and therefore also for this analysis of the aetiology of Gilgal, the *terminus ante quem* is marked by the birth of the Hebrews' national consciousness and the recognition of the feast of Passover as the key event in the cult calendar.[145] The fragment mentioning the sons of Israel for whom the stones raised in Gilgal were to be "a sign" and "a memorial" (Josh 4:6-7, 21-22) in the future is related to the fragment about descendants who are to remember the covenant between the tribes inhabiting both sides of the Jordan, set down in the narrative about the building of the altar in Josh 22.

In *Sefer ha-Yamim* the motif of the circumcision performed in Gilgal is omitted (Joshua § E-G).[146] Bearing in mind the relationships between the MT, LXX, the biblical texts and Qumran and the Samaritan literature, we can accept that the biblical information about circumcision is of late origin.[147]

---

143. The form of words in Josh 5:2-3 seems to be used very precisely, in a technical context, as opposed to the generalised formulation of Gen 17:1-27.

144. The fragment in question has been extensively analyzed by Langlamet, *Gilgal*, esp. 123-38.

145. Thompson, *Early History of the Israelite People*, 353-99, and *The Bible in History*, 62-69.

146. Macdonald, *The Samaritan Chronicle*.

147. For a discussion of the links between the biblical and the Samaritan literatures, see Bruce K. Waltke, *ABD*, *s.v.* "Samaritan Pentateuch."

Manuscripts containing fragments of the book of Joshua, dated close to 100 BCE, have been found in Qumran. The text, though very fragmentary, is nonetheless important evidence for the story's originality. After a description of the crossing of the Jordan and the raising of the twelve stones (*nota bene*, the name "Gilgal" does not appear), a fragment appears in the manuscript which in the MT and LXX is to be found at the end of ch. 8 (vv. 34-35). In the MT and LXX these verses concern the reading of the Law by the altar built on Mt Ebal, near Shechem.[148]

An analogous motif linking the raising of stones in Gilgal with a ritual performed in the vicinity of Shechem can be found in *Liber Antiquitatum Biblicarum*: "Et descendit Ihesus in Galgala, et edificavit sacrarium lapidibus fortissimis, et non intulit in eos ferrum sicuti preceperet Moyses. Et statuit lapides magnos in monte Gebal et dealbavit eos et scripsit super eos verba legis manifesta valde. Et congragavit omnem populum in unum, et legit in aures eorum omnia verba legis" (*LAB* 21:7). There is no mention here of circumcision or of celebrating Passover.

All this allows us to suppose that the biblical narrative about the founding by Joshua of a sanctuary in Gilgal arose only in the Hasmonean era. The fact that the place cannot be located stems from its being a purely literary creation. In the story's original version, Gilgal was to be found close to Shechem, but after modification it was situated on the banks of the Jordan. The birth of such a story can be readily explained by the growth in tension between the Jerusalem centre and the capital of the Samaritans which was becoming its rival, namely, Shechem.

The conflict between the Jews and the Samaritans was not—as has been mentioned above—as intense as Flavius Josephus presented it, and took the form both of political activity and propaganda, working on religious awareness. An indication of the political conflict was the destruction by John Hyrcanus of the Samaritan temple on Mt Gerizim (126 BCE), though we do not know the real reasons and motives that drove the Jews to perform this act of destruction. The argument that it was an attempt to eliminate a sanctuary that was a rival to Jerusalem appears mistaken in light of the fact that it was during John Hyrcanus's time that sacral investments were made in Beer-sheba and Lachish. Some other political activity, maybe even the impediments put in the way of restoring the walls of Jerusalem, noted in the book of Nehemiah, appear to explain the rivalry between the two centres during the Persian period much better. I do not think that any religious sub-texts should be read into Sanballat's dealings. The conflict between the two societies could

---

148.   See Abegg, Flint and Ulrich, *Dead Sea Scrolls Bible*, 201-202.

not have been as intense as might emerge from a superficial analysis of the New Testament, as evidenced by the fact that the Samaritans participated alongside the Jews in the rising against the Romans (66–70 CE).[149]

Examining the biblical and apocryphal writings from the point of view of the attitude they present to this conflict, one sees huge differences in the approach to the centre at Shechem. The anti-Samaritan trend is what probably helped to make the book of *Jubilees* omit naming the place of Joseph's burial (*Jub.* 46:1-9). This same tradition caused the removal from the MT of virtually all traces indicating that the tomb of the patriarchs was situated in Shechem. In my view, the account in Josh 4:1-5, 12 that Gilgal lies on the Jordan, which contradicts Deut 11:30, is a manifestation of that same tendency.[150]

Thanks to a contrasting tradition, information about the making of a covenant by Joshua in Shechem has been preserved (Josh 24), as has that of the interment of Joseph's remains there. The same attitude is evident in the fragment of the Eupolemos's work placing Abraham's meeting with Melchizedek in Shechem. We can read into this either a lack of a Jewish–Samaritan conflict or—as in the case of Josh 24—the existence of deeper reasons which did not allow the history of the covenant and of Joseph's grave to be separated from Shechem.

The creation of an image of a military-religious leader and the simultaneous retention of the pivotal role of the priests indicate that the probable beginning of the story about the ritual in Gilgal occurred in Hasmonean times. The kings of this dynasty had to preserve the tight links with the hieratic group and to build the monarchy's authority on the foundation of the temple's authority. It seems that the Hasmonean conquests and ideology were reflected by the religious message of the book of Joshua.[151] The state invokes the tradition of the twelve tribes, the powerful one-person leadership sanctioned by divine anointing (a continuation of the role of Moses). Joshua the commander, to a greater extent than the kings of the books of Kings, more than David and Solomon, combines the traits of monarch and priest. It may well have been this joining of secular and priestly power, revealed during the rituals

---

149.   All the evidence of the relations between the Samaritans and the Jews has been collected and annotated by Crown, "Redating the Schism"; see also Hjelm, *The Samaritans*.

150.   See Josh 12:23 in the LXX version where "Gilgal" is translated as "Galilee."

151.   John Strange, "The Book of Joshua: A Hasmonaean Manifesto?," in A. Lemaire and B. Otzen (eds.), *History and Traditions of Early Israel: Studies Presented to Eduard Nielsen*, VTSup 50, Leiden, 1993, 136-41.

in the ceremonies associated with the making of the covenant in Gilgal, that was so attractive to the Hasmoneans.

The story of the founding of Gilgal did not come out of nothing. Borrowings from known biblical motifs can be seen in it. Thus, the account of the crossing of the Jordan is copied from the description of the crossing of the Red Sea (see Josh 24), the account of the sanctuary in the vicinity of the Jordan has its equivalent in the description of the altar of testimony (Josh 22), and the Passover motif and the circumcisions are also taken from the story about the Israelites' exodus from Egypt.

I suspect that the purpose of including the Passover celebrations and the act of circumcision in Gilgal was merely to emphasise the sacral nature of the circle. The derivative nature of both of these rituals allows us to suppose that the name "Gilgal"—or rather "*Galgal"—was associated with, as its etymology suggests, a stone circle. Clear traces have been preserved in the Bible and in the apocryphal literature linking Gilgal with Shechem. Assuming that "Gilgal" was not the original proper name of the place by the Jordan but a technical term (similar to *bamah*) for a holy circle, the question we need to ask is whether the testimonies outside the description of the sanctuary's origins that mention Gilgal allow us to locate that *galgal* in the vicinity of Shechem. What we need to establish is whether this term was not perhaps the proper name of some object in the region of Shechem (like, for instance, the Palatine in Rome, Wawel in Kraków or the Tower in London). If we were to accept that Josh 4:1-5, 12 is about an imagined, fictional holy circle transported from Shechem to the Jordan, then other references to Gilgal in this book should remain consistent with that version. Gilgal is mentioned most frequently in 1 and 2 Samuel and denotes the place where the Israelites meet "before God" or before Saul. But it is not possible to establish precisely its location on the basis of these texts. In 1 Sam 7:16, Gilgal is mentioned alongside Bethel and Mizpeh—places where Samuel sat in judgment. The only typographic clue is in 2 Sam 19:15. From the fact mentioned there that it was the people of Judah who met in Gilgal to greet the king and to accompany him across the Jordan, we can infer that the place was situated within or in the proximity of the territories of that tribe. The book of Nehemiah (12:29) mentions, along with Beth-Gilgal, Geba and Azmaveth, towns situated in northern Judah and Benjamin. Micah (6:5) speaks of Gilgal in a context connected with the story from the book of Numbers about the city of Shittim and the crossing of the Jordan, but it is not clear which place it is referring to. Three times (Judg 2:1; Amos 5:5; Hos 4:15) Gilgal is mentioned alongside Bochim, Bethel and Beth-aven respectively. The prophets' announcements (Hos 4:15;

Amos 4:4; 5:5) are, however, directed against centres in Israel but mention only Samaria and Bethel. In the books of Hosea and Amos the name "Shechem" appears only once (Hos 6:9) and that in a completely neutral context. Could it be that the name "Gilgal" concealed a holy place in the vicinity of Shechem, which would explain the lack of references to Shechem in the prophecies?

The following words of Samuel reveal a strong association between Gilgal and kingship: "…'Come, let us go to Gilgal and there reaffirm the kingship'" (1 Sam 11:14). It is this very context—proclaiming someone king and renewing the institution of monarchy—that could suggest that we are dealing with a centre like Shechem here. The third chapter of the book of Judges describes the deeds of Ehud, who killed Eglon, king of Moab. The killing took place at the court of the monarch, and it is hard to explain what, in this context, is signified by the words: "After Ehud had presented the tribute, he sent on their way the men who had carried it. At the idols near Gilgal he himself turned back and said, I have a secret message for you, O king" (Judg 3:18-19). Since he was paying tribute at the court of the king of Moab, why did he go all the way to Jordan? It could be that the word "Gilgal" in this verse does not refer to the place indicated by the aetiological story, but to some cult object (with idols) to be found close to the king's court. Similar doubts concerning the location of Gilgal are evoked by the mention in the book of Hosea (12:11) where the prophet mentions Gilead.

On the basis of the biblical material, we cannot state that "Gilgal" is only a term to describe some kind of cult place. We can, however, accept that originally it did denote such sanctuaries and that, in time, it became a term from which the proper name of various places was formed.[152] The proper name of many places in Palestine was derived from the sacred circle, testimony of the great popularity of this cult stone construction. The biblical references to Gilgal, associated with the figures of Samuel and Saul, could be an indication that this place was located in Judah. From Judg 13:19 we might infer that Gilgal was situated in Moab, while from Hos 12:11 we could conclude that it was in Gilead. The bottom line is that all the biblical references to Gilgal can be interpreted in this way.

My own view is that the story under consideration, written down in the book of Joshua (4:1-5, 12), is dealing with an old tradition connecting the name "Gilgal" with a stone circle of a cult nature. Unable to establish which of the existing (?) places called "Gilgal" the author of this story means, we can accept, following the account in Deut 11:30, that the place where Passover was celebrated and the circumcisions

152. Kotter, "Gilgal (place)," mentions five places given the name "Gilgal."

performed was Gilgal near Shechem. A further argument is provided by the news that the circumcisions were carried out on Mt Haaraloth (Josh 5:3). If we were to accept the author's account that the whole event took place on the banks of the Jordan, then we would seek in vain—not only is Mt Haaraloth not there; there is, in fact, no hill at all.[153] The information about a hill close by seems to increase the probability that this most important *gilgal* was found in the vicinity of Shechem and the hills of Ebal and Gerizim.

---

153.   Henry O. Thompson, *ABD, s.v.* "Gibeath-Haaraloth (place)," mentions the impossibility of identifying this hill.

8.

Holy Places in Transjordan: Galeed—Mahanaim—Penuel

The Bible provides information about several cult centres located in the territory of Transjordan and in the vicinity of the Jordan. Unfortunately, their location is uncertain. Nevertheless, the function of the aetiological myths associated with them is so important in the body of the Bible that some attention needs to be accorded them.

The Bible treats Gilead, the name borne by territories east of the Jordan in the middle of its course, somewhat ambiguously. At times it acknowledges this region as belonging to the Israelites, at others it suggests it is distinct. Nevertheless a detailed analysis of the available data allows us to ascertain Gilead's independence from the territories inhabited by the Israelites. The epigraphical evidence provided by the Mesha stele shows a struggle for influence in the region of Gilead between Moab and Israel in the middle of the ninth century BCE.[1] There is no doubt that in the times of Omri and his immediate successors Israel maintained certain influences over the territories lying to the east of Jordan. It was probably in the time of the Assyrian expansion that this region fell under the sovereignty of the Aramaeans. Nadav Na'aman concluded that, on the basis of the inscription of Rezin, we can establish that the southern boundary of the Aramaean possessions went as far as Abel-Shittim, on a level with Jericho.[2] If that is so, then the (hypothetical) end of the Hebrew influence in Gilead would fall in the third quarter of the eighth century BCE. Analyzing biblical texts, Na'aman also reached the conclusion that the influence of the Hebrews in the time of

---

1. *KAI* 181; see the discussion in Miller and Hayes, *A History of Ancient Israel and Judah*, 267-87.

2. N. Na'aman, "Rezin of Damascus and the Land of Gilead," *ZDPV* 111 (1995): 105-106, and also the bibliography given there.

the divided kingdom reached as far down as the River Jabbok. The Bible associates these territories with Ammon.[3]

Galeed (Mizpah), like Penuel and Mahanaim, has not been positively identified archaeologically. The form "Mahanaim" is grammatically dual. This fact has persuaded scholars to look for two settlements situated close to one another. There is a lot to be said for the suggestion that Penuel or Mahanaim is to be associated with modern-day Tell edh-Dhahab el-Gharbi.[4] It is located on the northern bank of the River Jabbok at a point where the river forms an S-shaped meander. On its southern bank are the remains of a smaller settlement: Tell edh-Dhahab esh-Sherqiyeh. The history of settlement in both tells is not known to a satisfactory degree, but even the fragmentary information available to us is very intriguing. Specifically, no traces of settlement have been found there dating from the Middle or the Late Bronze Age, yet there is evidence of one from the Early Bronze Age, from the Iron Age I and II, as well as the Hellenistic, Roman and Byzantine periods.[5] From the end of the eleventh century BCE the town on Tell edh-Dhahab el-Gharbi was an important metallurgical centre. Strong Philistine influences (for instance the numerous ceramic finds) are visible in this region, and this could be connected to the exploitation of the rich deposits of iron ore to be found in this region.[6] The Bible provides a lot of information about the strategic importance of this region, linked to its position on the Israelite–Ammonite border and maybe to the iron ore deposits themselves.[7] Mahanaim and Penuel are mentioned on the Sheshonq inscription in Karnak, commemorating the Palestine campaign of 935 BCE.[8]

The three passages discussed below appear one after another to form an extensive fragment of the epic of Jacob. The location of places lying east of the Jordan is based on the biblical narrative according to which Jacob came upon the house of Laban in Paddan-Aram (פדנה ארם = Μεσοποταμία / Μεσοποταμία Συρία, Gen 28:2, 5-7) to Haran (חרן = Χαρραν, Gen 29:4-5). The term "Paddan-Aram" appears in the MT only

---

3. *Ibid.*, 112-13.

4. R.L. Gordon and L.E. Villiers, "Telul edh Dhahab and its Environs Surveys of 1980 and 1982: A Preliminary Report," *Annual of the Department of Antiquities of Jordan* 27 (1983): 275-89; R.A. Coughenour, "A Search for Mahanaim," *BASOR* 273 (1989): 57-66 (59-60); D.V. Edelman, *ABD*, *s.v.* "Mahanaim (place)" (which also contains a bibliography).

5. Gordon and Villiers, "Telul edh Dhahab"; Edelman, "Mahanaim (place)."

6. Coughenour, "A Search for Mahanaim," 61-63.

7. See the figure of Barzillai (ברזלי) in 2 Sam 19:31-39; the name derives from the noun ברזל, "iron."

8. M. Ottosson, *ABD*, *s.v.* "Gilead (place)"; Edelman, "Mahanaim (place)."

in Gen 28, whereas "Haran" appears in as many as ten places (Gen 11:31, 32; 12:4, 5; 27:43; 28:10; 29:4; 2 Kgs 19:12; Isa 37:12; Ezek 27:23). On each occasion the LXX version of the name is Χαρραν, a form that appears in Gen 36:26 and 1 Chr 1:41 as the name of a person. In Amos 1:5 the Greek form Χαρραν is used with reference to Damascus (Χαρραν = ארם).

The distance between Haran and Gilead, described in Gen 31:23 ("he pursued Jacob for seven days and caught up with him in the hill country of Gilead") is not precise, indicating only that two places were a long way apart.

The biblical narrative describing Abraham's journey from Ur to Haran, and the fact that it was from Haran that Rebekah, Rachel and Leah—wives of patriarchs—originated, appears to be meaningful. Garbini demonstrated that the choice of Haran as a place of rest by Abraham on the road from Ur to Canaan was not the result of any sympathy for the Aramaeans but for political reasons. According to Garbini, it was in the period of the Babylonian captivity that Haran was chosen as a stage in Abraham's journey because it was the traditional centre for the cult of Sin, which the Babylonian King Nabonid transformed into one of the most important religious centres.[9] If that really was so, then we could date the origins of this narrative's motif, which makes the Aramaean city of Haran the destination of the patriarchs' wanderings, in the period of the Babylonian captivity.[10]

Gilead / Galeed / Mizpah

Aetiology

Genesis 31:43-55:

> (43) Laban answered Jacob, "The women are my daughters, the children are my children, and the flocks are my flocks. All you see is mine. Yet what can I do today about these daughters of mine, or about the children they have borne? (44) Come now, let's make a covenant (ברית), you and I, and let it serve as a witness (לעד)[11] between us." (45) So Jacob took a

---

9.   Garbini, *Storia e ideologia*, 111-23. For more on the dating of the story of Abraham in the times of the Babylonian captivity, see Van Seters, *Abraham in History and Tradition*; Thompson, *The Historicity of the Patriarchal Narrative*, *passim*.

10.   E. Blum dates this Haran layer differently, pointing to the period between 721 BCE and the captivity of the sixth century; see D.J. Wytt-Williams, *The State of the Pentateuch: A Comparison of the Approaches of M. Noth and E. Blum*, BZAW 249, Berlin, 1997, 127.

11.   Lit. "as a witness" or "for the purpose of witnessing."

stone (אבן) and set it up as a pillar (מצבה). (46) He said to his relatives, "Gather some stones." So they took stones (אבנים) and piled them in a heap (ויעשׂו־גל), and they ate[12] there by the heap. (47) Laban called it Jegar Sahadutha (יגר שׁהדותא), and Jacob called it Galeed (גלעד).[13] (48) Laban said, "This heap (הגל) is a witness (עד)[14] between you and me today." That is why it was called Galeed. (49) It was also called Mizpah (והמצפה), because he said, "May the Lord keep watch (יצף) between you and me when we are away from each other. (50) If you ill-treat my daughters or if you take any wives besides my daughters, even though no-one is with us,[15] remember that God is a witness (עד) between you and me." (51) Laban also said to Jacob, "Here is this heap (הגל), and here is this pillar (המצבה) I have set up between you and me. (52) This heap is a witness, and this pillar is a witness, that I will not go past this heap to your side to harm you and that you will not go past this heap and pillar to my side to harm me. (53) May the God of Abraham and the God of Nahor," the God of their father, "judge between us." So Jacob took an oath in the name of the Fear of his father Isaac. (54) He offered a sacrifice (זבח) there in the hill (בהר) country and invited his relatives to a meal. After they had eaten, they spent the night there. (55) Early the next morning Laban kissed his grandchildren and his daughters and blessed them. Then he left and returned home.

Biblical Information

The toponym "Gilead" (גלעד) appears quite often in the Bible: a total of 110 times.[16] The LXX denotes it with the term Γαλααδ, and the Vulgate with "Galaad." This term applies to a region and not to a town. Yet the reference in Judg 10:17 indicates that it is describing a settlement, not a region: "When the Ammonites were called to arms and camped in Gilead, the Israelites assembled and camped at Mizpah." So, an equivalent to

12. Lit.: "they ate there on this heap (mound)."
13. גל עד = גלעד, "The Heap (Mound) of Witness."
14. The verb יצף and the name "Mizpah" are derived from the same root צפה, "to guard."
15. N.H. Snaith, "Genesis XXXI 50," *VT* 14 (1964): 375, suggests that in v. 50, instead of עמנו, we should read it as עמנו (in keeping with 2 Sam 10:12 and 1 Chr 19:13; Jer 46:16), which gives the following meaning: "when none of the people from the family of our (father) is looking, god will be witness." Another who wrote about this verse is J. Paradise, "What Did Laban Demand of Jacob? A New Reading of Genesis 31:50 and Exodus 21:10," in M. Cogan, B. Eichler and J. Tigay (eds.), *Tehillah le-Moshe: Biblical and Judaic Studies in Honor of Moshe Greenberg*, Winona Lake, 1997, 91-98; the author understands Jacob's undertaking as assuring the daughters of Laban exclusive inheritance.
16. 53 times with the definite article, and 47 times without an article; see Ottosson, "Gilead (place)."

Gilead is Mizpah—most certainly a town, not a region. In non-biblical sources the name "Gilead" appears as early as in Ugarit texts and in the Assyrian inscription at Nimrud.[17] According to the list of Israelite tribes and the division of Canaan, the lands lying to the east of the Jordan (from north to south) were occupied by half the tribe of Manasseh and by the tribes of Gad and Reuben. Most of the area denoted by the term "Gilead" is the lot of Manasseh.

The territory of Gilead was certainly an autonomous region. The genealogy of Machir, the father of Gilead (Num 26:29; 32:39-40; Deut 3:15; Josh 17:1) provides evidence of this, as does the role ascribed to the region by the story of the beginnings of the unified state: Saul strengthened his authority by conquering the Ammonites in Gilead, and his son Ishbosheth was proclaimed king of the northern tribes, including Gilead (2 Sam 2:8-10). The Ammonites must have played a considerable part in this territory since Rehoboam, king of Israel, was half-Ammonite: "His mother's name was Naamah; she was an Ammonite" (1 Kgs 14:31). We discover in 2 Kings (15:29) that "in the time of Pekah king of Israel, Tiglath-pileser king of Assyria came and took Ijon, Abel Beth Maacah, Janoah, Kedesh and Hazor. He took Gilead and Galilee, including all the land of Naphtali, and deported the people to Assyria." This conquest occurred in 732 BCE.[18]

It would seem that the Gileadites formed a separate people in the ethnic mix of Palestine. Evidence of this is manifested in the fact that differences in dialect exist between them and the Ephraimites:

> The Gileadites captured the fords of the Jordan leading to Ephraim, and whenever a survivor of Ephraim said, "Let me cross over," the men of Gilead asked him, "Are you an Ephraimite?" If he replied, "No," they said, "All right, say 'Shibboleth'." If he said, "Sibboleth," because he could not pronounce the word correctly, they seized him and killed him at the fords of the Jordan. Forty-two thousand Ephraimites were killed at that time. (Judg 12:5-6)

From the reference in the book of Hosea—"Is Gilead wicked? Its people are worthless!" (12:11)—it emerges that in that time (that is, the eighth century BCE) the territory of Transjordan was the subject of

17. *Ibid.*: "Outside the Old Testament the word is found in Ugaritic, Text 170 as a *nomen loci*, in Text 301 as a personal name, and in a royal Assyrian inscription from Nimrud, K 2649/III R 10, 2 'the town of *ga-al-ʾa-a-(za)*,' possibly identical with Ramoth-gilead."

18. See N. Na'aman, "Forced Participation in Alliances in the Course of the Assyrian Campaigns to the West," in M. Cogan and I. Eph'al (eds.), *Ah, Assyria... Studies in Assyrian History and Ancient Near Eastern Historiography Presented to Hayim Tadmor*, Jerusalem, 1991, 80-98 (91-94).

prophetic interest, and mentioning Gilead alongside Gilgal and Ephraim could indicate that it was considered to be part of the Israelite state.

The name "Galeed" appears exclusively in the aetiology associated with Jacob and Laban.

"Mizpah" (מצפה) is a toponym of some popularity in Palestine, and its etymology is associated with the root צפה, "to guard," "to observe." The most important centre of that name is in the territory of Benjamin.[19] In Gilead's Mizpah, mentioned in the book of Genesis (ch. 31), and identified with the Mizpah mentioned in the story of Jephthah and his daughter (Judg 12:7), the Israelites gathered before their battle with the Ammonites (Judg 10:17; 11:29). There must have been a sanctuary there since, "Jephthah went with the elders of Gilead, and the people made him head and commander over them. And he repeated all his words before the Lord in Mizpah" (Judg 11:11).[20] The narrative about Jephthah is somewhat inconsistent: first, we get the assurance that, as an exile, Jephthah lived in the land of Tob (Judg 11:3); then there is talk of his house in Mizpah (Judg 11:34) and his burial in "one of the cities of Gilead" (Judg 12:7). Menahem Haran is inclined to see in this biblical motif the trace of an open sanctuary in Mizpah, but not of a temple.[21]

The motif of Jephthah's deeds and his conflict with the Ammonites mentioned above was most probably derived from oral accounts of the people of Transjordan. What we have here is a local hero placed in a Transjordanian world. The question of Jacob's links with this territory is somewhat different.

One of the preserved fragments of the work of Eupolemos, a historian living in the second century BCE, contains a letter from Solomon to Suron, king of Tyre and Sidon. In it, he talks of disseminating a proclamation to various regions asking for a supply of materials and people to help in the building of a temple. Mentioned in turn were: Galilee and Samaria, and then the lands of the Moabites, Ammonites and "Galaad-ites" (γέγραφα δὲ καὶ τὴν Γαλιλαίαν καὶ Σαμαρεῖτιν καὶ Μωαβῖτιν καὶ 'Αμμανῖτιν καὶ Γαλαδῖτιν χορηγεῖσθαι αὐτοῖς τὰ δέοντα ἐκ τῆς χώρας...).[22] Naming "Galaad" alongside Moab and Ammon indicates that it was an autonomous country, independent of Israel. Unfortunately, there is no way of establishing whether the text cited in Eupolemos's work is talking about the author's times (that is, the middle of the second century BCE), or whether the author was drawing on some earlier

---

19. Cf. P.M. Arnold, *ABD*, s.v. "Mizpah (place)."
20. Arnold (*ibid.*) considers that this refers to Mizpah in the land of Benjamin.
21. Haran, *Temples and Temple Service*, 56-57.
22. Denis, *Fragmenta Pseudepigraphorum*, 182; Jacoby, *FGrHist*, 723, F 2.

historiographic work and relating an older history. All that can be said with certainty is that Gilead was not an integral part of the territory inhabited by the Israelites and the awareness of this fact found expression in Eupolemos's text. Drawing on the information from the Mesha stele and on what has been said about the times of Hosea, and also rejecting the secondary nature of the passage Hos 12:12,[23] it is tempting to reconstruct the links between Israel and the territories of Transjordan at various times. Before the Assyrian conquests at the end of the eighth century BCE, Gilead was in the sphere of influence of the northern kingdom. From the fall of Samaria to the Hasmonean expansion its links with Israel were virtually completely severed. This was the state of affairs during the rule of the Babylonians and the Persians. The Jews subjugated these territories (at least in part) only after Eupolemos's time, that is, at the end of second century BCE.

John Kloppenborg's view is that the attitude of the inhabitants of Judah and Israel toward Gilead changed over time: during the period of the First Temple, Gilead and the other territories in Transjordan were treated as an integral part of Jewish possessions (see Pss 108:9; 135:11-12); in the post-exile period, Gilead became an unclean territory (cf. Ezek 47).[24]

It seems that 1 Chr 15 well documents the deeds of the peoples inhabiting Transjordan well. Verses 1-10 relate to the Reubenites who, after overcoming the Hagarites, colonised the whole eastern part of Gilead, while vv. 11-17 relate to the descendants of Gad. Of fundamental significance is the information that: "All these were entered in the genealogical records during the reigns of Jotham king of Judah and Jeroboam king of Israel" (v. 17). From this it emerges that the inclusion of the people of Transjordan among the tribes living on the eastern banks of the Jordan took place only (!) in the middle of the eighth century BCE.[25] The earlier period was probably characterised by tensions between the Israelites and the Aramaeans, proof of which may be the references to the wars between Ahab and Benhadad.[26] According to the Chronicler, links with the Gileadites were severed during the Assyrian expansion:

---

23. Cf. Whitt, "The Jacob Tradition."

24. Kloppenborg, "Joshua 22," 360.

25. See G. Galil, *The Chronology of the Kings of Israel and Judah*, Leiden, 1996; Miller and Hayes, *A History of Ancient Israel and Judah*. Galil dates the reign of Jotham in Judah as 758/7–742/1 BCE, and of Jeroboam II in Israel as 790–750/49; Hayes and Miller gives the dates respectively as ?–742 and 785–745. According to Galil, the two monarchs' reigns coincided in the years 758/7–750/49.

26. Ahab is presented in the Bible as one of "the worst" kings of Israel and that is why its testimony of his victory over the Aramaeans has great historical significance (1 Chr 20).

But they were unfaithful to the God of their fathers and prostituted themselves to the gods of the peoples of the land, whom God had destroyed
before them. So the God of Israel stirred up the spirit of Pul king of
Assyria (that is, Tiglath-pileser king of Assyria), who took the Reubenites, the Gadites and the half-tribe of Manasseh into exile. He took them
to Halah, Habor, Hara and the river of Gozan, where they are to this day.
(1 Chr 5:25-26)

If we wanted to establish a putative time for the beginnings of a tradition
about the links between Israel and Gilead exclusively on the basis of the
book of Chronicles, we would have to point to a short period between
760 and 730 BCE.

The making of the covenant between Jacob and Laban is described in
the book of Genesis (31:43-55). Jacob, a patriarch of the Hebrews who,
as Israel, is an eponymous hero, is set alongside Laban, personifying the
Aramaeans (cf. Gen 25:20; 28:5; 31:20, 24). Several motifs typical of a
story about the establishment of a holy place appear in the aetiology of
Gilead: the heroes make a covenant with one another (v. 44), they set up
a מצבה (v. 45), they call on God, or gods, in making an oath (v. 53), they
make a sacrifice (v. 54), and receive a blessing (v. 55). Three proper
names appear: Yegar-Sahadutha, Galeed (v. 47) and Mizpah (v. 49). The
name "Mizpah" is linked with צפה, a verb used in this verse and meaning "to guard," "to look after."[27] The name "Galeed" is connected to
the narrative's recurring motif of building a mound as witness (גל עד).
The name Yegar-Sahadutha is the Aramaic equivalent of "Galeed."[28]
M. O'Conner's view is that they could all have existed alongside one
another and been interchangeable.[29] *Vetus Latina* introduces a semantic
differentiation between the names given by Jacob and Laban: "Et vocavit
illum Laban, Acervum testimonii, et Jacob vocavit illum, Acervum
testis." This differentiation is also present in Jerome's translation
although it is not the same as that of *Vetus Latina*: "Uem vocavit Laban
tumulus Testis et Iacob acervum Testimonii uterque iuxta proprietatem
linguae suae."

These doublings in the text give us reason to wonder what the original
shape of the story might have been. A stone pillar is a doubling of a heap
or mound of stones, a feast on the heap is the equivalent of a feast on a
hill or mountain, while the names "Yegar Sahadutha" and "Galeed"

27. J. Briend, "Genèse 31,43-54: Traditions et rédaction," in M. Carrez, J. Doré
and P. Grelot (eds.), *De la Tôrah au Messie. Études d'exégèse et d'herméneutique
biblique offertes à Henri Cazelles pour ses 25 années d'enseignement à l'Institut
Catholoque de Paris (October 1979)*, Paris, 1981, 107-12 (108).
28. Y. Kobayashi, *ABD, s.v.* "Yegar-Sahadutha (place)."
29. O'Conner, "The Etymologies of Tadmor," 245.

reproduce the name "Mizpah." Bearing in mind that the whole narrative revolves around the activity of piling up a mound, we would have to accept that the original story dealt with Mizpah, the erection of a pillar and a feast on the hill. A later layer consists of the elements linking the narrative to Galeed (Gilead);[30] the Laban motif is also presumably secondary.

Emanuel Tov noted that though we would expect the LXX to give a transliteration, it does in fact translate the term used in Gen 31:48: הַגַּל הַזֶּה עֵד, "[may this] heap be witness."[31] The whole of v. 48 in the LXX is as follows: εἶπεν δὲ Λαβαν τῷ Ιακωβ ἰδοὺ ὁ βουνὸς οὗτος καὶ ἡ στήλη αὕτη ἣν ἔστησα ἀνὰ μέσον ἐμοῦ καὶ σοῦ μαρτυρεῖ ὁ βουνὸς οὗτος καὶ μαρτυρεῖ ἡ στήλη αὕτη διὰ τοῦτο ἐκλήθη τὸ ὄνομα αὐτοῦ Βουνὸς μαρτυρεῖ. It is difficult to judge whether the reason why the translators undertook a translation here instead of a transliteration was the role played in the story by the reference to "a heap of witness."

Verse 44 has created some problems for commentators because of the inconsistency of grammatical forms: next to the feminine noun "covenant" (בְּרִית) the verb "to be" (הָיָה) appears in the third person singular masculine. Francisco O. Garcia-Treto suggested that the word עֵד be changed to עַד. He based his reconstruction on the fact that there is evidence in Aramaic epigraphy that the word carries the meaning "agreement," "pact."[32] However, Garcia-Treto's argument turns against him, for he has shown that the morpheme עַד is a part of the name "Gilead." Nor is this a surprise. The authors of Gen 31:43-55 do not employ the common toponym "Gilead," whose building block is the morpheme עַד postulated by Garcia-Treto, but consistently resort to the name "Galeed," thereby underlining the use of the morpheme עֵד. By turning away from the use of the proper name in its traditional form (here Gilead) the authors have clearly indicated to the readers or listeners a meaning other than the one which is directly suggested by the name. There can be no question of an emendation of עֵד to עַד since the essence of the whole story is to emphasise the word עֵד, "testimony, witness." The grammatical inconsistency could, nevertheless, be a trace of some editorial change in the text. It is possible that a motif indicating Gilead was originally added to the story about Mizpah, the raising of a pillar there, and the feast on

30. F.O. Garcia-Treto, "Genesis 31:44 and 'Gilead,'" *ZAW* 79 (1967): 15, indicates the secondary nature of vv. 47-48; cf. Briend, "Genèse 31,43-54...," 109-11.

31. Tov, *The Greek and Hebrew Bible*, 175.

32. Garcia-Treto, "Genesis 31:44," 13-17; this hypothesis was also accepted by Briend, "Genèse 31,43-54," 111.

the hill, after which revisions were made changing this toponym to "Galeed" in order to emphasise the role of the noun עֵד.

"Witness" (עד) is key to the whole narrative related to Galeed. In it, it is explicitly stated that the raised heap (הגל, vv. 48 and 51) and the pillar (המצבה, vv. 51-52) "will be witness"; at the same time, it contains the comment that "God is witness" (אלהים עד, v. 50). This duality could be the result of two different traditions laid on top of each other. The agreement between Jacob and Laban is reminiscent of a pact made at a frontier. A tangible trace of this, as well as a sign denoting a frontier post, is the stone pillar or heap. This would make the sense of the following sentence obvious: "Here is this heap (הגל) and here is this pillar (המצבה), I have set up between you and me. This heap is a witness, and this pillar is a witness, that I will not go past this heap to your side to harm you and that you will not go past this heap and pillar to my side to harm me" (Gen 31:51-52). The procedure of making a covenant is sanctioned by religious acts in the form of a sacrifice, a feast and calling upon God. A feast as an element accompanying the formation of an alliance or some other political agreement is mentioned in the aetiological myth of Beer-sheba and in the covenant between Moses and his father-in-law Jethro: "Then Jethro, Moses' father-in-law, brought a burnt offering and other sacrifices to God, and Aaron came with all the elders of Israel to eat bread with Moses' father-in-law in the presence of God" (Exod 18:12).[33]

The only trace of the history of the beginnings of Galeed has been preserved in the motif concerning the stone heap or mound, which in itself was not a sacral object. The stone heap (הגל) could originally have simply marked a frontier point. If what was present there in the initial narrative was not a heap but a pillar, then we will have the anticipated sacral element because המצבה is a house of god.[34] Could it be that the stone pillars which Jacob put up so frequently not only symbolised a theophany but were also representations of a god? Could it be that the vertically laid stone in some way made a god present?[35]

The other traditional aspect in the story is that God is the guarantor of the agreement.[36] Verse 50 uses the phrase "God witness" or "God testimony" (אלהים עד). What is interesting is the description of god summoned as a witness during the oath-taking: "May the God of Abraham

---

33. Cf. G.E. Mendenhall, *ABD*, *s.v.* "Midian (person)."

34. See the chapter concerning Bethel, Chapter 3.

35. De Vaux, *Ancient Israel*, 2:285-86, believes that מצבה, even if it had the form of an unhewn stone, represented a male god.

36. E.T. Mullen, Jr, *DDD*, *s.v.* "Witness," 1703-705 (and the bibliography there).

and the God of Nahor, the God of their father, judge between us. So Jacob took an oath in the name of the Fear of his father Isaac" (Gen 31:53). This enigmatic description does not indicate Yahweh, Elohim or any concrete manifestation of the god El known from the deeds of the patriarchs. There is quite a helpful pointer to the identity of the deity standing as witness in the very word "witness" or "testimony" (עד). In the MT v. 44 it sounds as follows: ועתה לכה נכרתה ברית אני ואתה והיה לעד ביני ובינך (lit. "Therefore go, let us transact[37] a covenant: I and you, in order that [he] be a witness between us"). In the LXX this same fragment has the following sense: νῦν οὖν δεῦρο διαθώμεθα διαθήκην ἐγὼ καὶ σύ καὶ ἔσται εἰς μαρτύριον ἀνὰ μέσον ἐμοῦ καὶ σοῦ εἶπεν δὲ αὐτῷ ἰδοὺ οὐθεὶς μεθ᾽ ἡμῶν ἐστιν ἰδὲ ὁ θεὸς μάρτυς ἀνὰ μέσον ἐμοῦ καὶ Σοῦ. The second part of the verse corresponds to v. 50 of the MT. I suppose that the use here of the verb "to be" in the third person singular is completely justified and does not require a change of the noun from עֵד to עֵד, in view of the fact that the subject of the second part of the sentence is understood and, on the basis of v. 50, can be deduced to be God.[38] E. Theodore Mullen has pointed to two biblical statements which assert that a summoned heavenly witness was a being other than Yahweh.[39] The first is the proclamation of God placed in a Psalm: "his [David's] line will continue forever and his throne endure before me like the sun; it will be established for ever like the moon, the faithful witness in the sky" (כירח יכון עולם ועד בשחק נאמן = καὶ ὡς ἡ σελήνη κατηρτισμένη εἰς τὸν αἰῶνα καὶ ὁ μάρτυς ἐν οὐρανῷ πιστός) (Ps 89:36-37).[40] The other is a fragment of the book of Job (16:19), which mentions a heavenly advocate: "Even now my witness is in heaven; my advocate is on high."[41] The Hebrew text is constructed from a nominal sentence: גם־עתה הנה־בשמים עדי ושהדי במרומים (lit. "And now therefore in the heavens my witness, and my witness up on high"). In this verse, just as in Gen 31:47, the same pair of words has been juxtaposed: עד and שהד. These very denotations are used to explain the etymology of the proper names: יגר־שהדותא and גלעד (Gen 31:47) in the narrative about the covenant struck between Jacob and Laban. Both words have identical meanings and the only difference is that עד is a Hebrew word and שהד is Aramaic.

---

37. The verb "to cut" is used here which, in conjunction with the word "covenant" creates the idiom "to make a covenant."

38. This was the view of, among others, Speiser, *Genesis*, 247-48.

39. Mullen, "Witness."

40. See P.G. Mosca, "Once Again the Heavenly Witness of Ps. 89:38," *JBL* 105 (1986): 27-37, for the role of the moon as a witness.

41. The LXX reads καὶ νῦν ἰδοὺ ἐν οὐρανοῖς ὁ μάρτυς μου ὁ δὲ συνίστωρ μου ἐν ὑψίστοις.

From what has been said already we can draw the following conclusions. First, the transcendental witness does not have to be identical
with Yahweh. Secondly, he is always located in heaven.[42] Thirdly, both
Gen 31 and Job 16:19 connect Hebrew and Aramaic vocabulary, which
could be an echo of a real covenant (peace accord) between the Hebrews
and the Aramaeans drawn up in the sight of a god known to both of
them. If we follow Raffael Pettazzoni's theory, then we would have to
say that the attribute of the god called as a witness is his heavenly nature,
and from that his omniscience. If the being עד in Ps 89:38 and Job 16:19
is not identical with Yahweh, then it is possible that the custom of summoning a heavenly being as a witness goes outside the cult of Yahweh
and refers to an older, more universal idea of a god of heaven. The Bible
often ascribes omniscience to god, while such texts as Gen 4:9 ("Then
the Lord said to Cain, Where is your brother Abel?") could be evidence
of the fact that Yahweh does not know everything. And "partial or
relative omniscience is a contradiction of terms."[43] Pettazzoni does not
deny Yahweh's omniscience,[44] but mentions other gods of the Western
Semitic pantheon who were characterised by omniscience.[45] Obvious
candidates for the role of god-witness include the all-knowing El and
Baal-Shamin ("Lord of the Heavens"). Pettazzoni's view is that the god
whose image is on the portrait drawn by Micah and adopted by the
Danites,[46] as also on the statue prepared for the Jerusalem Temple by
Manasseh (2 Chr 33:7, 15), and particularly the image brought to
Samaria from Tyre by Ahab (1 Kgs 16:29-33) is characterised by
omniscience, expressed by its many faces (*tetramorfos/tetraprosopos*).[47]

A helpful trail in the identification of the god summoned as a witness
could be the God of the covenant mentioned in the Bible. What is
interesting, however, is that the term ברית is applied not to Yahweh, but
to Baal.

Baal Berith—"Lord of the Covenant" (בעל ברית = Βααλ διαθήκην /
Βααλβεριθ)[48]—is mentioned in Judg 8:33 and 9:4, and the temple of El
Berith (בית אל ברית = Βαιθηλβεριθ) in Judg 9:46. The name Βαιθηλβεριθ
also appears in Judg 9:50. All of these references apply to the god
worshipped in the vicinity of Shechem.

---

42. R. Pettazzoni, *The All-Knowing God*, London, 1956, 17-21.
43. *Ibid.*, 20.
44. *Ibid.*, 92-111.
45. *Ibid.*
46. See the chapter concerning Dan.
47. Pettazzoni, *The All-Knowing God*, 87-89.
48. The Vulgate reads "Baal foedus" and "Baalbrith."

There is disagreement among scholars as to the god in question here. Is it one and the same as the god referred to as Baal in some places, and as El in others? There are also conflicting opinions regarding the relation between them and Yahweh and his part in the biblical covenant made with the people.[49] Even without adopting an unequivocal view on these matters, we can still shed new light on it. There is no doubt that the god linked with the word ברית was associated with the covenant. The version of his name in the LXX (Βααλβεριθ, Judg 9:4), as well as the use of the term Βααλβεριθ, indicate that the morpheme ברית was part of a complete name or title of the god. However, looking for connections between this god and the covenant made with the Israelites is unfortunately a largely speculative venture. It is my contention that it would be more useful to consider the god ברית in the role of guardian, a guarantor of the covenant rather than as one of the parties of such an agreement.

The god summoned as a witness of the covenant becomes the עד of the agreement. The semantic link between the act of making the covenant and the god who is its witness appears to be obvious. If our reading of Gen 31:44 is correct, then we can put forward—at the same time remembering the summoning of אלהים עד (Gen 31:50)—the hypothesis that "the God of Abraham and the God of Nahor, the God of their father" (v. 53) is, in the form of אלהים עד, the equivalent of the god ברית. If in turn we accept that Pettrazzoni is right in describing the characteristics of god-guardian of the covenant, then most appropriate here would be the Tyrian "God of heaven." This would indicate that Baal-Shamin equals Baal Berith (from Judg 8–9) equals אלהים עד (from Gen 31).

Identifying the god who plays the leading role in the aetiology of the pact between the Israelites and the Aramaeans (or Transjordanian tribes) in this way suggests a profound conclusion, namely, that the covenant made on the Jordan or in the territories of Transjordan should be associated with the god worshipped in Shechem.

Further speculations are, unfortunately, highly hypothetical. As a religious centre of Israel, Shechem played an important role until the end of the eighth century BCE, and then again in the Hellenistic era.[50] If the god guarding the covenant between the Israelites and the tribes of Transjordan was indeed the god ברית worshipped in Shechem, then the association of this god with the act of making this covenant would need to be dated before the fall of Israel in the eighth century BCE, or in the Hellenistic era. The existence of links between Israel and the territories

49. For an extensive discussion of the various standpoints, see T.J. Lewis, *ABD*, *s.v.* "Baal-Berith (Deity)."

50. I say more on this subject in the chapter about Shechem.

on the east of the Jordan can be demonstrated by archaeological finds as well as on the basis of the biblical tradition locating the tribe of Manasseh on both banks of the Jordan, a tradition which clearly points to a unity of these territories.[51] It could be that the motif underlining the part played by a god and his possible connections with Shechem, the main centre of Israel, in the covenant made with the Transjordanians, is a trace of a historical explanation aimed at showing the "affiliation" of the tribes living on both sides of the river.

Demetrius's silence on the subject suggests that the motif of Jacob's covenant with Laban is a late inclusion in the biblical narrative. This third-century historian writes about the births of Jacob's children during the patriarch's stay with Laban, then adds: "πορευομένω δ' αὐτῶ εἰς Χαναὰν ἄγγελον τοῦ θεοῦ παλαῖσαι καὶ ἄφασθαι τοῦ πλάτους τοῦ μηροῦ τοῦ 'Ιακώβ τὸν δὲ ναρκήσαντα ἐπισκάζειν."[52] Thus Demetrius omits the entire theme of Gen 31, as well as the description of Jacob's meeting with Esau. Immediately after the scene of Jacob leaving Laban and his battle with the angel, Demetrius includes the information about the patriarch's arrival in Shechem followed by the story about Dinah (fr. 2.8-9). This choice of material could be the result of the selective nature of Demetrius's work, or of the fact that there was a different version of the Jacob epic known in the third century BCE. If the narrative about the covenant in Galeed was not, at that time, associated with the person of Jacob, then maybe the story did not exist at that time. However, an *argumentum ex silencio* is too slender a proof to sustain more serious theories.

The book of *Jubilees* presents the deeds of Jacob and his parting from Laban in a rather different way:

> During the seventh year of the fourth week Jacob returned to Gilead on the twenty-first day of the first month. Laban pursued him and found Jacob on the mountain of Gilead on the thirteenth (day) in the third month. But the Lord did not allow him to harm Jacob because he had appeared to him at night in a dream, and Laban told Jacob. On the fifteenth of those days Jacob prepared a banquet for Laban and all who had come with him. That day Jacob swore to Laban and Laban to Jacob that neither would commit an offense against the other on the mountain of Gilead with bad intentions. There he made a mound as a testimony; for this reason that place is named the mound of testimony after this mound. But at first the land of Gilead

---

51. In attempting to establish the date of the pact between the Israelites and the Transjordanian tribes, I would not be inclined to follow Speiser (*Genesis*, 251) in dating it in mid-second millennium, but rather to opt for the period of the height of the northern kingdom's power, namely, the ninth to eighth centuries BCE.

52. Denis, *Fragmenta Pseudepigraphorum*, 176; Jacoby, *FGrHist* 722, F 1 [7,1]).

> was named the land of *Rafaem* because it was the land of Rafaim. The
> Rafaim were born giants whose heights were ten cubits, nine cubits, eight
> cubits, and (down) to seven cubits. (*Jub.* 29:5-9)

This version underlines the frontier-peacemaking nature of the Jacob–
Laban pact, mentioning only the mound or the heap of stones. The
reference to the giants of Refaim and their successors the "evil and
sinful" Amorites (*Jub.* 29:11), indicates that, to the author of the book of
Jubilees, the territory of Galeed was decidedly alien.

Assuming that the story about the covenant made between Jacob and
Laban in Galeed documented the factual extent of the Jewish state, we
can deduce that it happened either in the period before 722 BCE, and in
fact even before the year 750, or in the times of the Hasmonean expansion during which, by dint of military conquests, the Jewish state subjugated the territories of Gilead towards the end of the second century BCE.

The use of the phrase "The God of Abraham and the God of Nahor,
the God of their father" and the mentioning of God who was the "fear of
his father Isaac" (v. 53) point to the late origin of this text. This is
because the name "Nahor" appears only in obviously late texts (Gen 11;
24:10, 15, 47; 29:5; Josh 24:2; 1 Chr 1:26).

Attention needs to be drawn also to the phrase "the Fear of his father
Isaac." The MT reads וישבע יעקב בפחד אביו יצחק ("Jacob took an oath on
the fear of his father Isaac," Gen 31:53), and the LXX reads καὶ ὤμοσεν
Ιακωβ κατὰ τοῦ φόβου τοῦ πατρὸς αὐτοῦ Ισαακ. The form of words
פחד יצחק (φόβος Ισαακ) appears only in Gen 31:42 and 53. The noun
פחד, "fear," derived from the root פחד, "to fear," "to be afraid," appears
with this meaning quite commonly in the MT, but in two places it is used
in a way that indicates that we are dealing with the personification of
fear. The places in question are Ps 91:5 ("You will not fear the terror of
night [לא תירא מפחד לילה],[53] nor the arrow that flies by day"[54]) and Job
15:21 ("A dreadful sound [קול־פחדים][55] is in his ears: in prosperity the
destroyer shall come upon him").[56]

The name Zelophehad[57] (צלפחד) provides an additional argument.
Analysis of this name reveals that it consists of two words. The first

53. The LXX reads οὐ φοβηθήσῃ ἀπὸ φόβου νυκτερινοῦ.
54. I would like to thank Dr Maciej Münnich for drawing my attention to this
place.
55. Lit.: "Voice of fears"; cf. the LXX reads ὁ δὲ φόβος αὐτοῦ ἐν ὠσὶν αὐτοῦ.
56. Verse 22 reads: "He despairs of escaping the darkness; he is marked for the
sword." Attention needs to be drawn in this context to the appearance of the noun
"darkness" (חשׁך), which has a symbolic link with fear.
57. Num 26:33; 27:1, 7; 36:2, 6, 10, 11; Josh 17:3; 1 Chr 7:15. See M.A. Taylor,
ABD, s.v. "Zelophehad (person)."

morpheme is derived from the root צלל, "to be black," and the second is the noun פחד, "fear," "terror," which gives us "fear is black," but can also be read theophorically as "פחד is black." Following this track we would have to ascertain that פחד is a description of a deity. There are many occasions when the MT uses the conjunction פחד־יהוה,[58] which is usually translated as "the fear of the Lord," but maybe what has been preserved here is the title of a terrifying god, "fearful Yahweh."[59]

The presence and function of the noun "testimony" (עד) has persuaded Robert Boling to claim that the story about the building of an altar in Josh 22:10-34 could be a mirroring of the aetiological narrative associated with the pact struck between Laban and Jacob.[60] Regardless of whether the story about the altar of עד came into being under the influence of Gen 31 or of some tradition associated with a holy place in the vicinity of the Jordan, it is incontrovertible that the noun "testimony, witness" (עד) appears frequently in biblical texts dealing with accounts of the Transjordanian tribes.[61]

The book of Joshua (ch. 22) provides evidence of the significance of the covenant between the Israelites and the population of the eastern side of the Jordan in its story about the origins of, and reasons for, the construction of the altar dubbed "Witness." Its location is not entirely clear. Attempts have been made to identify it with the holy place in Gilgal, but there are elements in the story which arouse suspicions that it is the same as the place where Laban and Jacob made the pact described in Gen 31.

Joshua 22:10-34 reads:

> When they came to Geliloth near the Jordan[62] in the land of Canaan, the Reubenites, the Gadites and the half-tribe of Manasseh built an imposing altar (מזבח גדול למראה) there by the Jordan. And when the Israelites heard that they had built the altar on the border of Canaan at Geliloth near the Jordan on the Israelite side, the whole assembly of Israel gathered at Shiloh to go to war against them. So the Israelites sent Phinehas son of Eleazar, the priest, to the land of Gilead—to Reuben, Gad and the

58. 1 Sam 11:7; 2 Chr 14:13; 17:10; 19:7; Isa 2:10, 19, 21. The LXX uses two different forms: ἔκστασις κυρίου (1 Sam 11:7; 2 Chr 14:13; 17:10) and φόβος κυρίου (2 Chr 19:7; Isa 2:10, 19, 21).

59. For more on this subject, see M. Rose, *ABD*, *s.v.* "Names of God in the O.T."; E. Puech, *ABD*, *s.v.* "Fear of Isaac."

60. R. Boling, *Joshua: A New Translation with Notes and Introduction*, Garden City, NY, 1982, 516-17.

61. The aetiology of the altar עד, is treated in the section on Gilgal in Chapter 7.

62. Translator's note: the KJV gives "And when they came unto the borders of Jordan" here.

half-tribe of Manasseh. With him they sent ten of the chief men, one for each of the tribes of Israel, each the head of a family division among the Israelite clans. When they went to Gilead—to Reuben, Gad and the half-tribe of Manasseh—they said to them, "The whole assembly of the Lord says: 'How could you break faith with the God of Israel like this? How could you turn away from the Lord and build yourselves an altar in rebellion against him now? Was not the sin of Peor enough for us? Up to this very day we have not cleansed ourselves from that sin, even though a plague fell on the community of the Lord! And are you now turning away from the Lord? If you rebel against the Lord today, tomorrow he will be angry with the whole community of Israel. If the land you possess is defiled, come over to the Lord's land, where the Lord's tabernacle stands, and share the land with us. But do not rebel against the Lord or against us by building an altar for yourselves, other than the altar of the Lord our God. When Achan son of Zerah acted unfaithfully regarding the devoted things, did not wrath come upon the whole community of Israel? He was not the only one who died for his sin'." Then Reuben, Gad and the half-tribe of Manasseh replied to the heads of the clans of Israel: "The Mighty One, God, the Lord! The Mighty One, God, the Lord (אל אלהים יהוה)! He knows! And let Israel know! If this has been in rebellion or disobedience to the Lord, do not spare us this day. If we have built our own altar to turn away from the Lord and to offer burnt offerings and grain offerings, or to sacrifice fellowship offerings on it, may the Lord himself call us to account. No! We did it for fear that some day your descendants might say to ours, 'What do you have to do with the Lord, the God of Israel? The Lord has made the Jordan a boundary between us and you— you Reubenites and Gadites! You have no share in the Lord'." So your descendants might cause ours to stop fearing the Lord. That is why we said, "Let us get ready and build an altar—but not for burnt offerings or sacrifices." On the contrary, it is to be a witness (עד) between us and you and the generations that follow, that we will worship the Lord at his sanctuary with our burnt offerings, sacrifices and fellowship offerings. Then in the future your descendants will not be able to say to ours, "You have no share in the Lord." And we said, "If they ever say this to us, or to our descendants, we will answer: 'Look at the replica of the Lord's altar, which our fathers built, not for burnt offerings and sacrifices, but as a witness between us and you'. Far be it from us to rebel against the Lord and turn away from him today by building an altar for burnt offerings, grain offerings and sacrifices, other than the altar of the Lord our God that stands before his tabernacle." When Phinehas the priest and the leaders of the community—the heads of the clans of the Israelites—heard what Reuben, Gad and Manasseh had to say, they were pleased. And Phinehas son of Eleazar, the priest, said to Reuben, Gad and Manasseh, "Today we know that the Lord is with us, because you have not acted unfaithfully towards the Lord in this matter. Now you have rescued the Israelites from the Lord's hand." Then Phinehas son of Eleazar, the priest, and the leaders returned to Canaan from their meeting with the Reubenites and Gadites in

Gilead and reported to the Israelites. They were glad to hear the report and praised God. And they talked no more about going to war against them to devastate the country where the Reubenites and the Gadites lived. And the Reubenites and the Gadites gave the altar this name: "A Witness (עד) Between Us that the Lord is God (יהוה האלהים)."

This story demonstrably emphasises the separate nature of the tribes beyond the Jordan and makes the altar named Ed (עד), raised almost as a memorial (mound) by Jacob and Laban, a sign of their accord (Gen 31). Even though three tribes are mentioned, Gad, Reuben and Manasseh, the geographic references indicate only Gilead.

The fragment from the book of Joshua quoted above has given rise to a huge amount of writing devoted mainly to attempts at locating the altar. According to N.H. Snaith, it should be identified with the altar in Gilgal.[63] Nevertheless, his assertion that the object found on the western bank of the Jordan could have performed the role of a religious centre for Transjordanian tribes is unconvincing. More satisfactory is the explanation put forward, in his criticism of Martin Noth's theory, by John S. Kloppenborg.[64] Martin Noth held the view that Josh 22:10-34 is a remnant of an old tradition which contained the aetiological story in whose final version, in v. 34, the proper name was omitted.[65] My own view is that the appearance of analogous phrases (see Gen 28:19; 35:15; Judg 6:24 and others) does not allow us to claim that a proper name has been omitted from v. 34.[66] The entire narrative, after all, focuses on the term עד, a key term here. Kloppenborg demonstrates that the text under consideration is strongly influenced by priestly redaction. This can be seen in the emphasis placed on the role of Phinehas and the idea of the unclean nature of Gilead, where the cult of Yahweh could not be practised. This authorial attitude to the territories lying to the east of the "border" River Jordan is, according to Kloppenborg, typical for the period of the captivity.[67]

Kloppenborg asserts that ch. 22 of the book of Joshua is not an original work from the times of the Second Temple and that its authors drew on older sources.[68] Their fundamental aim was to show that the

---

63. N.H. Snaith, "The Altar at Gilgal: Joshua XXII 23-29," *VT* 28 (1978): 330-35.

64. Kloppenborg, "Joshua 22," 347-71; this work gives an account of the earlier discussion.

65. *Ibid.*, 355-62.

66. Kloppenborg, "Joshua 22," 368, talks about the "falling out" of the name of the altar in v. 34; he suggests that the original names took the form: מזבח־עד, עד or מזבח־גלעד.

67. *Ibid.*, 355-62.

68. *Ibid.*, 365-70.

altar built by the tribes living beyond the Jordan did not possess full rights to be a centre for the cult of Yahweh. Because he focuses exclusively on the theological-cultic aspect of the story, which incidentally was the subject of interest to the editors, he ignores the question of the relationship of the Transjordanian tribes with the Israelites of which that very altar was supposed to be the witness (עד). After all, it is the altar which plays the main part in this story, whose aim it is to inflate the meaning of the agreement made and sanctioned on a sacral-ritual basis. Underlining this altar's inferiority to legal altars is undoubtedly not the story's main theme. Kloppenborg writes that there is no way of showing the influences between the text of Josh 22 and Gen 31, but he does not reject such a possibility. A strong argument in favour of such an interdependence is the importance given in both stories to the meaning of עד. It does seem that Josh 22 is dependent on a tradition found in the story about the building of a mound (heap) in Gilead. We can posit such a hypothesis, basing it simply on discussions aimed at establishing the probable time of the origins of the tradition which became the source of Gen 31:43-55, put alongside Kloppenborg's conclusions about the date of the redaction of the book of Joshua. The primary story was about a cult place found near the Jordan, built as a memorial to the agreement of a political alliance between the Transjordanian tribes and the tribes dwelling on the western banks of the river. It probably came into being in the middle of the eighth century BCE, and its first literary image is the story of the pact between Jacob and Laban (Gen 31). Joshua 22 was probably formed on the basis of the story about Jacob, of which the analogous application of the noun "witness" is evidence. The enlargement of the role of the priests and the emphasis on the sacred nature of the Promised Land indicate that the time of the story's creation is the period of the developed theocracy. There is, however, no way of establishing whether this text was written in the Persian or Hellenistic period.

Mahanaim

Aetiology

Genesis 31:55–32:3:

> Early the next morning Laban kissed his grandchildren and his daughters and blessed them. Then he left and returned home. Jacob also went on his way, and the angels of God (מלאכי אלהים) met him. When Jacob saw them, he said, "This is the camp (מחנה) of God!" So he named that place Mahanaim (מחנים). Jacob sent messengers ahead of him to his brother Esau in the land of Seir, the country of Edom.

Biblical Information

The name "Mahanaim" appears, in addition to the fragment cited above, several times in the Bible (see Josh 13:26, 30; 21:38; 2 Sam 2:8, 12, 29; 17:24, 27; 19:33[32]; 1 Kgs 2:8; 4:14; 1 Chr 6:65).

Joshua 13:24-28 talks about the division of land between the tribes of Israel:

> This is what Moses had given to the tribe of Gad, clan by clan: The territory of Jazer, all the towns of Gilead and half the Ammonite country as far as Aroer, near Rabbah; and from Heshbon to Ramath Mizpah and Betonim, and from Mahanaim to the territory of Debir; and in the valley, Beth Haram, Beth Nimrah, Succoth and Zaphon with the rest of the realm of Sihon king of Heshbon (the east side of the Jordan, the territory up to the end of the Sea of Kinnereth). These towns and their villages were the inheritance of the Gadites, clan by clan.

Joshua 21:38-40 concerns the assignment of towns wherein the Levites were to live: "from the tribe of Gad, Ramoth in Gilead (a city of refuge for one accused of murder), Mahanaim, Heshbon and Jazer, together with their pasture-lands—four towns in all. All the towns allotted to the Merarite clans, who were the rest of the Levites, were twelve." This information is repeated in 1 Chr 6:65.

2 Samuel 2:8-11 describes the proclamation of Ishbosheth, son of Saul, as king:

> Meanwhile, Abner son of Ner, the commander of Saul's army, had taken Ishbosheth son of Saul and brought him over to Mahanaim. He made him king over Gilead, Ashuri and Jezreel, and also over Ephraim, Benjamin and all Israel. Ishbosheth son of Saul was forty years old when he became king over Israel, and he reigned two years. The house of Judah, however, followed David. The length of time David was king in Hebron over the house of Judah was seven years and six months.

The references in 2 Sam 2:12 and 29 concern David's conflict with Abner and Ishbosheth whose quarters and supporters were in Mahanaim.

2 Samuel 17 talks about the conflict between David and Absalom during which David receives support from the inhabitants of Mahanaim (vv. 24 and 27). When Absalom took refuge in the land of Gilead, David in pursuit of him

> …came to Mahanaim, Shobi son of Nahash from Rabbah of the Ammonites, and Makir son of Ammiel from Lo Debar, and Barzillai the Gileadite from Rogelim brought bedding and bowls and articles of pottery. They also brought wheat and barley, flour and roasted grain, beans and lentils, honey and curds, sheep, and cheese from cows' milk for David and his people to eat. For they said, "The people have become hungry and tired and thirsty in the desert." (2 Sam 17:27-29)

2 Samuel 19:32 mentions the provision of sustenance for David and his warriors by Barzillai in Manahaim, while 1 Kgs 2:8 refers to David's flight to that town.

1 Kings 4:14 contains a fragment of a list of King Solomon's governors, among whom is "Ahinadab son of Iddo—in Mahanaim." This shows that this town was the capital of one of the twelve provinces of Solomon's kingdom.

These biblical quotations are evidence that Mahanaim was an important administrative centre.[69] The town is mentioned in the context of armed conflicts: the battle for the throne between David and Ishbosheth (2 Sam 2:8-11, 12, 29), and also Absalom's rebellion (2 Sam 17:24, 27; 1 Kgs 2:8). It was there, too, that one of Solomon's twelve governors was supposed to reside (1 Kgs 4:14).

The mention of Mahanaim among the Levite towns (Josh 21:38; 1 Chr 6:65), and also the inclusion of the information about the proclamation of Ishbosheth as king there, proves that it performed an important role as a religious centre where the Levites performed their cult. The regal proclamation of Jehu (2 Kgs 9:13), of Joash (2 Kgs 11:14-15), or the anointing of Saul (1 Sam 9:19–10:1) and David (1 Sam 16:3-5, 13) are accompanied by elements of a religious cult and, one might allow, all took place "in the sight of God." The proclamation of Ishbosheth as king, cited above, must also have taken place in a holy place and the ritual was assuredly accompanied by sacrifices.

A comparison of the Greek and Hebrew texts reveals an inconsistency in the rendering of the name of the place Mahanaim. Its Greek form, Μααναιμ, appears in Josh 13:30 and 1 Chr 6:65, while the form Μααναιν is found in Josh 13:26 and 1 Kgs 4:14. A third form, Μαναϊμ, appears in 2 Sam 17:24, 27; 19:33, while yet another form, Μαναεμ, appears in 2 Sam 2:8, 12 (added to which in this version of the story v. 29 uses the common noun "camp": ἐκείνην καὶ διέβαιναν τὸν Ιορδάνην καὶ ἐπορεύθησαν ὅλην τὴν παρατείνουσαν καὶ ἔρχονται εἰς τὴν παρεμβολήν).

In 1 Kgs 2:8 the Hebrew term מחנים corresponds to the Greek denotation παρεμβολή, "camp," used in the plural (lit.: "David took an oath in Mahanaim/two camps"). Considering that the taking of an oath is associated with a place of a cult (let us simply recall Absalom's oath in Hebron), the reading of Mahanaim as a place appears to predate that of it as a camp (by implication: a military camp), allowing an oath to be made there in the face of god.

Josephus, in *Jewish Antiquities*, carried out a significant re-interpretation of the passage about the naming of the place Mahanaim, emphasising

---

69. Coughenour, "A Search for Mahanaim," 58.

the nature of a vision: "Jacob now pursuing his journey to Canaan had visions which inspired him with good hopes for the future; and he called that spot 'God's camp'" (*Ant* 1.20.1). Undoubtedly rationalising the biblical narrative, Josephus changed the waking vision into a dream vision (φαντάσματα).

Commentators have wondered how this "camp of God," which became the word-source of the name "Mahanaim" (two camps), can be envisaged. Linking the etymology of the name "Mahanaim" with either the vision of the angels as an army of god, or with the division made by Jacob of the land into smaller "camps," is merely the purest guess-work by commentators. It is most likely that this duality in the proper name is connected to the proximity of two settlements on the banks of the Jabbok (Tell edh-Dhahab el-Gharbi and Tell edh-Dhahab esh-Sherqiyeh).

Penuel

Aetiology

Genesis 32:22-32:

> That night Jacob got up and took his two wives, his two maidservants and his eleven sons and crossed the ford of the Jabbok. After he had sent them across the stream, he sent over all his possessions. So Jacob was left alone, and a man (איש) wrestled with him till daybreak. When the man saw that he could not overpower him, he touched the socket of Jacob's hip so that his hip was wrenched as he wrestled with the man. Then the man said, "Let me go, for it is daybreak." But Jacob replied, "I will not let you go unless you bless me." The man asked him, "What is your name?" "Jacob," he answered. Then the man said, "Your name will no longer be Jacob, but Israel, because you have struggled with God (אלהים) and with men and have overcome." Jacob said, "Please tell me your name." But he replied, "Why do you ask my name?" Then he blessed him there. So Jacob called the place Penuel (פניאל) saying, "It is because I saw God face to face (פנים אל־פנים) and yet my life was spared." The sun rose above him as he passed Penuel, and he was limping because of his hip. Therefore to this day the Israelites do not eat the tendon attached to the socket of the hip, because the socket of Jacob's hip was touched near the tendon.

Biblical Information

In the MT the name "Penuel"—when applied to a place—appears additionally in Judg 8:8, 9, 17 and in 1 Kgs 12:25, and as a proper name of two people in 1 Chr 4:4; 8:25.

The book of Judges mentions Penuel alongside Succoth, in the context of the war of Gideon with the Midianites, as one of two towns which not only refused to support Gideon but even refused to give bread to his army (Judg 8:8-9). Gideon promised that on his way back from conquering the Midianites he would destroy the fortress (המגדל) of Penuel. Verse 17 informs as of the fulfilment of the threat: "He...pulled down the tower of Penuel" (ואת־מגדל פנואל נתץ).

1 Kings provides alternative information on the aetiological theme linking Penuel (Peniel) with the person of Jacob. After the death of Solomon, when the kingdom disintegrated, Jeroboam, the new king of the northern kingdom "...fortified Shechem in the hill country of Ephraim and lived there. From there he went out and built up Peniel" (1 Kgs 12:25).[70]

1 Chronicles mentions someone called Penuel from the tribe of Judah (1 Chr 4:4) and a Penuel from the tribe of Benjamin (1 Chr 8:25). We have an interesting allusion here to 1 Kgs 12:22-33 where Jeroboam, king of Israel, when founding Penuel, is challenged by Rehoboam, the king of Judah and Benjamin (see 1 Kgs 12:23). The biblical evidence does not suggest that Penuel had any exceptional religious significance. There is no mention anywhere of any cult practised there. The only pointer suggesting a supposed religious function for this centre is a reference to Jeroboam making Penuel the capital of his kingdom or at least a royal residence. It is possible, however, that Penuel was never an important cult centre and functioned only in the reality of the myth associated with the deeds of the hero Jacob-Israel.

Hermann Gunkel has drawn attention to the strange nature of the unnamed deity with whom Jacob struggled.[71] He considers that Yahweh is Jacob's guardian deity whereas the being he struggled with is an inimical one, typical of a god of a lower order of the pre-Yahwistic religion of the Israelites.[72] Distancing himself from the claim that Jacob's nocturnal struggle is a reflection of a nightmare, Gunkel sees rather an analogy to the motif of a hero's battle with a wise man, a battle whose fruit was to be some gift (e.g. the gift of wisdom), and recalls, among others, the story of Menelaus and Proteus. He also claims that the reference to limping is an allusion to a cult dance (cf. 1 Kgs 18:26).

70. See the chapter about Shechem; Albertz, *A History of Israelite Religion*, 1:143 considers that Penuel was funded on an equal footing with Bethel and Dan as one of the traditional cult centres.

71. Gunkel, *Genesis*, 352-53.

72. *Ibid.*, 352.

In Gunkel's opinion, the etymologies of the names "Penuel," "Jabbok" and "Israel" are later additions to a much earlier story about the hero's battle. Added to this, the original story was separate from the Jacob–Esau narrative.

A similar interpretation of Jacob's struggle with the angel has been provided by B. Margalit,[73] who sees in this story an expression of the Israelites' nomadic mentality. His isolation, forced on him by a taboo associated with a physiological activity, made Jacob's withdraw from the camp. The hero's antagonist was supposed to have been a river demon. Margalit proposes this idea on the basis of the use in the text of the noun יָרֵךְ (usually translated as "hip joint"), which is derived from the recon-structed root יָרַךְ*, suggesting something convex. Margalit claims that it is not a hip joint or bone that is in question here, which does indeed have a shape consonant with the etymology of the word יָרֵךְ, but a buttock. The circumstances of Jacob's injury would thereby be very prosaic and be linked to a physiological action demanding the straining of his buttocks.[74] Margalit also inclines to the view that a significant role in this narrative is played by powers emanating from the underworld, the dead giving their blessing, and that the setting of the action—the valley of a river in Transjordan—was the domain of Mot.

The aetiology of Peniel (Penuel) is comprised, it seems, of two parts. The first is connected to Jacob's struggle with אֱלֹהִים / אִישׁ; the second to the name of a place.

Unlike any other biblical story, the narrative about Jacob's struggle is an obvious initiation scenario. All of the narrative's parts combine to produce a positively textbook definition of initiation:
1. the setting of the action: isolation, river (place of passage);
2. the time of the action: night;
3. battle with the unknown (stranger);
4. a physical trace of the duel: a damaged hip, limp;
5. change of name;
6. a culinary taboo as a social consequence of the cult hero's initi-ation.

There is evidence of the motif of Jacob's struggle with a supernatural being as early as the eighth century BCE. The reference in the book of Hosea leaves no room to doubt that it concerns the same mythical

73. B. Margalit, "Jacob and the Angel (Gen. 32:23-33) in Light of the Balaam Text from Deir 'Alla" (paper delivered at the 48 Colloquium Biblicum Lovaniense, Leuven, 28–30 July 1999).
74. Here, of course, is the end of any similarity with H. Gunkel's commentary.

happening: "He struggled with the angel and overcame him; he wept and begged for his favour" (Hos 12:4). It is unclear if the protagonist of this battle is Israel or Jacob, since v. 2 mentions both names. The mention of this myth in the book of Hosea, though very generalised, allows us to ascertain several significant differences from the version in Gen 32. First, the hero's antagonist is an angel,[75] and not אלהים / איש. Secondly, the hero who triumphed (ויכל[76]) cries and despairs (בכה[77]). Another reference in Hosea seems to be evidence of the existence as early as the eighth century BCE of a story about Jacob serving Laban in return for being given a wife: "Jacob fled to the country of Aram; Israel served to get a wife, and to pay for her he tended sheep" (Hos 12:13).

 Genesis 32:31 expresses a frequently repeated idea that the life of the story's hero is threatened because of his direct contact with a deity (see, *inter alia*, Gen 28:16-17; Judg 6:22-23). Emphasising the danger consequent upon contact with a supernatural being indicates unequivocally that the narrative's authors' intention was to underline the significance of the theophany itself.

 Steven McKenzie suggested an interesting hypothesis: that the fragment of Hos 12:4-5 was, in the prophet's text, a quotation from a poem performed during rituals in Bethel.[78] Convinced as he was that the Jacob motif penetrated the prophet's text from the epic tradition, McKenzie does not discuss its dependence on the version in Genesis.[79] I suspect that the difference in traditions should be underlined, but the material is insufficient to show to what extent they functioned independently of one another and to what extent one depended on the other.[80]

 Flavius Josephus in *Jewish Antiquities* altered the version of this myth only slightly. First of all, he called Jacob's antagonist a phantom

---

 75. S.L. McKenzie, "The Jacob Tradition in Hosea XII 4-5," *VT* 36 (1986): 311-22 (313), considers that in the pericope related to the struggle with a supernatural being, it was Israel who appeared and that in the original version the antagonist was אל. For McKenzie, it was only later that the place of God was taken by an angel.

 76. From the root יכל, "to overcome," "to conquer."

 77. From the root בכה, "to cry," "to despair," "to shed tears"; see, e.g., Gen 45:14—the weeping of Joseph and Benjamin; Exod 2:6—the crying of a child; Num 11:10—the people's crying; 2 Sam 19:2—the weeping of mourning.

 78. McKenzie, "The Jacob Tradition," 319-21.

 79. *Ibid.*, 321.

 80. Whitt, "The Jacob Tradition in Hosea," considers that both the references in the book of Hosea and the story in the book of Genesis draw on the same source which was the body of epics about Jacob and having a cult application in Bethel. Whitt sets the date of the passage in Hosea in the eighth century, and of the narrative in the book of Genesis in the seventh to sixth century BCE.

(φαντάσμα) and an angel of god (ἄγγελως θεοῦ); secondly he wrote that "the spectre, which now found a tongue and addressed him," implying that phantoms could also use their voice to speak in unrecognizable ways; thirdly, in Josephus's version, Jacob, seeing that he is dealing with a phantom (angel), asks for a prophecy which indicates that the epiphany of the supernatural being is linked to divination. Finally, assuredly seeking to rationalise the entire story, Josephus adds that: "Jacob, [was] delighted with the vision" (*Ant* 1.20.2). This interpretation was supposed to have made this narrative more credible for the audience, even though the result is that an inconsistency has arisen. Indeed, the event is supposed to have taken place during a vision, in other words, in a special state of consciousness, yet its consequence is very real: "Now when he felt pain, by this struggling, upon his broad sinew, he abstained from eating that sinew himself afterward."

This myth is also to be found in the preserved fragments of the work of Demetrius who summarises the biblical story, expanding the motif of the angel (ἄγγελος), the hero's wound, the limping and the change of name (Demetrius, fr. 2, 7). The setting of the events is not described in detail—all we are told is that it all happened on the road to Canaan and that after the struggle Jacob reaches Shechem (which corresponds to the content of Gen 33:18-20). As I mentioned earlier, the whole theme of Jacob's meeting with Esau is omitted.

In the version of Jacob's deeds collected in the book of *Jubilees*, on the other hand, immediately after the description of the pact made with Laban there is information about a meeting with Esau but no mention of the story of Mahanaim and Penuel (*Jub.* 29:5-13).

The initiation nature of the story of Jacob's struggle with an angel, and also the lack of information about the religious significance of Penuel, prove that the aetiological motif explaining the origins of this place are a later addition. Originally the story comprised a fragment of the mythological deeds of Jacob and as such could serve as a recipe for initiation (e.g. of warriors). Crucial was the setting of the action on a frontier. A precise location was not needed for the myth to function properly. I suspect that at the stage when the collection of myths (epic) about Jacob were systematised, the story of the initiation battle of the eponymous hero with a supernatural being was exploited in order to explain the place's name aetiologically. The story was ideally suited to incorporate the phrase "I looked on God face to face." Undoubtedly, more important than the aetiology of the place name is the origin of the hero's name—Israel.

9.
Conclusions and Summary

The aetiological myths of holy places discussed in this work form a unified body of sources. The Bible associates the beginnings of nine such places in various parts of Palestine with the patriarchs, with the times around the conquest of Canaan and with the period of Judges. Neither the books describing the deeds of David and Saul, nor the books of Kings, contain a separate aetiological myth. This in itself is enough to let us conclude that the books of Samuel and the books of Kings are texts of a different kind than the Pentateuch, the book of Joshua and Judges. It is tempting to apply the epithet "historiographical" to them. The concept would, however, need to be defined more precisely. Biblical historiography is unique in the Middle East where there is no work comparable to the description of the deeds of Judah and Israel.[1] Arnaldo Momigliano's theory that Greek and Jewish historiography have common roots in unpreserved Persian writings seems to be unwarranted.[2] Niels Peter Lemche's claims regarding the dependence of biblical historiography on the historiographic traditions of the Greeks and Romans require further study.[3] Even if the appearance of aetiological myths of holy places were an indicator applicable to these studies, we would still have to recognise the difference in kind between the Genesis–Judges collection and that of 1 Samuel–2 Kings. The Pentateuch, the book of Joshua as well as the book of Judges contain a record of the Israelites' mythical past and for

1. Van Seters, *In Search of History*.
2. A. Momigliano, "Biblical and Classical Studies. Simple Reflections upon Historical Method," *Annali della Scuola Normale Superiore di Pisa*, serie III, 11 (1981): 25-32; *idem, The Classical Foundations of Modern Historiography*, Berkeley, 1990, 5-28.
3. Lemche, *The Israelites in History and Tradition*; but particularly "Ideology and the History of Ancient Israel," *SJOT* 14 (2000): 165-93; see also Edelman (ed.), *The Fabric of History*; Davies, *In Search of "Ancient Israel"*; Fritz and Davies (eds.), *The Origins of the Ancient Israelite States*; Grabbe (ed.), *Can a "History of Israel" Be Written?*

this reason they should not be analyzed as works of historiography. Since the events and personages described there belong to the world of myth, that is to say, to the religious world of the authors' sensibility, we cannot regard them as a record of a historical reality.[4]

Analyzing all the aetiologies to be found in the collection Genesis–2 Kings, Friedemann W. Golka concluded that the corpus is divided into two parts. The first, which contains many aetiologies, consists of Gen 1:1–1 Sam 27:6, and the second, which contains none, runs from 1 Sam 27:7 to the end of 2 Kings. He concluded that what we are dealing with from the book of Genesis through to nearly the end of 1 Samuel is a tribal tradition whereas in the later sections of the deuteronomistic collection we have a historiography, the work of Israelites within a state organisation.[5] Although Golka's assessment of the presence of aetiologies in the Pentateuch and the DtrH coincides with mine, the conclusions we draw from it are different. According to Golka, the literary genres of the Bible evolved; the record of the Israelites' literary output from the pre-tribal period was collected in Genesis–1 Samuel and then, in the kingdom of David and Solomon, a new way of writing developed, namely, historiography.

This naïve assertion is completely unwarranted, and a comparison with Greek literature reveals how arbitrary it is. If this suggestion were true, then, staying with the example of Greece, we could expect there to be numerous aetiologies in ancient times and a lack of them in classical historiography. Whereas the fact is that the reverse is true: the Greek epic is almost entirely devoid of aetiological stories, whereas they play an important part in the works of Herodotus, and are very numerous indeed in the works of Diodorus and Pausanias. There is here, therefore, no evolution of literary type—from tribal literature frequently making use of aetiology, to refined historiography reluctant to resort to such tools. Sometimes it can even appear that the more inexplicable the phenomena under discussion were, the more eagerly did the writers resort to aetiological myths. A period must have elapsed between the origins of an institution and the creation of its aetiology, long enough to allow the reasons for its origins to be forgotten. Although I agree that the body of biblical sources of interest to us here does divide into two parts, I would not draw from this the conclusions that Golka proposes. There is a qualitative difference between the Genesis–Judges and the 1 Samuel–2 Kings collections, but that does not in itself allow us to speak of the evolution

---

4. From this perspective, the works of *inter alia* W.F. Albright, J. Bright and A. Alt seem to be anachronistic.

5. Golka, "Aetiologies," 43-44.

of literary genres. They are collections of different styles and different principles. The former contains mythological works constructing the Israelites' past in ancient times, the latter contains historiographic works (the fact that the texts are not always credible is not significant here). Two different genres, bringing with them two different formal methods, do not necessarily indicate two different eras, nor even different authors.

Before I proceed to the summary of, and the conclusions drawn from, the analysis of the myths discussed in this work, I would like to present several specific findings regarding holy places as subjects of mythic narratives. The chapter devoted to the sanctuary established by Gideon presents a thesis concerning the artificially created name "Ophrah." On the basis of the version of this name found in the LXX (Εφραθα), I inferred that the altar built by Gideon was to be found in the vicinity of Bethlehem. The remains of the citadel there correspond to the details described in the aetiology: that the altar was located on the top of the fort. The royal citadel was built very close to Bethlehem, in today's Ramath Rahel, the very place where biblical tradition locates the tomb of Rachel. I have tried to show in which period this "removal" of the tomb from Benjamin's territory to that of Judah took place. This process, along with the intrusions into the myth of Gideon in Εφραθα, was linked to the expansion of the tradition of the house of David. Two elements proved to be key to the dating of the mythical story about Gideon's altar: the existence in Ramath Rahel of a citadel, and the time when the biblical editors propagating the Messianistic theology associated with a descendant of David worked. The citadel, which served initially as a defensive structure then as a royal residence, existed from the ninth or eighth century BCE until the beginning of the sixth century BCE. The first story of Gideon and the Yahweh altar should be dated in this period. The dating of the process of expanding the ideology of the house of David is harder, though it is probable that the times of the Babylonian captivity and the beginnings of the Persian period will be involved. The addition of references linking the figure of Gideon with Abiezer seems to have been made at this same stage, as was the interpolation of the information about Gideon coming from the family of Manasseh (Judg 6:15). The final interference in the text of the myth, the one leading to the change of name from אפרתה to עפרה, must have taken place after the separation of the LXX manuscript tradition.

Another important aetiological myth is the story about Gilgal. The inaccuracies in the location of this sanctuary (on the banks of the Jordan, *vis-à-vis* Jericho or close to Shechem) and its lack of identification have led me to conclude that the term "Gilgal" was not, initially, a toponym but a technical term signifying a holy circle. In its original form, *galgal*, this term could well have referred to many places, while the most important sanctuary named thus was to be found in Shechem. In Chapter 7 I attempted to gather data indicating the secondary nature of the story. The similarities in the narratives between the crossing of the Jordan and the crossing of the Red Sea or the celebrations of the first Pesach in Canaan with the account of the beginnings of Pesach in Egypt allow us to infer that the story in the book of Joshua (4:1-5, 12) is secondary in relation to the story of the deeds of Moses. Elements such as the elevation of the role of the priests, the emphasis on the association of all twelve Israelite tribes and also the figure of Joshua himself—as a military and a religious leader—force us to acknowledge that its origins fall at some time in the Hasmonean era. Another fact encourages this dating, namely, that during the second century BCE the conflict between the Samaritans and the Jews strengthened. This could have influenced the minimisation of Shechem's religious significance.

The story about the origins of the Transjordanian cult centre described as "Galeed" is closely linked with *galgal. The name Galeed, associated with the region of Gilead, comprises the word גל, "mound," and עד, "testimony." The origins of this sanctuary, situated on the frontier and most probably on the Jabbok, are associated with the figures of Jacob and Laban. The singularity of this place stems from its frontier situation: the mound in question (גל) was raised as a mark of the border accord between the Hebrews and the Aramaeans. The story of the building by the Transjordanian tribes of an altar named עד (Josh 22) takes up the same ritual theme. It seems pointless to search for this object since, in my view, the description of its construction is simply an echo of the theme of the story of Galeed's origins and does not refer to any actually existing cult place. Just as the story of Galeed contains contradictions (the altar and the mound of stones) which testify to the ancient provenance of the original story, so the narrative in the book of Joshua about the raising of the altar seems to be describing merely a literary (mythical?) reality. The emphasis in this current of tradition on the exceptional—in religious terms—status of the Holy Land, on its purity and on the special role of the priests, indicates that this narrative is of late derivation.

In the Introduction I posed several questions which became the stimulus to an analysis of the stories about the origins of holy places. One of them applied to the probable time of the creation of the aetiological myths associated with the stories. Before I answer these questions I have to set down some reservations. It is not possible to analyze the history of myths in the same way as one can study the history of nations or states. The reality of a myth exists initially in the minds of people, while the historian is dealing with the written record of that consciousness. The question of how long and since when a myth is propagated orally cannot be answered. The lack of sources makes it impossible to carry out methodologically accurate studies. Some mythical motifs in the aetiologies of holy places could well have functioned independently of the stories in which they finally appeared. In addition, entire myths could have been exploited separately from their context in the Bible. It was possible to base the date of their origin on the assumption that the conclusions refer only to myths which are strongly linked to the place being described. This meant that cases where a myth explained the origins of a place X and was subsequently associated with place Y should be excluded. I suspect that such things did happen, though not very often. They did so for two reasons: (1) myths are an expression of people's religious consciousness, which is by its nature conservative (the survival of the cult of the sacred tree in Mamre) and resistant to change; (2) aetiological myths of holy places are in large measure created in language derived from a ritual associated, I suggest, with the sanctuary in question. Accepting these assumptions allows us to explain those cases where the Bible gives us an obvious transmission of mythic motifs and where we find the elements of the mythology of one centre appearing in another. Such a literary device was possible because the subjects were descriptions of non-existent sanctuaries. It was possible for such borrowings to be accepted because the centre described (created) had no myths or rituals of its own. Albeit the language of the myth in which the beginnings of a holy place was told revealed associations with other traditions, the fact that this was simply a literary reality meant that there was no conflict involved in the alignment with other, and the rejection of original, traditions. There is no doubt that each holy place, or—as Eliade believed—all reality, had its origins in myth. Religious society constructs an extended structure of myths which constitute the entirety of the world that surrounds it.

Attempts at dating the myths about the origins of holy places necessitate the establishment of the time when these sanctuaries functioned, and this is only partly possible because even the most thorough historical and archaeological reconstruction can only ever be a reconstruction based, obviously enough, on incomplete material. Despite the often very wide margin of error contained in every reconstruction of the past, archaeological finds do provide priceless material for the study of the history of holy places. Not all the sanctuaries discussed here have been discovered by archaeologists. Nor have thorough explorations been carried out everywhere. Despite the incomplete archaeological data and the even more fragmentary historical data, I have attempted to suggest the periods during which a given sanctuary could have existed. Even if it has not been possible to find a *temenos*, or any sacred objects or any traces indicating that a cult was practised there, I consider that the existence of a settlement is enough to assume that some kind of sanctuary did function there. Such an assumption does, of course, broaden the margin of error; in view of the selectivity of the data available, however, it proved to be essential.

One other assumption had to be made to establish a relatively accurate date for the origins of aetiological myths around holy places. In my view, mythical stories regarding real cult places arose when those places were under the management, or in the sphere of influence, of the people formulating the given myths. The creation of myths associated with the beginnings of a sanctuary was possible only when a specific group (the inhabitants of a town, a tribe or a people) knew that sanctuary and participated in the cult practised there. This assumption remains in force also in relation to the later developments of the mythical tradition in its literary form. The sacred places whose myths were systematised, edited or reshaped were exclusively those which continued to function and which remained in the hands of the people editing the myths. If a sanctuary ceased to exist, or was located "abroad," then its aetiologies would be senseless. Being a way of explaining a reality which no longer needed explanation, it would quite simply be excised from the text. An example to illustrate this is the Bible's lack of aetiology for Arad, Megiddo, Hazor or the important religious centre of Shiloh—omissions which came about because, at the time of the biblical text's editing, these sanctuaries did not exist, rendering any explanation of their origin pointless.

To a large extent it was analysis of the archaeological material that decided the dates of the beginnings of various aetiological myths. The list below shows the periods when the various centres with the sanctuaries in question were functioning:

Beer-sheba	ninth to seventh; second to first centuries BCE
Bethel	most probably uninterruptedly from tenth to first centuries BCE
Dan	ninth to tenth (eighth?); second to first centuries BCE
Gilead	ninth to eighth; first centuries BCE
Hebron	tenth to eighth; second centuries BCE
Ophrah-Ephrathah	ninth to seventh/sixth; second to first centuries BCE
Penuel	ninth to eighth; first centuries BCE
Shechem	tenth to eighth; third to second centuries BCE

It is not possible to establish that all the traditions began simultaneously. Where chronology is concerned, the data are of necessity approximate. Nevertheless, it is possible to reach certain conclusions on their basis. As the list above shows, there was a long period (ninth to eighth century BCE) during which all the sanctuaries were functioning. It must also be remembered that in this same period there were two separate states in existence: Israel and Judah. The testimonies of the prophets of the pre-exile epoch prove that there was considerable antagonism between the two kingdoms. To seek the beginnings of biblical traditions in the time of the divided monarchy would require us to assume that there was a supra-state link connecting all the Israelites.

Dan was probably the only sanctuary which was not controlled by the Israelites at the time. One can therefore suppose that it was during the period of the First Temple, in the ninth and eighth centuries, that stories about the origins of the other sanctuaries came into being. If that is the case, then did they function in the same form as is recorded in the Bible? I suspect that the answer to that is negative. While we cannot exclude the possibility that some stories about holy places did exist as early as the ninth or eighth century BCE, it is doubtful that they included all the elements that the myths we know contain. The aetiologies explaining the origins of Beer-sheba and Hebron are linked to the figure of Abraham. Yet, assuredly, the figure of Abraham the patriarch did not feature in Hebrew mythology as early as the years 900–700 BCE.[6] It is feasible that the story's hero was "transformed," but that seems implausible. Things are different in the myths associated with the figure of Jacob the patriarch, who appears in biblical texts from before the Babylonian captivity. I have tried to show that initially the aetiology of Galeed was associated with some relationship, of which we do not know the full details, between the Hebrews and the inhabitants of Transjordan in the middle of the eighth century BCE.

The aetiologies of Beer-sheba and Hebron can be of particular assistance in the establishment of the date of the composition of the book of Genesis. The generally accepted thesis is that the literary tradition describing the deeds of Abraham arose during, and just after, the Babylonian captivity. At the same time, we have concluded that the narrative about Abraham in Beer-sheba and the purchase of a tomb in Hebron could have arisen no earlier than the Hasmonean times. If we accept the first assumption, it follows that the story about the covenant in Beer-sheba (Gen 21:22-33 and the text of Gen 26:23-33 which is dependent

---

6. Garbini, *Storia e ideologia*; Van Seters, *Abraham in History and Tradition*; Thompson, *The Historicity of the Patriarchal Narrative*.

on it) and the extended narrative about the purchase of the grave in Hebron (Gen 23:1-20) arose only after 164 BCE; this is because during the Persian period and for most of the Hellenistic era the centres in Hebron and Beer-sheba were under the sway of the Idumaeans. This late dating is based, in turn, on the assumption that these works came into being thanks to increased politico-religious activity (no earlier than the years 180–170 BCE) which led to the Maccabean revolt. The closing date is defined by the manuscript testimonies (both biblical and apocryphal texts that show a close dependence on biblical texts, for instance the book of *Jubilees*). This would be—as the palaeographic evidence suggests— more or less the middle of the second century BCE (maybe the years 150–125 BCE?).

There are two other theories to explain the process by which these stories came into being. The first, somewhat vertiginous, theory assumes that the aetiological myth was picked up from the local, that is to say, Idumaean, population.[7] The second presupposes a modification of the thesis about the birth of the Abraham tradition during the captivity. Indeed, only by accepting that the figure of this patriarch functioned in the mythical imaginations of the Hebrews as early as the First Temple can the history of the sanctuaries be reconciled with the development of the mythic motifs of their origins.

The choice of any one of the theories presented here depends almost entirely on scholarly discretion, the world-view and scientific back-ground of those seeking to interpret the data. The source material is too flimsy to allow us to make a rational choice. Without pretending to formulate definitive statements, I can only express my subjective con-victions on this subject. It seems most probable to me that mythic motifs about the patriarch Abraham, a hero strongly linked with the world of southern Judah and the borders of the Negev desert, existed in ancient times—though it is impossible to establish whether this was the Bronze Age or the time of the First Temple. In the First Temple period not much importance was ascribed to him. Evidence of that is, *inter alia*, the lack of any references to him. He could have been a mythical ancestor of a group acknowledged locally; as a group's importance grew, so the cul-tural hero's status also increased. Initially, it was the eponymous hero Jacob-Israel who played the key role (cf. the idea associated with him of the twelve sons/tribes), as did the story of the exodus from Egypt (or the migration from the south), with which it was Moses who was chiefly

---

7. It must be remembered that the references to Philistines and Hittites which occur in the narratives do not necessarily apply to real Philistines and Hittites but could be a form of archaising applied to, for instance, the Greeks.

associated. Traces of these local traditions have survived, for example, in the book of Judges, although it can be supposed that most of this heritage of the Hebrews has been completely lost. I concur with the thesis that the motif of Abraham coming from Ur and journeying to Haran came into being in the times of the Babylonian captivity. It is surely the case that this figure evolved gradually until it finally assumed the position of the first of the patriarchs. The supra-ethnic character of Abraham and his ecumenical nature can be defended.[8] The phenomenon of the formation of a heroic figure who is outside the world of the ethnos and national religion does not fit easily into the Persian era, a time when the Jews were in constant conflict with the world around them. Equally improbable is the early Hellenistic period. The Jews had to try to preserve their individuality under the rules of the Achaemenids, the Ptolemies and the Seleucids. Traces of ethnic exclusivity can be seen as late as the Hellenistic era (Demetrius and the book of Sirach). One can envisage the creation of a common patriarch only in a situation where the sense of threat to one's own individuality has been lifted and independence is evident. The literature of the Hasmonean era shows a coexistence of two ideologies. One of them, it seems, made of Abraham a patriarch of virtually all the known Jewish peoples. The other gave birth to a xenophobic attitude culminating in the idea that all foreign wives and the children born of them were to be banished (Ezra). The former resulted from the openness of the strongly Hellenised court elites in the Hasmonean times; the latter was the creation of a stratum of Jerusalem priests wanting disengagement.[9]

It is likely that we will never discover when a myth was formed. It seems to me, however, that we can set down the moment by which its presence in the religious consciousness, and effectively also in the biblical text, was well established. It is obvious that the Bible's authors used old sources during the forming of the Old Testament text, and that at a certain moment they selected some stories that were considered to be canonical, and removed others. The completion of this process, at least following the chronology presented above, took place in the second half of the second century BCE. At this time all the sanctuaries were within the borders of the Jewish state or in its sphere of influence.

It is not possible to set precise dates. We have to take into account the possibility that even sanctuaries far from the Jewish state could have

8. De Pury, "Abraham," 163-81.
9. To a large extent this division coincides with the division of the Sadducees and the Pharisees; the latter, hostile to the royal court, had a decisive influence on the form and content of the MT after 70 CE.

been of interest to the Jerusalem elites. Symptomatic of this are the examples of Beer-sheba and Dan. If we were to stick strictly to the assumption that a sanctuary's aetiological story makes sense only when its creators (or editors) can be present in the centres concerned, then we would have to accept that these texts came into being only after the Jews had taken possession of the territories around those towns, that is to say, after John Hyrcanus's conquest of Idumea (129–126 BCE) and the north-ward expansion of Galilee (probably in the reign of Alexander Jannaeus in the years 103–76 BCE). Setting the date of the biblical text's final redaction in this time would, however, meet with certain difficulties. I do not think that the only period we should consider is the one during which these sanctuaries were located within the Jewish state. It is possible to attempt a reconstruction of a Jewish ideology of the Hellenistic period postulating a return to the state of possession that pertained during the reign of David (regardless of whether that state was mythic or historical).

The myths about the beginnings of Beer-sheba and Dan had a meaning and sense for the Jews not only when those towns were part of their state, but also when they began their policy of expansion. It is most probable that this ideology was born only as late as the Maccabean revolt. It was then that, for the first time since the Babylonian captivity, the Jewish state won its independence and rapidly began to bring new territories under its control. The new leaders, being both head priests and military commanders, wielded both religious and secular power. Numismatic finds illustrate the process accompanying this accumulation of power. The first coins, modelled on Seleucid coins, contain the inscription "arch-priest,"[10] but already in those issued by Alexander Jannaeus a new nomenclature appears: βασιλεος Αλεχανδρος.[11] The Hasmoneans strove to harness religion for political ends, and this can be seen, among other ways, in their building works. It was during their rule that investments in Mamre, Beer-sheba and Lachish were made.

Any reconstruction of the ideologies accompanying the birth of a new state is difficult because it relies exclusively on assumptions. There are, however, several arguments which might strengthen the hypothesis that links the birth of a new way of thinking about Palestine with the Hasmonean period. Importantly, the Bible makes no mention of the

10. J. Sievers, *The Hasmoneans and their Supporters: From Mattathias to the Death of John Hyrcanus I*, Atlanta, 1990, 152-54; D. Mendels, *The Rise and Fall of Jewish Nationalism*, New York, 1992, 62-63.

11. E.M. Meyers *et al.* (eds.), *Ancient Synagogue Excavations at Khirbet Shema', Upper Galilee Israel 1970–1972*, Durham, NC, 1976, 150-51; pl. 6.1.8-12; see also Y. Meshorer, *Ancient Jewish Coinage*, vols. 1–2, New York, 1982.

residence and sanctuary of Tobiah in 'Araq el-Emir in Transjordan. This could be because in the Hasmonean (or priestly) ideology, the history of the family of Tobiah was not well received and because their residence no longer played any meaningful role in the middle of the second century BCE.[12] Yet, the fundamental proof that Hasmonean ideology influenced the final shape of the Bible is found in the biblical text itself. Thomas L. Thompson, as well as J. Maxwell Miller and John H. Hayes, have shown that a biblical chronology based on (among others) 400- and 80-year cycles is evident in the MT, and that it contains various events from the history and mythology of the Hebrews that occur at regular time intervals. The last of the events whose date derives from the cyclical nature of the deeds of the Hebrews is the purification of the Jerusalem temple in 164 BCE. This shows that this event "closed off" the biblical chronology.[13] There is, however, nothing to suggest that editorial interventions in the biblical texts did not proceed further during the Hasmonean times.

We can characterise the myths in question on the basis of this reconstruction. The aetiological myths about Beer-sheba, Dan, the stories about the sanctuaries in Transjordan, and, to some extent, the aetiology of the holy place in Hebron (Mamre), could have been useful in the second century BCE in the establishment of relations between the Jews and their neighbours. All of those sanctuaries were outside the jurisdiction of the Hebrews right until the Hasmonean expansion. It could be that underlining the role of the covenant between Israelites (Abraham, Jacob) and outsiders (Laban, Abimelech, the Anakim in Hebron) was supposed to sanction the relations with those societies which actually existed there. That does not mean that these aetiologies arose on an *ad hoc* basis, as an instrument serving the ideology or propaganda of the state. There must have been ancient templates in existence which probably underwent considerable reworking. For in every case, the aetiological stories refer to symbols which assuredly had a direct link to the rituals taking place in the sanctuaries which explain their beginnings.

The situation is different with Bethel and Ophrah (Ephrathah) because these centres were always under the control of the Israelites. Their aetiologies contain no motifs indicating a covenant or alliance. There is no mention of any feasts which could have symbolised an agreement between two sides. There are no figures appearing in them apart from the hero who builds the sanctuary and the divinity. In both cases, the aetiologies characteristically emphasise that a theophany is the event

---

12. Campbell, Jr, "Jewish Shrines."
13. Thompson, *The Bible in History*, 73-75; Miller and Hayes, *A History of Ancient Israel and Judah*, 58-59.

which sanctifies the future cult place. Both myths talk about the first sacrifices offered to God. I would be inclined to set the date of these stories' beginnings at a time before the Babylonian captivity, though a more precise dating (especially in the case of Bethel's aetiology, which contains the most archaic elements) is not possible.

Since I have ascribed such a significant role to the activity of the editors of the Hasmonean times, the question arises as to how the aetiologies of both these sanctuaries managed to survive. The simplest answer, which is determined by my reconstruction of the deeds contained in the narrative about Ophrah, comes down to the claim that it was the result of the great importance attached to them by virtue of their antiquity in the Hebrews' consciousness. If Ophrah is indeed Bethlehem, it would be impossible to conceive that a town of such importance in Jewish history should not have an aetiology of its sanctuary. The evidence provided by references to it in Hosea shows just how persistent was the memory of Bethel.

There are other, more hypothetical, answers to the question. We can envisage that the inclusion of old traditions into the biblical canon, despite their negative message from the viewpoint of Jerusalem's priests (as in the case of Bethel), was the consequence of pressure brought to bear by centres representing other interests or another tradition. Unfortunately, we cannot say whether or not Bethel was still a vibrant religious centre in the second century BCE. Nevertheless, what we can accept is that groups derived from these centres, or simply associated with them, did exist. Editors who were active in Jerusalem could have remembered the centres from which they had come and this would have inclined them to retain in the biblical text the motifs associated with those centres. This would explain why the Bible calls for the acceptance of just the one temple while at the same time talking about many other sacred places where legal cults were practised. This same contradictory approach can also be seen in the construction of the priests' genealogy. The descendants of Aaron, Moses and Zadok were conscious of differences between them and these are reflected in the Bible. An awareness of different ancestries could also have accompanied differences in traditions and a sense of attachment to different parts of the country.

It seems that the aetiologies of holy places in Shechem belong to both categories of aetiology—the "traditional" and the "politically useful." Old mythical motifs and the continuity of the cult, or at least the consciousness that the place's sanctity was maintained, influenced the universal awareness of Shechem's exceptional position. Ancient beliefs, according to which the hills surrounding the town contained the place devoted to the cult of the Supreme God, influenced the association of the covenant motif with Shechem (and its preservation in the Bible). Because the myth of the dying divinity was so deeply embedded in the Hebrews' consciousness, details recounting the burial of Joseph and mourning rituals in Shechem were retained. Additionally, the biblical texts show certain editorial interpolations which can be explained only by reference to the political situation, particularly the conflict between the Samaritans and the Jews, which started in the second century BCE.[14]

To conclude that the Hasmonean times were the period of the Bible's final redaction requires the presentation of material which can be used to determine the dates of the origins of biblical texts. The traditional dating of the Pentateuch and the remaining books of the Old Testament, as discussed in the Introduction, is based more on the assumptions and will of scholars than on source materials. By means of some well-dated relics, we can determine the *terminus ante quem* for six of the books of the Bible.[15] The dating of the oldest biblical manuscripts found in Qumran (4QSam[b], 4QJer[a], 4QEx[b]) is the second half of the third century BCE. The majority of Hebrew and Greek fragments of biblical writings found at Qumran are dated between the years 150 BCE and 68 CE. The date of the oldest papyri containing fragments of the Greek translation of Deuteronomy is considered to be the second century BCE. The apocryphal book of *Jubilees*, a work evidently relying on the canonical texts of the books of Genesis and Exodus, judging by the fragments found in Qumran which have been dated on the basis of palaeographically to about the year 100 BCE, probably came into being at the end of the second century BCE.[16] That is the source material allowing us to make relatively precise datings for these works in their entirety. In addition to this, we can look at what certain omissions might indicate. The Jewish historian Demetrius, who lived in the third century BCE, makes no reference to the text contained in the canonical version of the Bible. Also, some fragments of the work of Eupolemos, a historian active in the middle of the second century BCE, evidently conflict with the Bible's account. Furthermore, there is no source material outside the sphere of the Jewish tradition to confirm the fact that the Jews possessed a sacred text. This last argument, in view of

14. For an exhaustive discussion on this subject, see Hjelm, *Jerusalem's Rise to Sovereignty*.

15. I omit here the amulets of the seventh century BCE with an inscription containing a text analogous with Num 6:24-26.

16. There is some disagreement about the dating of this text. Mendels, *The Land of Israel*, 57-88, dates the book of *Jubilees* in the twenties of the second century BCE. J.A. Goldstein, *Semites, Iranians, Greeks, and Romans: Studies in their Interactions*, Atlanta, 1990, 161-79, suggests the years 169–167 BCE. For a synthetic overview, see VanderKam, "Jubilees, Book of."

the small amount of source information concerning the Jews available from before the first century BCE, is admittedly weak, though we should bear in mind that the Bible, as a religious-literary phenomenon, has no equivalent in the Graeco-Roman world and so the fact that the existence of a Jewish holy book is not mentioned does appear to be significant.

The considerations discussed bring me to an important question. My assertion is that the aetiological myths of sanctuaries operated in the language of the local rituals. How was it, then, that the editors of the Bible knew these rituals even though a given sanctuary lay outside the boundaries of the state at the time? We can resolve this uncertainty in two, not mutually exclusive, ways. The first is to assume a continuity of the mythical tradition stretching from the times of the early monarchy (or maybe even to the Bronze Age) all the way to the Hellenistic times. This would mean that the myths were not so much written in the second century BCE as recorded or rewritten. The second is to remember that the ancient world, even if it did organise itself into states, was not a world of visas and border crossings. Although there is no direct record to confirm the undertaking of pilgrimages to Palestinian territories during the Persian and the Hellenistic periods, there is no way that we can exclude the possibility of such practices. The sanctuary at Arad, active in the time of the First Temple and located far from any human settlements, functioned as a place of pilgrimage. The finds at Kuntillet 'Ajrud, associated with the crafts of the northern monarchy, provide the strongest evidence of the existence of pilgrimages to holy places.[17] Whether by pilgrimages or by remaining in touch with the local populace, the editors of the Bible could get to know the ritual associated even with very distant sanctuaries.

The exploitation of aetiological myths associated with the sanctuary at Shechem, as well as the tradition linked with this centre, was characteristic of the process of including the religious sphere, an element of which was the biblical text, in political activity.

Shechem functioned as an important cult centre throughout almost the entire period of the First Temple, after which it was completely abandoned. Only towards the end of the fourth century BCE did settlement resume there. The conflict between the Jews and the Samaritans was not as strong as some commentators believed (if we accept the assertions of Josephus), though we cannot deny the existence of tension between the two groups.[18] It is true that the Jews destroyed the temple on Mt Gerizim,

17. Compare the mention of pilgrimages from Israel to Jerusalem (1 Kgs 12:27-28), and also the information about Elijah's journey in the desert (1 Kgs 19:2-7).
18. Cf. Crown, "Redating the Schism," 17-50.

but we should not look for religious motives for this attack. We cannot explain John Hyrcanus's campaign against Shechem as a drive to establish just one cult place for all Jews because the sanctuaries in Beersheba and Lachish arose during his reign. On the other hand, we do have Eupolemos's text, which indicates that Shechem was the place where Abraham and Melchizedek met; this would suggest an acceptance of the town's religious importance.[19]

A hostility to Shechem and the Samaritans living there could well have been the cause of the creation of the entity which became Gilgal on the Jordan. The same considerations led to the removal from the Old Testament of traces of the tradition linking Shechem with the tomb of the patriarchs.[20] On the other hand, the account of the covenant before God and of Joseph's tomb in Shechem was retained. This is evidence, in my view, that the scale of the Jewish–Samaritan conflict was smaller than is generally supposed, and that these two religious elements—Joseph's grave (his and no other patriarch's) and the promise made before God—were particularly, though not exclusively, linked to the cult in Shechem.

In the history of biblical Israel, only in the period of the First Temple and in the Hasmonean times did conditions exist favouring the creation and cultivation of stories about the beginnings of sanctuaries other than Jerusalem. Although the existence of biblical aetiologies in their final form before the Babylonian captivity does seem highly improbable, nevertheless we cannot negate the possibility that their beginnings could have stretched back to those times. The final recording in writing and inclusion of them in the biblical text was, in my view, the work of editors active between 160 and 100 BCE. The situation of Palestine at the time of the Hasmonean expansion—the resurgence of the ideas of monarchy colliding with the growth of significance of the priestly elites, as well as the absorption of new territories and the necessity to clarify relations with other peoples—all influenced scriptural scholars in their work on the biblical text.

In his brilliant work on Jewish literature of the second century BCE, Doron Mendels has shown how greatly the political and religious realities of the age influenced its writing.[21] Various apocryphal works, several

---

19. For a discussion on the text left by Eusebius (*Praep. Evan.* 9.17.2-9) and the claim by some that it is Eupolemos' original text, see Garbini, "Eupolemo storico giudeo," 613-34; and also my article, "(Pseudo-)Eupolemos, Shechem and the Methodology of the Use of Biblical and Jewish Hellenistic Writers" (forthcoming).

20. This tradition is preserved in Acts 7:16.

21. Mendels, *The Land of Israel*; see also *idem, The Rise and Fall of Jewish Nationalism*, and "Creative History in the Hellenistic Near East in the Third and Second Centuries BCE: The Jewish Case," *JSP* 2 (1988): 13-20.

canonical books (Sirach, Tobias, Esther, the Maccabees) and Jewish historiography written in Greek can be interpreted in the light of contemporary political events. Mendels' insight is accurate, though it does not explain how the book of Genesis, so close to the text of the apocryphal book of *Jubilees*, came to be written. The *Testament of the Twelve Patriarchs* emphasises the dominant position of the Levites, but how should we explain the same tendency in the book of Joshua? Mendels has stopped short of an important statement—namely, that it is not just the texts he discusses that have their roots in the Hasmonean era, and that time also left its mark on the biblical text, on three books especially: Genesis, Joshua and Judges. Mendels applies his argument to the book of *Jubilees*, but it also applies to large fragments of the book of Genesis. It is as valid for apocryphal as it is for canonical literature. Moving the date of the final redaction of the three books (Genesis, Joshua and Judges) to a later time allows us to avoid the inconsistencies contained in a study which omits these texts.

After discussing many stories that explain the causes of and circumstances surrounding the origins of holy places, we may be now attempt a summing up, and a reply to the question of how, and by recourse to what collection of mythic concepts, these aetiologies were constructed.

The table overleaf displays the relationship between holy places and the figures and the biblical traditions present in their aetiologies. The beginnings of the sanctuaries are linked with the deeds of the patriarchs, Joshua and the judges. Of the patriarchs, Isaac plays the smallest role, appearing only in the reprised version of the aetiology of Beer-sheba. Abraham is the founder of Beer-sheba and of Hebron and plays a secondary part, in relation to Jacob-Israel, in the history of Bethel and Shechem. The figure of Jacob is associated with the origins of Bethel, Gilead (Galeed), Penuel and Shechem. Of the stories contained in the book of Joshua, the only original story is the narrative about the covenant on Mt Ebal and Mt Gerizim in Shechem. Accompanying the description of this ritual is an important reference to the burial of Joseph's remains in Shechem. The story of the construction of a sanctuary in Gilgal (Josh 4:1-5, 12) appears to be a literary fiction and not the aetiology of a real cult place, and the same is true of the story about the building of an עד altar (Josh 22:10-33), which duplicates the story of Jacob in Gilead. The aetiologies of holy places in the book of Judges relate to Gideon in Ophrah (Ephrathah) and the Danites migrating north and founding the town of Dan on the ruins of Laish (Judg 18:1-31).

*A Table of Biblical Stories Containing
the Aetiologies of Holy Places*[22]

	Abraham	Isaac	Jacob	Joshua	Judges
Beer-sheba	Gen 21:22-33	*Gen 26:23-33			
Bethel	*Gen 12:8-9 *Gen 13:3-4		Gen 28:10-22 Gen 35:1-15		
Dan					Judg 18:1-31
Gilead			Gen 31:43-55	*Josh 22:10-33	
Gilgal				**Josh 4:1-5, 12	
Hebron	Gen 13:18 Gen 23:1-20				
Ophrah (Ephrathah)					Judg 6:11-32
Penuel			Gen 32:22-32		
Shechem	*Gen 12:4-9		Gen 33:18-20 Gen 35:1-4	***Josh 24:1-28, 32	

22. * indicates a secondary tradition; ** by the aetiology of Gilgal indicates the narrative's secondary nature in relation to the aetiology of Shechem; *** by the aetiology of Shechem indicates its secondary nature in relation to the tradition of the book of Deuteronomy.

I should close this analysis of myths about the establishment of holy places by making a few comments about the manner in which these works were constructed. The collection of mythic concepts appears, in this instance, to be quite compact.[23] Apart from stories related to Hebron, Ophrah and Shechem, all the aetiologies contain information about the name etymology or the circumstances in which the name was given to a holy place. The motif of a divine epiphany is missing in only two cases. The motif which could be described as the establishment of legal relations between the parties participating in the mythical event appears very frequently. This can take the form, for example, of the swearing of an oath (a promise of success) by a supernatural being.

Several elements recur in descriptions of the beginnings of these holy places: a tree, מצבה, a stone mound (גל), an altar and a grave all arranged in a specific, logical way. Trees accompany places of burial (Bethel, Hebron, Ophrah = Ephrathah = Bethlehem, Shechem); their presence can also indicate that the cult is chthonic in nature (Beer-sheba); מצבות accompany sacred trees only in Bethel and Shechem. The myth about Penuel is exceptional because of its standing as a place of initiation where there is no reference to a cult. Nor is reference made to an altar or an offering, a מצבה or a sacred tree marking out the holy ground. What we find in this story is confirmation of the thesis that Penuel played no part in sacrificial cult practices and was exclusively a place—be it real or symbolic—associated with initiation practices.

In descriptions of the origins of holy places, what appears most often is information about the beginnings there of a cult practice: the offering of a sacrifice, a ritual feast or some other ritual act, such as the raising of an altar or calling the name of the Lord, which may be linked to the presence of priests there. The consecration of such a place is commutable with the beginnings of a cult. What follows from this is that the performance of a cult marked out the holiness of a place, though of course it could be argued that the process worked in reverse: the fact that a given piece of ground was regarded as holy led to the introduction of a cult there.

References to altars (מצבות), trees and graves appeared in myths because most probably these objects actually did exist in the sanctuaries in question. What we have to consider, however, is what lay at the root of the concept of the epiphanies of supernatural beings in holy places. It seems unreasonable to wonder whether the revelation of a supernatural being was a real or a fabulous occurrence as far as the authors were

---

23. See the Appendix.

concerned. The very definition of myth suggests that the fact that the epiphany was recorded in writing showed a belief in its reality. My own view is that we can assume that what influenced descriptions of epiphanies were certain concepts associated with religious experiences. There are, in fact, two possibilities: the theophanies refer either to oracles, where the presence of the divinity or its messenger is something natural, or to the imagined world associated with the cult of a holy place. In the former case the epiphany would be the consequence of a mystical experience by the seer or prophet who had asked questions of the divinity. A reply given by the divinity presupposes a direct or indirect manifestation of its will. The manifestation of its will reveals, in turn, not only the existence and activity of the divinity, but also a working relationship between God and man. The existence of such a relationship is just one step away from the idea of a divinity revealing not only its will but also its own self.

According to Benedict Otzen, the descriptions of the visions of a temple found in apocryphal literature are an account of the priests' mystical experiences.[24] This view argues against the dominant assumption in the literature that all mystical experiences are of prophetic origin. Otzen holds that the fundamental characteristic of the visions described is their content, dominated by a concept of the temple and the presence in it of the glory of God. One can accept Otzen's explanations and see the priests' experience as the source of the literary tradition of many apocrypha. But these visions differ from the epiphanies described in the aetiological myths of holy places because what is emphasised is not the person of the divinity or its messenger, but the temple and the successive paradisal levels leading closer and closer to the divinity. "The Angel of God" from Penuel or Ophrah is a figure "proving" its supernatural nature whereas the visions of the temple assume *a priori* that the object being seen is but the source of the *sacrum*. The phenomenon which Otzen describes does not, it seems to me, apply to the myths under discussion in this work. The theophany in Bethel could be the only one regarded as an example of priestly experiences. Assuming that theophanies stemming from priestly experiences always adopt a similar form, we need to ask what inspired the theophanies described in our myths. We need to look for the sources of this inspiration outside the practice associated with the cult of the temple. The area where such concepts might well have their origin is the broadly interpreted world of divining.

24. B. Otzen, "Heavenly Visions in Early Judaism: Origin and Function," in Barrick and Spencer (eds.), *In the Shelter of Elyon*, 199-215.

If it is not the cult of the temple which inspires the descriptions of theophanies but rather mantic practices, then the material under discussion leads to one important conclusion. As I have mentioned, there is a strong link between the appearance of trees in cult places and the chthonic aspect of those places (a grave or the cult of a chthonic divinity). In the stories we also see a correlation between a theophany and the presence of trees and graves (Bethel, Hebron, Ophrah = Ephrathah = Bethlehem, Shechem). If the suggestion linking theophanies with mantic practices is correct, then it follows that there is an interdependency of a divinity revealing its own self and a holy place designated by the presence of a grave or a sacred tree. Furthermore, this leads to an additional conclusion about the association of divination with the cult of the dead and of gods of the underworld.[25] Holy places marked out by the existence of a contact with the underworld (grave) are areas where the divinity reveals itself. It can then be assumed that a theophany requires the establishment of contact with the underworld. This can be achieved either by getting to know the will of a chthonic god directly or by asking the dead as intermediaries between the world of people and the god of the underworld. Bearing in mind the presence of a cult of a chthonic god (Beer-sheba), it is my opinion that divination is based on contact with the dead as beings who know the truth and are able to share with people information about the will of the divine being.

In the light of the linking in the Bible of theophanies with the presence of trees and graves, we need to ask about the function of trees in divination. The most obvious association seems to be the linking of the oak of Dodona with the oracle of Zeus. This, however, is not a full analogy because the Hebrews' mantic practices relied on asking questions of the dead and not in reading and interpreting signs emanating from the God of heaven. In its symbolic meaning, a tree could have denoted the place of contact with the underworld, with the world of the dead. All the biblical references to trees located in holy places should be analyzed from this point of view. Assuredly, the sacred groves also symbolised the world of the dead.[26] The wide extent of sacred trees and groves, as well as אשׁרות—in both the real Palestinian landscape and in the mythic-historical descriptions of the deeds of the Hebrews—indicates the popularity of the cult of chthonic gods. In this context, the attempts of

25. For more on the subject of necromancy among the ancient Hebrews, see van der Toorn, *Family Religion*, 231-35; see also Garbini, *I Filistei*, 216-21.

26. As mentioned earlier, according to A. Lemaire and E. Lipiński the term אשׁרה denotes sacred groves. G. Garbini, *Note di lessicografia ebraica*, Brescia, 1998, 102-104, associates the term עב with sacred groves.

the Bible's editors to diminish the role of sacred trees in biblical tradition, to erase traces of the chthonic nature of places of ritual, and to eliminate references to the existence of a cult of the dead of divination and of the chthonic aspect become understandable.

On the basis of the material incorporating the aetiological myths of holy places we can try to answer one other important question concerning the existence and extent of the idea of monolatry. The biblical idea regarding the exclusivity of Jerusalem as a legal cult place is a conclusion drawn on the basis of references in the Pentateuch and in the texts of the prophets, always bearing in mind that the latter need to be treated as manifestations of Yahwistic propaganda which, by its nature, was concentrated in Jerusalem. In the writings of the prophet Amos there is still no trace of any thought of making of Jerusalem a place of exceptional religious significance (see Amos 7:10-17). The concentration on Jerusalem of the prophets of the Persian era is the result of the territorial diminution of the Yehud province, and the suggestion that its cult is exclusive (which older commentators sought) is not confirmed by the material of the Pentateuch.[27]

The existence of a temple on Elephantine in the fifth–fourth century BCE, of temples on Mt Gerizim (fourth to second centuries BCE) and in Leontopolis (second century BCE to first century CE),[28] as well as cult places in 'Araq el-Emir, Beer-sheba, Dan, Hebron and Lachish, all prove that a "legal" Yahwistic cult was practised in centres other than Jerusalem.[29] At the same time scholars interpret this as being in conflict with the ideology of the priests of Jerusalem. We have to bear in mind that if our conviction about the editorial interventions during the Hasmonean period is correct, then it was none other than the priestly elites of Jerusalem who decided the final shape of the biblical account—accepting the sacred and exceptional quality of Beer-sheba, Bethel, Dan, Hebron and Shechem. In my view, we should not differentiate between the sacredness

---

27. B. Halpern, "The Centralization Formula in Deuteronomy," *VT* 31 (1981): 20-38; J.G. McConville, "Faces of Exile in Old Testament Historiography," in J. Barton and D.J. Reimer (eds.), *After the Exile: Essays in Honour of Rex Mason*, Macon, GA, 1996, 27-44 (39-41); I. Hjelm, "Cult Centralization as a Device of Cult Control?," *SJOT* 13 (1999): 298-309; J. Milgrom, "Does H Advocate the Centralization of Worship?," *JSOT* 88 (2000): 59-76.

28. See Josephus, *War* 7.420-32; *Ant* 13.62-73.

29. See J. Frey, "Temple and Rival Temple—The Cases of Elephantine, Mt. Gerizim, and Leontopolis," in B. Ego *et al.* (eds.), *"Gemeinde ohne Tempel / Community without Temple." Zur Substituierung und Transformation des Jerusalemer Tempels und seines Kults im Alten Testament, antiken Judentum und frühen Christentum*, Tübingen, 1999, 171-203; Campbell, Jr, "Jewish Shrines."

of the patriarchal sanctuaries and the sacredness of the centre in Jerusalem in Hasmonean times. The sacredness of the former and of the Jewish state's capital are both equally valid legally. How, then, can the exclusivity of the cult of Jerusalem be reconciled with the sanctioning of the sacredness of other centres?

If these stories about the origins of cult places other than Jerusalem served, among other things, propaganda purposes, it would mean that the traditions of competing centres were exploited as tools in political machinations. If the underlining of the legality of cult places and their affiliation to a national tradition (e.g. by association with the deeds of the patriarchs) served political ends, then it could be that there were none of the religious tensions which one might anticipate if their aetiologies had been used to weaken the position of Jerusalem. The recounting or creating of stories about these centres could well have been a purely political argument separate from any internal religious tensions.

I am convinced that the thesis about Jerusalem's exclusivity as a cult place cannot be backed up, just as it cannot be denied that the motif emphasising its exceptional nature is present in Jewish thought. This, however, is a result of the extension of the Messianic idea of the house of David. The idea that Jerusalem is unique developed only after the destruction of the Temple (70 CE), when a real national tragedy coincided with a newly defined religion. The end of the cult of Jerusalem denoted the beginning of Judaism. The end of Yahwism came with the entrance of Titus's soldiers into the Holy of Holies. This event opened the door to Judaism with its cult of the synagogue, its rabbis and the Holy Torah.

Appendix

The main elements of the myths

The holy places	Altar	Sacrifice / calling of God's name	Grave	Monument / stone mound	Tree	Oath	Theophany	Etymology of the place name
Beer-Sheba	+	Chthonic			Tamarisk	+	+	+
Bethel	+	+ Libation	+ Deborah		Oak	+	+	+
Dan	Monument	Priest		Monument				+
Gilead	+	+ Sacrifice and Meal	Stone Mound	+		+		+
Gilgal	+	Passover and Circumcision		+		+	Cratophany	+
Hebron	+	Meal	+		Oak	God's promise	+	
Ophrah	+	+ Sacrifice	+		Oak	God's promise	+	
Peniel						Blessing	+	+
Sychem	+	Burying of the Gods	+	+	Oak	+	+	

Bibliography

Abegg, M., P. Flint and E. Ulrich, *The Dead Sea Scrolls Bible*, New York, 1999.

Abel, F.-M., *Géographie de la Palestine*. Vol. 1. *Géographie physique et historique*, Paris, 1933.

— *Géographie de la Palestine*. Vol. 2. *Géographie politique. Les villes*, Paris, 1938.

Ackerman, Susan, *Under Every Green Tree. Popular Religion in Sixth-Century Judah*, HSM 46, Atlanta, 1992.

Aharoni, Y., "Beersheba, Tel," in *EAEHL*, 1:167.

— "The Citadel of Ramat Rahel," *Archaeology* 18 (1965): 15-25.

— "Excavation at Ramat Rahel," *BA* 24, no. 4 (1961): 98-118.

— "Ramat Rahel," in *NEAEHL*, 3:1261-67.

Aharoni, Y. et al., *Excavations at Ramat Rahel: Seasons 1959 and 1960*, Rome, 1962.

— *Excavations at Ramat Rahel: Seasons 1961 and 1962*, Rome, 1964.

Aharoni, Y. (ed.), *Beer-sheba I: Excavations at Tel Beer-sheba 1969–1971 Seasons*, Tel Aviv, 1973.

Ahlström, G.W., "Was Gad the God of Tell Ed-Duweir?," *PEQ* 115 (1983): 47-48.

Albertz, R., *A History of Israelite Religion in the Old Testament Period*, vols. 1–2, Louisville, 1994.

Alt, A., *Die Ursprünge des israelitischen Rechts*, Leipzig, 1934.

Amit, Yairah, "Bochim, Bethel, and the Hidden Polemic (Judg 2,1-5)," in Gershom Galil and Moshe Weinfeld (eds.), *Studies in Historical Geography and Biblical Historiography: Presented to Zechariah Kallai*, VTSup 81, Leiden, 2000, 121-31.

— "Hidden Polemic in the Conquest of Dan: Judges 17–18," *VT* 40 (1990): 4-20.

Hidden Polemics in Biblical Narrative, Biblical Interpretation Series 25, Leiden, 2000.

Applebaum, S., *ABD*, *s.v.* "Ramat el-Khalil."

Arbeitman, Y.L., "Detecting the God who Remained in Dan," *Henoch* 16 (1994): 9-14.

— "The Hittite is Thy Mother: An Anatolian Approach to Genesis 23," in Y. Arbeitman and A. Bomhard (eds.), *Bono Homini Donum: Essays in Historical Linguistics in Memory of J. Alexander Kerns*, Amsterdam, 1981, 889-1026.

— "Minōs, the Ὀαριστής of Great Zeus, ά, ά, and ὁ-Copulative, the Knossan Royal Titulary and the Hellenization of Crete," in Arbeitman (ed.), *A Linguistic Happening*, 411-62.

Arbeitman, Y.L. (ed.), *A Linguistic Happening in Memory of Ben Schwartz*, Louvain-la-Neuve, 1988.

Arnold, P.M., *ABD*, *s.v.* "Mizpah (place)."

Aspesi, F., "Precedenti Divini di 'adama," *Studi Epigrafici e Linguistici (sul Vicino Oriente antico)* 13 (1996): 33-40.

Astour, M.C., *ABD*, *s.v.* "Aner (person)."

Athas, G., *The Tel Dan Inscription: A Reappraisal and a New Interpretation*, JSOTSup, 360, London, 2003.

Auld, A.G., "Gideon: Hacking at the Heart of the Old Testament," *VT* 39 (1989): 257-67.

Bächli, Otto, "Zur Lage des alten Gilgal," *ZDPV* 83 (1967): 64-71.

Bailey, R.C., *ABD, s.v.* "Jerubbešet."

Barag, D., "New Evidence on the Foreign Policy of John Hyrcanus I," *Israel Numismatic Journal* 12 (1992–93): 1-12.

Barr, J., "Seeing the Wood for the Trees? An Enigmatic Ancient Translation," *JSS* 13 (1968): 11-20.

Barrick, W.B., "Burning Bones at Bethel: A Closer Look at 2 Kings 23, 16a," *SJOT* 14 (2000): 3-16.

Barrick, W.B., and J.R. Spencer (eds.), *In the Shelter of Elyon: Essays on Ancient Palestinian Life and Literature in Honor of G.W. Ahlström*, JSOTSup 31, Sheffield, 1984.

Bartlett, John R., *Edom and the Edomites*, JSOTSup 77, Sheffield, 1989.

— "Edom in the Nonprophetical Corpus," in Diana Vikander Edelman (ed.), *You Shall Not Abhor an Edomite for He is Your Brother: Edom and Seir in History and Tradition*, Archaeology and Biblical Studies, 3, Atlanta, 1995, 13-21.

Baruch, Y., "Hebron, ed-Deir," *Excavations and Surveys in Israel* 14 (1994): 121-22.

Bauer, U.F.W., "A Metaphorical Etiology in Judges 18:12," *Journal of Hebrew Scripture* 3 (2001): online: http://www.arts.ualberts.ca/jhs/.

Beentjes, Pancratius C. (ed.), *The Book of Ben Sira in Hebrew: A Text Edition of all Extant Hebrew Manuscripts and a Synopsis of all Parallel Hebrew Ben Sira Texts*, VTSup 68, Leiden, 1997.

Beit-Arieh, I., "The Edomite Shrine at Horvat At Qitmit in the Judean Negev: Preliminary Excavation Report," *Tel Aviv* 18 (1991): 93-116.

Bennett, Bouce M., Jr, "The Search for Israelite Gilgal," *PEQ* 104 (1972): 111-22.

Bič, M., "Bet'el—Le sanctuaire du roi (Géographie et théologie de l'Ancient Testament)," *ArOr* 17 (1949): 46-63.

Bickerman, E.J., "The Altars of Gentiles: A Note on the Jewish 'Ius Sacrum,' " in *Studies in Jewish and Christian History*, vol. 2, Leiden, 1980, 324-46.

Binger, Tilde, *Asherah: Goddesses in Ugarit, Israel and the Old Testament*, JSOTSup 232, Sheffield, 1997.

Biran, A., *ABD, s.v.* "Dan (place)."

— "To the God who is in Dan," in Biran (ed.), *Temples and High Places*, 142-48.

Biran, A. (ed.), *Dan I: A Chronicle of the Excavations, the Pottery Neolithic, the Early Bronze Age and the Middle Bronze Age Tombs*, Jerusalem, 1996.

— *Dan II: A Chronicle of the Excavations and the Late Bronze Age "Mycenaean" Tomb*, Jerusalem, 2002.

— *Temples and High Places in Biblical Times: Proceedings of the Colloquium in Honor of the Centennial of Hebrew Union College–Jewish Institute of Religion. Jerusalem, 14–16 March 1977*, Jerusalem, 1981.

Biran, A., and J. Naveh, "An Aramaic Stele Fragment from Tel Dan," *IEJ* 43 (1993): 81-98.

Black, M., *The Book of Enoch or I Enoch: A New English Edition*, Studia in Veteris Testamenti Pseudepigrapha 8, Leiden, 1985.

Blenkinsopp, J., "Bethel in Neo Babylonian Period," in O. Lipschits and J. Blenkinsopp (eds.), *Judah and the Judeans in the neo-Babylonian Period*, Winona Lake, 2003, 93-107.

— "The Judaean Priesthood during the Neo-Babylonian and Achaemenid Periods: A Hypothetical Reconstruction," *CBQ* 60 (1998): 35-43.

Bloch-Smith, Elizabeth, *Judahite Burial Practices and Beliefs about the Dead*, JSOTSup 123, Sheffield, 1992.

Bohak, G., "Classica et Rabbinica I: The Bull of Phalaris and the Tophet," *JSJ* 31–32 (2000): 203-16.

Boling, R.G., *Joshua: A New Translation with Notes and Introduction*, Garden City, NY, 1982.

— *Judges: Introduction, Translation, and Commentary*, AB 6A, Garden City, NY, 1975.

Bombelli, Luciano, *I Frammenti degli storici giudaico-ellenistici*, Genoa, 1986.

Briend, J., "Bethléem-Ephrata," *Le Monde de la Bible* 30 (1983): 29.

— "Genèse 31,43-54: Traditions et rédaction," in M. Carrez, J. Doré and P. Grelot (eds.), *De la Tôrah au Messie. Études d'exégèse et d'herméneutique biblique offertes à Henri Cazelles pour ses 25 années d'enseignement à l'Institut Catholoque de Paris (October 1979)*, Paris, 1981, 107-12.

Brown, J.P., "The Mediterranean Vocabulary of the Vine," *VT* 19 (1969): 146-70.

Bruneau, P., "'Les Israélites de Délos' et la juiverie délienne," *Bulletin de Correspondance Hellénique* 106 (1982): 465-504.

Campbell, E.F., "Jewish Shrines of the Hellenistic and Persian Periods," in F.M. Cross (ed.), *Symposia Celebrating the Seventy-fifth Anniversary of the founding of the American Schools of Oriental Research*, Cambridge MA, 1975, 159-67.

— *Shechem II: Portrait of a Hill Country Vale. The Shechem Regional Survey*, Atlanta, 1991.

— "Shechem, Tell Balatah," in *NEAEHL*, 4:1354.

Campbell, E.F., and G.R.H. Wright, *Shechem III: The Stratigraphy and Architecture of Shechem/Tell Balâtah*. Vol. 1, *Text*. Vol. 2, *Illustrations*, Boston, 2002.

Carr, David M., "Genesis 28,10-22 and Transmission-Historical Method: A Reply to John Van Seters," *ZAW* 111 (1999): 399-403.

— *Reading the Fractures of Genesis: Historical and Literary Approaches*, Louisville, 1996.

Carstens, P., "The Golden Vessels and the Song of God: Drink-offering and Libation in Temple and on Altar," *SJOT* 17 (2003): 110-40.

Carter, Charles E., *The Emergence of Yehud in the Persian Period: A Social and Demographic Study*, JSOTSup 294, Sheffield, 1999.

Cassuto, U., *A Commentary on the Book of Genesis*, vol. 2, Jerusalem, 1964.

Cathcart, K.J., "The Trees, the Beast and the Birds: Fables, Parables and Allegories in the Old Testament," in J. Day, R.P. Gordon and H.G.M. Williamson (eds.), *Wisdom in Ancient Israel: Essays in Honour of J.A. Emerton*, Cambridge, 1995, 212-21.

Cazelles, H., *ABD*, s.v. "Bethlehem."

Childs, B.S., "The Etiological Tale Re-examined," *VT* 24 (1974): 387-97.

— "A Study of the Formula 'Until this Day,'" *JBL* 82 (1963): 279-92.

Clarke, E.G. (ed.), *Targum Pseudo-Jonathan of the Pentateuch: Text and Concordance*, New Jersey, 1984.

Coats, G.W., "Parable, Fable, and Anecdote: Storytelling in the Succession Narrative," *Interpretation* 35 (1981): 368-82.

Cook, Stanley A., *The Religion of Ancient Palestine in the Light of Archaeology*, London, 1930.

Cooke, A.B., *Zeus: A Study in Ancient Religion*, vol. 3, Cambridge, 1940.

Coughenour, R.A., "A Search for Mahanaim," *BASOR* 273 (1989): 57-66.

Cowlay, A., *Aramaic Papyri of the Fifth Century B.C.*, Oxford, 1923.

Craigie, P.C., *Psalms 1–50*, WBC 19, Waco, TX, 1983.

Cross, Frank Moore, *Canaanite Myth and Hebrew Epic: Essays in the History of the Religion of Israel*, Cambridge, MA, 1997.

Crouch, J.E., "Demetrius the Chronographer and the Beginnings of Hellenistic Jewish Historiography," *Kwansei Gakuin University Annual Studies* 30 (1981): 1-14.

Crown, A.D., "Redating the Schism between the Judaeans and the Samaritans," *JQR* 82.1-2 (1991): 17-59.

Cryer, F., *Divination in Ancient Israel and its Near Eastern Environment: A Socio-Historical Investigation*, JSOTSup 142, Sheffield, 1994.

Currid, J.D., "A Note on the Function of Building 5900 at Shechem—Again," *ZDPV* 105 (1989): 42-46.

Curtis, J.B., "An Investigation of the Mount of Olives in the Judeo-Christian Tradition," *HUCA* 28 (1957): 157-80.

Dahood, M., "Ugaritic and the Old Testament," *Ephemerides Theologicae Lovenienses* 44 (1968): 35-54.

— "Hebrew–Ugaritic Lexicography XII," *Biblica* 55 (1974): 387.

Dalglish, E.R., *ABD*, *s.v.* "Bethel (deity)," 1:706-10.

Davies, Philip R., *In Search of "Ancient Israel,"* JSOTSup 148, Sheffield, 1992.

— "Josiah and the Lawbook," paper presented at the European Seminar on Historical Methodology, Berlin, July, 2002.

— "The Place of Deuteronomy in the Development of Judean Society and Religion," in *Recenti tendenze nella ricostruzione della storia antica d'Israele. Roma, Convegno internazionale, 6–7 Marzo 2003*, Rome, 2005, 139-55.

Day, John, "Asherah in the Hebrew Bible and Northwest Semitic Literature," *JBL* 105 (1986): 385-408.

De Moor, Johannes, *The Rise of Yahwism: The Roots of Israelite Monotheism*, 2nd edn, Leuven, 1997.

Dempster, S.G., *ABD*, *s.v.* "Elhanan."

Demsky, A., "House of Achzib: A Critical Note on Micah 1:14b," *IEJ* 16 (1966): 211-15.

Denis, Albert-Marie (ed.), *Fragmenta Pseudepigraphorum Quae Superunt Graeca*, Pseudepigrapha Veteris Testamenti Graece, 3, Leiden, 1970.

De Vaux, Roland, *Ancient Israel*, vols. 1–2, New York, 1965.

— *Les sacrifices de l'Ancien Testament*, Paris, 1964.

Derfler, Steven, *The Hellenistic Temple at Tel Beersheva*, Lewiston, 1993.

— "A Terracotta Figurine from the Hellenistic Temple at Tel Beer-sheba," *IEJ* 31 (1981): 97-99.

Dever, W.G., "Archaeology and the Ancient Israelite Cult: How the Kh. El-Qom and Kuntillet 'Arjud 'Asherah' Texts have Changed the Picture," *Eretz Israel* 26 (1999): 9-15.

— "'Asherah, Consort of Yahweh? New Evidence from Kuntillet Ajrud," *BASOR* 255 (1984): 21-35.

— *ABD*, *s.v.* "Beitin, Tell (place)," 1:651-52.

— "Iron Age Epigraphic Material from the Area of Khirbet el-Kom," *HUCA* 40–41 (1969–70): 139-204.

Dicou, Bert, *Edom, Israel's Brother and Antagonist: The Role of Edom in Biblical Prophecy and Story*, JSOTSup 169, Sheffield, 1994.

Doran, R., "Jewish Hellenistic Historians before Josephus," *ANRW* 20.1: 246-97.

Dothan, M., "The Excavations at Nahariyah," *IEJ* 6 (1974): 14–25.

Dothan, Trude, *An Introduction to the Literature of the Old Testament*, Oxford, 1897.

— *ABD*, *s.v.* "Philistines (Archaeology)."

— *The Philistines and their Material Culture*, New Haven, 1982.

Dozeman, Thomas B., "The Yam-Sup in the Exodus and the Crossing of the Jordan River," *CBQ* 58 (1996): 407-16.

Driver, G.R., "Brief Notes (Part 3): Two Gods (HW and MWT) in Proper Names," *PEQ* 77 (1945): 5-14.

Dyk, P.J. van, "The Function of So-Called Etiological Elements in Narratives," *ZAW* 102 (1990): 19-33.

Edelman, Diana Vikander, *ABD*, *s.v.* "Mahanaim (place)."

Edelman, Diana Vikander (ed.), *The Fabric of History: Text, Artifact and Israel Past*, JSOTSup 127, Sheffield, 1991.

Eissfeldt, O., "Gilgal or Shechem?," in J.I. Durham and J.R. Porter (eds.), *Proclamation and Presence: Old Testament Essays in Honour of Gwynne Henton Davies*, London, 1970, 90-101.

— *Molk als opferbegriff im punischen und hebräischen, und das ende des gottes Moloch*, Halle, 1935.

Eliade, Mircea, *Patterns in Comparative Religion*, New York, 1974.

Emerton, J.A., "Gideon and Jerubbaal," *JTS* NS 27 (1976): 289-312.

— "New Light on Israelite Religion: The Implications of the Inscriptions from Kuntillet 'Arjud'," *ZAW* 94 (1982): 2-20.

— "Yahweh and his Asherah": The Goddess or her Symbol?," *VT* 49 (1999): 315-37.

Erling, B., "First-Born and Firstlings in the Covenant Code," in *Society of Biblical Literature 1986 Seminar Papers*, SBLSP 25, Atlanta, 1986, 470-78.

Fensham, F.C., "The First Ugaritic Text in *Ugaritica* V and the Old Testament," *VT* 22 (1972): 296-303.

Ferch, A.J., *ABD*, *s.v.* "Beer-elim," 1:640.

Ferris, P.W., Jr, *ABD*, *s.v.* "Hebron (place)."

Finkelstein, I., *The Archaeology of the Israelite Settlement*, Jerusalem, 1988.

Finkelstein, I., and N. Na'aman (eds.), *From Nomadism to Monarchy: Archaeological and Historical Aspects of Early Israel*, Jerusalem, 1994.

Fitzmyer, J.A., *The Genesis Apocryphon of Qumran Cave I: A Commentary*, Rome, 1966.

Fleischer, G., "Jakob träumt. Eine Auseinandersetzung mit Erhard Blums methodischem Ansatz am Beispiel von Gen 28,10-22," *BN* 76 (1995): 82-102.

Fowler, M.D., "A Closer Look at the 'Temple of El-Berith' at Shechem," *PEQ* 115 (1983): 49-53.

Frazer, James George, *Folk-Lore in the Old Testament*, 3 vols., London, 1919.

Fretz, M.J., and R.I. Panitz, *ABD*, *s.v.* "Caleb (person)."

Frey, Jena Jörg, "Temple and Rival Temple—The Cases of Elephantine, Mt. Gerizim, and Leontopolis," in B. Ego, A. Lange and P. Pilhofer (eds.), *"Gemeinde ohne Tempel / Community without Temple." Zur Substituierung und Transformation des Jerusalemer Tempels und seines Kults im Alten Testament, antiken Judentum und frühen Christentum*, Tübingen, 1999, 171-203.

Fritz, Volkmar, and Philip R. Davies (eds.), *The Origins of the Ancient Israelite States*, JSOTSup 228, Sheffield, 1996.

Galil, Gershom, *The Chronology of the Kings of Israel and Judah*, SHANE 9, Leiden. 1996.

Garbini, Giovanni, "Eupolemo storico giudeo," *Atti della Accademia Nazionale dei Lincei, Rendiconti 9/9, fasc. 4* (1998): 613-34.

— *History and Ideology in Ancient Israel*, New York, 1988.

— *I Filistei. Gli Antagonisti di Israele*, Milano, 1997.

— *Il ritorno dall'esilio babilonese*, Brescia, 2001.

— "L'iscrizione aramaica di Tel Dan," *Rendiconti della Accademia Nazionale dei Lincei* series 9, vol. 5, 1994: b. 3, 461-71.

— *La religione dei Fenici in Occidente*, Dipartimento di studi orientali. Studi semitici, NS, 12, Rome, 1994.

— *Myth and History in the Bible*, London, 2003.

— *Note di lessicografia ebraica*, Brescia, 1998.

— *Storia e ideologia nell'Israele Antico*, Brescia, 1986.

— "Sul nome antico di Ramat Rahel," *Rivista degli Studi Orientali* 16 (1961): 199-205.

García Martínez, F., and E.J.C. Tigchelaar (eds.), *The Dead Sea Scrolls Study Edition*, Leiden, 2000.

Garcia-Treto, F.O., "Genesis 31:44 and 'Gilead,'" *ZAW* 79 (1967): 15.

Goldstein, Jonathan A., *Semites, Iranians, Greeks, and Romans: Studies in their Inter-actions*, Brown Judaic Studies 217, Atlanta, 1990.

Golka, F.W., "The Aetiologies in the Old Testament, pt. 1," *VT* 26 (1976): 410-28.

— "The Aetiologies in the Old Testament, pt. 2," *VT* 27 (1977): 36-47.

Gordon, R.L., and L.E. Villiers, "Telul edh Dhahab and its Environs Surveys of 1980 and 1982: A Preliminary Report," *Annual of the Department of Antiquities of Jordan* 27 (1983): 275-89.

Gordon, R.P., *1 & 2 Samuel: A Commentary*, Exeter, 1986.

Görg, M., *ABD, s.v.* "Beth-Millo (place)."

Gottwald, N., *The Tribes of Yahweh*, New York, 1979.

Goulder, Michael D., *The Psalms of Asaph and the Pentateuch. Studies in the Psalter, III*, JSOTSup 233, Sheffield, 1996.

Grabbe, Lester L. (ed.), *Can a "History of Israel" Be Written?*, JSOTSup 245, Sheffield, 1997.

Gray, John, *The Legacy of Canaan: The Ras Shamra Texts and their Relevance to the Old Testament*, VTSup 5, Leiden, 1957.

Grossfeld, B., *The Targum Onqelos to Genesis*, The Aramaic Bible 6, Edinburgh, 1988.

Grottanelli, C., "Giuseppe nel pozzo, I. Un antico tema mitico in Gen. 37:12-24 e in RV I 105," *Oriens Antiquus* 17 (1978): 107-22.

— "Giuseppe nel pozzo, II. Il motivo e il suo contesto nel folklore," *Oriens Antiquus* 22 (1983): 267-90.

— "The Ogygian Oak at Mamre and the Holy Town of Hebron," *Vicino Oriente* 2 (1979): 39-63.

— "Santuari e divinitŕ delle collonie d'occidente," in R. Kuntzmann (ed.), *La religione fenicia. Matrici orientali e sviluppi occidentali. Atti del Colloquio in Roma (6 marzo 1979)*, Rome, 1981, 109-37.

— "Spunti comparativi per la storia biblica di Giuseppe," *Oriens Antiquus* 15 (1976): 115-40.

Gunkel, Hermann, *Genesis*, Göttingen, 1901.

Gunn, D.M., "Narrative Patterns and Oral Tradition in Judges and Samuel," *VT* 24 (1974): 296-317.

Haag, H., "Gideon—Jerubbaal—Abimelek," *ZAW* 79 (1967): 305-14.

Haak, R.D., *ABD*, *s.v.* "Altars."

Hadley, Judith M., *The Cult of Asherah in Ancient Israel and Judah: Evidence for a Hebrew Goddess*, Cambridge, 2000.

— "The Khirbet el-Qom Inscription," *VT* 37 (1987): 50-62.

— "Some Drawings and Inscriptions on Two Pithoi from Kuntillet Ajrud," *VT* 37 (1987): 180-213.

Hagan, H., "Deception as Motif and Theme in 2 Sm 9–20; 1 Kgs 1–2," *Biblica* 60 (1979): 301-26.

Hallo, W.W. (ed.), *The Context of Scripture*, Leiden, 1997.

Halpern, B., "The Centralization Formula in Deuteronomy," *VT* 31 (1981): 20-38.

Hamilton, J.M., *ABD*, *s.v.* "Kiriat-Jearim (place)."

— *ABD*, *s.v.* "Ophra."

Handy, L.K., *ABD*, *s.v.* "Shalom."

Haran, Menahem, "Temples and Cultic Open Areas as Reflected in the Bible," in Biran (ed.), *Temples and High Places*, 31-37.

Haran, Menahem (ed.), *Temples and Temple-Service in Ancient Israel: An Inquiry into the Character of Cult Phenomena and the Historical Setting of the Priestly School*, Oxford, 1978.

Hayward, C.T.R., "Jacob's Second Visit to Bethel in Targum Pseudo-Jonathan," in Davies (ed.), *A Tribute to Geza Vermes: Essays on Jewish and Christian Literature and History*, JSOTSup 100, Sheffield, 1990, 175-92.

Hayward, R., "Abraham as Proselytizer at Beer-sheba in the Targums of the Pentateuch," *JJS* 49 (1998): 24-37.

Healey, J.F., *DDD*, *s.v.* "Tiraš," 1642-45.

Held, M., "Pits and Pitfalls in Akkadian and Biblical Hebrew," *JANESCU* 5 (1973): 173-90.

Hepper, F.N., and S. Gibson, "Abraham's Oak of Mamre: The Story of a Venerable Tree," *PEQ* 126 (1994): 94-105.

Herion, G.A., *ABD*, *s.v.* "Chesil (place)."

Hertzberg, H.W., *I & II Samuel: A Commentary*, Philadelphia, 1964.

Herzog, Zeev, "Israelite Sanctuaries at Arad and Beer-Szeba," in Biran (ed.), *Temples and High Places*, 120-22.

— "Tel Beersheba," in *NEAEHL*, 1:173.

Herzog, Zeev (ed.), *Beer-Sheba II: The Early Iron Age Settlements*, Tel Aviv, 1984.

— "Tel Beersheba," in *NEAEHL*, 1:167-73.

Hesrin, R., "A Note on the 'Lion Bowls' and Asherah," *The Israel Museum Journal* 7 (1988): 115-18.

Higgins, R.A., *Catalogue of Terracottas in the Department of Greek and Roman Antiquities, The British Museum*, vol. 1, London, 1954.

Hillers, D.R., *ABD*, *s.v.* "Micah, Book of."

Hjelm, Ingrid, "Cult Centralization as a Device of Cult Control?," *SJOT* 13 (1999): 298-309.

— *Jerusalem's Rise to Sovereignty in History and Tradition*, JSOTSup 404, London, 2004.

Hoffman, Y., "Aetiology, Redaction and Historicity in Jeremiah XXXVI," *VT* 46 (1996): 179-89.

— "A North Israelite Typological Myth and a Judaean Historical Tradition: The Exodus in Hosea and Amos," *VT* 39 (1989): 169-82.

Hollander, H.W., and M de Jong, *The Testaments of the Twelve Patriarchs: A Commentary*, SVTP 8, Leiden, 1985.

Hooke, Samuel H., *The Labyrinth*, London, 1935.

— *Myth and Ritual*, London, 1933.

— *Myth, Ritual, and Kingship. Essays on the Theory and Practice of Kingship in the Ancient Near East and in Israel*, Oxford, 1958.

Houtman, C., "What did Jacob see in his Dream at Bethel? Some Remarks on Genesis 28,10-22," *VT* 27 (1977): 337-51.

Howard, D.M., Jr, *ABD*, *s.v.* "David (person)."

Huehnergard, J., "Biblical Notes on Some New Akkadian Texts from Emar (Syria)," *CBQ* 47 (1985): 428-34.

Huffmon, H.B., *DDD*, *s.v.* "Shalem," 1428-31.

Hunt, M., *ABD*, *s.v.* "Aner (place)."

— *ABD*, *s.v.* "Moreh (place)."

Hurwitz, V.A., "Who Lost an Earring? Genesis 35:4 Reconsidered," *CBQ* 62 (2000): 28-32.

Husser, J.-M., "Les métamorphoses d'un songe. Critique littéraire de Genèse 28,10-22," *RB* 98 (1991): 321-42.

Ibañez Arana, A. "Las etiologías etimológicas del Pentateuco," *Scriptorium Victoriense* 10 (1963): 241-75.

— "La narración etiológica como género literario bíblico," *Scriptorium Victoriense* 10 (1963): 161-76.

Irwin, B.P., *ABD*, *s.v.* "Mahaneh-Dan (place)."

Jacobson, D.M., "The Plan of the Ancient Haram el-Khalil in Hebron," *PEQ* 113 (1981): 73-80.

Jamme, A., "The Bethel Inscribed Stamp Again: A Vindication of Mrs. Theodore Bent," *BASOR* 280 (1990): 89-91.

Jamme, A., and G.W. Van Beek, "Herion," *BASOR* 163 (1961): 15-18.

Jones, Gwilym H., *The Nathan Narratives*, JSOTSup 80, Sheffield, 1990.

Josephus, Flavius, *Jewish Antiquities*, trans. H.St.J. Thackeray, London, 1958–65.

— *The Jewish War*, trans. H.S.J. Thackeray, LCL, Harvard, MA, 1997.

Kalimi, I., "Zion or Gerizim? The Association of Abraham and the Aqeda with Zion / Gerizim in Jewish and Samaritan Sources," in M. Lubetski, C. Gottlieb and S. Keller (eds.), *Boundaries of the Ancient Near Eastern World: A Tribute to Cyrus H. Gordon*, JSOTSup 273, Sheffield, 1998, 443-57.

Kallai, Z., "Beth-El - Luz and Beth-Aven," in R. Liwak and S. Wagner (eds.), *Prophetie und geschichte Wirklichkeit im alten Israel*, Köln, 1991, 171-88.

— "Rachel's Tomb: A Historiographical Review," in J. A. Loader and H.U. Kieweler (eds.), *Vielseitigkeit des Alten Testaments. Festschrift für Georg Sauer zum 70. Gebertstag*, Frankfurt, 1999, 215-23.

Katzenstein, H.J., *ABD*, *s.v.*, "Philistines (History)," 5:326-28.

Kelso, J.L., "Bethel," in *EAEHL*, 1:190-93.

— "Bethel," in *NEAEHL*, 1:192-94.

King, P.J., *ABD*, *s.v.*, "Jerusalem," 3:747-66.

— "The Third Campaign at Bethel," *BASOR* 151 (1958): 3-8.

— "The Fourth Campaign at Bethel," *BASOR* 164 (1961): 5-19.

Kelso J.L. (ed.), *The Excavation of Bethel (1934–1960)*, AASOR 39, Cambridge, MA, 1968.

Kisch, Guido, *Pseudo-Philo's Liber Antiquitatum Biblicarum*, Notre Dame, IN, 1949.

Klein, M.L., "The Aramaic Targumim: Translation and Interpretation," in *Interpretation of the Bible: International Symposium on the Interpretation of the Bible*, Ljubljana/Sheffield, 1998, 317-31.

Kloppenborg, S., "Joshua 22: The Priestly Editing of an Ancient Tradition," *Biblica* 62 (1981): 347-71.

Knauf, Ernst Axel, "Bethel: The Israelite Impact on Judean Language and Literature," in O. Lipschits and M. Oeming (eds.), *Judah and the Judeans in the Persian Period*, Winona Lake, IN, 2006, 291-349.

— "Eglon and Ophrah: Two Toponymic Notes on the Book of Judges," *JSOT* 51 (1991): 25-44.

— *DDD*, *s.v.* "Qos," 1272-78.

— *ABD*, *s.v.*, "Toponyms and Toponymy," 6:601-605.

— "Who Destroyed Beersheba II?," in U. Hübner and E.A. Knauf (eds.), *Kein Land für sich allein. Studien zum Kulturkontakt in Kanaan, Israel/Palästine und Ebirnâri für Manfred Weippert zum 65. Geburtstag*, OBO 186, Göttingen, 2002, 181-95.

Kobayashi, Y., *ABD*, *s.v.* "Yegar-Sahadutha (place)."

Kokkinos, N., *The Herodian Dynasty: Origins, Role in Society and Eclipse*, JSPSup 30, Sheffield, 1998.

Kotter, Wade R., *ABD*, *s.v.* "Gilgal (place)."

Kraeling, E.G.H., "The Early Cult of Hebron and Judg. 16,1-3," *The American Journal of Semitic Languages and Literatures* 41 (1924/1925): 174-78.

Kraft, R.A., "'Ezra' Materials in Judaism and Christianity," in H. Temporini and W. Haase (eds.), *Aufstieg und Niedergang der Roemischen Welt: Geschichte und Kultur Roms im Spiegel der Neueren Forschung*. II. *Principat 19.1 Religion*, Berlin, 1979, 119-36.

Kraus, H.-J., "Gilgal. Ein Beitrag zur Kulturgeschichte Israels," *VT* 1 (1951): 181-91.

Landes, G.M., "Report on an Archaeological 'Rescue Operation' at Suwwanet eth-Thaniya in the Jordan Valley North of Jericho," *BASORSup* 21 (1975): 1-22.

Langlamet, F., *Gilgal et les Récits de la Traversée du Jourdain (Jos.,III-IV)*, Cahiers de la Revue Biblique 11, Paris, 1969.

Langston, Scott M., *Cultic Sites in the Tribe of Beniamin: Beniaminite Prominence in the Religion of Israel*, Frankfurt, 1998.

Lasine, S., "Melodrama as Parable: The Story of the Poor Man's Ewe-lamb and the Unmasking of David's Topsy-turvy Emotions," *HAR* 8 (1984): 101-24.

Laundeville, D.F., *ABD*, *s.v.* "Gideoni (person)."

Leach, E. *Genesis as the Myth and Other Essays*, London, 1969.

Lemaire, André, "Les inscriptions de Khirbet el-Qom et l'Asherah de YHWH," *RB* 84 (1977): 595-608

— "Who or What was Yahweh's Asherah? Starling New Inscriptions from Two Different Sites Reopen the Debate about the Meaning of Asherah," *BAR* 10.6 (1984): 42-51.

Lemche Niels Peter, *The Canaanites and their Land: The Tradition of the Canaanites*, JSOTSup 110, Sheffield, 1990.

— *Early Israel: Anthropological and Historical Studies on the Israelite Society before the Monarchy*, VTSup 37, Leiden, 1985.

— "Ideology and the History of Ancient Israel," *SJOT* 14 (2000): 165-93.

— *The Israelites in History and Tradition*, London, 1998.

Lengauer, W., "Dionysos dimorphos," *Kwartalnik Historii Kultury Materialnej* 1–2 (1998): 87-92.

— "Dionizos rogaty," in *Nunc de Svebis dicendum est. Studia archaeologica et historica Georgio Kolendo ab amicis et discipulis dicata*, Warsaw, 1995, 157-60.

Lewis, T.J., *ABD*, *s.v.* "Baal-Berith (Deity)."

Lewy, H., "Origin and Significance of the Mâgên Dâwîd: A Comparative Study in the Ancient Religions of Jerusalem and Mecca," *Archiv orientálni* 18 (1950): 330-65.

Lewy, J., "Les textes paléo-assyriens et l'Ancien Testament," *Revue de l'Histoire des Religions* 60 (1934): 29-65.

— "The Šulmân Temple in Jerusalem," *JBL* 59 (1940): 519-22.

Lichtenstein, M.H., "The Poetry of Poetic Justice: A Comparative Study in Biblical Imagery," *JANESCU* 5 (1973): 255-65.

Liid, D.C., *ABD*, *s.v.* "Silla (place)."

Liphscitz, N., and Y. Waisel, *The Botanic Material of Iron Age I*, in Herzog (ed.), *Beer-sheba II*, 116-17.

Lipiński, E., "'Anaq–Kiryat 'Arba'–Hebron et ses Sanctuaires tribaux," *VT* 24 (1974): 41-55.

Lipschits, O., " 'From Geba to Beersheba': A Further Consideration," *RB* 111 (2004): 345-61.

Liverani, M. "Le Chêne de Sherdanu," *VT* 27 (1977): 213.

— "Memorandum on the Approach to Historiographic Texts," *Orientalia* 42 (1973): 178-94.

Livingston, D., "Further Considerations on the Location of Bethel at El-Bireh," *PEQ* 126 (1994): 154-59.

— "One Last Word on Bethel and Ai—Fairness Requires No More," *BAR* 15 (1989): 11.

Loewenstamm, S.E., "The Death of the Patriarchs in Genesis," in B. Uffenheimer (ed.), *Bible and Jewish History: Studies Dedicated to the Memory of J. Liver*, Tel Aviv, 1971, 110-13, 119.

Long, Burke O., *The Problem of Etiological Narrative in the Old Testament*, BZAW 108, Berlin, 1968.

Loretz, O., "ADN come epiteto di Baal e i suoi raporti con Adonis e Adonaj," in *Adonis. Relazioni del colloquio in Roma 22–23 maggio 1981*, Rome, 25-33.

Lowery, K.E., *ABD, s.v.* "Jerubbaal."

— *ABD, s.v.* "Sheshai (person)."

Luker, L.M., *ABD, s.v.* "Ephrathah."

Lust, Johan, and Marc Vervenne (eds.), *Deuteronomy and Deuteronomic Literature: Festschrift C.H.W. Brekelmans*, Leuven, 1997.

Lyke, Larry L., *King David with the Wise Woman of Tekoa: The Resonance of Tradition in Parabolic Narrative*, JSOTSup 255, Sheffield, 1997.

Macalister, S., *The Excavation of Gerer 1902–1905 and 1907–1909*, vol. 2, London, 1912.

Macdonald, John (ed.), *The Samaritan Chronicle No. II (or: Sepher Ha-Yamim) from Joshua to Nebuchadnezzer*, Berlin, 1969.

Mader, E., *Mambre. Die Ergebnisse der Ausgrabungen im heiligen Bezirk Ramet el-Halil in Südpalä stina 1926–1928*, vols. 1–2, Freiburg, 1957.

Magen, I., "Garizim, Mount," in *NEAEHL*, 2:484-93.

— "Mamre," in *NEAEHL*, 3:939-42.

Malamat, A., "The Danite Migration and the Pan-Israelite Exodus-Conquest: A Biblical Narrative Pattern," *Biblica* 51 (1970): 1-16.

Manor, D.W., *ABD, s.v.* "Laish."

Marcos, N.F., "Nombres proprios y etimologias populares en la Septuaginta," *Sefarad* 37 (1977): 239-59.

Mare, W.H., *ABD, s.v.* "Millo."

Margalit, B., "Jacob and the Angel (Gen. 32:23-33) in Light of the Balaam Text from Deir 'Alla" (paper presented at the 48 Colloquium Biblicum Lovaniense, Leuven, 28–30 July 1999).

Martin-Archard, R., *ABD, s.v.* "Isaac."

Martone, Corrado, *The Judaean Desert Bible: An Index*, Turin, 2001.

Matthews, V.H., *ABD, s.v.* "Abimelech."

McCarter, P.K., Jr, *II Samuel: A New Translation with Introduction, Notes and Commentary*, AB 9, Garden City, NY, 1984.

McConville, J.G. "Faces of Exile in Old Testament Historiography," in J. Barton and D.J. Reimer (eds.), *After the Exile: Essays in Honour of Rex Mason*, Macon, GA, 1996, 27-44.

McGarry, S.E., *ABD, s.v.* "Beth-Anoth (place)."

McKenzie, Steven L., "The Jacob Tradition in Hosea XII 4-5," *VT* 36 (1986): 311-22.

McKenzie, Steven L., and Thomas Römer (eds.), *Rethinking the Foundations: Historiography in the Ancient World and in the Bible. Essays in Honour of John Van Seters*, BZAW 294, Berlin, 2000.

Mendels, Doron, "Creative History in the Hellenistic Near East in the Third and Second Centuries BCE: The Jewish Case," *JSP* 2 (1988): 13-20.

— *The Land of Israel as a Political Concept in Hasmonean Literature: Recourse to History in Second Century B.C. Claims to the Holy Land*, Texte und Studien zum antiken Judentum 15, Tübingen 1987.

— *The Rise and Fall of Jewish Nationalism*, New York, 1992.

Mendenhall, G.E., *ABD*, s.v. "Midian (person)."

Meshel, Z., "Did Yahweh Have a Consort?," *BAR* 5, no. 2 (1979): 24-35.

— *Kuntillet 'Ajrut: A Religious Center from the Time of the Judean Monarchy on the Border of Sinai*, Jerusalem, 1978.

Meshorer, Y., *Ancient Jewish Coinage*, vols. 1–2, New York, 1982.

Meyer, M., and P. Mirecki (eds.), *Ancient Magic and Ritual Power*, Leiden, 1995.

Meyers, E.M. *et al.* (eds.), *Ancient Synagogue Excavations at Khirbet Shema', Upper Galillee Israel 1970–1972*, Durham, NC, 1976.

Niesiołowski-Spanò, Ł., "Stan badań nad historią i religią starożytnej Palestyny," *Przegląd Historyczny* 91 (2000): 435-49.

— "Where to Look for Gideon's Ophra?," *Biblica* 86 (2005): 478-93.

Milgrom, J., "Does H Advocate the Centralization of Worship?," *JSOT* 88 (2000): 59-76.

Milik, J.T., "Les papyrus araméens d'Hermoupolis et les cultes syro-phéniciens en Égypte perse. 2 Dieu Béthel," *Biblica* 48 (1967): 565-77.

Millard, A.R., "YH and YHW Names," *VT* 30 (1980): 208-12.

Miller, J. Maxwell, and J.H. Hayes, *A History of Ancient Israel and Judah*, Philadelphia, 1986.

Mitchell, T.C., "Judah Until the Fall of Jerusalem (c.700–586 B.C.)," *CAH* 3.2:390-91.

Momigliano, A., "Biblical and Classical Studies: Simple Reflections upon Historical Method," *Annali della Scuola Normale Superiore di Pisa, serie III* 11 (1981): 25-32.

— *The Classical Foundations of Modern Historiography*, Berkeley, 1990.

Mosca, P.G., "Once Again the Heavenly Witness of Ps. 89:38," *JBL* 105 (1986): 27-37.

Moscati, S., A. Ciasca and G. Garbini, *Il Colle di Rachele (Ramat Rahel). Missione Archeologica nel Vicino Oriente*, Rome, 1960.

Mowinckel, S., *He that Cometh*, Oxford, 1956.

— *The Psalms in Israel's Worship*, Oxford, 1962.

Muchowski, Piotr, "Dwie kluczowe kwestie badawcze w studiach nad rękopisami biblijnymi z Qumran," *Studia Judaica* 4.1-2 (2001): 27-43.

Muilenburg, J., "The Site of Ancient Gilgal," *BASOR* 140 (1955): 11-27.

Mullen, E.T., Jr, *DDD*, s.v. "Witness," 1703-705.

Münnich, M., "Azazel—nowe interpretacje," *Ruch Biblijny i Liturgiczny* 55.2 (2002): 89-108.

Myers, J.M., "Edom and Judah in Sixth-Fifth Centuries B.C.," in Hans Goedicke (ed.), *Near Eastern Studies in Honor of William Foxwell Albright*, Baltimore, 1971, 377-92.

Na'aman, N., "Beth-aven, Bethel and Early Israelite Sanctuaries," *ZDPV* 103 (1987): 13-21.

— "Forced Participation in Alliances in the Course of the Assyrian Campaigns to the West," in M. Cogan and I. Eph'al (eds.), *Ah, Assyria… Studies in Assyrian History and Ancient Near Eastern Historiography Presented to Hayim Tadmor*, Jerusalem, 1991, 80-98.

— "The Law of the Altar in Deuteronomy and the Cultic Site Near Shechem," in McKenzie and Römer (eds.), *Rethinking the Foundations*.

— "Rezin of Damascus and the Land of Gilead," *ZDPV* 111 (1995): 105-106.

Naeh, S., and M.P. Weitzman, "Tiroš—Wine or Grape? A Case of Metonymy," *VT* 44 (1994): 115-20.

Nielsen, E., "The Burial of the Foreign Gods," *StTh* 8 (1955): 103-22.

— *Shechem: A Traditio-Historical Investigation*, Copenhagen, 1955.

Nielsen, Kirsten, *DDD*, s.v. "Terebinth."

— *There is Hope for a Tree: The Tree as Metaphor in Isaiah*, JSOTSup 65, Sheffield, 1989.

Noort, E., *The Traditions of Ebal and Gerizim: Theological Positions in the Book of Joshua*, in Johan Lust and Marc Vervenne (eds.), *Deuteronomy and Deuteronomic Literature: Festschrift C.H.W.Brekelmans*, Leuven, 1997, 168-80.

Noth, M., *Das System der Zwölf Stämme Israels*, Stuttgart, 1930.

Noy, Tamar, "Gilgal," in *NEAEHL*, 2:517-18.

— "Gilgal I: An Early Village in the Lower Jordan Valley—Preliminary Report of the 1987 Winter Season," *The Israel Museum Journal* 7 (1988): 113-14.

— "Ten Years of Research in the Area of Gilgal, Lower Jordan Valley," *The Israel Museum Journal* 4 (1985): 13-16.

O'Brien, Mark, *The Deuteronomistic History Hypothesis: A Reassessment*, OBO 92, Göttingen, 1989.

O'Conner, M., "The Etymologies of Tadmor and Palmyra," in Arbeitman (ed.), *A Linguistic Happening*, 235-54.

Oesterley, W.O.E., *Sacrifices in Ancient Israel: Their Origin, Purposes and Development*, London, 1937.

Ofer, A., "Hebron," *NEAEHL*, 2:606-609.

Olyan, Saul M., *Asherah and the Cult of Yahweh in Israel*, Atlanta, 1988.

Ottosson, M., *ABD*, s.v. "Gilead (place)."

Otzen, B., "Heavenly Visions in Early Judaism: Origin and Function," in Boyd Barrick and Spencer (eds.), *In the Shelter of Elyon*, 199-215.

Paradise, J., "What Did Laban Demand of Jacob? A New Reading of Genesis 31:50 and Exodus 21:10," in M. Cogan, B. Eichler and J. Tigay (eds.), *Tehillah le-Moshe: Biblical and Judaic Studies in Honor of Moshe Greenberg*, Winona Lake, 1997, 91-98.

Perrot, C., and P.-M. Bogaert (eds.), *Pseudo-Philo: Les Antiquités Biblique*, SC 229-30, Paris, 1976.

Pettazzoni, Raffaele, *The All-knowing God*, London, 1956.

— *Wszechwiedza bogów*, Warsaw, 1967.

Pitt-Rivers, J. *The Fate of Shechem or Politics of Sex: Essays in the Anthropology of the Mediterranean*, London, 1977.

Pope, Marvin H., *Song of Songs*, AB 7C, Garden City, NY, 1977.

Popko, Maciej, *Religions of Asia Minor*, Warsaw, 1995.

— *Wierzenia ludów starożytnej Azji Mniejszej*, Warsaw, 1989.

Porten, B., *Archives from Elephantine: The Life of an Ancient Jewish Military Colony*, Berkeley, 1968.

Porten, B., and A. Yardeni, *Textbook of Aramaic Documents from Ancient Egypt*, 4 vols., Jerusalem, 1986-99.

Puech, E., *ABD*, s.v. "Fear of Isaac."

Pury, A. de, "Abraham: The Priestly Writer's 'Ecumenical' Ancestor," in McKenzie and Römer (eds.), *Rethinking the Foundations*, 163-81.

— *DDD*, s.v. "El-Oam," 549-55.

— "Le raid de Gédéon (Juges 6,25-32) et l'histoire de l'exclusivisme yahwiste," in T. Römer (ed.), *Lectio Difficilior Probabilior? L'exegèse comme expérience de décloisonnement. Mélanges offerts à Françoise Smyth-Florentin*, Heidelberg, 1991, 173-205.

Pury, A. de, T. Römer and J.-D. Macchi (eds.), *Israel Constructs its History*, JSOTSup 306, Sheffield: Sheffield Academic Press.

Rabin, C., "Hittite Words in Hebrew," *Orientalia* 32 (1963): 137-38.

Rad, von Gerhard, *Das formgeschichtliche Problem des Hexateuches*, Berlin, 1938.

— *Genesis: A Commentary*, London, 1956.

— *Old Testament Theology*, trans. D.M.G. Stalker, New York, 1962.

Ribichini, Sergio, *Adonis. Aspetti 'orientali' di un mito greco*, Rome, 1981.

— *Adonis. Relazioni del colloquio in Roma 22–23 maggio 1981*, Rome, 1984.

Robertson Smith W., *The Religion of the Semites: The Fundamental Institutions*, New York, 1959.

Rogerson, J.W., *Myth in Old Testament Interpretation*, BZAW 134, Berlin, 1974.

Röllig, W., *DDD*, *s.v.* "Bethel," 173-75.

Rooke, D.W., "Kingship as Priesthood: The Relationship between the High Priesthood and the Monarchy," in J. Day (ed.), *King and Messiah in Israel and the Ancient Near East: Proceedings of the Oxford Old Testament Seminar*, JSOTSup 270, Sheffield, 1998, 187-208.

Rose, M., *ABD*, *s.v.* "Names of God in the O.T."

Rosenbaum, M., and A.M. Silbermann (eds.), *Pentateuch with Targum Onkelos, Haphtaroth and Rashi's Commentary*, Jerusalem, 5733 (1973/74).

Ross, A.P., "Jacob's Vision: The Founding of Bethel," *Bibliotheca Sacra* 142 (1985): 236-37.

Roth, W., "You are the Man! Structural Interpretation in 2 Samuel 10–12," *Semeia* 8 (1977): 1-13.

Rudman, D., "The Second Bull in Judges 6: 25-28," *Journal of Northwest Semitic Languages* 26 (2000): 97-103.

Sabbatucci, D., "Il problema storico-religioso di Adonis: confronto tra il momento frazeriano e il moderno," in *Adonis. Relazioni del colloquio in Roma 22–23 maggio 1981*, 17-24.

Sabourin, L., "L'étiologie biblique," *BTB* 2 (1972): 201-206. English version "Biblical Etiologies," *Biblical Theology Bulletin* 2 (1972): 199-205.

Schäfer, Peter, *The History of the Jews in Antiquity: The Jews of Palestine from Alexander the Great to the Arab Conquest*, Luxemburg, 1995.

Schley, D.G., *ABD*, *s.v.* "Abiezer."

Schoors, Antoon, "The Bible on Beer-sheba," *Tel Aviv* 17 (1990): 100-109.

Schmidt, Brian B., *Israel's Beneficent Dead: Ancestor Cult and Necromancy in Ancient Israelite Religion and Tradition*, Forschungen zum Alten Testament 11, Tübingen 1994.

— "The 'Witch' of En-Dor, 1 Sam. 28, and Ancient Near Eastern Necromancy," in M. Meyer and P. Mirecki (eds.), *Ancient Magic and Ritual Power*, Leiden, 1995, 111-29.

Schmidt, F.W., *ABD*, *s.v.* "Sallu (person)."

Schmitz, P.C., *ABD*, *s.v.* "Sidon (place)."

Schofield, A., and J.C. VanderKam, "Were the Hasmoneans Zadokites?," *JBL* 124 (2005): 73-88.

Scobie, C.H.H., "The Origins and Development of Samaritan Christianity," *NTS* 19 (1973): 390-414.

— "The Use of Source Material in the Speeches of Acts III and VII," *NTS* 25 (1979): 399-421.

Scurlock, J., "167 BCE: Hellenism or Reform?," *JSJ* 31 (2000): 125-61.

Seters, J. van, *Abraham in History and Tradition*, New Haven, 1975.

— "Divine Encounter at Bethel (Gen 28,10-22) in Recent Literary-Critical Study of Genesis," *ZAW* 110 (1998): 503-13.

— *In Search of History: Historiography in the Ancient World and the Origins of Biblical History*, New Haven, 1982.

— "Joshua 24 and the Problem of Tradition in the Old Testament," in Boyd Barrick and Spencer (eds.), *In the Shelter of Elyon*, 139-58.

— *The Life of Moses: The Yahwist as Historian in Exodus–Numbers*, Kampen, 1994.

— *Prologue to History: The Jahwist as Historian in Genesis*, Louisville, 1992.

Sievers, J., *The Hasmoneans and their Supporters: From Mattathias to the Death of John Hyrcanus I*, Atlanta, 1990.

Simon, U., "The Poor Man's Ewe-Lamb: An Example of Juridical Parable," *Biblica* 48 (1967): 207-42.

Simons, J., *The Geographical and Topographical Texts of the Old Testament: A Concise Commentary*, Leiden, 1959.

Skehan, P., E. Ulrich and J. Sanderson (eds.), *Discoveries in the Judaean Desert 9, 4: Qumran Cave 4—Palaeo-Hebrew and Greek Biblical Manuscripts*, Oxford, 1992.

Smith, Mark S., *The Early History of God: Yahweh and the Other Deities in Ancient Israel*, San Francisco, 1990.

Smith, Morton, *Palestinian Parties and Politics That Shaped the Old Testament*, New York, 1971.

Snaith, N.H., "The Altar at Gilgal: Joshua XXII 23-29," *VT* 28 (1978): 330-35.

— "Genesis XXXI 50," *VT* 14 (1964): 375.

Soggin, J.A., "Appunti per lo studio della religione d'Israele in epoca pre-esilica," in V. Angelo (ed.), *Biblische und Judaische Studien. Festschrift für Paolo Sacchi*, Frankfurt, 1990, 55-63.

— "Jacob in Shechem and in Bethel (Genesis 35:1-7)," in M. Fishbane and E. Tov (eds.), *Sha'arei Talmon: Studies in the Bible, Qumran, and the Ancient Near East Presented to Shemaryahu Talmon*, Winona Lake, 1992, 195-98.

— "La radice TMN—'Nascondere,' 'Seppelire' in ebraico," in P. Franzaoli (ed.), *Atti del secondo congresso internazionale di linguistica Camito-Semitica. Firenze 16–19 aprile 1974*, Quaderni di Semitistica 5, Florence, 1978, 241-45.

— "'La sepultura della Divinità' nell'iscrizione di Pyrgi (Lim.8-9) e motivi paralleli nell'Antico Testamento," *Rivista degli Studi Orienatli* 45 (1970): 245-52.

Sozomen, Hermias, *Ecclesiastical History*, repr., Kessinger Publishing Co., 2004.

Sperber, Daniel, *The City in Roman Palestine*, New York, 1998.

Sperling, S.D., "Joshua 24 Re-examined," *HUCA* 58 (1987): 119-36.

Spina, F.A., "The Dan Story Historically Reconsidered," *JSOT* 4 (1977): 60-71.

Stager, L.E., and S.R. Wolff, "Child Sacrifice at Carthage: Religious Rite or Population Control?," *BAR* 10 (1984): 31-51.

Steiner, R.C., "New Light on the Biblical Millo from Hatran Inscriptions," *BASOR* 276 (1989): 15-23.

Strange, J., "The Book of Joshua: A Hasmonean Manifesto?, in A. Lemaire and B. Otzen (eds.), *History and Traditions of Early Israel: Studies Presented to Eduard Nielsen*, VTSup 50, Leiden, 1993, 136-41.

— "The Philistine City-States," in M.H. Hansen (ed.), *A Comparative Study of Thirty City-State Cultures*, Copenhagen, 2000, 129-39.

Stuart, D., *Hosea–Jonah,* WBC 31, Waco, TX, 1987.

Tadmor, Miriam, "Female Cult Figurines in Late Canaan and Early Israel: Archaeological Evidence," in Tomoo Ishida (ed.), *Studies in the Period of David and Solomon and Other Essays: Papers Read at the International Symposium for Biblical Studies, Tokyo, 5–7 December 1979*, Tokyo, 1982, 139-73.

Tal, Abraham, *The Samaritan Pentateuch. Edited According to Ms6 (C) of the Shekhem Synagogue*, Tel Aviv, 1994.

Tal, Abraham (ed.), *The Samaritan Targum of the Pentateuch: A Critical Edition*, vols. 1–3, Tel Aviv, 1980–83.

Taylor, M.A., *ABD, s.v.* "Zelophehad (person)."

Teixidor, Javier, *The Pagan God: Popular Religion in the Greco-Roman Near East*, Princeton, 1977.

Thackeray, H.S.J. (trans.), Josephus, *The Jewish War* (LCL).

Thompson, Henry O., *ABD, s.v.* "Gibeath-Haaraloth (place)."

— *Mekal: The God of Beth-Shan*, Leiden, 1970.

Thompson, Thomas L., *The Bible in History: How Writers Create a Past*, London, 1999.

— *Early History of the Israelite People, From the Written and Archaeological Sources*, SHANE 4, Leiden, 1992.

— *The Historicity of the Patriarchal Narrative: The Quest for the Historical Abraham*, BZAW 133, Berlin, 1974.

Tigay, Jeffrey H., *You Shall Have No Other Gods: Israelite Religion in the Light of Hebrew Inscriptions*, Harvard Semitic Studies 31, Atlanta, 1986.

Toews, W.I., *ABD, s.v.* "Eshcol (place)."

Tomal, Maciej, *Język hebrajski biblijny*, Warsaw, 2000.

Toorn, van der, Karel, *Family Religion in Babylonia, Syria and Israel: Continuity and Change in the Forms of Religious Life*, SHANE 7, Leiden, 1996.

— "Herem-Betel and Elephantine Oath Procedure," *ZAW* 98 (1986): 282-85.

— "The Nature of the Biblical Teraphim in the Light of the Cuneiform Evidence," *CBQ* 52 (1990): 203-22.

Tov, Emanuel, *The Greek and Hebrew Bible: Collected Essays on the Septuagint*, VTSup 72, Leiden, 1999.

Tromp, Nicholas J., *Primitive Conceptions of Death and the Nether World in the Old Testament*, Biblica et Orienatalia 21, Rome, 1969.

Tronina, A., *Biblia w Qumran*, Kraków, 2001.

Tsevet, M., "Ishboshet and Congeners: The Names and their Study," *HUCA* 46 (1975): 71-87.

— "Studies in the Book of Samuel, II," *HUCA* 33 (1962): 107-18.

Van Beek, G.W., and A. Jamme, "An Inscribed South Arabian Clay Stamp from Bethel," *BASOR* 151 (1958): 9-16.

Van, Zyl A.H., *The Moabites*, Leiden, 1960.

VanderKam, J.C., *ABD*, *s.v.* "Jubilees, Book of."

VanderKam, J.C. (trans.), *The Book of Jubilees*, CSCO 511, Scriptores Aethiopici 88, Leuven, 1989.

Walsh, Carey Ellen, *The Fruit of the Wine: Viticulture in Ancient Israel*, Harvard Semitic Monographs 60, Winona Lake, 2000.

Waltke, Bruce K., *ABD*, *s.v.* "Samaritan Pentateuch."

Webb, Barry G., *The Book of the Judges: An Integrated Reading*, JSOTSup 46, Sheffield, 1987.

Weitzman, S., *ABD*, *s.v.* "Heshmon (place)."

— "Reopening the Case of the Suspiciously Suspended Nun in Judges 18:30," *CBQ* 61 (1999): 448-60.

Wellhausen, Julius, *Die Composition des Hexateuchs und der historischen Bücher des Alten Testaments*, Berlin, 1899.

— *Prolegomena zur Geschichte Israels*, Berlin, 1883. English edition, *Prolegomena to the History of Ancient Israel*, New York, 1957.

Wevers, John William, *Notes on the Greek Text of Genesis*, Atlanta, 1993.

Whitley, C.F., "The Sources of the Gideon Stories," *VT* 7 (1957): 157-64.

Whitt, W.D., "The Jacob Traditions in Hosea and their Relation to Genesis," *ZAW* 103 (1991): 18-43.

Wiggins, Steve A., *A Reassessment of "Asherah": A Study According to the Textual Sources of the First Two Millennia B.C.E.*, AOAT 235, Neukirchen–Vluyn, 1993.

Wilfall, W., "The Sea of Reeds as Sheol," *ZAW* 92 (1980): 325-32.

Wolff, Hans Walter, *Joel and Amos: A Commentary on the Books of the Prophets Joel and Amos*, Philadelphia, 1977.

Wright, G. Ernest, "The Samaritans at Shechem," *HTR* 55 (1962): 357-60.

— "Shechem," in *EAEHL*, 4:1083-94.

— *Shechem: The Biography of a Biblical City*, New York, 1965.

Wright, G.R.H., "Joseph's Grave under the tree by the Omphalos at Shechem," *VT* 22 (1972): 476-86.

— "The Mythology of Pre-Israelite Shechem," *VT* 20 (1970): 75-82.

Wyatt, Nick, "The Meaning of El Roi and the Mythological Dimension in Genesis 16," *SJOT* 8 (1994): 141-51.

— *Myths of Power: A Study of Royal Myth and Ideology in Ugarit and Biblical Tradition*, Ugaritisch-Biblische Literatur 13, Münster, 1996.

— "Where did Jacob Dream his Dream?," *SJOT* 2 (1990): 44-57.

Wynn-Williams, Damian J., *The State of the Pentateuch: A Comparison of the Approaches of M. Noth and E. Blum*, Berlin, 1997.

Xella, Paolo, "L'Episode de Dnil et Kothar (KTU 1. 17 [=CTA 17] v 1-31) et Gen. XVIII 1-6," *VT* 28 (1978): 483-88.

Yadin, Y., "An Inscribed South-Arabian Clay Stamp from Bethel?," *BASOR* 196 (1969): 37-45.

Yarden, L., "Aaron, Bethel, and the Priestly Menorah," *JJS* 26 (1975): 39-47.

Yee, Gale A. "Ideological Criticism: Judges 17–21 and the Dismembered Body," in *Judges and Method: New Approaches in Biblical Studies*, Minneapolis, 1995, 146-70.

— *ABD*, *s.v.* "Jezebel."

Youngblood, R., *ABD*, *s.v.* "Elkanah."

Younker, R.W., *ABD*, *s.v.* "Beth-Haccerem."

— *ABD*, *s.v.* "Ramat Rahel."

Zadok, Ran, *The Pre-hellenistic Israelite Anthroponymy and Prosopography*, Leuven, 1988.

Zertal, A., "Ebal, Mount," in *NEAEHL*, 1:375-77.

— *ABD*, *s.v.* "Ebal, Mount (place)."

Indexes

Index of References

Index of Authors

LaVergne, TN USA
04 April 2011
R6105700001B/R61057PG222112LVX2B/2/P

9 781845 533342